ISRAEL

Ancient Land, Young Nation

Books by Oden Meeker

ISRAEL: ANCIENT LAND, YOUNG NATION
ISRAEL REBORN
THE LITTLE WORLD OF LAOS
REPORT ON AFRICA

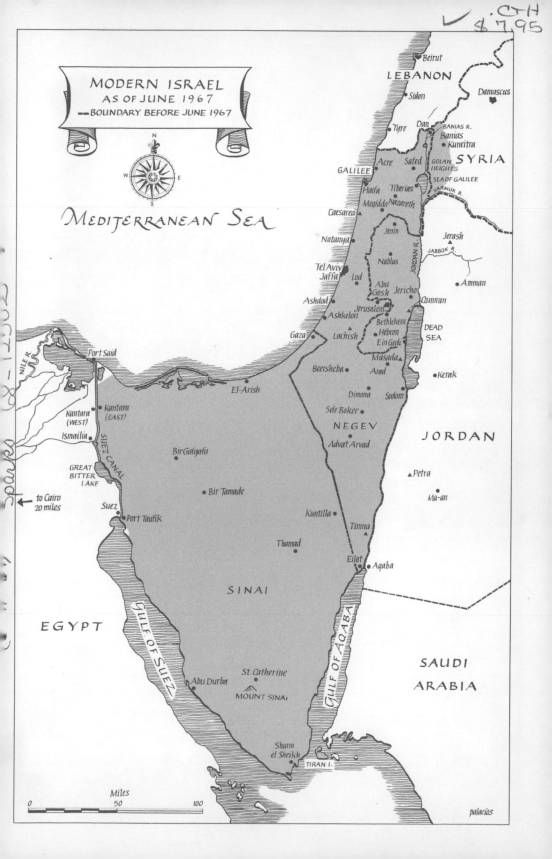

MODERN ISRAEL
AS OF JUNE 1967
-- BOUNDARY BEFORE JUNE 1967

MEDITERRANEAN SEA

LEBANON

Beirut

Sidon

Damascus

Tyre

Dan

BANIAS R.

Banias

Kuneitra

SYRIA

Acre

Safed

GOLAN
HEIGHTS

GALILEE

SEA OF GALILEE

Haifa

Tiberias

YARMUK R.

Caesarea

Megiddo

Nazareth

Natanya

Jenin

Jerash

JORDAN R.

JABBOK R.

Tel Aviv
Jaffa

Nablus

Lod

Amman

Abu
Gosh

Jericho

Ashdod

Qumran

Jerusalem

Ashkelon

Bethlehem

Gaza

Lachish

Hebron

Ein Gedi

DEAD
SEA

Beersheba

Masada

Arad

Kerak

Dimona

Sodom

Sde Boker

JORDAN

NEGEV

El-Arish

Port Said

Advat Arvad

Petra

Kantara
(WEST)

Kantara
(EAST)

Ma-an

Ismailia

SUEZ CANAL

Bir Gafgafa

GREAT
BITTER
LAKE

NILE R.

to Cairo
20 miles

Suez

Bir Tamade

Port Taufik

Kuntilla

Timna

Thamad

Eilat

Aqaba

SINAI

SAUDI

ARABIA

GULF OF SUEZ

GULF OF AQABA

Abu Durba

St. Catherine

MOUNT SINAI

EGYPT

Sharm
el Sheikh

TIRAN I.

Miles

0   50   100

palacios

ISRAEL

ANCIENT LAND, YOUNG NATION

by Oden Meeker

New York
CHARLES SCRIBNER'S SONS

for Maddy Brennan
with love and affection

PREFACE

CARE had sent me first to Laos, and then to Hong Kong, then to India, and next, to Israel.

For a year before we first went to Israel in late 1960, when my wife Bertie and I knew it was to be our home, we read everything we could: the Bible, the long, terrible and extraordinary history of the Jews, their tribal migrations, their kingdoms, their exile and their return; the pyrotechnic rise of Islam and its sudden surge from the Middle East through a good part of our world. We read about Arab and Jewish refugees; about ancient wars and modern hostilities; the efforts to make the desert green again on both sides of a maddening, crazy-quilt frontier.

In spite of all our preparation, Israel remained eternally surprising.

For its people, for its enemies and for its friends, it had become a kind of emotional crucible.

Now, looking back, I want to try to recapture how it looked and felt. This was, and it is still, a time of the return to Israel of the Jews, of the return of those exiled for two thousand years and more. It is a time of the flood tide of immigration, of help from overseas, and of attack as well from every neighbor. When we lived there, it was also the time of the capture, the trial and execution of Adolf Eichmann, of the emotional response of those who mourned six million Jewish dead, and the time of the pilgrimage of Pope Paul VI to the Holy Land.

The execution and the pilgrimage seemed to me to be the two poles. Most of the time, we lived closer to the center of this small world, absorbed with the daily business of working with the new Israelis, wondering whether the fragile armistice would hold.

We wondered how the Jews as a people had survived at all. The

Canaanites and the Moabites and the other Hebrew-speaking peoples of the Bible had vanished, at one with the Phoenicians, the Etruscans and all the others who live now only in museums.

The Jews, after some centuries of wandering, weakened by attack from without and by dissension from within, after servitude in Egypt and captivity in Babylon, conquest by Rome and dispersal of most of them for nearly two thousand years—this extraordinary people had encountered nearly every nuance of hostility from those others with whom they lived: from faint dislike, to mass murder. How the Jews, as one of this world's many small, distinctive groups, had managed to retain their separate identity, how they had survived (a small nucleus, always, in Israel), and how at last the others had returned to their ancient home in Israel, and how the State of Israel itself has survived, all this to me remains a sort of miracle.

Of perhaps seven million Jews in Western Europe, there were left at the end of the Second World War some eight hundred thousand, of whom four hundred and fifty thousand lived in England.

More than fifty million persons left their homes following the end of the Second World War, the greatest migration of human beings yet known. Most of them were refugees. Now, some twenty years later, there were even more refugees than there had been in 1945.

More than a year after the war's end, after the fires of the Nazi death camps burned no longer, there were still a quarter of a million Jews among the displaced persons held in those same camps, awaiting a chance of emigration. On one occasion, a large group of Jews attempting to enter Palestine in defiance of the regulations of Great Britain (responsible under a League of Nations Mandate for government of the territory) were returned to their original camp in Germany.

There were six hundred and fifty thousand Jews in Palestine in 1948 at the end of the British mandate. Fifteen years later, the State of Israel had accepted well over a million more refugees and immigrants, and the end was nowhere in sight: There still existed the dangers and the difficulties that followed the establishment of the state against almost insuperable odds. What had gone before, and just the fact that the Jews were here at all, seemed to me to make it a happy return.

CONTENTS

ISRAEL

ISRAEL

Ancient Land, Young Nation

1/ THE KALEIDOSCOPE

I n the Holy Land, that part of it which belonged to Israel, everything looked green and peaceful.

The reality was infinitely complex, difficult to absorb and to understand. Woven into the daily life of the country were four thousand years and more of history: a series of great and ancient civilizations, mass murder in Europe, a tidal wave of refugees, the vast, and often violent, energies released with the birth of three of the world's great religions.

The visitor lands at the airport near Tel Aviv in Lod, the Lydda of St. George who was born and was buried there, until one day not too long ago his bones were ceremoniously removed to Greece. Understanding of contemporary Israel grows suddenly with the shock of recognition by the newcomer that many of his neighbors, the people he sees in the street, are survivors of the concentration camps, have tattooed numbers on their arms.

Looking back, I see Israel in a kaleidoscope held to the light, slowly turning, the jagged mosaic of bits of colored glass, harsh reds and greens and yellows and purples sharply, sporadically shifting, yet always forming a pattern.

At the airport at Lod or the docks at Haifa we saw the clusters of immigrants, robed and bearded patriarchal figures from North Africa, standing bewildered among bags and bales and boxes and families. Then, a little later, I remember the children of these refugees, chatting easily in Hebrew on their way to kindergarten, completely at home in this world new to their parents.

I remember the homicidal buses that roared down the roads of Israel, and sometimes when they stopped, the snatches of classical music floating through the drivers' windows. Music is a part of the daily nourishment of the country.

Sometimes it is the contrasts one remembers. I remember one lazy, warm, spring holiday morning in our garden, looking up to see jet planes streaking by overhead to join Israel's Independence Day Parade: the French Mystères and Super-Mystères and the supersonic Mirages which looked like deadly flying triangles. Though I have an irrational prejudice against military machinery, I was glad to see them, for the country was twelve miles wide where we lived, a little north of Tel Aviv, and there were a fair number of MIG jets just across the Egyptian frontier not far to the south.

The paradox of this land, fertile once again with its new towns in the desert and its patchwork of green fields, is the curious balance between war and peace. With the great white cotton clouds floating overhead in a sky of Mediterranean-blue, and the green and brown patches of field in the gentle hills of Galilee and Judah, all seems tranquil. Bright red or yellow tractors, towering cotton-picking machines move along the rows; others reduce hay to neat, six-sided bales. Then one notices the hay is being stacked, guarded by a girl wearing faded army fatigues and carrying an Israeli submachine gun. The flocks of Biblical sheep are tended by shepherds with rifles over their shoulders. By the shores of the Sea of Galilee, a few yards from the Syrian border, the tractors were armored, and the children in an agricultural settlement there played near the entry of an air-raid shelter, always ready for the siren which sent them scrambling to safety—until the great guns and the mortars which for nineteen years sporadically had shelled them from the heights above were silenced when the Israelis took these positions during the Six Day War of June, 1967.

The deeply tanned young farmers and construction workers, men stripped to the waist in country or city when it's hot, are building the new Israel. They wear short shorts and faded blue cloth caps like deep-cupped mushrooms, the national *kova tembel* or "idiot's hat," rather like an American gob's cap with the brim turned down. You can see these new Israelis in the fields, constructing the new towns, driving the trucks on the desert roads winding south. They have physical toughness and easy confidence.

As I remember Israel, everybody always seemed to be hiking somewhere. Boy Scouts, Girl Scouts, primary-school students, secondary-school students, university students, boys and girls in military service are all on the road. They trek over the hills of Galilee, scale the faces of the cliffs that ring the Dead Sea.

Every year in Israel at the time of the Four-Day Route March, on a sort of competitive pilgrimage with prizes for first arrival, fastest march and so on, bands from the collective and communal settlements, children, undaunted grandfathers, English postmen, Africans in robes, blond Dutch undergraduates, athletic teams and special delegations from filling stations and the clerical staffs of banks march from all over Israel to hike up the winding road that leads through the Judean hills to Jerusalem.

At the other end of the Israeli spectrum from the hikers and the tanned workers in the fields are the pallid small boys and the men wearing the traditional curling locks before the ears who live in the ultra-Orthodox quarters of Jerusalem and just outside Tel Aviv, the boys with small black skullcaps and the men with broad-brimmed black hats, crowns undented, and the long black Eastern European coats called kaftans whose skirts fall well below the knees. These are the bearded, thin, and sometimes hooknosed, men—those whom enemies of the Jews have so often caricatured—who are themselves sometimes litigious and intolerant, but for the most part studious, otherworldly, inoffensive and deeply, deeply religious. It would be difficult to think of Israel without them.

5

The same vitality seems to animate the recluses, fierce scholars and Orthodox religionists, and the Israeli farmers and construction workers, or the leathery old men driving two-wheeled kerosene carts pulled by mules or diminutive donkeys, which share downtown traffic with American tail-finned cars.

I remember the disarming offhandedness of many of those charged with running the country, this coupled with a passion to get things done or, sometimes, just to make a point in a discussion. I remember a general healthiness which puts to shame most of us brought up in big cities. And, most especially, I remember a smiling, often laughing people. And there was a feeling of tremendous physical energy.

What are the keys to Israel? . . . What is it that makes the Jews who live there not only Jews but Israelis?

Religion shared with other Jews dispersed throughout the world outside Israel, that part of Jewry called the Diaspora, is surely the strongest factor for the believing Jew, the agnostic and the atheist alike. Inextricably bound up with Judaism and its history is the history of the Jewish people as a group apart from others, throughout much of the Christian era in many parts of the world forced to live in separate communities; and the other side of this coin of segregation, the burning determination of Jewish leaders and the ghetto communities themselves to retain their own, distinctive way of life.

Together with religion is consciousness of Jewish culture as a separate, splendid thing in itself. And in its return to Israel, Jewish culture has undergone a sea change, or perhaps reversion to its ancestral origin. For here, as the visiting Gentile notes, Jews no longer seem "Jewish" in the faintly invidious sense of the word as it is sometimes used. In Israel, Jews are no longer fighting, reflexively defensive, against an alien and often hostile majority among whom they live in the Diaspora. In Israel, the Jewish people finds itself once again at home. Sometimes brusque, Jews here also seem easy and confident in their approach to others, Jew or Gentile, and one can feel it.

Israel is a collection of minorities coming from remarkably disparate backgrounds. Except from Laos, Tibet, Bhutan and a few geographical curiosities like the Ifni Enclave, the exiles who have returned to Israel come from nearly every country in the world. I can remember an alert, youngish Russian refugee porter at the railway

6

station in Haifa who began a chat in excellent Mandarin; fortunately, the train pulled out before I ran out of what polite Chinese small talk I could remember, left over from working for CARE in Hong Kong.

Ironically, one major, almost overriding, factor holding together this bright, quick, hard-working and fantastically variegated collection of Jews from all over the world, with different educations, different food, different ideas, is pressure from the outside. With the exception of the Mediterranean Sea, Israel is surrounded by the lands of an enemy sworn to destroy her.

It is always Israel on guard that I remember. It is the young conscripts hiking, looking like nothing so much as a bunch of Senior Scouts. It is the younger, paramilitary outfit called Gadna in which high school boys and girls are sent on hikes and archeological digs, taught camping and the use of light arms. It is Nahal, an élite but non-privileged group of young men and women volunteers who do their thirty-six or twenty months' military service, respectively, in one of the more dangerous frontier and farming settlements.

Above all, one is struck by the part women play in the security and defense of the country, from the tawny, handsome Yemenite policewomen who look particularly striking in their deep-blue and white uniforms much like those of the American WAVES, to the girls in the Israeli Army, Navy and Air Force, including a couple who had been fighter pilots during the War of Independence.

The River Jordan at the extreme east of the country begins just to the north in Syria where three streams on the snowy slopes of Mount Hermon plunge two thousand feet in a very few miles down to the Sea of Galilee in Israel, itself only twelve miles long, but mountain-ringed and tempestuous. Then at the end of the Sea of Galilee is the Jordan, scarcely more than a large brook, with bosky banks, the water dappled with sunlight shining through the trees. I see it wandering on its path through the poplars, oleanders and papyri, meandering past the banks where John baptized Jesus, until at last the Jordan enters the Dead Sea, thirteen hundred feet below sea level, and the lowest spot on the earth's surface where men work. Here, the white-rimmed evaporation pans and the deeper water are brilliant, shining blue-green and deep-amethyst against the chalky buff of the jagged mountains that surround the sea.

What is it about the River Jordan—among all the other extraordinary things in the Holy Land—which has so seized men's imaginations? My first reaction was surprise and a little disappointment seeing this tiny stream where I had expected something roughly the size of the Mississippi (a friend named Lisa Stephenson, who was then ten years old and Junior Diving Champion of India, and I once swam across it and back, with me puffing, in less than five minutes). Yet the Jordan is one of the things we remember most vividly about our stay in Israel. Here hundreds of thousands of pilgrims from the Christian world have come to be baptized. I can think of no other river and few other subjects about which so many songs have been sung. As these lines are being written, American folk songs composed by those most deeply involved in the struggle for civil rights in the United States refer again and again to Israel, to the Valley of the Shadow, and to the River Jordan.

These are the shifting bits of colored glass in the kaleidoscope that combine to make Israel: religion and history and pioneers and refugees, the defense forces and the desert. Sometimes it is the desperation and the nowhere else to go. It is the arts and the intellectual vitality. Above all, it is the language and the army—the miracle of a dead language brought back to life; in Israel, almost everyone learns Hebrew, one more bond to bring this disparate group together. And almost everyone does military service, and not grudgingly, either—even those girls who are automatically excused if they come from Orthodox religious families, but who in a surprisingly large number of cases feel it their duty to do a twenty months' hitch in Israel's defense forces, just as does the majority of the population. I thought one of the most fascinating photographs in the Israel government's archives was that of the last Jewish soldier to leave the Old City of Jerusalem when it was evacuated following orders from the new Israeli Government under pressure from the advancing Arab armies: he was a blond young theological student, curling earlocks and all. In practice, the defense force of Israel is the population itself, and anyone doing service in his or her late teens comes out an Israeli, no matter how recent a newcomer to the country.

The newcomers come from anywhere and everywhere. The last fragment catching my eye in the kaleidoscope as it turns is, again, the ships and the planes bringing the Israelis home after their long exile. My wife and I were at the airport often enough meeting guests and friends of CARE not to be surprised at the surprise of passengers on Israel's national airline, El Al, who, en route, had found themselves suddenly and without warning landing at European airports not on their itinerary, because a group of refugees had unexpectedly appeared—often released without explanation or expectation from one of the Eastern European countries, and now awaiting passage to Israel.

For the Jews returning to Israel—and any Jew anywhere may come—there are no invisible diplomatic officers like the one in whose anteroom the refugees wait in Menotti's opera *The Consul* . . . who can grant visas to the desperate and the fleeing, if he will, but who never, never comes. . . .

2/ THE NEIGHBORS

J ust a few miles west of Lod is the Mediterranean, and along its shore about twenty minutes' drive from Tel Aviv is Nof Yam, the quiet, small community where we lived. Here, a gently rolling strip of sand dunes patchily covered with coarse grass, succulents, and wind-flattened scrub ended at an abrupt, deeply eroded bluff falling a hundred feet or so to a sandy shore. Following the curves of the coastline south, one can see the toy smokestacks of the electric company at the mouth of the diminutive Yarkon River in Tel Aviv, and beyond around the bay, the mosques of the older, sister city of Jaffa, the port whence Jonah sailed to be swallowed by the whale. From Tel Aviv north as far as our village, there were blocks of housing here and there, dull but modern, mixed with private villas and diplomatic residencies, occasionally punctuated by a resort hotel.

Nof Yam, with its modest gardens and shaded streets winding through the six blocks or more from the sea to the Haifa Road, was a microcosm, a cross-section of the Jewish communities returned to Israel from across the world. In the one-storey rows that made up Nof Yam's refugee transit camp or *ma'abara*, a little barracks-like and yet with many small gardens and individual touches, there lived families from Morocco, Algeria, Tunisia, Iraq and Egypt, many from Hungary and Poland, Austria and Germany, a few from Turkey, Mexico and almost anywhere else one could think of. The brass nameplates on some of the doors were in Arabic, the first language of numbers of newcomers from North Africa and the Middle East. Often, French was the second language, and Hebrew, acquired by most in intensive courses at language schools called *ulpanim*, was third. Many girls and boys really learned Hebrew during military service.

From the refugee camp sheltered in the lee of the last sandy, wooded ridge leading to the Mediterranean, it was five minutes' walk inland up the opposite slope of dunes to the local movie house. Here were heard, in addition to all the languages of the *ma'abara*, a dozen other tongues, including a good deal of English, some Russian, and intermittent Swahili from the East African students studying government administration, hotel management and other skills at nearby schools. The movie audience was a mixture of farm hands and hydraulic engineers, hotel staff, housewives, students, scientists, salesmen, soldiers on furlough, members of the coöperative rural settlements, doctors, drivers, and almost every sort except perhaps tourists. The film fare was as varied as its neighborhood audience: Israeli and French newsreels, westerns, men from outer space and other Hollywood high adventure for the junior matinees, experimental films, horror films, the exploits of spies and sleuths, musicals, psychological melodramas—a fair sampling of what the world's movie makers offer. All but the shortest films were crudely cut, with the result that the plot sometimes took surprising turns, but this gave us something to talk about when during intermission we bought ice cream, nuts, beer and the Israeli pop called *gazoz*—or after the audience had streamed away into the night, on foot or bike, in Jeeps, pick-ups, small European or some-

11

times the larger, American cars. Some of the audience rode away on the same brightly enameled yellow or blue tractors with which they would be at work in the fields early in the morning.

The Nof Yam movies were very much a part of the community. It was probably inevitable that the contemporary wave of Biblical epics should wash up on our neighborhood wide screen, and perhaps not too surprising that there should be apparent acceptance of the happily idiotic American and Italian rewriting of the Scriptures.

It was even more understandable that there should be shown numbers of films about the world of Adolf Hitler, about the German invasions, the resistance movements, the death camps and the hunt for the war criminals who had created them. Throughout the three years we lived among the people of Nof Yam there was scarcely a day when some small incident in the daily routine didn't remind my wife and me of what our neighbors had survived.

I doubt that either of us can forget the evening when the film was *Judgment at Nuremberg*, in which testimony that a young German Jew had been sterilized by the Nazis was the key to the story. It struck us as well done, and harrowing. Then, when the lights went up, we saw sitting near us with her husband a woman who was a friend and neighbor, a youngish, attractive housewife who had in fact been sterilized.

This was life in our village: calm and sunny at first appearance, with the inhabitants quietly busy; small houses, and shady lanes, close to the fields that surrounded the community, to the cliffs and the sea; a village friendly to strangers, and curious, but not insistent; people surprisingly open about themselves and their own lives. Gradually, one became aware of how much lay beneath the surface. The scream of planes overhead and the sharp tremors that shook the neighborhood during coastal defense practice were reminders of how precarious was the peace. A neighbor frequently seen was suddenly absent, and we learned that so-and-so was not well, had had to return to the hospital for shock treatment in an attempt to cope with an emotional and mental legacy of the concentration camps.

At our nearest corner, behind a neat green border of lawn grown in the sand, was the neighborhood clinic of the General Federation of Labor's Kupat Cholim, offering crowded, overworked, but generally comprehensive, medical facilities to all its subscribers, about eighty per cent of the country's population. Here at the neighborhood clinic, the benches were full of mothers and children, elderly immigrants, laborers, most of our small world. Among those helping were Nurse Anna Frank, a jovial, outgoing, dark-haired matron, very much in evidence, and Albert Cohen, a young gynecologist and general practitioner with black-rimmed glasses, a shock of black hair and an intense but cheerful manner in spite of the one thousand patients and more whom he looked after (a greater number than the health service asked him to serve, but this was his choice).

Dr. Cohen spoke to his patients in Hebrew, French, Turkish and English, the last of which he was learning from a Californian neighbor on the same street. Receiving patients until long after nightfall, and swiftly plowing his way through the sea of papers which seem one of the modern symptoms of sickness was the clinic's manager, Ja'acov Medina, a slight, wiry man, fond of jokes, with a high forehead and grey-white hair brushed back to an electric confusion in the rear, in his early sixties but looking a good deal younger. He seemed always ready to help the unending line of people at our clinic, one of the three for which he was responsible. He had come to this job after arriving in the new State of Israel from Yugoslavia nearly destitute, working first as a manual laborer, then in an ordnance plant.

Mr. Medina liked to be called Jacques, perhaps in memory of the year he had spent as a young man in Paris learning French. His life, like many others we came to know well, before he came to Israel had been such a bewildering succession of buffets and escapes, harrowing experiences, sometimes with comical but still dangerous interludes, that it was a surprise to see him at all. A Jewish officer in the Royal Yugoslav Army during the Second World War, his life was saved, ironically, because he was almost immediately captured by the Germans. During the four years he was transferred from one prisoner-of-war camp to another, he taught himself English to add to the languages he already knew, Serbo-Croatian, German, French, Italian and Spanish, with some Russian and Polish. He liked to practice speaking English with us, though

13

sometimes ghosts of his other tongues appeared: "You will some more coffee?" He was intense, conscientious, funny and extremely articulate.

To lend a hand to Bori Breiner, taking care of the house on our arrival but who could spare only two mornings a week from her nearby farm, Jacques produced a friend of his family, Zahava Suisa, who could come to work for us a few hours every day. Bori and Zahava made a highly competent, delightful and original pair, particularly helpful to us since we wanted time for our own work: Bertie is a painter, and had plunged into the creation of vivid, tropical gouaches, working at an accelerating tempo; and since we first knew we were coming to Israel, a year before leaving India, I had been gathering material for a book on Israel.

Bori was a small, spare, quizzical, tense person with dark-brown hair in a chopped bob, grey-green eyes, a long face and an extraordinarily wide frame of reference. She spoke Serbo-Croatian, Hungarian, German and Hebrew, but understood most European languages, and used such Americanisms as "twist," "sex appeal" and "gangster." Zahava, by contrast, though she had grown up in Morocco, was fluent in French university slang and Parisian argot, a medium-short, rounded girl with light strawberry-blonde hair, piled up in a beehive or teased like a lion's mane. She was pretty enough to be crowned Miss New Year's Eve at a local resort hotel, but this didn't inhibit her sustained assaults on our floors and our wash and anything else in the house that needed cleaning. She was sunny, artless and open, and the only person we've ever known who actually put her head down and her finger in her mouth when she giggled. She giggled often. Also, she was hopelessly flirtatious. Bertie and I used to tease her that, when she ran out of mailmen, laundrymen and meter checkers, she would begin to vamp Neer Goldberg, a tow-headed four year old who ferociously tricycled up and down the street in front of our house everyday.

"Pure gold," said Jacques Medina approvingly when introducing Zahava. In Hebrew, Zahava meant "gold," as did her earlier Arabic name of Zari. We called her Zahava and Zowie. One of seventeen children of the same mother, she had grown up in the Franco-Arabic world in which lived most of the Jews of Morocco. Her father had worn the hooded Moroccan robe, and with his family lived in Agadir in the cool twilight of a large Arab house with many rugs and the cages of songbirds which he particularly fancied. At fourteen, Zahava had been married by her family to a suitable much older man. She had two sons, Chaim and Zion. She had, in her way, emancipated herself, coming with her two children but without her husband to Israel via France, traveling with a brother who was now a policeman in Haifa. In March of 1960, less than nine months before we arrived in Israel, Zahava's husband was among the twelve thousand killed in the earthquake of Agadir, leaving her a widow at twenty-three.

Bori, whom we inherited with the house, was engagingly homely, but had a small, trim figure and, according to Bertie, the best pair of legs in Israel. She was obviously a lady, and her children markedly better-mannered than most of the people we met in this still rough, frontier society. Somehow, this had been salvaged from a girlhood spent in concentration camps. Born in Yugoslavia in 1927, Bori had been taken with her family in 1942 to Auschwitz. There, her parents were sent to the gas chambers, while Bori and a sister, now living in Tel Aviv, were saved to work. Bori survived the camps of Auschwitz and Ravensbrück, married Itzhak Breiner, a Yugoslav somewhat older than she, who had lived through the war years in a Russian labor camp. Together they had come to Israel to join the *moshav* of Rishpon across Haifa Road and a little north of where we lived—with no previous experience farming, making a go at raising chickens and cows, strawberries and grapes. They had two children: Shoshana, a quiet, well-mannered girl of about sixteen, who was without the prickliness of many of the Israel-born, and who was about to study drafting; and Reuben, a happy scrawny fellow of nine who loved all automobiles and was enchanted by our Christmas tree, his first. (Bori said that in Yugoslavia she and her family customarily enjoyed the holidays with Christian friends.)

Breiner, whom Bori never called by any other name, was a small, thin man with a long, thin face, glasses, a large nose, hazel eyes, indeterminate brown hair, a deeply red-brown neck from working in the sun, a small man but unconquered, nervous yet trusting and friendly. Like Bori, he loved jokes.

We used to wait for Breiner and his horse and vegetable wagon to come clopping along Rehov Hapoel where we lived. Someone from our place would join the housewives descending on his cart, armed with string bags, weighing the merits of tomatoes, spring onions, celery, parsley and dill, lettuce and romaine, avocados, celeriac, new potatoes, turnips, kohlrabi, artichokes, corn, oranges, lemons, grapefruit, grapes, melons, peaches and strawberries, all in their season.

When Breiner's horse came ambling down the street, his wife often would be working in the kitchen which faced the road. The morning light streamed through the kitchen window, bright and cheerful, ever-changing as the breeze from the sea played in the leaves of the shade trees overhead. We seemed far from Auschwitz, that great complex of gas chambers, crematoria and work camps where had died three million of the six million Jews lost in Europe. It had been a nightmare, peopled by ghosts now dead some twenty years. The survivors, most of them, seemed outwardly happy. But I never got used to the sight, when she reached up to open the kitchen window, of the camp number tattooed on Bori's left arm.

3/ MORE NEIGHBORS

O ur house in Nof Yam was really half of a double house, but with a feeling of privacy provided by a ten-foot hedge of scarlet hibiscus, and salmon-and-yellow lantana. The house itself was an indifferent grey stucco with a sloping terra cotta tile roof, but we had painted the shutters, the front gate, and the window trim and doors of the garage alongside the front garden the bright, chalky-blue used in Arab and Jewish villages as protection against the evil eye.

Inside were the small kitchen, two bedrooms and a long living room at whose western end was a picture window framing a much longer expanse of neatly cropped crab grass, the only green cover we could find which flourished on the dunes. In defiance of the

New Testament injunction, our house, literally, was built upon the sand, but here grew oranges and lemons and tangerines, three frangipani which we had planted, guavas and pine trees, pink and white periwinkles, geraniums, violets, pansies, snapdragons and poinsettias, scattered through the small garden in front of the house, lining the hedges, in beds in front, or beside the walk that wound from the front door through a dark green hedge to the road, or behind the house in the long garden that led toward the sea.

Looking down the long living-room walls, dead-white behind splashes of tropical color that were the Thai silk cushions scattered on the light wicker furniture from Hong Kong and Laos, the bronzes, ceramics and ivory, oddments we'd brought with us from the tropics of Africa and Asia and the Americas, we could see through sliding glass doors or our large window some of the wonderful profusion of birds and beasts and plants and flowers to be found here at the corner of Asia, Africa and Europe.

There were the small, reddish, soft-buff and grey turtle doves from the Song of Solomon; the African bulbuls, yellow-vented and tawny, whose pointed black caps were like cowlicks brushed forward; the metallic green-and-blue-black sunbirds hovering before the opened flowers in the garden; and, sometimes, the stubby, brilliantly handsome blue-green and chocolate Smyrna kingfishers.

A few yards from our back window, the ground tilted briefly, rather like the ha-ha in an old-fashioned English garden. Above the abrupt slope of grass was an octagonal summer house, made of widely spaced diagonal branches running between the uprights. All was interlaced with a bignonia creeper with bright orange blossoms, white jasmine, and everywhere were vines, grape leaves and tendrils winding from an ancient root big enough to climb on, at the far end of our arbor. One hundred and twenty-six boughs, bark and all, had been used by Bertie in the making of our summer house after termites had made off with most of the original structure, and as far as we could determine, it corresponded nicely to the huts, called booths or tabernacles, described in the book of Leviticus, in which the Lord told Moses all the Children of Israel must dwell during the autumn week of the Hebrew harvest-home, as they had in the years of their flight from Egypt.

The Feast of the Tabernacles is still celebrated each year with the creation of temporary shelters of green boughs in memory of

the Exodus and the Wilderness. Hanging from the boughs overhead are pomegranates and other fruits, sometimes with bottles of
wine. In these shelters called *sukkoth* which give their name to the
holiday, people take their meals during the harvest festival. Our
own individual *sukka* was rich in falling twigs, termite dust and a
variety of insects which inhibited picnicking, but we used to like
to sit on Bertie's three white wooden benches which lined the
bower, watching the play of the sunlight on the leaves, and the
hummingbirds and the other visitors. The hoopoe, that extraordinary
bird, did a kind of hesitation walk across the lawn, probing the
earth for insects with its long, slender, slightly curved bill. The
hoopoe was about seven inches long and reminiscent of our blue
jay in form, but with head, breast and upper back orange dusted
with cinnamon, and with zebra black-and-white wings, back and
tail; its black-tipped orange crest rose on its head with interest or
alarm. We liked its fine scientific name, *Upupa epops*.

Also, we liked to see the occasional chameleon, pea-green most
of the time, with a bony, helmeted head and with puffed, in-
dependently swivelling eyes and a long, superbly prehensile tail of
much use as it moved with great deliberation from branch to branch.
The hedgehogs came out only at night, and, when caught in the
beam of a flashlight while questing for dinner about our *sukka*,
would curl up into a snug ball, a little prickly but possible to
handle, and perfectly immobile if we carried one into the house
for a moment to show to our kittens.

The cats of Nof Yam were a part of the landscape. At the
house of a friendly couple named Glück, on a corner across the
road from the clinic, there were usually from a dozen to twenty-
six cats—gangs of mewling, patchy, blue-eyed kittens crowded
around an enamel dish of bread and milk, tawny cats sitting on
the wall, crouching among the plants in the flower beds, cats
everywhere. But Israel Glück and his wife Marta, gentle, kindly
people who were both survivors of Auschwitz, were animal lovers
in general and cat lovers in particular, though most of the people
here seemed moderately indifferent to domestic animals, and particularly unattracted by cats. Still, there were a lot of cats in
Nof Yam.

It all had begun with a cat whom we called The Schnorrer, a
tough vagabond who seemed more than a little daft and who

came to us for handouts as she worked her way through the whole neighborhood with the same hardluck story. She presented us with three kittens, born in a packing crate on our back porch: a smoky female we called Shadow; an amazed-looking little tom called Popeye whose fur was haphazardly white and black, as though he'd been caught in a fight between two house painters; and another small white-and-reddish marmalade tom called Gingy, which is the standard Arab and Hebrew nickname for Red.

Other cats disappeared, but Gingy remained with us, becoming larger and larger, and fading to a yellowish buff with large white patches, rather like light scrambled eggs. He was now twelve pounds or more of overstuffed tom with impressive whiskers, big, flat cheek pads which reminded me of those of an orangutan, and, at times, a baleful, misleadingly malevolent expression, for his chief interests were food, affection, sleep, more affection, and—far down the list—an occasional night or two of tomcatting.

Across the narrow, shady lane which ran past our front door lived Mischa Rakir, the cellist who had traveled with the Israel Philharmonic during the War of Independence. He and his wife were a plump, comfortable couple in middle years, who had a few black cats of their own, a geometrically tidy garden, and the sort of neighborliness that led Mrs. Rakir to come and plant bright beds of pansies along our winding front walk once when we were out of the country, and led them both one Christmas to march into our house and begin singing "Silent Night" and other German carols. Mischa Rakir, it turned out, had traveled from Russia to study music in Germany, where he met his wife. The Rakirs lost their only child, a son, fighting with the Israeli forces.

A bit down our street and beside the clinic was Victor's kiosk, a small white box of a general store in which a stream of children and their mothers and neighbors bought bread and petits pains, soft white cheese, fat, knobbly kosher pickles and dark olives ladled from enameled vats and wide-mouthed jars, salami, bologna and a variety of lunch meats, noodles and dehydrated chicken-soup mix (it made an excellent base for Chinese soups with dried mushrooms), the floppy, slippery Israeli mushrooms which looked like something to avoid when taken from the tin, but which were surprisingly good. In Victor's small space, in every corner, under the shelves and the counter, behind the building, and stacked to the ceiling were as many oddments as to be found in a large market: Israeli brandy and sweet Israeli wines, coconut, ice cream, yogurt and sour cream, pickled chili peppers, anchovy paste, the pastes called *humus* and *tehina* made of ground chick peas and sesame seed and served with unleavened Arab flatbread, candles and laundry soap, everything one could think of—all quickly found, wrapped in a scrap of Hebrew newspaper and delivered by Victor, a small, slender, friendly type, near-sighted, swarthy, with close-cropped, crinkled hair, and the movements of an unusually nervous humming bird.

The never-failing neighborhood amusement, and that of the rest of the country, was the *kumsitz*, which means to come and sit. It was at its best on the beach. Here we found ourselves below the jagged limestone bluffs atop which sat the deserted mosque of Sidna Ali, named after a thirteenth-century Moslem warrior who fell fighting the Crusaders. At sunset, the mosque's minaret was silhouetted against the yellow, orange and violet and smudgy blue-black sunset, clouds of dull cotton white-edged with grey low against the horizon as the sun slipped into the sea. As the darkness deepened, here and there along the shore there were bonfires flaming high nearby and glowing and winking in the distance. Our neighbors asked us to join them roasting hot dogs and drinking beer and pop, singing, and occasionally swimming. (It wasn't the twenty to forty people drowned each year which kept us swimming in the sunlight; we were just unable to jump into the cold night water and declare it bracing.)

Those at the beach were for the most part groups of young Israelis, spending a good part or sometimes all of the night on the sand. Off and on there would be the steady clap and driving rhythm of the *hora* as the dark, gesticulating figures of dancers revolved around the fires. This was the national dance, taken from one in the Balkans and now an inescapable part of Israel at home and abroad, much as the Arab *filafeel*—pungent combinations of tomatoes, onions, scraps of meat and spices stuffed in an opened half-round of unleavened bread—had now become the Hebrew cousin *felafel*, the national dish of this new country, and so thoroughly a part of the nation that it would be difficult to imagine surviving without it.

In Israel, entertainment begins about nine o'clock with coffee and cakes, when parents would have finished their dinner and seen their children securely in bed and asleep before starting out for the evening. There's seldom a place in the budget for baby-sitters, but children are safe. The idea of a dinner party as such was relatively rare. I accepted one elaborate, formal invitation in both Hebrew and English from a relatively affluent club to join them for a banquet, and the "banquet" consisted of a couple of hours of speeches ending with the inevitable cup of coffee and piece of cake.

No one, even the doctors, seemed to have much money. People became jolly or disputatious, but not from drink, for the society as a whole was most temperate. Wines and spirits seemed to be available at every candy store and lunch counter, but trade was not brisk. Even the Jews from Dublin were notably abstemious. Some guests might take one or possibly two drinks during the evening, and that was that.

Even with the spring festival of Purim with its Hebraic scriptural injunction that one should become drunk (some anthropologists believe this may be connected with other vernal fertility rites with carousing and general carrying-on), we only twice in three years in Israel saw people in public who appeared to be so.

Purim commemorates the salvation of Israel in Persia by Queen Esther from the wicked Hamman, and on the streets of Tel Aviv we encountered small children dressed as angels, cowboys, generals, rabbits and butterflies with gauzy wings. There were twenty-odd other occasions for civic rejoicing. As in Jewish communities throughout the world, there was a great deal of warmth and humor and family affection, enough so that it spilled over to embrace visitors, and we found ourselves included, with invitations for everything from a newborn son's *brith*, the circumcision and namegiving on his eighth day in this world, to funerals and mourning in which one felt a sense of terrible family-tribal loss, where the body was buried in a winding sheet. (Only the military were permitted coffins, out of consideration of the feelings of the survivors faced with violent death and, here, holes were bored in the coffin to conform with the Biblical injunction that the body must rest in the earth.) The body must be buried before sundown, if possible, and, if not, on the day following death. Burial services are simple.

Moslem circumcision comes in the seventh month. Both Jew

and Arab were surprised to learn that, in a place like New York, male children, including Buddhists, are automatically circumcized unless their parents specifically object.

The next great event in the life of a Jewish boy comes at the age of thirteen with his *bar mitzvah* when he assumes a man's full religious responsibilities, and when, in ambitious, affluent communities, *bar mitzvah* receptions may turn into examples of competitive social display not unlike some of the debutante superlaunchings in the United States.

The Jewish wedding, like the simple *bar mitzvah,* can be most affecting, with a rectangular canopy supported on four poles above the bride and groom, who take from the rabbi a glass of wine together to seal their pledge to share whatever life may bring; and where the glass is broken to symbolize the destruction of the Jewish Temple in Jerusalem.

Shavuoth in May or June is the Hebrew harvest festival, with small, smaller and smallest school children wearing circlets of green garlands round their heads, as they trooped down the road past our windows carrying baskets of flowers nestled in greenery, on their way to school or proudly back to their parents. Then, around Christmas, comes the festival of Hannukah, with a nine-branched *menorah*, the traditional Jewish candelabrum, instead of the usual seven. This is in memory of the single small cruse of oil supposed to have burned miraculously without replenishing for eight days during rededication by the Maccabees of the Temple in Jerusalem. And since the first Hannukah candle, called the messenger, or beadle, is used to light all the others, one more each night, on the eighth night all nine candles are burning. Through windows and on the roofs in the cities and towns, in the hamlets and the isolated frontier villages, there are thousands upon thousands of lights everywhere.

Yom Kippur, the Day of Atonement, is the holiest of all the days in the Hebrew Year. It is a solemn and thoughtful holy day, observed with fasting, with neither work nor travel. One walks to the synagogue, and the feeling about strict observance of Yom Kippur is such that on one occasion, when the Canadian ambassador, Margaret Meagher, an agreeably rangy, highly professional career diplomat, at home in the suburbs, was told by telephone of the arrival of a cable in code from her government, she hiked all the way into the Canadian chancery in Tel Aviv to decode it, and discovered, predictably, that it was notice of a routine matter to be taken care of later. The point is that the ambassador would not dream of offending the feelings of her neighbors or of anyone else whom she might chance to meet by driving on Yom Kippur. One exception, of course, even on Yom Kippur, is Israel's defense forces. Jacques Medina's eldest son Chaim, who worked as an army driver, had rocks thrown through his windshield by angry ultra-Orthodox religionists on two successive Yom Kippurs when he was on duty; the rocks stopped only on the third year when, following his father's advice, Chaim put a hand-lettered sign on the windshield saying ARMY DUTY.

Yom Kippur is a time for meditation, repentance and reconciliation with God..On our last Yom Kippur in Israel, I was asked by Israel and Dorothy Naor to go with them and their children to services at one of the three Reform synagogues in a country which is overwhelmingly Orthodox. In the United States there are more Reform congregations than Orthodox or Conservative, and here across the highway from Nof Yam, in another village called Kfar Shmariyahu, the rabbi conducting the most solemn service of the year was a young American. The congregation among whom we sat came from many countries, a gathering of people with a great variety of backgrounds. Still, it seemed a close-knit community, and there was a great feeling of humanity, even on this day. People were easy with each other and with strangers, not afraid to joke or smile before or after the service, but all concerned, believing and deeply moved. So was I.

On Yom Kippur, Bertie had stayed at home with visiting friends, but during our last Passover in Israel we joined Danny Shimshoni and his wife Rose, both of whom had come to Israel from the United States, their children, Jonathan, Mihail and Abigail, and other friends for Seder supper on the first eve of the eight holy days.

At the beginning of this Seder supper with which Passover begins, Jonathan as the eldest son of the family was asked by his father, "Why is this night different from all other nights?"

"Because we were slaves unto Pharaoh in Egypt, and the Eternal, our God, brought us thence with a mighty hand and an outstretched arm. . . ."

We ate the unleavened bread called matzoth, symbolizing the

flight, the Exodus of the Jews from Egypt, carrying with them only dough without yeast, Passover's "bitter herbs" of horseradish or lettuce, parsley, and the *haroseth* paste of apples and nuts in memory of the mortar used by the Jews as laborers in bondage to the Egyptian pharaohs. There was an egg, and a lamb's shankbone to represent the traditional sacrifices of the Paschal lamb. Then during the Seder there are the four cups of wine, each to hold as much as an egg and a half, and to be drunk at appointed moments during the service. Traditionally, an extra glass of wine is poured for the prophet Elijah, and the door left ajar for him to enter, for it is he who, one Passover, will arrive to announce the coming of the Messiah.

Rather than sitting upright at the table, we sipped our Seder wine reclining on our left elbows, this in celebration of deliverance from bondage in Egypt where this sort of ease was reserved for the masters. At intervals, portions of the Passover service were read, and I was asked to read a passage in English.

It has often been said, "More than Israel kept the Sabbath, the Sabbath kept Israel."

Observance of the High Holy Days and the other festivals, with their inseparable joining of Jewish ethics and religion, history and legend is the rule, even for those Jews who think of themselves as non-religious. For children, it is an introduction and then a continuing education in that culture into which they were born. The presence of children, their sharing in traditional Jewish ceremonial, is remarkable, important and warming to someone from less closely knit, northern societies. So is the determination, the intensity of community feeling. To me, these help explain the survival of the Jews as a people against impossible odds.

4/ GOING TO JERUSALEM

I srael is small, a scant eight thousand square miles, roughly the size of El Salvador, the smallest of the Latin Americas, or of Massachusetts, the sixth smallest of the United States. It is two hundred and sixty miles from north to south, and seventy miles wide at its widest, in the northern Negev. But the visitor to the Holy Land travels four or five millennia backward and forward in time. Jericho, a part of the Hashemite kingdom of Jordan until its capture by Israeli troops during the Six Day War, and not far from Jerusalem or from Bethlehem, may be the oldest city on earth, inhabited some nine thousand years ago. In Israel, the traveler cannot escape the story of Solomon and the Queen of Sheba, who is supposed to have landed near Eilat, traveling north to Jerusalem to meet him. According to the First Book of Kings, this was a part of her quest to acquire the wisdom of the greatest rulers. And according to Ethiopian tradition, the Queen of Sheba was so taken with Solomon that she had by him a son, Menelik, ancestor of the Ethiopian dynasty founded in the thirteenth century, B.C. Descent is claimed by Haile Selassie, on whose imperial arms is a line in Hebrew, and among whose titles is that of Conquering Lion of Judah. It was in Jerusalem that he took refuge following the Italian invasion of his country in 1935.

As long as man can remember or discover, Jerusalem has been at the crossroads, on the caravan routes throughout the Middle East and on to Africa and Asia; near the coast that led to Europe; in the path of the great migrations of tribes and peoples. Jerusalem is one of the first known of man's settlements. Through the centuries, it was taken and plundered by the Egyptians, conquered and the Temple destroyed by the Babylonians, taken by the Greeks under Alexander the Great, made tributary to Syria, besieged and conquered by the Roman legions in seventy A.D., and the Temple again destroyed. With the rise of Islam in the seventh century, it fell to the Caliph Omar; its possession became the dream of medieval Europe whose chivalry and whose rabble swarmed through the Holy Land in ten crusades until Jerusalem was taken in 1099 and made the capital of the short-lived Crusader Kingdom. At one time or another, the city was taken by the Persians, the Mongolians and the Turks. At one time or another, the conquerors slew every Jew, every Christian or every Moslem who could be found within the city walls.

With all this turbulence, Jerusalem remained the goal of pilgrims. Of Chaucer's Wife of Bath, "Thryce hadde she been at Jerusalem." Now it is the jet-propelled tourist in search of the Holy Land. Very many come.

Robert Payne has written in *The New York Times Book Review* that, "In the Middle Ages, when men set out on pilgrimage to Jerusalem, they would sell their possessions, say farewell to their families and count it a blessing if they returned alive. They walked or rode by slow stages, and there was time enough to stare. Each country they passed through was like a cloak they wore around their shoulders. . . .

"We who fly from New York to Lydda in a single hop, and find ourselves half an hour later safely installed in Jerusalem. . . . I have

27

seen men 'doing' the Sea of Galilee, speeding round the lake at 50 miles an hour," continued Mr. Payne, pointing out that in one frenetic afternoon, the tourist can touch base at the Mount of Beatitudes, Tiberius, Nazareth and six other holy places. "It can be done, and there is no law to prevent it. . . . But in the Holy Land the camel's pace is too fast. . . . Around the Sea of Galilee, certainly, it is best to walk slowly, and there is no harm in walking barefoot."

Whatever transport the traveler may use to reach Galilee or Jerusalem (there are few donkeys and fewer camels now), whether he goes to Galilee by air or bus or the crowded collective taxi called *sherut* (often an overage model bought after years of faithful service in New York), or to Jerusalem by car or by the rickety railway that runs up through the gorges of the Judean Hills, sandy sometimes, then grey-green and stony as the train rattles along, the hills weather-worn but still steep—however he may first come—there is for almost every visitor a feeling of expectancy. Going to Jerusalem. It is an extraordinary and a moving experience to come on it as the late afternoon light is caught in the warm Jerusalem stone.

Leaving the sea, the road leads west across the fertile coastal plain, through the formerly Christian Arab town of Ramle, a center well endowed with mosques and churches, including the Monastery of St. Nicodemus.

Like the ruins of an Arab village at the turn-off for Lod Airport as one leaves Tel Aviv, Ramle was one of a handful of strategic Arab-held positions which straddle the route to Jerusalem. Like most of the others, it was taken without the attempt at negotiation and compromise that marked much of the Jews' approach to the opposing Arabs during the earlier stages of the struggle; rather this was the hard and simple decision of the Israeli forces fighting for the survival of their state that destroyed or cleared these few enemy guardians of the way to the Holy City.

The exception was Latrun. Defended by the British-trained and British-led Arab Legion whose fighting qualities are still respected by the Israelis, Latrun was the site of a French Trappist monastery and agricultural school founded three-quarters of a century ago, overlooking the ruins of a medieval fortress which pilgrims believed to be the home of St. Dismas, the Good Thief. The site commands the approaches below and the road leading up to Jerusalem, and during their War of Independence it was this strong point that Israeli forces were charged with taking. Many of the troops had just landed at Haifa from the ships crowded with immigrants waiting offshore for the hour of independence. Young men from a bewildering diversity of countries and speaking many languages, numbers of them without the rudiments of military training, were issued weapons and ammunition, sent up the road that leads to Jerusalem, and told to take Latrun. Often, officers' commands were unintelligible to their men. Many were killed. Latrun held, and remained in Jordanian hands for nineteen years until taken by the Israelis during the Six Day War.

Here Joshua, pursuing the five Canaanite and Jebusite kings joined against him, commanded the sun and the moon to stand still. The large building of the Trappist monastery on the hills rising opposite is dark in the evenings except for the gleam of an occasional candle or kerosene lantern.

Along the road as it begins to mount the Judean Hills, after passing the crossroads commonly known as Samson's Inn, at the spot where Samson is believed to have strangled a lion, there are left, here and there along the mountain road, among the most moving memorials that I have ever seen to those who have died in war: simply the burned-out, rust-colored shells of armored cars and other vehicles which had been caught in convoys attempting to relieve Jerusalem during the War of Independence. On some of the lifeless cars were memorial wreaths, turned brown by time and sun and rain, left there by the comrades and friends and families of those who had died in them here in the Jerusalem Corridor.

Making it a little easier to accept this sharp reminder are the trees, many millions of them, planted in the woods of evergreens along the way, a part of the continuing effort to make green again these rocky, denuded hills which had been cut over for so many centuries. Here, tourists, official visitors, those who wished Israel well, or friends or relatives from overseas themselves plant trees or ask that it be done for them by Keren Kayemeth, the agency responsible for the purchase and reclamation of land in Israel. There is a Forest of Costa Rica, a Forest of the Red Army and a forest for almost any nation or group one could think of.

Nearly a hundred million trees have now been planted since Israel's independence, and a good many during earlier periods of Jewish colonization. Some of the forests are now half a century old. Together, they make the difference between the green mantle beginning to cover more and more of the Israeli side of the frontier and the brown lands of Jordan.

As the road climbs to the gentle heights before Jerusalem, this becomes more apparent as the traveler looks across the valley which at some imperceptible point becomes another country. In fact, two frontier markers were put up by a joint survey team following the armistice of 1949, but suddenly the demarcation ceased, on the grounds that this would admit the existence of the new State of Israel.

Past one of the last of the hills before Jerusalem is Abu Ghosh, a small Arab village nestled in a hollow between the hills just to the right of the curving road. It seemed a poor, straggling village now, but from the mid-eighteenth century until about 1834, the Sheikhs of Abu Ghosh had been the terror of the pilgrims' path, seizing many of them and holding them in an underground crypt of the old church-fortress there until ransom could be sent from Jerusalem nearby. Originally built during the eighth and ninth centuries by the Arabs as a resting place or *khan* for travelers, the place was seized in the mid-twelfth century by the Knights Hospitallers who built there a fortress with its crypt over an ancient fountain and cistern. The Sisters of Saint Joseph of the Apparition built on the same ruins of an earlier Byzantine church a new church called Mary Ark of the Covenant, for it was here the Ark holding the sacred Covenant between God and the Hebrew people had rested on its way to Jerusalem from Beit Shemesh, the Biblical Canaanite and Philistine city.

Two years before the first voyage of Columbus and the expulsion of the Jews from Spain, the Franciscan fathers who then ran the hospice were massacred by the Moslems, and the place was abandoned by the Crusaders. Still, occasional pilgrims to Jerusalem found shelter at Abu Ghosh, as did Nicholas Christopher Radziwill, prince of Poland, on July the ninth in 1583.

Then in 1873, the French Ambassador to the Sublime Porte in Constantinople secured from the Turkish Sultan the French title to the church at Abu Ghosh as part of an arrangement in which the French Franciscans yielded to the Greek Orthodox Church all Franciscan claims to the Church of Saint George in Lydda, or Lod (if this seems a bit complicated, it is relatively simple and straightforward contrasted with the history of most antiquities in the Holy Land). The French flag now flies over the church in Abu Ghosh, as it does over a few other extraterritorial bits of France, technically French soil, still to be found throughout the Holy Land. The present Sheikh of Abu Ghosh and his tribe have opened an agreeable open-air restaurant across the highway from their village, and there sell Arab food and the standard Israeli beer and brandy. And it was the decision of the tribe during the War of Independence to throw in their lot with that of the Jews and to fight the Arab Legion (there is extant a photograph of the Sheikh wearing the uniform of Irgun, the underground Jewish terrorist organization). At any rate, the Sheikh is now the beneficiary of an agreement with the Rabbinate by which, during Passover, he assumes legal title, for a small fee from each of the owners, to all food either in Israel or even on its way to Israel, which does not meet the strict and special kosher standards for Passover—its ownership on paper by a non-Jew evidently satisfying Orthodox rabbinical interpretation of Old Testament dietary law.

The road from the sea past Samson's Inn and Beit Shemesh, past Abu Ghosh and on to the outskirts of Jerusalem's New City is traveled now by a multitude of Jewish and Christian pilgrims. Not a few of the visitors are Moslem members of African governments. The flags and the bunting and the banners across the entrance to the city are of many new nations and in many languages.

One of the last times we looked back at the city, there was an almost perfect rainbow curving down over the stony hills to one of the little white villages in the valley.

5/ THE GOLDEN CITY

The late-afternoon sunlight, clear and golden against the warm stone of the city, was Jerusalem to me, as I suppose it has been to poets and painters, pilgrims and prophets through the centuries. There would be long shadows on the Mount of Olives rising from the Old City, then with the gently rolling Judean Hills stretching through Jordan, the Dead Sea hidden among them, to the steep slopes of the Transjordanian Plateau rising abruptly in Syria beyond, deeply wrinkled and tawny, with reddish-purple folds like a great relief map.

If at every few paces in the Holy Land might be found reminders of our own turbulent family history over the past three and a half millennia—Judeo-Christian and Graeco-Roman, with all the tributaries that feed into these streams—then in Jerusalem itself memories come crowding.

In Jerusalem, above all, some quick, delighted recognition—a phrase, a story we'd known all our lives—would bring us back to the Bible, inextricably interwoven with the words we use every day. Writing in *The Psalms for the Common Reader* of the songs sung by the early pilgrims to Jerusalem, Mary Ellen Chase says, "The sight of the Holy City upon its hills was the climax to all such pilgrimages. . . . When they first saw its buildings against the sky, its walls, and above all, its Temple, the pilgrims burst forth exultantly: I will lift up mine eyes unto the hills!"

She continues with the pilgrims' song of joy at arriving at Jerusalem, their goal:

> Our feet shall stand within thy gates, O Jerusalem!
> Jerusalem is builded as a city that is compact together:
> Whither the tribes go up, the tribes of the Lord,
> Unto the testimony of Israel,
> To give thanks unto the name of the Lord!

and she comes at last to a psalm, the eighty-fourth, not usually included in the pilgrims' psalter, but one which she believes has caught, in the simplest, most understandable yet compassionate language, the joy and the wonder of what was to the pilgrims their home on this earth:

> Yea, and the sparrow hath found a house,
> And the swallow a nest for herself where she may lay
> her young!
> Even thine altars, O Lord of hosts, my King and my God.

Something of this was felt by many, perhaps by most, of those coming to Jerusalem. The *Guide to the Holy Land* published there in 1946 by the Franciscan Press recalls those of the Middle Ages who kept vigil throughout the night before entering the city, and "Then they descended from their horses and kneeling in the dust, recollected themselves in fervent prayer and meditation." The churchly guide goes on to ask something of the same vigil, recollection, meditation and prayer of those who now came to the city.

Much the same is still true for men of all persuasions, for an agnostic, or for a hard-shelled fundamentalist Protestant: whatever one's convictions, there is here the most intense sense of faith on the part of the believers, of feeling of history, that one could find. In Arabic, Jerusalem is called simply: *El Quds*, The Holy.

Fighting between Arab and Jew had flickered and flared sporadically and with increasing ugliness over the past decade under the British Mandate, until by 1947 Arab marauders and Jewish resistance fighters, Jewish terrorists and Arab terrorists tried by violence, each side to make irrevocable its position, to intimidate the people of the country, more particularly, their British rulers.

Before the last governor of Palestine sailed from Haifa in 1948 at midnight on May the fourteenth, terrorists of both sides had stepped up the tempo. On Sunday the thirtieth of the preceding November, the day following the United Nations vote to partition Palestine into separate, sovereign Arab and Jewish states, Arabs sacked the New City's commercial center and attacked outlying Jewish settlements. Thus began the Battle of Jerusalem.

The Arab states and the militant Arab forces within Palestine (the moderates had long since been silenced and had lost whatever authority among their own people they once had) rejected passionately the U.N. recommendations, or any solution which would give the Jews control over any portion of the land which the Arabs insisted was theirs alone. The twenty-five hundred inhabitants of the Jewish quarter of the Old City, mostly rabbis and religious students and their families, were cut off. The Jews moved quickly to protect the New City. The truncated concrete cones of tank traps called dragons' teeth were made ready to close the approaches coming up from the Old City, and long coils of barbed wire were strung out next to one another along some of the thoroughfares until, with their parallel rows of barbed curls, they looked like satanic exercises in penmanship. Fifty-two persons were killed in an explosion set off at the English-language Jewish daily *Palestine Post*, blasting a great hole at the side of Ben Yehuda Street and leaving one wall torn away, and the rooms, like a stage set, open to the air—an act blamed variously on the Arabs and on British deserters who sympathized with their cause or both.

More lives were lost in a less successful attack on the fortress-like Jewish Agency buildings. In an action for which the small but militantly extremist group known as the Stern Gang took credit, Jewish terrorists dressed as Arabs delivered milk cans full of nitroglycerin to the King David Hotel, blowing up one wing and killing over a hundred persons, Christian, Moslem and Jew, including nearly half of the senior British staff in Palestine. This last outrage alienated many of the more moderate Jews overseas as well as non-Jewish friends of Israel. It also gave warning of the struggle within the ranks of the Jews between the violently extremist and the more disciplined groups fighting for independence.

Attacked from three sides by the Egyptian Army and the Jordanian Arab Legion, the Jews of Jerusalem managed to beat back the Egyptians, but faced furious bombardment and determined assault by the Legion. During the first three weeks, more than ten thousand shells hit Jerusalem. Water supply to the New City was cut, the road to the coast blocked. There was no electricity, no oil, no wood. Hospitals were jammed with the sick and wounded, emergency cases, the most serious among the civilian and military casualties. A great part of all medical supplies and equipment was at Hadassah Hospital on Mount Scopus, beyond the Old City, and encircled by Arab forces. Among the Jews, ammunition was low. Water and bread were strictly rationed, and as the months wore on there was near-famine. On the twenty-eighth of May in 1948, the surviving Jews in the Old City surrendered to the Arab Legion. The twenty-eight synagogues in the Old City's Jewish Quarter were destroyed.

Finally, a new path bypassing Latrun was cut through the Judean Hills, joining the main road to the coast on the plain near Samson's Inn. It was nicknamed the Burma Road, and up it were carried food and ammunition just before the first armistice in June. One thousand four hundred and ninety Jews were known dead. But the Jewish survivors held most of the Jerusalem in which they lived.

There was another flurry of fighting during that same June of 1948, followed by a final armistice which confirmed division of Jerusalem into two, hostile cities.

All this was but the latest in a long series of invasions, sieges, battles and civil strife in the Holy City—assaulted, among others, by the Egyptians, the Hebrews under David, the Babylonians, the Persians, Greeks, Romans, Byzantine Christians, Mamelukes, Tartars,

Mongols, the Turks, and finally by the British in 1917, ending four centuries of Ottoman Turkish rule, and nearly thirteen centuries of almost uninterrupted Moslem domination.

When the rabbi-physican-scholar Moses ben Nachman, also known as Nachmanides, arrived in Jerusalem in 1267, twenty-three years after the Tartar invasion, he found left in the city only two Jewish families out of a population of two thousand. But after the expulsion of the Jews from Spain in 1492 and from Portugal four years later, these Sephardic Jews scattered throughout the rest of the world and the Jewish population of Jerusalem grew in the next eight years to a respectable one thousand five hundred. With the relative tolerance following Ottoman conquest in the early sixteenth century and the rebuilding by Suleiman the Magnificent of the Old City and its walls approximately as they are today, increasing numbers of Jews and Christians came to live in their own communities among the holy places. Whatever the vicissitudes of fortune, even among the ruins of the Temple, even during times of exile and transportation of most of the Jews to Babylon or Rome, even following massacre and pillage and banishment without the city's walls, since the time of David three thousand years ago, groups of Jews have striven tenaciously to live their lives in and around their Holy City.

What the visitor encounters in Jerusalem is a quiet, peaceful city of light, warm stone among the hills, very much the center of the government of Israel, an ancient seat of Hebrew learning and culture whose history the contemporary State of Israel draws on for guidance in the day-to-day management of its affairs. The visitors themselves seem aware of their heritage. Tired as the tourists might be, and deluged with a confusion of names and dates of five millennia, each in his own way is somehow caught up in the timelessness of the city.

Atop Mount Zion is first of all the Cenacle, a small, simple, handsome building of Jerusalem stone, in whose upper storey Christ and his Apostles are thought to have taken their Last Supper—now generally believed by Biblical scholars to have been the Seder supper of the Jewish Passover. Next door to the Cenacle on Mount Zion is the Church of the Dormition, a heavy neo-Romanesque basilica at the supposed place of the death of the Virgin Mary. A neighboring shrine is the supposed site of the Tomb of David.

From the churches on Mount Zion, past the guttering candles

placed by the reverent in niches around the courtyard of the official Tomb of King David, beyond its minaret with a view over the Old City next door and the great golden dome of the Mosque of the Dome of the Rock, the steps lead down the mountainside, past the little kiosk which sells souvenirs and supplies skullcaps for males visiting the Jewish holy places. There is the original, authentic Valley of Hell, Gehennah: peaceful and quiet in the sunlight, a small valley with a gentle slope on which are a few small houses, modest yet clean and decent, and with small flower gardens and vegetable patches about them. One remembered, driving over a sort of causeway that spans the valley, that this was, without any doubt, the site of the pre-Hebrew gods we know as Baal, into whose brazen bellies infants were thrown as propitiatory sacrifice.

Tourists come in droves in chartered buses, in private cars, often hitchhiking—the tanned boys and girls carrying rucksacks usually heading for one of the student hostels, or across the road from the King David to the YMCA. The last is an incongruous, fako-hokum Moorish building which always reminded me of a Shriners' temple: two large wings, colonnaded, with rounded arches, and rising at the center, a tall, domed minaret named Jesus Tower, at two hundred and sixty feet the highest structure in the city. It has little balconies like those used by a muezzin to call the Moslem faithful to prayer, and affords an unrivaled view of all the city.

With the annual invasion of tourists, the Holy Land in the past few years has seen the greatest influx of foreigners since the arrival of the Crusaders during the Middle Ages. It is an invasion considerably better disposed toward the inhabitants. About half of those who come to Israel are not Jews. Jerusalem is awash with Asians and Africans in saris and jodhpurs, caracul hats and the handsome robes which the new nations have adopted as their national dress. Then there are the battalions of comfortable Jewish business and professional families on sentimental journeys from London's northern boroughs or from New York's Bronx and Queens.

Throughout the year, there are two thousand and more African, Asian and Latin American students at Hebrew University in Jerusalem and throughout the country, just as there are a thousand or so Israelis training and teaching others abroad. And, as there have been throughout the centuries, there is a stream of Jewish Orthodox religious scholars come to pray and study in the Holy Land, above all in Jerusalem: both pale little boys and their fathers with curling sidelocks, the men with rather unorganized beards, and males of all ages with broad-brimmed black hats and the sober kaftans of Eastern Europe, the coats that reach below the knees. Except for the accents among the Britons or Americans, they are interchangeable in appearance with the ultra-Orthodox Israelis of the Meah Shearim—the Hundred Gates.

Off go the visitors every day to comb Jerusalem, Americans in cottons and lightweight miracle fabrics during the summer, some in expensive, slubbed Italian silks, many wearing sports shirts and duck-billed straw hats as though on leave from Florida and California. English accents range from Oxonian to Harvard, Australian, Cockney, Russian, German and Yiddish. Even though the few winter months remain raw and dismal in defiance of the Government Tourist Corporation's "Follow the Sun to Israel" posters, the tourist season grows longer and longer and busier and busier, building up to a crescendo as Easter and Passover came in the spring each year. The tourists survey the legislature, the Knesset, and children playing about the massive bronze seven-branched candelabrum, a traditional Hebrew menorah made by the British sculptor Benno Elkan and given to Israel by the British Parliament. They make their way through the tombs of the Sanhedrin, the ancient Hebrew court of justice; a whirl through Hebrew University with its handsome modern buildings and synagogue which looks like a curving low mushroom; past the supposed site of the tomb of John the Baptist in the small village of Ein Kerem on the hillside, and, next to it, to see the glorious stained-glass windows of Marc Chagall at the Hadassah-Hebrew University Medical Center—twelve brilliantly luminous windows with creatures and objects and symbols depicting the twelve tribes of Israel, infused with the ever-changing light of Jerusalem, now obscure, now flooded with warmth that brings alive the intense, deeply poetic, and essentially Hebraic religious world of Chagall.

After working for two years on the windows in the atelier in Paris of his colleagues, Jacques Simon, Charles Marq and Brigitte Simon, the artist said at the time of the windows' inaugural in Jerusalem in February of 1962:

"How is it that the air and earth of Vitebsk, my birthplace, and of thousands of years of exile, find themselves mingled in the air and earth of Jerusalem?"

He spoke in Yiddish. Chagall asked, "How could I have thought that not only my hands with their colors would direct me in my work, but that the poor hands of my parents and of others and still others who with their mute lips and their closed eyes, who gathered and whispered behind me, would direct me as if they also wished to take part in my life? . . .

"I feel as if colors and lines flow like tears from my eyes, though I do not weep. . . .

"I saw the hills of Sodom and the Negev, out of whose defiles appear the shadows of our prophets in their yellowish garments, the color of dry bread. . . . I have heard their ancient words. . . . Have they not truly and justly shown in their words how to behave on this earth and by what ideal to live?"

During the Six Day War, when his stained-glass windows were endangered and one slightly damaged by a bomb blast, Chagall gallantly urged Israel to get on with fighting the war without worrying about his work, adding that, if his windows were lost, he would replace them with better ones.

The visitors moved with purpose through the supposed tomb of the family of Herod with its great round and flat rolling stone like that used to seal the tomb of Christ; the tomb of Theodor Herzl, the journalist from Vienna who became so inflamed by the injustice of the Dreyfus trial that he spent the rest of his life on the momentarily surprising but, in the end, singularly successful struggle for the idea of a Jewish state to which the Jews would return as a people once again reunited.

One can see in Jerusalem the Biblical Zoo, dingy but with happily appropriate quotations from the Bible: "The Great Crocodile That Lieth in the Midst of His Streams—Ezekiel 29, 3." The zoo and the other metropolitan attractions and amenities are agreeable, but closer to the heart of most of the people who come to see Jerusalem are those philanthropies which they as foreign friends of Israel have undertaken to support: the Baby Home of WIZO (Women's International Zionist Organization), the religious schools, the trade schools, the university, the old people's homes—a thousand and one places that a tightly knit group with a strong social conscience and, above all, a strong feeling of compassion would support.

So it is with the Jews of England and France and America and all the other countries who have returned to live in Israel, who come in flights and clouds as tourists, who through the centuries have supported the pious communities of Jews living in the Holy City, whose benefactions have given Jerusalem everything, from the small schools and orphanages endowed in a relative's memory, to the gleaming, thirty-million-dollar Hadassah Hospital complex and the blocky, domed, neo-Turkish structure of the Chief Rabbinate, Hechal Shlomo, dramatically illuminated at night, the deep, floodlit entrance with its tall and slender columns, the play of light in the line of windows high above the street and on the building. Here and there and everywhere are the little painted signs and the engraved bronze plaques in honor of the unending list of donors. It is a standing joke at Hebrew University that each flower in its ornamental bed carries the name of its sponsor, on a proper and appreciative little label.

Not far from the King David Hotel and the YMCA, one comes upon a large windmill built of fieldstone, its skeleton sails idle now and partly broken: it is a curious landmark, and the reminder of one of the first Jewish settlements outside the walls of the Old City, an idea of Sir Moses Montefiore, a British philanthropist who encouraged the Jewish community to move beyond the confines of the Old City walls to the west, then open country and now the New City, the Jerusalem which became the capital of the State of Israel.

Until the middle of the nineteenth century, most of the Jews of Jerusalem remained huddled in the Old City, fearful of living outside the walls. It took the combined efforts of Sir Moses Montefiore and Judah Touro, an American merchant and philanthropist who had helped to build the Bunker Hill Monument, to create the new Jewish settlements. Sir Moses's windmill, intended to give employment to the Jews of the city, was not a commercial success, but gradually new colonies were established—first settled with poor families who were given free lodging and a small allowance to stay in what to them seemed the inhospitable wilds.

The maps carried by contemporary tourists still reflect this patchwork settlement. In the Old City, there is a Moslem quarter, a Christian quarter, a Jewish quarter and an Armenian quarter. In the New City, there is a German colony, a Greek colony, and a Bukharan quarter where the Jews from Central Asia are among the most enthusiastic in celebrating the Simhat Torah, the festival of the Rejoicing of the Law each year at the end of Sukkoth, singing in the streets, dancing and revolving with the great scrolls on which are written the first five books of the Bible, as the year of the reading of the Pentateuch in the synagogues ends, and the scrolls are rewound, for the reading to begin again for the next year.

In Meah Shearim itself, now become the bastion of Orthodoxy against the steady encroachments of the changing times, life goes on in good part as it did in the ghettos of Central and Eastern Europe: a self-contained community ranging from old-fashioned faithful Jews to the belligerently pious whose most extreme members refuse to recognize the State of Israel in which they live, on the grounds that only the Messiah may reestablish Eretz Israel—and who provided a serious security problem during the 1948 Battle of Jerusalem when some of their number attempted to join King Abdullah of Jordan (he refused them), and others intermittently tried to break through the impious Israeli lines to throw in their lot with the Jordanians. It should be said that Meah Shearim and its inhabitants took the hardest shelling from the Jordanian side, and they were caught between the forces of a state which they considered immoral and irreligious, and its enemies who were trying to destroy it.

In Meah Shearim, the community remains walled off from its surroundings, for security, and houses are built next to one another around a large courtyard, each again walled off from its neighbors, and each with its own water supply, ritual baths and synagogues. Along the flagged streets of Meah Shearim, stone sidewalks raised a bit and overhung with balconies and canopies over shops, walk somberly dressed rabbis and their congregations, the beards of some of the older men streaked with grey; on some, the fringes of the *tallith*, the striped black-and-white prayer shawl, may be seen beneath rusty jackets. Some of the men carry scuffed, imitation-leather briefcases. One is reminded, inevitably, of the extraordinarily poor Jews of New York's Lower East Side in an earlier era, of parts of Brooklyn and the Bronx.

The Jews in Jerusalem live partly in a past of the Old Testament. But much of it is the heritage of four hundred and some years of Turkish rule, and some years under the British Mandate. The walls of heavy stone blocks which still surround the Old City have all the defenses of a mediaeval city: the towers and embrasures, the merlons sheltering the defenders and the crenels for archers or the showering of rocks upon the enemy, the slits, called machicolations, for scalding besiegers with boiling water or searing them with molten lead.

Here and there along the ruins of the walls of the Old City are the slender, spindle-like minarets of Turkish times, one marking the site of the palace of Herod the Great, and another now called the Tower of David. Some buildings are vestiges of the foreign consular period in the city when great European powers, as in China, maintained their own little extraterritorial domains with their own post offices, their own guards, their own courts empowered to try their own citizens as well as those others to whom that nation extended its protection, as did the British government to the Jews in the Holy Land during the first part of the nineteenth century. All of this was completely without the jurisdiction of the government of Turkey, until the First World War the sovereign power in the land.

Perhaps the most striking reminder of those days of capitulary rights was the Russian Compound, where once camped the Assyrian Army of Sennacherib which in 701 B.C. unsuccessfully tried to take the city; where Pompey's Roman legions gathered to besiege and capture Jerusalem in 70 A.D.; where now are bivouaced a few of the Israel government offices without a home of their own, the Israel government's press offices, and a ghost of the Russian Orthodox past in the Byzantine ecclesiastical architecture.

Another ghost of the past in the New City, and one not easily recognizable, is the railway station, built by the French in the eighties, and where arrived in exile in 1936 His Imperial Majesty Haile Selassie I of Ethiopia, accompanied by the Empress whom the world's reporters insisted on calling the second Queen of Sheba.

It is all part of the web of what Jerusalem has been and is. There was a city of sorts here some five thousand years and more before our era. There was an Egyptian governor of Jerusalem about 1500 B.C., and the city's inhabitants were the object of the Egyptian Middle Kingdom's Pharaoh's ire a hundred years later when a classical Execration Text was impressed on a clay figure, hurling abuse at the Pharaoh's enemies—in this case, the Habiru, or Hebrews. The name Jerusalem was there first mentioned.

Here, David united all Israel into one kingdom in 1000 B.C. Alexander the Great conquered the city and established a tiny tributary kingdom inherited by the Greek Ptolemies who ruled over Egypt. In Jerusalem, the Jews rebelled in 66 A.D. against their Roman masters. Four years later, the capital was retaken and occupied by the Roman Tenth Legion Fretesis whose emblem was a ship and, of all things, a wild pig. Jewish Jerusalem was plowed under, a market, a forum, a theater, baths and a Temple of Aphrodite were built in the new Aelia Capitolina which was laid out on the traditional lines of a Roman camp, square and with two roads intersecting at right angles—still roughly the form of present-day Jerusalem's Old City. Jerusalem became a remote, obscure provincial city of the Roman Empire. Circumcized males were forbidden within its precincts, where were banned not only traditional Jews but also Jewish Christians, and this meant most of the early followers of Christ. It was at this point that Christian leadership and the recording of the traditional history of the Christian holy places passed to the new Christians of non-Jewish extraction.

There is in Jerusalem almost too much to remember. Of all the cities of ancient times, Jerusalem alone has been described in such detail. From the year 33 A.D. through 1878, some 3,515 authors busied themselves with writings on the Holy Land. The next three-quarters of a century saw, according to one conservative estimate, another quarter of a million titles added to the bibliography. In the past decade or so, the pace has further quickened with an avalanche of new works following the discovery of the Dead Sea Scrolls and the curiosity, the excitement and the tremendous interest aroused by this new light thrown on the Bible, on the daily life of the Jews and the Jewish Christians about the time of Christ. "Of the making of books there is no end" is the simple statement of Ecclesiastes.

To the visitor, this superabundance was at once exhilarating and bewildering. Everywhere the past is still alive. Perhaps all signs have vanished of the Mongols' invasion and capture of Jerusalem in 1244 A.D., probably the most abysmal time in the city's long history of conquest, plunder and destruction; but the Church of the Holy Sepulchre, completed in the first half of the fourth century, is a living part of the Old City, as is the Mosque of the Dome of the Rock, dedicated at the end of the seventh century after the city's conquest by the Caliph Omar a half-century earlier. The invasions of the Persians, the Egyptians, the Turks and the Crusaders have all left their mark on the population. Napoleon got no further to Jerusalem than Acre on the coast, now an easy drive, but before Haile Selassie, Richard the Lion Heart was here as was his chivalrous opponent Saladin, and Suleiman the Magnificent, and Saint Helena, the mother of the Emperor Constantine, who conquered under the sign of the cross and forcibly converted the Roman Empire to Christianity. And then, two years after the new state had declared its independence, Jerusalem once again was made the capital of Israel.

6/ JERUSALEM ETERNAL

I'm not quite sure what I expected to find in Israel and especially in Jerusalem—certainly more than just another country and just another city, so inextricably is Jerusalem interwoven with our culture and our heritage, our history for the past three thousand years and more.

Patrick O'Donovan, a correspondent for the London *Observer* with long experience in Africa and Asia, a consummate stylist and perceptive writer, has summed up in a single short essay called "The Unique Land" what he has learned, felt and come to believe about Jerusalem and Israel after a series of visits in recent years:

> There is no significant part of Western or Arab civilization that has not played its part here. . . .

From the great Latin hymns of the Roman Church to the Byzantine Greek delight in the concept of the City of God to the cool imagery of the seventeenth-century English religious poets to the Negro spirituals to the ecstatic poetasters of fundamental Protestantism, this is the place that has loomed in imagination and imagery.

O'Donovan keeps returning to the theme:

Here, there is a prevalent and continual sense of mission. . . . Despite the unprecedented horror of their history, these Jews seem to feel that they owe something to this land and that it owes almost nothing to them.

For me, the special quality of Israel and Jerusalem is part of our common heritage, above all through the King James Version of the Bible which for three centuries and a half has shaped the language and the thought of the English-speaking world as no book is likely to do again. Then, there are the memories of ancient-history courses in school and college, though I must confess that the long and complex chronicles of the Semites and their neighbors—the ancient Hebrews, the Canaanites, Moabites, Hittites, Midianites, Edomites, Phoenicians, Assyrians, Babylonians, Hyksos, Egyptians, Ethiopians, Greeks and Romans—were more than a little blurred around the edges by the time I first reached the Holy Land; and even now, if I don't keep reading, I have to go back and look everything up.

Throughout the past two thousand years and before, no city has been so visited and written about, the goal of so many pilgrimages, the subject of so many paintings, poems and prayers, as Jerusalem. "Nowhere in the world are there more religious associations," says a British compendium called *Places*, "not at Rome, nor at Mecca, nor at Delphi. . . ."

Though its exact date has been lost long since in the mists of memory, the three-thousandth anniversary of the coronation of King David is being celebrated in Jerusalem these days. It was a city long before David captured it from that branch of the Canaanites known as the Jebusites, who called it Jebu. Its settlement as a town has been traced as far as the third millennium B.C., a thousand years earlier, during the Bronze Age and contemporary with the Old Kingdom in Egypt. That of the neighboring Jericho, near the Dead Sea, goes back at least to 8000 B.C., according to the remarkable work there of the archeologist Kathleen Kenyon and her colleagues. The first villages in this land are thought to have been settled ten thousand years B.C. or so.

Where to start? So much has happened in the history of this extraordinary city, there is so much to learn, that it seems there is no beginning and no end. Sir Winston Churchill once said that, next to that of England, the map he knew best in the world was that of the Holy Land. This feeling of old familiarity was what struck me first and most forcibly in Jerusalem, in all of Israel. Here, in our civilization, is where it all began. There come crowding memories of the Hebrew tribes escaped from Egyptian bondage, wandering in the wilderness of Sinai until at last they came to the Promised Land; of the psalmists and the prophets and the kings; of the conquering ancient armies, the Babylonian captivity and the long exile in the Roman world, the great Temple built by Solomon in Jerusalem, destroyed by the Babylonians and built once again by the exiles returning from Babylon; the ministry of Christ in Jerusalem and his crucifixion there; the Crusaders, and the Moslems who defeated them; the wars of 1948, 1956 and 1967, which finally again secured to the Jews their own land, Israel.

Every day at every few steps, there is a reminder of all that has gone before. Instead of Gideon Bibles, hotel rooms are furnished with the standard Old Testament translation by the Jewish Publication Society of America called "The Holy Scriptures"—Hebrew and English side by side—and a very great number of passages identical with those of the King James Version, whose language, the Society's editors say, "can never be surpassed." Mary Ellen Chase, in her extremely helpful work *The Bible and the Common Reader*, says directly:

> The language of the Bible . . . has placed its indelible stamp on our best writers from Bacon to Lincoln. . . . Without it there would be no *Paradise Lost*, no *Samson Agonistes*, no *Pilgrim's Progress*; no William Blake, or Whittier, or T. S. Eliot as we know them; no Emerson or Thoreau, no Negro Spirituals, no Address at Gettysburg. Without it the words of Burke and Washington, Patrick Henry and Winston Churchill would miss alike their eloquence and their meaning.

In this book and in her later *Life and Language in the Old Testament*, Miss Chase mentions a few of the Biblical phrases which are a part of our daily speech: "We are *hewers of wood and drawers of water*; earn our bread by the *sweat of our faces*. . . . We sit in *sackcloth and ashes*, eat *sour grapes*; discover that like the leopard we cannot *change our spots*; long to be *giants in the earth*, but are satisfied if we can but *quit ourselves like men*. . . . Also, we suffer *a thorn in the flesh* or *a millstone around the neck*, and we escape *by the skin of our teeth*. We say that *our spirit is willing but our flesh is weak*; in moments of anger we remember that *a soft answer turneth away wrath*."

From the roof of the convent of Notre Dame de France, overlooking the Old City and the Mosque of the Dome of the Rock, the place of the ascent of Mohammed to Heaven after his famous night ride from Arabia, one can see at the same time in the grounds now surrounding the mosque the place of the threshing floor bought from the Jebusite Ornan by David to erect an altar to the Lord; the site where David's son Solomon built the First Temple with its Holy of Holies which sheltered the Ark of the Covenant for three centuries and a half until pillaged and destroyed by the soldiers of Nebuchadnezzar of Babylon. There are memories of the destruction of Herod's Second Temple and the worship of Greek and Roman gods on this site which was the capital of the Crusaders' short-lived Kingdom of Jerusalem in the twelfth century, when the Knights Templar converted the mosque into their headquarters and patterned all their churches in Europe after it, under the impression it had once been Solomon's.

The persistence of sacred sites as sacred in spite of changes of master, of doctrine, or the uprooting and death of whole religions is beautifully illustrated in the Holy Land where the "high places" sacred to the early Israelites and to the tribes before them are now the sites of church and mosque as well as synagogue. The thirty-five acres of the Dome of the Rock, with its surrounding terraces, shrines, fountains, arcades, walls, gates, the Aqsa Mosque and the Dome of the Chain and other outbuildings (known together as Haram es-Sherif, the Noble Sanctuary), cover the twenty-six acres of the earlier Temple. The sacred Rock itself, an uneven stone surface rising from the floor of the mosque, and surrounded by an iron grille left by the Crusaders, is thought to be the tip of Mount Moriah, the hill where God commanded Abraham to sacrifice Isaac, then relented. On the stone, believers are shown the imprint of the hand of the Archangel Gabriel, who pressed down to prevent the Rock from loyally following Mohammed to Paradise. The Prophet had arrived astride his marvelous mount Al Buraq, which means "lightning," a horse with rainbow wings and the head of a woman, flying in the night to meet Allah and receive the wisdom of Solomon.

In a grotto under the Rock, visitors are shown the spot where Abraham, David, Solomon, Elijah and Mohammed are all said to have prayed, and the impression of Mohammed's turban in the stone ceiling where the prophet hit his head. This intertwining of legend and history of Islam, Christianity and Judaism and the beliefs which preceded them, the overlapping of holy places in the Holy Land is typical of this crossroads of the world, and nowhere more so than in Jerusalem. If the architecture of the Dome of the Rock has been copied by Christian churches throughout Europe, Temple Church in London and Aix-la-Chapelle in Paris among them, then the mosque itself was derived in good part from the design of the Church of the Holy Sepulchre nearby.

To add to the confusion, there are three different Christmases in the Holy Land: that of December twenty-fifth; then another on January seventh celebrated by the Russian, Greek and Syrian Orthodox Churches as well as the Egyptian and Ethiopian Copts; and a last Christmas on January nineteenth for the Armenians. Easter is relatively uncomplicated, though it sometimes falls about the same time as Passover and when this happens, all hotel rooms are jammed.

At Passover, the approximately four hundred Samaritans gather at Nablus. These are all that remain of the once numerous people of Samaria who gave their name to "the good Samaritan" of the Bible. This followed the Samaritans' long feud with the Jewish majority following the return of the latter from exile in Babylon and their refusal to let the Samaritans help with the building of the Second Temple. The Samaritans, nevertheless, continued to look upon themselves as true Jews. They accepted only the five books of Moses. At dawn on the day of Passover, the Samaritans still sacrifice the Paschal lamb at services on Mount Gerizim, near Nablus and fourteen miles north of Jerusalem.

The hadj, or pilgrimage to Mecca and Medina in Saudi Arabia

which each true Moslem must try to make at least once in his life-time, may also come at about the same time as Easter (the dates of some religious holidays vary by as much as nearly five weeks from year to year, depending on calculations based on the lunar-solar calendar). Neither Jordan nor Saudi Arabia before 1968 permitted Moslem Arabs under Israeli jurisdiction to cross their borders to make the hadj, though in the Saudi economy religious pilgrimage is second only to oil. Still, at this time of year, the streets of Jordanian towns were clogged with tourist buses flying green Islamic flags and crammed with pilgrims from Lebanon, Syria, Iraq, Jordan and other parts of the Moslem world, all bound on the pilgrimage to Mecca and Medina, as enjoined by the Prophet Mohammed, who was born in Mecca in 570 A.D. and died in Medina in 632 A.D. To complete the confusion, Medina turns out to be a Hebrew name meaning "state," left over from the pre-Islamic days when that city was founded as a Jewish trading post.

Tourists—who began to return to Jerusalem in 333 A.D.—now num-ber a third of a million in Israel annually. On Friday evenings, some weary tourists wend their way back to their hotels from Gethsemane, the Via Dolorosa and the maze of the Old City, and others in the New City are preparing to set out on the famous tour of some of Jerusalem's four hundred and fifty synagogues. Often it is led by Yeheskel Friedmann, a meter reader for the Jerusalem Electric Corporation.

The trippers' cars which cluster around the holy places bear license plates from Denmark, the Netherlands, Texas and Virginia. There is, as a rule, an eddy of people outside Damascus Gate and a constant stream in and out through the great archway, under the crenelated battlements of the Old City. Inside the gate there is the Sûq, or market, looking like the Casbah in the movie *Algiers*, with crooked, narrow streets flagged or cobbled, with shafts of sunlight cutting through the shadow of the stone buildings on either side, splashing on the enclosed dark wooden balconies over-head and on the canvas awnings sheltering the hole-in-the-wall shops at every step.

Seated at café tables along the narrow streets, substantial Arabs wearing tassled dark-red fezzes smoke hookahs and drink small cups of coffee. Making their way along the streets are the immemorial,

Biblical donkeys, weighted with saddle bags on either side, and often enough carrying a heavy owner. In the crowd are Arab women in black, a few tattooed on the forehead above the headcloth half drawn over the lower face. There is always a scattering of European and American visitors, priests, nuns, the occasional scholar, retired businessmen and housewives from the cities of the Western world.

Throughout Jerusalem are signs of what Professor Melville Herskovits of Northwestern University calls transculturation. Here, some Moslem women wear stiletto heels and needle-toed shoes, and a few of the small daughters of the classical Arabs are dressed in bright-red tights. Many of the Arab children turn out to be blue-eyed and with blond or gingery-red hair. Equally, a newsreel of Israeli soldiers could often seem an equally suitable illustration for the Swiss Army. Foreigners are apt to be surprised at first at the occasional appearance of blue-eyed blonds among the Arabs, or their frequency among the Jews, forgetting for the moment that, even before the recent return of a million and a quarter Jews from a hundred nations, this land bridge between Asia, Africa and Europe has seen human migration, conquest, deportation and colonization since the beginning of recorded history.

Probably the greatest monument to acculturation in all of the divided city is its newest caravansary, the Hotel Jerusalem Intercontinental, a Pan American Airways affiliate, built toward the top of the Mount of Olives above the Jewish cemetery. (I had been worried about the cemetery, and was relieved to learn that the hotel's excavation had disturbed nothing more than a handsome, tawny Byzantine mosaic, now mounted vertically as a screen in the entry.) Here, while the façade is the familiar warm, golden Jerusalem stone, the overall décor of the public rooms is neo-Moorish with a sure, light use of the arabesque. It was very well done, too, giving lie to the canard that American hostelries overseas must be endless repetitions of the great American motel.

I think that one factor encouraging this impression may be the relative unawareness of many observers that cultural borrowing is a continuing business, and the jazziness of some of the latest imports from the U.S.A. may be a little unexpected. The eye is caught by bar and coffee-shop lists offering Manhattans and Screwdrivers, Swankburgers and Hobo Special sandwiches, milk shakes, Pepsi-

Colas, and the Jordan Valley Banana Split; a display card advertised the Arab combo providing the evening's music: Solomon & His Twisters.

By contrast, the flavor of the region is well expressed in the Intercontinental's Middle Eastern cuisine, with succulent combinations of lamb, chicken, lemon, rice, tomatoes, onions, eggplant, artichokes, grape leaves, sesame, chick peas and pine nuts. The print on several of the menus is superimposed on subdued, greenish-grey reproductions of Frederick Catherwood's steel engravings of life in Jerusalem a century ago. Light dances through a thousand perforations in the great brass Arab chandeliers overhead.

Here, looking out from the dining room called the Seven Arches, down the Mount of Olives across most of Jerusalem, lights winking in the Old City and the New, when the sentries were at their posts even during the days when the city was divided, there was never any line at all to be seen in the night.

7| PILGRIMS AND PROMOTION

C ontemporary tourists are descendants of all those who have made their way to Jerusalem throughout the centuries, drawn for many of the same reasons. A recent recounting, *The Spring Voyage* by Miss R. J. Mitchell, draws on the journals of half a dozen pilgrims traveling to the Holy Land in 1458 with the Earl of Worcester, a Fellow of Eton, and with Italian, German and Dutch companions, friends, family and priests to the number of a hundred and fifty or so: the voyage from Venice to Haifa was five weeks by car and by sail, seven weeks to return without bad winds; but at a time when the Moslem overseers of Jerusalem were appreciative of the tourist trade, as were the officers of the Republic of Venice where travelers embarked. Pilgrims some five hundred years ago

53

were offered a tour with transportation, lodging, taxes and baksheesh included in the overall charge. Guides to Jerusalem were provided without extra cost. Guides were forbidden to accept commissions from shops recommended. Tipping was discouraged, and, at times, even prohibited.

Three and a half centuries later, a surgeon named F. B. Spilsbury who served aboard the man-of-war H.M.S. *Le Tigre* during the 1799 and 1800 British campaigns "for the Defence of the Ottoman Empire," produced after his return to England the almost obligatory journal of his travels, *Picturesque Scenery in the Holy Land and Syria.* During these two expeditions under Sir Sydney Smith against the forces of Napoleon which had already conquered Egypt and captured Jaffa, Dr. Spilsbury and a small party of sailors obtained permission from the ferocious Pasha of Acre, Al Jazzar, the Butcher, to travel inland to Jerusalem, and, with a collapsible steel boat, to descend the River Jordan from the Sea of Galilee to the Dead Sea. It may be that Dr. Spilsbury was sufficiently discouraged by the deaths from disease of several of his companions—a not unusual hazard for European and American travelers in the East until our own day. In any event, his enthusiasm for this "country made classical by Profane Histrys as well as Venerable by Holy Writ" was restrained. While cataloguing the wonders of the land "and many other sacred curiosities" in Jerusalem, he found "the reflections of former eminence . . . now a melancholy spot inhabited by nothing but a few miserable Arabs." The familiar self-assurance of Europeans in the Holy Land pervades the doctor's journals: he and his party proceeded to the "concurring acclamations of the grateful natives."

By the middle of the nineteenth century, through the pious, English-speaking world, where in many homes the chief, or only, book for generations had been the Bible, there existed an almost inexhaustible audience thirsty for descriptions of the Holy Land. W. H. Bartlett, one of the most popular British delineators of the foreign scene, addressed himself to the Holy Land with handsome rag-paper volumes suitably embellished with woodcuts and steel engravings and with titles like *Forty Days in the Desert; or On the Track of the Israelites* and *Walks about the City and Environs of Jerusalem.* They are very good, detailed, a bit stuffy, paternally

Victorian, and not expensive now, even in their original editions. I like to keep a copy of *Walks about Jerusalem* as a more or less modern guide to the Old City.

In June of 1867 there sailed from the United States the first American guided tour, one hundred and fifty passengers aboard the side-wheeler *Quaker City* for a ten months' "Pleasure Excursion to the Holy Land, Egypt, the Crimea, Greece and Intermediate Points of Interest." The average age of the tourists was fifty, and they paid $1,250 each, plus five dollars in gold daily for all expenses on shore. Among them was the thirty-two-year-old Mark Twain, reporting the trip for the *Daily Alta California,* the *New York Tribune* and the *New York Herald.* His pieces became *The Innocents Abroad; or, The New Pilgrims' Progress,* published two years later. They have a good deal to tell us about tours and tourists and the Holy Land a hundred years ago and in our own time.

Writing of "The Grand Holy Land Pleasure Excursion," Mark Twain described this party of Americans:

> The incorrigible pilgrims have come in with their pockets full of specimens broken from the ruins. . . . They broke off fragments from Noah's tomb; from the exquisite sculpture of the temple of Baalbec; from the houses of Judas and Ananias in Damascus; from the tomb of Nimrod the Mighty Hunter . . . and now they have been hacking and chipping these old arches here that Jesus looked upon . . . . Heaven protect the Sepulchre when this tribe invades Jerusalem!

His fears were well founded. For centuries, churchly custodians at the Holy Sepulchre sold chips of stone there to the faithful.

In the Greek Chapel of the Holy Sepulchre, Mark Twain observed:

> . . . a short column that arises from the middle of the marble pavement and marks the exact *center of the earth.* . . . From under this column was taken the dust *from which Adam was made.* . . . Not far away . . . Adam himself . . . lies buried. . . . The tomb of Adam! How touching it was, here in a land of strangers, far away from home, and friends, and all who cared for me, thus to discover the grave of a blood relation. True, a distant one, but still a relation.

55

What he took to be the manufacture and promotion of holy relics roused Mark Twain even more satisfactorily. Of St. Helena, who had no difficulty in locating the three original crosses when she visited the Holy Land, Mark Twain mused while visiting in the Church of the Holy Sepulchre.

> St. Helena, the mother of Constantine, traveled all over Palestine and was always fortunate. Whenever the good old enthusiast found a thing mentioned in her Bible, Old or New, she would go and search for that thing until she found it. If it was Adam, she would find Adam; if it was the Ark, she would find the Ark. . . .

Since Mark Twain's time, the discovery, production and sale of sacred relics and holy souvenirs has kept pace with the tide of trippers to the Holy Land. It is true that enthusiasm has declined for the carrying off and enshrining in European churches of the supposed limbs and fingers and nails and other bits of saints, and trade in the innumerable bits of wood alleged to be part of the True Cross has come to a standstill. Instead, the mass production foreshadowed by the latter has become a reality. Tourists in Jerusalem and in Bethlehem are pursued by runners offering business cards ornamented with the Wise Men's Star, printed in blue and with a tail like a comet sailing over pressed wild flowers, sometimes with the announcement that these have been placed on the Holy Manger in the Church of the Nativity. Dealers such as the Oriental Souvenir Shop and the Holy Manger Store, both of Milk Grotto Street in Bethlehem, advertise Bibles bound in mother-of-pearl or in olive wood and emblazoned with Crusaders' crosses, as well as crèches, crucifixes, rosaries, medals, stars, icons, daggers, toy wooden camels, cut-rate Oriental rugs, Holy Land color slides, Crusaders' jackets, and more flower cards. The Milk Grotto is a Franciscan chapel southeast of the Church of the Nativity, and the source of the soft white stones preserved in numbers of European churches as the Virgin's Milk. This follows the belief that some drops of the Virgin's milk turned the stone white. Throughout the centuries, women have come to pray in the grotto, then grind some of the white stone into their drink as an aid to lactation. Apparently the stone is harmless.

Religious-goods industries seem to thrive wherever there are shrines and pilgrims. In Bethlehem and the Old City of Jerusalem, small Bibles, missals and Books of Common Prayer faced with olive wood have sold so many hundreds of thousands of copies by this time that it seems unlikely there would be a twig left on the Mount of Olives if this were the only source of supply, as the buyer is assured. Similarly, in the New City, so many little muslin sacks allegedly filled with earth taken from Mount Zion are sold to tourists that one feels that, by rights, there should now be there a great crater instead of a hill.

Coarsely woven shrouds are still available at places like the Greek Orthodox supply shops in the Old City, but it is doubtful that demand such as it is is as great as it was in preceding centuries when pious Christians of many persuasions were accustomed to buying their shrouds relatively early in life, traveling with them, wearing them for baptism in the River Jordan and, at last, being buried in them. Water from the River Jordan still sells as briskly as it ever did, and pilgrims carry it home with them for family baptisms.

There is a persistent story, which I have never been able to confirm but which is far from implausible, that before 1948 an Arab citizen of Haifa made a small fortune by bottling municipal tap water which he then sold as straight from the river.

When I sent an exceedingly modest contribution (perhaps this was the trouble) to the Gene Ewing Revival Crusades of Dallas, Texas, together with their coupon labeled "Clip out for your souvenir water from the Jordan River and Rush . . ." the postman brought me one quarter of a cc. of holy water in a small vial wrapped in cardboard. It didn't stop there, for I was then on the list, and kept in pretty constant awareness of my parlous state by a stream of tracts, gospel magazines and solicitations signed Bro. Gene Ewing, who is also the leader of Campmeeting Revival, Inc. and editor of a periodical called *Revival Crusades, The Magazine of Prayer and the Blessed Old Bible,* published by Victory Tabernacle, Inc.

Another appeal, and one I think fairly representative of those which flood the mails each day, came from Kash D. Amburgy, billed as "The Country Preacher from So. Lebanon, Ohio—Pastor—Evangelist—Radio Speaker—Businessman—Holy Land Tour Conductor," who offered to take me for $1,495 on a Holy Land tour that included not only Jordan, Israel, Egypt, the Lebanon, Syria and Turkey, but included England, Italy, France, the Netherlands, Switzerland, West Germany and East Berlin. Kash D. Amburgy's is but one of the hundreds of such tours that leave the United States each year, headed for the Holy Land, school teachers and ministers from the country's small towns prominent among them.

It is not surprising that so many clergymen and teachers should be attracted to the Holy Land. But I don't believe I had realized, before living in Israel for a bit, and then looking for signs of curiosity or interest when back in the United States on leave, just how deep and abiding in our nation is interest in the Bible, in Bible stories, in the places of the Bible. At least it isn't so obvious from the vantage of New York or Washington or the other big cities. Nor from the newspapers nor the favorite family magazines. Nor from often-remarked closer association in our times with church and synagogue. Rather, I've found more enthusiasm for the old-time religion, and consequent interest in the Holy Land, in the small town and gospel radio stations, many of which are powerful and reach a very large audience indeed. Also from the evangelist publications whose circulation is unknown but phenomenal. Between them, they account for many of the latter-day pilgrims.

On a simpler plane, the deluge of quasi-Biblical films continues, with contributions from everyone from John Huston to a recent Mr. Universe in the pay of the Italian cut-rate spectacular industry. By now it has become an art form with a discipline of its own as tight and familiar as the sonnet, yet perhaps with more in common with its cousins, the western, the spy, cops-and-robbers, horror, and army-navy-air force films. First-run Biblical spectaculars play the more opulent movie houses with reserved seats and inflated prices. This goes on until the superannuated Biblical epics, chopped rather haphazardly, and laced with commercials, end up on the early-morning television treadmill.

Twentieth Century-Fox's version of the Bible (as distinct from the King James or the Douay) in *David and Bathsheba*, with Gregory Peck, Susan Hayward and James Robertson Justice, strikes me as dead average: archers and foot soldiers wear standard medieval-Hollywood helmets; Goliath of Gath appears to be a monster left over from a thriller in outer space; and the Ark carrying the Ten Commandments, surmounted with graven images in clear defiance of Hebraic law, seems designed by the Wing Ho Novelty Co. of

Hong Kong. There is a noticeable absence of prayer throughout. On the telecast I saw, between each snippet of story, there were up to seven commercial announcements. These were accompanied by ads for other films. No doubt, this thundering lack of taste is familiar, but there is something in the Biblical movie which brings out the worst in everyone.

However they come and for whatever reason, visitors can hardly remain unaffected by the general air of pilgrimage and religiosity—both holy and commercial—with which they are surrounded. Or unaware that every third doorway in the Old City seems to be that of a travel agency or a dealer in objects of piety. The traveler's eye is caught by notices such as "Cable: HOLYTOURS." Or:

TRAVEL WISELY

with

THE GUIDING STAR AGENCY

Activity comes to a semi-standstill at the time of Israel's triennial International Bible Contest, with two hundred and fifty or more press, radio and television correspondents and up to a couple of dozen contestants from as many countries descending on Jerusalem for the quiz. There are special editions of the daily papers, tens of thousands listening to the broadcasts over Kol Israel which makes tapes for sending to other countries, and at least three thousand on hand for the finals, which last from five to seven hours—the President, the Prime Minister and the Speaker of the House all on hand, and sometimes submitting their own questions. Interpreters responsible for translating the questions into Finnish, French, Portuguese, Afrikaans or whatever is required are locked up for thirty-six hours in advance, lest they reveal the answers. The first year my wife and I were in Israel, the contest was won at two-twenty in the morning.

The places of the Bible and those famous in history have drawn the most remarkably variegated groups of visitors—the devout, the idiosyncratic, the studious, the curious, the political. Living in Israel is a group of Seventh Day Adventists dedicated to tilling the soil of the Holy Land until the day of the Second Coming, which they judge near at hand—counting among other portents the fact that the State of Israel was established and managed to survive.

Throughout all that is called the Holy Land—across Sinai, which is the Asian extension of Egypt, and the length of Israel, Jordan,

Lebanon and parts of Syria and Iraq—there are monasteries and nunneries, sheltering little bands from a multitude of Christian sects and a good number from the Moslem world, dedicated to the preservation of the shrines, or keeping vigil there. Monasteries still cling to cliff-faces, and there are still hermits in the caves in the cliffsides.

Most of the newcomers in the land—almost everyone—goes to Jerusalem. Besides the better-known Christian churches and the smaller, more obscure sects, and the usual guardians of the holy places of Islam, there are uncountable, miniscule Christian cults, and a raggle-taggle of rather kindly eccentrics attracted to the Holy Land from far away. One pale, uncertain-looking person turned up in Jerusalem wearing a sort of doublet emblazoned with a great Crusader's cross, and when asked what religious group he represented, the man in costume said that he really didn't know too much about it yet, as this particular sect, with the aim of collecting funds for work in the Holy Land, had been founded only recently, and that he himself had been recruited three weeks before in London.

There is something about the Holy Land which seems to attract people of strong, and sometimes spectacular, religious persuasion. During the days of the Mandate, an elderly British woman in Jerusalem was celebrated for rising early in the morning and going out through the fields with a thermos of hot tea and some biscuits, suitable for refreshment for the Saviour in case of the Second Coming.

Of all the pilgrim's goals, the Holy Sepulchre is, usually, the greatest anti-climax. Almost theatrically so. The main façade is much as the Crusaders built it in 1144, but with the improvements and the restorations of the ages the great church looks as though it were permanently under construction. Shaken by earthquakes and built on ground already honeycombed with rock tombs, crypts and cisterns, the structure had settled perilously when the British authorities shored it up between 1935 and 1944 with metal scaffolding inside and out; but unfortunately, with the sharp change in Jerusalem's temperature between day and night, the metal expands and contracts, loosening the same stonework it was meant to reinforce. At the same time, it is feared if the scaffolding were removed without elaborate and extremely costly reconstruction, the church would collapse. Meanwhile, the façade, looking as though it were about to topple over on the throngs of worshippers below, is propped up by an intricate, high triangular network of steel girders and struts, buttresses and jacks, broad at the base, rather like a piece of the Eiffel Tower which had unaccountably lost its way.

Accretions to the façade over the past sixteen centuries—once the eye can be distracted from the scaffolding—appear to be windows and doors irregularly latticed, sealed with planks or bricks, ladders leading from one height to another, and, on holy days, a swarm of celebrants massed on the roof, sitting in the windows and clustered on the ledges.

Inside the Church of the Holy Sepulchre, on its roofs and all about, the rival Christian sects of the Franciscans, representing the Roman Catholics, or Latins as they are known here, the Greek, Russian, Armenian and Syrian orders, and Egyptian Copts all carry on their holy offices, each jealously guarding, reinforcing or improving its own precedence and privilege at the churches, shrines and other holy places—all hotly contested. In the middle of the Rotunda of the Church of the Holy Sepulchre is the sepulchre itself, the stone on which the body of Christ lay from Good Friday until Easter Sunday, now the Fourteenth Station of the Cross, and protected with marble against the ubiquitous vandals. Surrounding the sepulchre is the Edicule, a little building within a building. Capped with a cupola and ornamented with heavily worked balustrades and cornices, the Edicule is so small that only four worshippers may enter at the same time. Services here are restricted to the Greeks, the Armenians and the Roman Catholics, who are also responsible for care of the profusion of pictures, lamps and giant candelabra which decorate the Edicule, all numerically divided between the sects. The Egyptian Copts are relegated to a chapel behind the Edicule. The Ethiopian Copts, who formerly enjoyed the privilege of serving within the church, have now been reduced to the roof of St. Helena's Chapel, overhead, "having lost their position through poverty, in 1633," according to *The Pilgrim's Companion in Jerusalem and Bethlehem* by Stewart Perowne. "The Georgians had lost theirs from the same cause four years earlier, and have disappeared altogether," adds Mr. Perowne.

For the Roman Catholics, Greek Orthodox, Syrian Catholics, Egyptian Copts and Armenians alone, a condensation of the former Turkish government's regulations determining precedence and privilege for these particular denominations—whose priests may be where at what time, using exactly what candles, carpets, coverings, icons, censers and other equipment for religious ceremonials—covers sixty-four printed pages in Arabic and English. Of the twin doors at the entry to the Church of the Holy Sepulchre, that on the right has been closed since the time of Saladin, and the key to the other has been kept by a Moslem family since 1244; another Moslem family has the privilege of opening the door. Both families must be paid each morning by the Latins, the Greeks and the Armenians before the place is opened.

This patchwork of claims, concessions, dispensations and tradition in time has acquired the authority of customary law throughout the Holy Land. But the brothers and the fathers to which these apply are, some of them, a disputatious and turbulent lot. Far more difficult for the authorities to cope with than the flood of lay visitors are the suspicious, litigious and occasionally violent resident clerics belonging to a galaxy of competitive Christian religious establishments. There are sporadic scuffles, and sometimes a real fracas, at which point the police have had to be sent for to keep order. One Christmas while we were in Jerusalem, two of the Eastern sects got into an unholy row over their respective rights to circumnambulate a holy spot on the rooftop of the Holy Sepulchre. They ended up in a melee, throwing empty wine bottles at one another.

In spite of this sectarian squabbling, in spite of the credulity of visitors looking for miraculous keepsakes and the predictable preparedness of the purveyors of religious articles in bulk, perhaps the abiding significance of all this is the simple faith of the pilgrims.

Of the holy places mainly free from these rivalries and temper tantrums, one of the most soothing is the Garden of Gethsemane, at the foot of the Mount of Olives and on the grounds of a Roman Catholic basilica, Byzantine in style and with a frieze in shining golden mosaic. Among the flowers are the giant, dark grey-green, gnarled trunks of eight ancient olive trees, still sprouting feathery pale green shoots, and revered by the many who believe that they were alive at the time Christ walked in the garden here. (Father Eugene Hoade's *Guide to the Holy Land* notes that there used to be a ninth olive tree, but this was stolen.)

Even here all is not entirely peaceful, for on the wooded slope over-

looking the basilica are the gold onion domes of the Russian Orthodox Church of St. Mary Magdalen, a dependency of the Imperial
Russian Palestine Society, which owns a fair part of the Mount of
Olives, with the Convent of Eleon at its top and that of Gethsemane
below, together with its own Garden of Gethsemane. (It's notable
that holy places often come in multiples, with a choice between
rival sites.) This is where the confusion begins again, for the Soviet-
controlled Moscow Patriarchate claimed inheritance of all Russian
Orthodox holdings in the Holy Land. Israel agreed, buying from
the Soviet government all their extensive secular holdings for three
million dollars, two-thirds in oranges, one-third in cash, and leaving
to the Moscow Patriarchate the religious properties such as the convent at Ein Kerem and the cathedral in the New City's Russian
Compound. On the arrival of an archimandrite, an abbess and
twenty-eight nuns from Moscow, some of the older nuns who had
served there since Czarist days fled to Jordan, while the twenty who
remained were obliged to accept Soviet passports.

The issue was more complicated on what used to be the Jordanian
side of Jerusalem where the Greek Orthodox Patriarchate strongly
supported the Moscow claim and a Russian Orthodox nun called
Sister Seraphima, a United States citizen who was formerly the
Russian Princess Marie Poutiatin, lived near the Church of the
Holy Sepulchre, and zealously worked for installation of the Soviet
hierarchy in Jerusalem. At the same time, Mother Mary, the British-
born abbess of the Convent of the Garden of Gethsemane, and
others there and at the Convent of Eleon, have remained strongly
anti-Communist and anti-Soviet, supported by the Metropolitan
Anastasi of the Russian Orthodox Church in America and by King
Hussein's declaration that there would be "no change" in administration of the convents on the Mount of Olives. This was all before
the third round of Arab-Israeli fighting, the Israeli occupation of the
Old City, the Russian break with Israel, and the Israeli promise that
shrines in the Old City will be accessible to all and will remain
the responsibility of the appropriate religious authorities. (Communist or anti-Communist Russian Orthodox authorities?) If the sects,
nationalities and politics involved here seem interwoven in a semi-
lunatic way and beyond disentanglement, I can only say that it all
seems not unusual for the Holy Land. By the time this appears in

print, I suspect, the whole politico-religious landscape will have undergone ever further convolutions, but that is in the nature of the land.

All the while that Christian pilgrims travel to the Church of the Nativity in Bethlehem and the Church of the Holy Sepulchre in Jerusalem, there is a constant stream of Moslem pilgrims to Jerusalem's Mosque of the Dome of the Rock and its neighbor, Al-Aqsa. On these grounds is also the Dome of the Chain, a small, graceful, open-air pavilion whose octagonal upper portions and cupola are supported by seventeen pillars in two concentric circles, all supposedly visible from any side. The Dome of the Chain served as a treasury and as a model for the Dome of the Rock built in 691 by the Umayyid Caliph of Damascus, Abdul Malek ibn Marwan. The Chain refers to the belief that those testifying here before the tribunal of David were made to grasp a great hanging chain and that this magically lost a link if a person lied.

The Dome of the Chain, the Dome of the Rock and Al Aqsa are all distinguished by arabesques, caligraphy, intricate mosaics, sixteenth-century Persian and Turkish titles beautifully glazed in buff, navy, white, turquoise, coral and pale-lime. Thanks to some two million dollars worth of restoration over the past few years, the Dome of the Rock is now in far better shape than the Church of the Holy Sepulchre, with more tile from Turkey, marble from Italy, Greece and Belgium, and a new golden dome, even though this is of anodized aluminum in place of the gilded lead roof judged to be in danger of collapse. But even the Dome of the Rock has its problems, for the Rock itself held such fascination for Crusaders that they chipped off pieces and bought others for their weight in gold from the priests there, to carry home. In the end, the Rock was covered with marble like the Holy Sepulchre, to save it from disappearance.

The Dome of the Rock, surrounded by Al Aqsa and the Dome of the Chain, the surrounding shrines, domes and minarets, has become the holiest place in Islam after the Kaaba in Mecca (a simple, rectangular building housing a black stone which is believed inherited from pre-Islamic times), and the great mosque of Mecca, which together with the Mosque of the Dome of the Rock is among the first of the mosques which led to the Moslems' great contribution to the world in architecture.

There is another Moslem holy place of extreme veneration nearby: the great mosque of Ahmed Jazzar Pasha in Acre which is modeled after St. Sophia in Istanbul. In Acre is preserved a single hair of the beard of the Prophet—one of the few claimed anywhere. It is kept in a box in a cage with pea-green bars, and may be seen once a year by the throngs of faithful who assemble for this privilege. But these are Israeli Arabs. Those in the surrounding states may not pass.

The Arab boycott instituted in 1951 which threatens economic reprisal to anyone doing business with Israel, to anyone doing business with anyone doing business with Israel, to businesses using the Star of David as a trademark, to anyone with the temerity to hire Jewish executives, and so on through a long list of similar sins, all has been largely ineffective, to judge by the goods and services usually available on both sides of the frontier. Blacklisting, by the Arab Boycott Committee, of Ford and Coca-Cola made the headlines (*COLA NON GRATA*), but at the same time, the large insurance companies, eighty international banks, and well over a hundred American concerns including most automobile manufacturers, air and shipping lines, motion picture and recording companies, distillers, wire services, newspaper, magazine and book publishers, and everybody from General Electric to Old Dutch Cleanser continued to do business on both sides.

The techniques used by the Boycott Committee to intimidate traders with Israel are interesting. Announcements are made of removal from the black list of firms which were never on it in the first place. Letters of enquiry are sent to companies which have never invested in Israel and which are not likely to do so—represented as a great victory over the Zionists.

When Chase Manhattan and Conrad Hilton held out firmly, the Boycott Committee gave up with the limp explanation that Chase's business in Israel was "only of a banking nature," and that the Tel Aviv Hilton was permissible since it would just drain money from Israel.

Application of the boycott has been erratic. Both Jordan and Egypt have welcomed Jewish movie makers, and Jordan not only granted permission to shoot *Lawrence of Arabia* on location near the port of Aqaba at the southern tip of the Negev Desert while the Jewish producer Sam Spiegel lived on his yacht offshore, but accorded Mr. Spiegel a guard from the Arab Legion.

Fulminations against the Jews in general and Israel in particular have not prevented Egypt from buying ten million Organon oral contraceptive pills from the Organon Factories in Oss, Netherlands, an organization founded and owned in good part by a Jewish Dutch family named van Zwanenberg. In early 1966, when an Austrian herpetologist named Friedrich Kniezanrek was bitten in Ma'an Jordan by a horned viper (*Aspis cerastes cerastes*, probably the species which bit Cleopatra), he was taken through Mandelbaum Gate in still divided Jerusalem to Beilinson Hospital in Israel, where specific antivenin was available. Herr Kniezanrek recovered, and the news stories describing his recovery mentioned that he had been given in Jordan an antivenin received from the Pasteur Institute in Paris, which in turn was supplied with venom from the Beilinson Hospital in Israel.

One of the most distressing boycott enforcements which I've seen so far was that suffered by Lee Griggs, Yale, 1951, who in the same year was hailed before the authorities in Beirut. They wanted to listen to each one of his collection of phonograph records, suspicious of Zionist propaganda since his Yale Glee Club recording carried the university crest with its traditional line of Hebrew. A compromise was effected, and the authorities burnt the offending cardboard cover, while Griggs, '51, kept the record with the suspicious "Whiffenpoof Song."

Frontiers, too, are subject to other unorthodox departures and arrivals. Probably one of the most spectacular was made in that same busy early 1966, when affable Abie S. Nathan, the proprietor of the California Restaurant and Bar in Tel Aviv, on the last day of February, in fulfillment of an election promise when he ran unsuccessfully for the legislature, took off in a rented two-seater, single-engine 1927 Stearman biplane, painted white and marked PEACE in Hebrew, Arabic and English and headed for Egypt with peace petitions for President Nasser. A somewhat surprised staff at the Port Said airport declined to let Mr. Nathan proceed to Cairo, and suggested instead that he fly back to Israel. Mr. Nathan countered by maintaining that his batteries and fuel were too low for the trip. The Egyptians, appearing harassed, now offered Mr. Nathan gasoline, batteries and a jet escort as far as the border if he would only leave the following morning. He was dispatched and returned safely, to find himself even more of a celebrity than when he left. Many of his fellow citizens had a good deal of sympathy with his quixotic effort to bring peace to the neighbors.

Undoubtedly the most sensational method of getting human beings quietly across frontiers came to light on November seventeenth, 1964, at the Fiumicino Airport outside Rome in the person of Mordechai Luk—apparently the last of a series of people who had occupied the same space—who turned up in a trunk marked DIPLOMATIC MAIL and addressed to the United Arab Republic's Minister of Foreign Affairs. Luk, it appeared, was a twenty-nine-year-old, Morocco born Israeli with a wife and children in Tel Aviv who had crossed the Gaza frontier and volunteered for Egyptian espionage. A jazzy type who favored dyed blond hair and heavy Hollywood sunshades, a dark suit and shirt with a shiny cream-colored tie, he was said to speak Arabic, Hebrew, French, Spanish, Italian and English. Luk was assigned to Naples where he collected from labels of shipments at the port the names of firms dealing with Israel, and these he reported to the Arab Boycott Committee.

During his sixteen months in Naples, Luk apparently fancied himself as something of a man about town, becoming engaged to at least two Neapolitan girls. Then, when he approached his superiors at the Egyptian Embassy in Rome and began to argue about pay, he was given drugged coffee, clapped in a specially fitted trunk, and shipped to Cairo.

The trunk was a handsome one in red leather with brass bindings, run up especially for the Egyptian Embassy by a firm in Perugia, fitted with a stool, arm rests, foot holders, head clamp and air holes. It arrived at the airport in good time to catch the United Arab Airline's evening flight to Cairo, but, unfortunately for the shippers, the plane was two hours late, and Luk's drugs began to wear off. Customs officials routinely checking diplomatic cargo that November seventeenth were disconcerted to hear muffled bumping and faint cries of "Assassins! Assassins!" from inside the trunk.

On being questioned, the embassy men explained that the trunk was full of musical instruments, which explained the noise. When officials seemed dubious, the shippers quickly reloaded the trunk on their truck and disappeared into the night.

There followed a Keystone Cops chase, during which the trunk was captured and the reluctant traveler unpacked.

The Egyptian diplomats involved were asked please to leave Italy. Mr. Luk is now serving a reduced, ten-year sentence at a maximum-security prison at Ramle in Israel.

What has fascinated me is the report of the Rome police. Laboratory tests of bloodstains and hair found inside the trunk showed that, indisputably, these were from other persons. The trunk had been flying back and forth for some time.

8| THE METROPOLIS:

TEL AVIV AND
JAFFA AND
THE OUTSKIRTS OF TOWN

Lying roughly halfway down Israel's Mediterranean Coast, Tel Aviv occupies an odd position: it has not the physical charm of Haifa, nor its civilized pace. It has not the frontier bravado of towns like Beersheba and Eilat. It lacks the beauty of Jerusalem's golden stone, the Judean hills, that city's feeling of history, and the magical evocation of the very name "Jerusalem" to the people of a good part of this world.

Tel Aviv remains the manufacturing and the commercial center of the nation. It is a transportation hub, and a communications center. It is military headquarters. The main offices of the all-important Israeli coöperatives are here. Since it was the first capital, many foreign missions are still based here. The city is hospitable to the arts. It probably welcomes more tourists and more immigrants than any other part of Israel. I have never heard anyone describe Tel Aviv as beautiful. But it can be an exciting place to live.

Tel Aviv is a busy, bustling and brash city whose inhabitants, like those of Manhattan, are so single-mindedly intent about their own business that the visitor risks being run over by pedestrians. This is not to be taken personally.

By long odds the most popular recreation is the movies, and most of these are in Tel Aviv. It is estimated that the per capita attendance in Israel is the highest in the world. Something like five hundred foreign films are imported annually from the United States, France, Britain, Italy, the U.S.S.R., Sweden, Turkey, and a few from Egypt, through intermediaries. Foreign producers will make a dozen films on location in Israel in a given year, in addition to a good number of documentaries and TV films. There are two Israeli newsreels. Of the seven repertory companies open all year round in Tel Aviv, the three most famous, Habimah, Kameri, and Ohel are subsidized by the government, but only to less than one-half of one per cent of their total budgets. This accounts, according to New York *Playbill*'s Hy Kalus for their "furious production schedules." Organized half a century ago, with the blessing of Stanislavsky and the Moscow Art Theatre, and moving some ten years later to Israel, Habimah has presented *Who's Afraid of Virginia Woolf?* in their large hall in Tel Aviv, while *Photo Finish* was being presented by another of their companies in a smaller theater upstairs, and a third company was playing *A Comedy of Errors* in Jerusalem at the same time.

There is experimental theater in Israel, a couple of hundred amateur groups, and troupes touring kibbutzim and settlements of newcomers with plays in a dozen languages. There are good Hebrew translations of Shakespeare, Molière, Tolstoi, Shaw, Ionesco, O'Neill, Sartre, Inge, Brecht, Miller and Albee, but it has been a general observation by Mr. Kalus and others that, as he puts it, "Israeli playwrights still have to come to grips with the problems of their own society."

The same comment might be made of Israeli music, dance, and graphic arts, in that they all tend to be international rather than indigenous in their technique, notwithstanding the fact that mediocre painters continue to turn out genre pictures of the Orthodox community much appreciated by a large, middle-class audience and the Yemenite Inbal Dance Troupe has turned to Hebrew tradition for *The Story of Ruth* and other Biblical themes in its extremely popular ballets. Popular song writers tend to set appropriate portions of the Song of Songs to music.

Faces of Israel, a sprightly review which has helped tourists in recent years learn something of the country, gives an idea of its extraordinarily cosmopolitan origins in its title song, which goes in part:

> We're British and we're Chilean,
> And he is a Brazilian.
> From Pakistan, Afghanistan, and
> I don't know from where I am.
> And he was born in Sweden!
> Alle zeinen Yidden?
> Alle zeinen Yidden!

The Israel Philharmonic Orchestra, which is considered to be one of the finest anywhere, has twenty-seven thousand subscribers, the equivalent of just under or just over two million subscribers in the United States or the Soviet Union. Other symphonic orchestras are maintained by the Gadna Youth Corps, the Defense Forces, and the municipalities of Haifa and Ramat Gan. Many communal settlements and towns maintain other ensembles, chamber-music groups and, altogether, about one hundred and twenty choirs. Weekly concerts are also given by the fifty-member symphony of the state broadcasting service, Kol Israel, one of whose chief duties it is to encourage and to present Israeli compositions. You can hear almost anything on the Israeli radio, including an all-Arab orchestra playing Ravel's *Bolero*.

The Philharmonic's ten-month season is supposed to be the world's longest. As a matter of principle, one-third of the time is spent playing in smaller settlements, but its home remains Tel Aviv.

This is true of much of the creative work in the country. In Tel Aviv, twenty-five newspapers are printed daily in ten languages, and according to the count of Robert St. John, there are more than one hundred bookshops and bookstalls in Allenby Road in Tel Aviv, between them selling these and others of the three hundred and forty weekly, fortnightly, monthly and quarterly Israeli magazines, in addition to the something like two thousand books which are published every year in the country. Altogether, UNESCO estimates, Israel has the second highest per capita consumption of books in the world, second only to Scandinavia.

If there are more book stores in Tel Aviv than movies and drugstores combined, there are over a thousand cafés and restaurants, serving young people, courting couples, young matrons with baby carriages, architects, lawyers, journalists, kibbutzniks and moshavniks from the communal settlements upcountry, politicians, intellectuals, and any of the numberless and overlapping other groups which take their tea or coffee, ice cream, or *gazoz* at any of the special places which they have staked out for their own. For men, the combination of briefcase and khaki shorts—often the ballooning British Colonial variety—is common enough, and shirt sleeves are almost *de rigueur*. A friend who happens to like neckties has reported that he and many others of his persuasion were for years intimidated by the Israeli stereotype of the tieless pioneer and Premier Ben-Gurion and many of his Cabinet appearing almost always in open-necked shirts.

Flying in over the aquamarine sea, the white beaches and the bluffs and the green of Israel beyond, one may wonder after trundling into town on the airport bus, surrounded by row on row of colorless blocks in which the people live, whatever happened to the Mediterranean? In a discouragingly familiar manner, Jews returning from northern countries to Palestine have brought their inappropriate northern architecture with them. It's too bad in a way, for architects could draw on some of the characteristics of classic Moslem hot-country architecture, evolved to meet the demands of the climate: thick walls, high ceilings, colonnades and overhanging projections above windows to give shade, tiles, breezeways, patios, greenery, perhaps a fountain, louvers or *brisesoleils* of one sort or another—in short, *cool*. All this is nothing new. Of particular importance is the attention paid to the prevailing winds, the seasons, the angle of the sun at different times of day. But it's a long struggle, and meanwhile the new buildings have air conditioners like little excrescences sticking out of their sides.

Some fifty years ago, when the first settlers drew lots among the sand dunes of the Mediterranean just north of Jaffa, Tel Aviv was planned as a garden suburb of that city, already some four thousand years old. For nearly a decade longer, both Arab and Jewish communities were to live under the four-centuries-old Ottoman Turkish rule.

During the First World War, most of the settlers of Tel Aviv were dispersed by the Turks, only a few watchmen being left behind. Then, beginning with the British Mandate in 1921, Tel Aviv began to expand in every possible direction. Except that its inhabitants did little about their seashore. Boulevards ran parallel to the coast so that the buildings lining them effectively cut out the sea breeze and the view of the Mediterranean, screening from the city what could be an incomparable blessing. For years, sixteen pipes have spilled the sewage of the municipality a hundred and fifty to four hundred and fifty yards off shore; extending the disposal to a safe-enough distance so that the beaches will once again be unpolluted has been a major effort of American aid.

There has been in Tel Aviv no town planning worth the name, nor a particular flavor or great charm as in the old towns such as Sfad, nor the buildings of the beautiful, warm Jerusalem stone for generations made obligatory by the government in that city.

Down the centers of Tel Aviv's boulevards march giant, heavy pylons carrying electric power, left over from the days when they were laid out across the sand dunes. Streets are lined with row on row of blocky, unimaginative concrete buildings, punctuated with little boxy balconies. There are some with a certain style, there is hope in the opportunity afforded by the building needed by the fast-growing University of Tel Aviv, but there is evident little of the architectural excitement of the Hebrew University and the Israel Museum in Jerusalem. Like much of New York, Tel Aviv is a builder's rather than an architect's town. Here, even the details are tacky. From the façades of moderately expensive apartment houses in the middle of the city sprout poles from which the laundry flaps. In front of houses in the suburbs are permanent concrete blocks housing garbage cans.

Commenting that Tel Aviv, unlike other Israeli cities, is a specifically Israeli growth, David Pryce-Jones in his *Next Generation* says flatly: "The one town where one might hope and expect to find some indication or reflection of the new Israeli society turns out to be a characterless and featureless extension in concrete, a willful, tiny Los Angeles. The new rich, most of the five hundred acknowledged millionaires, have come in on the land boom and their exploitation of the economic and real-estate factors which govern the urgent housing problem has negated the attempt to create something organic, a town of people gathered for communal purposes."

The same applies to sculpture and to décor. There are some lively murals in the new hotels, and I remember with particular affection the sculpture of a small rearing lion battling a larger one, representing Israel versus Britain, outside a movie house in the neighboring town of Ramat Gan. The widespread use of lithographs, original drawings and paintings in offices of all sorts is commendable. But— in contrast to the handsome, intelligent and truly informative exhibitions at the Israel Museum—that at the much-praised Helena Rubinstein Pavilion in Tel Aviv, even for the Van Gogh show, as far as general display and lighting went, is enough to make the angels weep.

When Bertie and I first learned we were to go to Israel for CARE, fantasies possessed us of an international cuisine prepared by skilled chefs returned from Shanghai, Leningrad, Budapest, Vienna, Paris and Rome. As it turned out, the language of the menus was international, but the general impression was that all the chefs and restaurateurs had had their taste buds removed by the immigration authorities upon arrival. "Generally, the food is very bad," says David Catarivas's impressionist, excellent guide, *Israel*. "But the Israelis somehow manage to give the meal an Israeli flavor by drinking, for example, orange juice with their meat." The orange juice is likely to be canned rather than fresh, even though the guest may be surrounded by orange groves.

One curious result of the haphazard growth of Tel Aviv is its relative lack of parks and green places, strange for a community whose settlers came from Russia and Eastern Europe, Central Europe and England.

A glance at a map of Tel Aviv and Jaffa brings a flood of memories and associations with the Bible, of the exile of so many of the Israelites, and of their fight for independence.

To start with, there is Jerusalem Boulevard, and Mount Zion Boulevard, King Saul Boulevard, Solomon Road and Prophets' Street. In Jaffa, at the southern end of Tel Aviv, there is a Japheth Street, named after the son of Noah from whom this four-thousand-year-old community may have taken its own name. Then there is in Jaffa harbor Andromeda's Rock where that Ethiopian princess was chained by a sea monster until rescued by Perseus, who waved the Medusa's head at the monster, snake curls and all, turning it to stone, whereupon he married Andromeda and they both lived happily ever after and had constellations named after them. The tradition that Jaffa was the center of the work of the Apostle Peter is remembered in a church named after him not far from Andromeda's Rock. A few blocks to the south is another church named after St. Anthony, the third-century Egyptian who first lived alone in the desert, then invented the original monastery.

A little to the north on the map are Allenby Road and King George Street, commemorating the ruler of England at the time Britain assumed its Mandate, and Field Marshal Sir Edmund Allenby, Viscount of Megiddo and Commander-in-Chief of Britain's Egyptian Expeditionary Force in the First World War, which captured Gaza, Beersheba and Jerusalem before driving north to take Damascus and Aleppo. Allenby Bridge at twelve hundred feet below sea level on the road between Jerusalem and the Jordanian capital of Amman, and wrecked during the third round in the Israeli-Arab Wars, was named in his honor.

To the east on the map of Tel Aviv lie streets named after two of the most illustrious parents (for there were many fathers and mothers) of the reborn State of Israel: Theodor Herzl and Chaim Weizmann.

Ever since the First World Zionist Congress in 1897 at Basle, it seems that either Herzl himself or his portrait was present, the noble head with dark, deep-set eyes, a Roman nose and an almost theatrically handsome long black beard. Herzl was the lawyer, dramatist and journalist for the Viennese *Neue Freie Presse* who was so shaken by the wave of anti-Semitism in 1895 at the trial of the French Army captain Alfred Dreyfus when that captain was accused on the basis of forged evidence of betraying his country, selling military secrets to the Germans, publicly degraded and sent to Devil's Island, accompanied by cries of "Death to the Jews!" It took the combined efforts of Anatole France, George Clemenceau, Jean Juarès and Émile Zola, whose front-page open letter to the President of France, "J'Accuse . . . !"—which obliged Zola to flee the country—before Dreyfus was released twelve years later from the infamous island prison.

Herzl returned home two years later, wrote his pamphlet *The Jewish State,* and thus became the father of political Zionism. He traveled to petition the Sultan of Turkey, the British statesman Joseph Chamberlain, the king of Italy, the Czar of Russia—even during a year of great massacres of the Jews in that country—the Pope, the Kaiser and any others whom he thought could help his cause in resettling his people in their homeland. Herzl did not receive much encouragement from the powers that were, but as he had written in his diary after the First Zionist Congress, "At Basle, I founded the Jewish State. If I said this out loud today I should be greeted by universal laughter. In five years perhaps, and certainly in fifty years, everyone will perceive it."

He was wrong by one year. It was 1948, and not 1947, when the new Jewish State was proclaimed in Tel Aviv. Perhaps the best summation of the struggle in the years in between was that of Herzl in his novel, *Alt-Neuland,* written after a visit to Palestine, in which he said, "If you will it, it is no legend."

Following the death of Herzl in 1904, leadership of the Zionist movement passed to Weizmann, the modest, patriotic professor of chemistry at Manchester University, whose synthesizing of acetone in the First World War, and of rubber during the Second, put not only Britain but all of the Allies in his debt, and who, when offered what amounted to a blank check by the British government after the First World War, asked only "for something for his people," who was instrumental in securing the Balfour Declaration of 1917, committing the British government to establishment of a Jewish homeland in Palestine, and who ended as the first President of the State of Israel.

Not too far in Tel Aviv, either geographically or emotionally, from the streets named after Herzl and Weizmann, are those named for the settlers, the pioneers, and the fighters for Israeli independence. There is Jabotinsky, named after Vladimir Ze'ev Jabotinsky, founder in the First World War, with Joseph Trumpledor, of the Zion Mule Corps, which fought with the British at Gallipoli, and then which became the Jewish Legion, largely recruited in the United States and Canada, and among whose members were David Ben-Gurion and Itzhak Ben-Zvi. The legion fought on the Palestine front, earning the commendation of General Allenby.

There is a street called The Aliyah, the Hebrew term for "ascent," the word used here for immigration to Israel, particularly the six great waves beginning in the 1880s and 1890s of Jews fleeing the pogroms in Russia and Eastern Europe, continuing through the flight from the Nazi terror of Europe in the thirties to the post-independence rescue of remnants of the European Jewish communities, and of large sections of the Jewish populations of the Arab countries in North Africa and the Middle East.

There is another Tel Aviv street named after the Haganah, a self-defense force formed by early Jewish settlements as protection against hostile bands among the Arabs—a force which went underground at the time of the British occupation when it was declared illegal. It became most effective in helping "illegal immigrants" and, as guerrillas, in countering both Arab marauders and the British. Haganah came to the surface in 1948, just in time to meet the five invading Arab armies. It was and is probably the most youthful army the contemporary world has known.

There are also streets in Tel Aviv honoring latter-day Jewish poets, pamphleteers, Zionists and Judah the Maccabee, "The Hammer," an incomparable guerrilla leader who fell fighting the Syrians in 161 B.C., whose followers established the Hasmonean Dynasty, cleansed and rededicated the defiled Temple in Jerusalem. A plaque to Judah the Maccabee as a great military leader can be found at West Point. There is a boulevard in memory of Baron Edmond de Rothschild, who did much to encourage settlement in Palestine, and who made possible the vineyards and the wineries at Rishon-le-Zion, just south of Tel Aviv and one of the many places where Ben-Gurion worked. Herbert Samuel Esplanade along the shore in central Tel Aviv, just behind the opera house, the American Embassy, and the Dan Hotel, is named after the first British High Commissioner in Palestine under the Mandate, who was counted to have done a good job except that he tried so hard to be impartial that at one point he named as Grand Mufti of Jerusalem, Haj Amin-al-Husseini, who first led something like five thousand Arab terrorists in attacks on the Jewish colonies in Palestine, and who finally ended up recruiting for Hitler during the Second World War.

Another street carries the name of Eliezer Ben Yehudah, that extraordinarily single-minded philologist and lexicographer who came to Palestine in 1882 with the Russian immigrants known as Bilu, who by his fanatical insistence on speaking only Hebrew did a great deal to revive it as a spoken language after three thousand years. Just the street names of the villages and cities, the place names on the map of the land are themselves a sort of microcosm, a most evocative reminder of some of the things which have happened here in the past five thousand years.

In Tel Aviv alone, a name like Dizengoff, that of a major artery and the circle at the center of the town to which it leads, brings back memories of that meeting in 1908 of Meier Dizengoff and his fellows who hoped to found there in the sand dunes just to the north of Jaffa, by the sea but bleak and unrelieved by tree, bush or other vegetation, what they hoped would be a "garden suburb."

There are records of Egyptian rule of Jaffa about fifteen hundred B.C., and it had been the home of the tribe of Dan. It was the port for Jerusalem under the kings of Judah. Here, Hiram of Tyre sent his friend Solomon the cedars of Lebanon for the building of the Temple.

Jaffa had been governed by the Philistines (from whose name the word Palestine was taken), the Assyrians, the Persians and the Phoenicians. Under Roman rule, it was largely a Jewish city, with the seamen of Jaffa playing an important role in the great revolt against Rome. When they were conquered, the victory over them was celebrated with special memorial coins reading "Maritima Judea, the Victory at Sea." There was still in Jaffa a considerable Jewish community, even after the destruction of Jerusalem, and the end of the Bar Kochba revolt in 135 A.D.

The Jewish community of Jaffa was expelled or destroyed under Byzantine Christian rule, again under the Crusaders, and once again by Napoleon during his siege of 1799. At the beginning of the British Mandate, Jewish settlement in Jaffa continued, but stopped abruptly after the Arab riots of 1921. It grew worse with further Arab riots against the Jews in 1929, and those from 1936 through 1939, until the Jewish population had left.

After the 1947 U.N. resolution in favor of the establishment of a Jewish as well as an Arab State, Jaffa became a center for the forces of the invading Arab armies, who bombed, shelled and launched attacks on Tel Aviv from there until, after decisive counter-attack by the Jews in May of 1948, Jaffa surrendered on the thirteeenth of that month. Almost all of the thirty thousand Arab inhabitants fled. What survives is still the ancient Arab city, with more than five thousand Arab inhabitants, but largely occupied by the Jewish Israelis. It has become an intellectual center. There are artists and galleries, good Jewish and Arab writers of prose and poetry. There is a new Chinese restaurant in an old Turkish bathhouse. There are night clubs. Jaffa has gone through one more transformation in its millennial history.

The old sepia photographs which survive the times when Tel Aviv was a sand dune recall the days when, though some Arabs were violently opposed to further Jewish immigration, there was considerable give and take and even a good deal of friendliness between some of the Arabs and the Jews. In 1919, the Emir Feisal had welcomed Weizmann and the Zionist immigrants to Palestine as brothers. Moshe Sharett, head of the Jewish Agency and briefly Premier of Israel, was more than proud of a fine Oriental rug given him by his friend King Abdullah of Jordan. T. E. Lawrence had served as adviser and translator to the Emir at the Délégation Hedjazienne during the Paris Peace Conference, where he came to know and admire Dr. Weizmann, and when he wrote, in English and in his own hand, the 3 January 1919 letter to Justice Felix Frankfurter signed by Feisal and expressing the Arabs' "deepest sympathy" for the Zionist cause. Later, Lawrence, Feisal and Weizmann met secretly in Aqaba, and there the Emir reaffirmed his support of Jewish settlement in Palestine, while Lawrence turned out to be not only pro-Arab but strongly pro-Semitic in general, and warmly disposed toward the Jewish settlers.

Jewish lifeguards in the early days of Tel Aviv under the British Mandate wore fezzes with their bathing suits, and the Jewish settlements' watchmen, called *hashomrim,* wore great Cossack fur hats called *kalpaks,* all this a legacy from the Ottoman world. It should be noted that, until the defeat of the Turks in 1917, Moslems had

been permitted freedom of movement within all parts of the Ottoman Empire, extending from the Balkans to the state of Equatoria
in Central Africa. In Palestine itself, there was much hostility among
many Arabs toward new Jewish settlers, but also union organization
among both Jewish and Arab laborers. This did not endear them to
the Arab landowners.

After the years of work by Ben-Zvi and Ben-Gurion and their fellow
Zionists helping to create a new nation in their ancient home—then
came aid from the United Nations. It was the unanimous recommendation of the U.N. fact-finding committee in 1947 that the
British Mandate of Palestine be terminated, and that Palestine be
made independent. Most of the committee favored economic union,
but with political partition into separate Arab and Jewish states. On
American initiative and with Soviet concurrence, the General Assembly approved this recommendation. Britain announced that she would
give up her Mandate at midnight on May fourteenth, 1948. But since
Britain argued that she had only the agreement of the Jews and not
of the Arabs to help the United Nations make arrangements for an
orderly transfer of power, she felt unable to do anything to assist the
new states. If the Arabs were refused all of Palestine, as they asked,
they would have nothing to do with any part of it. The result, in a
land where the mandatory government now lived behind barbed
wire and nearly all administration had broken down while guerrilla
warfare and terror wracked the country, was close to chaos.

The Jewish Agency dealt directly with the British Mandatory
authorities, speaking for the Jews of Palestine. Had there been an
equivalent body representing Arab interests, a number of the British
government officers believed, then there would have been two responsible groups, Jewish and Arab respectively, to whom they could hand
over authority on leaving Palestine. But the Arabs had not created an
administration of their own as had the Jews. This deficiency coupled
with the political disarray of the Arabs, both in Palestine and in
the neighboring states, was seen as a factor contributing directly
to the war which followed. The only common denominator among
the Arabs, then as now, was hatred of Jews in general and the
Zionists in particular.

In an effort to help redress this lack of unity and constructive
purpose throughout the Arab world, feared to be potentially dangerous politically, Anthony Eden in 1941 announced full British support

of any plan for Arab unity commanding general approval. This policy was reaffirmed by Eden in the House of Commons two years later, and with his encouragement the Arab League was formed in 1945. Unfortunately, by this time the new, strongly nationalist feeling surging through the Arab states was coming to be expressed increasingly in almost anything anti-Colonial, anti-Western and anti-British.

Two days before the expiry of the British Mandate, Ben-Gurion's shadow government still had not made up its mind whether to accept international trusteeship as it was being urged to do by many of its friends, or to try to go it alone.

Golda Meir, the ardent trade unionist and schoolteacher from Milwaukee who was later to become Israel's Foreign Minister and to hold her own successfully against John Foster Dulles at the State Department and to opposing U.N. delegations during the 1956 crisis over Israel's invasion of Sinai, now made a secret visit to King Abdullah to solicit the coöperation of his country, then known as Transjordan, in carrying out the United Nations plan for partitioning Palestine into separate Jewish and Arab states. Mrs. Meir reported to her fellow members of the shadow government that Abdullah wanted all of Palestine, though he proposed allowing the Jews a certain autonomy, within their own province yet under his administration. His crack Arab Legion, British-trained and British-officered, commanded by Clubb Pasha, was at that moment prepared to attack the Jews, together with forces from Egypt, Syria, Iraq and Lebanon, with armed bands of Palestinian guerrillas and contingents from Saudi Arabia and the Sudan. Mrs. Meir made King Abdullah's position clear to her colleagues. They declared the new State of Israel. As it happened, the fifteenth of May was a Jewish Sabbath, and so they met at the Tel Aviv Museum at four o'clock in the afternoon of the fourteenth, just before the dusk which brought the holy day.

The new State was fortunate in the strength, the experience and the capacity of the members of the new provisional government. Ben-Gurion was there with his halo of white hair, looking a little odd wearing a dark suit and a tie for the occasion.

Sharett had been up all night working on the draft of the Declaration of Independence. The Director-and-Minister designate of Communications, David Remez, had been pleading in vain for weeks for the Cabinet to agree on a name for their new State. His job was to have the country's postage stamps printed. But he never found out in time. And so the first Israeli stamps are marked *Doar Ivri*, which means only "Hebrew Post." It didn't matter much, for they were on sale in good time on May fourteenth.

At the last meeting of the founding fathers, there were proponents of Zion as a name for the new country, of Eretz Israel, the State of Israel and especially of Judea, which seemed to be the favorite. Ben-Gurion carried the day with the one word "Israel."

All the while, the complex and efficient organization of the Jewish Agency had been training locomotive drivers, telephone operators who were to operate the new exchanges, a network of hospitals and clinics, a broadcasting service, and all the thousand and one things which go into the making of a state or even a small city. Men and women from seventeen to twenty-five were called up for service in the Jewish Defense Forces. Taxes were imposed. Those in charge stored fuel in easily accessible centers. And a woman named Hanna Eventov, described as "a shy, middle-aged employee of the Jewish Agency," organized volunteers who stole into No-Man's-Land where the Jerusalem Court House with its Supreme Court sat on the front line, and returned to the Jewish lines with the irreplaceable legal documents and files, using as porters Haim Cohn, later a Supreme Court Justice, and Shabtai Rosenne, later legal adviser to the Foreign Ministry.

The thirty-seven members who had assembled to proclaim a Jewish State formed from among its members a provisional government. When they had finished their deliberations, just a little before the dusk which heralded the Sabbath, they all signed their names to the new constitution of nine hundred and seventy-nine words, sparsely and well written, modeled in part on our own, and, among other things, extending the hand of friendship to the neighboring states which they knew surely were about to invade them. The band played the national anthem, "Hatikvah," which means "Hope," and the light blue-and-white flag with the Star of David of this youngest State was raised. The founders all went home to Sabbath supper.

All had been done in such haste, this rebirth of a State after one thousand eight hundred and seventy-eight years, there had been no time to letter the constitution. So the founding fathers put their signatures to a blank scroll of parchment. A Torah scribe was dispatched to the recesses of an underground vault and, during the next few days, filled in the text of the constitution, some days after Israel had become a political reality.

In the early hours of the morning, the Egyptian Air Force bombed Tel Aviv, and that day, the armies of the allied Arab nations crossed the border into Israel.

9/ THE COAST:

PHILISTIA, PHOENICIA, CAESAREA AND HAIFA

E xcept for Israel's extreme southern tip on the Gulf of Aqaba, the country's Mediterranean coastline is its only entry and exit from the outside world. From the Gaza border, it is one hundred and sixteen miles north to the high promontory called the Ladder of Tyre which marks the Lebanese frontier. The shore, except for the Bay of Haifa, is an almost straight line. The port of Tel Aviv is an open roadstead. Yet there were great ports here when Palestine was a crossroads of the ancient world. Chief among the southern ports were those of the Philistines. These were one of the "Peoples of the Sea," who appeared in these waters about 1200 B.C., when they invaded Egypt, were then driven back by Ramses III and settled in southern Palestine, the land to which they gave their name. Thereafter, during the times of Samson and King Saul and King David, the Philistines struggled with varying success with the Hebrews for control of the shore of the region then known as Canaan. The principal ports of the Philistines began with Gaza at the south, then, just to the north, Ashkelon, the birthplace of Herod the Great, a resting place of the Ark of the Covenant after it had been captured from the Hebrews by the Philistines, and later a great Greek city and port conquered by the Crusaders, and taken from them by the Mameluke slave kings of Egypt. The Philistines came from elsewhere in the Mediterranean, perhaps Crete, a non-Semitic people, often disparagingly described in the Old Testament as uncircumcized, to distinguish them from their Semitic neighbors. This seems a long way from the present use of the word Philistine to denote a person considered less cultured and intellectual than the speaker.

To the southeast of Ashkelon lay Gath, one of the Philistines' five self-governing cities, and celebrated for its giant Goliath slain by David. Goliath of Gath characteristically was clad in armor of bronze and iron, the importing and forging of iron then being a Philistine monopoly.

A little further to the north is the Philistine anchorage of Ashdod, now being made into a considerable port by the Israelis. Ashdod was an earlier resting place of the Ark after it had been taken from the Hebrews.

Then, north to Jaffa, which was the end of the territory of Philistia, altogether perhaps a third of what is now the Israeli coast. Another scant third of the way north along the coast lie the ruins of Caesarea, the great Roman city and port completed by Herod a few years before the birth of Christ, and serving for six centuries as the capital of Judea. A roughly equal distance north, and just below the Lebanese frontier, are Haifa with Acre across its bay, these marking the southern limits of the land of the Phoenicians, the greatest of the seafarers. In between, from north to south along the low bluffs, the dunes and rocks and beaches of this comparatively short stretch of coast, are the Crusaders' battlements, the mosques with slender minarets, and the Greek and Roman ruins falling into the sea. In the sands are coins of Greece and Rome and Judea and the lands from which the Crusaders came, mosaics where the cities stood along the shore, and in the waters of Caesarea, sometimes, the classical terra cotta storage vases called *amorphae* and Arab jewelry of filigreed gold, agate, carnelian and colored glass; and all along the shore, the bits of pottery that tell the story of the successive generations.

For the Peoples of the Sea and especially the Phoenicians, the oceans were their highways, but there were others who came down the Mediterranean littoral overland. One of the most intriguing of these and one about whom least is known were the Hyksos who ruled Egypt during the fifteenth and sixteenth dynasties, from 1700 to 1570 B.C. The Hyksos who invaded the Egyptian delta through Palestine were nomadic tribes with a strong Semitic element (the name Jacob is found on the scarabs inscribed in Egypt during their reign). Increasingly, students of the Bible are coming to believe that the story of Joseph and his family is intimately bound up with that of the Hyksos: if the Pharaoh himself were also an alien Semite, it would be more credible that Joseph, originally sold into servitude by his brothers, could rise to become master of the royal household. Further, it appears quite probable that the migration of Joseph and his family was but a part of a steady stream from Palestine southward to the delta during the brief reign of the Hyksos. The latter were a feudal, military caste far less numerous and less sophisticated than the Egyptians, but the Hyksos had one invincible advantage. They were skilled charioteers at a time when both chariots and horses were still unknown in Egypt. After little more than a century, the Egyptians rallied and expelled the Hyksos, in their anger obliterating all Hyksos inscriptions and almost every other record of their hated conquerors, then pursuing them into Palestine where the Hyksos held out for another three years until they were finally defeated, and disappeared from history.

For another four centuries the Hebrews remained in the Land of Goshen, that part of the eastern delta just across from Sinai, where traditionally they had come to graze their flocks in times of drought. Now they were gradually reduced to bondage, building towns and temples for the Pharaohs until finally delivered by Moses.

Making allowances for dates or years in the Bible being illustrative or symbolic rather than exact, there is still a curious lapse between the Hebrews' life with the Hyksos, the Egyptians meanwhile learning from the Hyksos the uses of horses and chariots, and the fact that it was apparently three to four hundred years later until the horse-drawn chariot was used in Israel. David himself rode a donkey, his soldiers were on foot. David's sons sometimes used horse and chariot, but it was not until the reign of Solomon that there was created a modern Hebrew army with, according to the Books of Kings, fourteen hundred chariots and twelve thousand horses. Scholars used to consider these, like many other Biblical statistics, as highly exaggerated. Then excavations at Megiddo, in the Valley of Jezreel northeast of Caesarea, revealed most extensive fortifications with accommodation in this one of Solomon's many "chariot cities" for five hundred horses and one hundred and fifty chariots. There is no record that his great horse-and-chariot force ever fought a campaign, but it must have added greatly to Solomon's prestige and his power. In the course of the digging, mostly by the Oriental Institute of the University of Chicago, nineteen other cities turned up, making twenty layers in all and dating back to 4000 B.C.

This Megiddo, where Pope Paul VI came through a specially opened chink in the barrier between Jordan and Israel on his visit of 1964, the first Pope since Peter to visit the Holy Land, lies astride some of the most ancient of the world's great military routes. It is itself the site of countless battles, commanding the way to Egypt and the south, and Damascus and Baghdad on the north and east. Allenby in 1917 made it his base for his Palestine campaign, fought the Turkish Army there, and was rewarded with the title of Viscount Allenby of Megiddo. It is the Biblical Armageddon of the Apocalypse, where it is predicted that, before Judgment Day, there will be a last great battle in the world between the forces of good and evil.

It used to take us about three-quarters of an hour driving from northern Tel Aviv up to the ruins of the Roman port of Caesarea. Along the way, one of the features of the landscape was not ruins left by the Peoples of the Sea, but the great hotels along the waterfront built by the peoples from across the sea, often Americans or South Africans in collaboration with Israelis. The bathing beauties who appropriately decorate the pools of the great hotels, and less often the beaches below, are so elaborately coiffed by Friday just before the Sabbath as to make it difficult if not impossible for the more dedicated among them actually to immerse themselves late in the afternoon or on the following holiday; but they sun themselves prettily, and do a delicate mannequin's stalk around the pool in wedgies. Nicely tanned, with ghostly pink or orange lips and nacreous long nails, they wear bikinis, balletic one-piece black suits or whatever may have been popular in the United States in recent months.

On exhibition are black-and-gold pumps, silver-and-gold spike heels and sometimes gold bathing suits. Bikinis continue to be popular, from the discreet, mature citizen's model to the basic triangle exposing dimples in the gluteus maximus. There are many heavily bronzed bathers in their middle years, not a few of them tourists, and among them a high incidence of barrel chests and matronly figures. Large diamond rings are not unknown with bathing costumes. On the umbrellas sheltering poolside tables there is a spattering of advertising for cordials and colas.

An occasional sunbather will wear a shiny white triangle stuck to the nose to prevent peeling, surrounded with generous applications of suntan oil or cream, and altogether giving the wearer the appearance of someone about to go onstage in a harlequinade.

The Sabbath is the great day, with throngs milling happily on the beaches below the luxury hotels. The last time I noticed, there were a number of high, pointy straw sombreros, looking as though the bathers were headed for a Mexican hat dance. Others among the visitors wore panamas or coconut straws, sometimes decorated with a Star of David or a *menorah*. *Kova tembels* in bright blue and orange, faded khaki, less-than-bright red or yellow, sometimes flowered, are always popular—plain for the citizens, or emblazoned with "Welcome to Tel Aviv" or some other motto for the tourists. Most Israelis consider a hat in the sun essential. Bertie and I were warned that we must not go out without protection, and when we remarked that we had been able to survive four years in India on the Gangetic plain without a hat, it was explained that this was entirely different, that the sun here in Israel was really dangerous.

Once I saw walking on the beach two students from the Afro-Asian Institute, one a Nepali wearing his national headgear, which looks rather like a squashed cloth pimento, and his companion, a Basuto from the country now known as Lesotho, his hat a handsome conical straw topped with a knob from which hung a short fringe of leather thongs.

Among the Israelis, most popular for both men and women, are gold Stars of David worn on fine gold chains around the neck; sometimes a gold pendant of the Tablets of the Law; frequently a single teardrop pearl for women; and occasionally, on men, a little gold horseshoe, or a Star of David within a horseshoe, which I suspect would not pass muster at the High Rabbinate.

Flying above the lifeguards' perches are pennants, blue-and-white indicating that surf and sea are safe, red-and-black warning against entering the water. These are not to be ignored, for the number of drownings each season seems out of all proportion to the population. This is partly because people will swim at night when they cannot see the signal; sometimes because girls from the stricter religious schools will be taken to bathe in sheltered places where their superiors and they may feel more modest (although there are "religious beaches" where certain days are reserved for swimming by men, and others for women only), and where they consequently find themselves without a guard in attendance; and perhaps most of all because the surf and the undertow along this coast can be treacherous.

The road north to Haifa, running along past the beaches and the great hotels, passes Natanya, which specializes in diamond cutting and polishing, one of the important centers for this work in the world and, with Tel Aviv, responsible for about a third of Israel's export income, or well over a hundred million dollars.

Beside the highway are the groves which supply the Jaffa oranges much favored in Europe, and on the road trundling north to Haifa are trucks full of slatted crates through which peek the bright splashes of orange. There is a steady stream of buses and taxis and jitneys and hired tourist cars, too, and the fearless military vehicles which are said to account for an unfair proportion of the highway accidents which make Israel's rate one of the highest in the world.

As for the taxi drivers, as a group they are smokers, and as far as I could make out, are in the habit of offering cigarettes to their passengers. Cars of the Israel Government Tourist Corporation are long, black, finned and have emblazoned on their sides the red-

and-white official insignia: the two robed and bearded figures sent by Joshua "to spy out the land," trudging along carrying between them a pole from which hangs a single great bunch of grapes, each the size of a cantaloupe.

Sprouting from the rooftops are little clusters of TV antennae, a portent of things to come, with educational television already well launched from Tel Aviv, and general television in Arabic and Hebrew now beginning, beamed at the formerly Arab territories taken in the Six Day War—this partly as an answer to the many thousands of sets already bought by individuals and by cafés for their patrons, and tuned into Cairo, Beirut and Damascus for a diet of Arabian Nights extravaganzas, heavy-lidded Egyptian soap operas, American westerns with Arabic subtitles and a full program of Arab propaganda.

One unfamiliarity which strikes the driver is the names of the gasoline stations along the road. They are called Delek or Paz or Sonol (née Sun Oil) or something not quite identifiable. This is the legacy of one of the few victories of the Arab boycott, when they blackmailed the large British, Dutch, and American companies into giving up their business in Israel, and the new distributors with new, or slightly new, names were organized with an infusion of emergency capital to handle petroleum products still being brought in, largely from Iran, and pumped up through the pipeline leading north to Haifa from the Gulf of Eilat.

Turning off the highway at Caesarea, busloads of tourists on their way to the Roman ruins pass the first and only golf links in Israel, supported by the Rothschilds and opened by them and the government in 1960 as the first part of a resort and new, small industrial town to be built here. At the seaside are the remains of six cities, one above the other, beginning with a prehistoric settlement. Of these, the greatest was Caesarea. Here, at the site of a fourth-century B.C. Phoenician port called Strato's Tower, most recently a part of the Hasmonean kingdom of the Maccabees, Herod the Great in the twelve years beginning in 22 B.C. constructed a deep-water port and metropolis, tactfully named after his patron Caesar Augustus, which became the capital of the province of Judea and the wonder of the coast.

There were ten great towers, and the Temple of Augustus, raised on a platform which contained two colossal statues of Rome and of the emperor, could be seen far out to sea. The semicircular walls enclosed a Roman city which stretched for about a mile along the coast. A drainage system used the tides to flush the city's streets.

If this Herod, the creator of Caesarea, is to be called Great, it must rest on his enthusiasm for creating magnificent public buildings and whole cities in the Greco-Roman idiom of his day, and his ability to walk the perilous political tightrope of his times. Nominally a Jew, Herod was in fact the son of a Nabataean mother and a father who, as Procurator of Idumaea, came from a family which had been converted to Judaism by the sword.

Just as his father, Antipater, had smoothly transferred his allegiance on the death of Pompey, the conqueror of Jerusalem in 63 B.C., to his rival, Julius Caesar, so his son Herod found no difficulty in successively transferring his allegiance to Caesar, to Antony, and then to Antony's rival Octavian, and finally to the deified Augustus Caesar for whom the new metropolis was named and who was to remain Herod's patron for the rest of his life.

On this coast almost without harbors, Herod built great breakwaters for his new port, with a narrow entrance at the northwest, protected against the prevailing winds and affording safe berth for the Roman galleys. The city for which this was the port was adorned with a theater, an amphitheater, a hippodrome seating twenty thousand, and the Temple of Augustus. There were higher and lower aqueducts bringing water from the slopes of the Carmel range and from the Crocodile River nearer by. The population of the city grew quickly to fifty thousand.

Herod had made his way to Rome and there, in 40 B.C., had himself proclaimed king of the Jews. He still was not popular with his new subjects, even after he had rebuilt in great splendor the Temple of Solomon in Jerusalem, then in ruinous disarray. For this he provided at his own expense ten thousand men to dress the great stones from which it was built, and had trained a thousand priests as masons so that they might build the sanctuary where only they might enter, stone by stone so that the devotions would not be interrupted for a single day. At the same time, backed by Cleopatra's redoubtable Gaulish bodyguard, which he managed to have Rome reassign to him, together with an army of German and Thracian mercenaries, he ruled mercilessly, dispatching any real or imagined rival. Among others, he murdered Mariamne, a Maccabean princess who was his favorite among his ten recorded wives, also her mother, his wife's guardian, his uncle, a number of Jewish scholars, a group of Pharisees who were roasted alive for having the audacity to remove the golden imperial eagle from the Temple at a time when Herod lay ill, and the inoffensive Hyrcanus II, an eighty-two-year-old Maccabean who had served as titular king and front man for Herod's father, who had actually run the country. A group of Judean noblemen were taken captive and held against the day of Herod's death, when they were to be slaughtered so that the kingdom might not rejoice.

If, as is generally now accepted, Christ was born in 4 B.C., then the King Herod responsible for the attempted massacre in Bethlehem of all children two years old and younger so that he might not be threatened by fulfillment of the prophecy that a descendant of David was to be born there and known as King of the Jews, would have been Herod the Great.

In the family tradition, one of Herod's surviving sons, Archelaus, while waiting for confirmation from Rome of his succession to his father, angrily slew some three thousand Jewish pilgrims assembled at the Temple in Jerusalem for the Passover. Another son, Herod Antipas, when rebuked by John the Baptist for marrying a woman named Herodias, formerly wife of still another brother, was incited by Herodias to have the offender decapitated and his head presented to her daughter Salome as a reward for her famous dance.

With the exile to Rome of Herod's weak and ineffectual son Archelaus, the great city of Caesarea became the seat of the Roman Procurators. From here the Procurator Pontius Pilate traveled to Jerusalem, as was his custom each year, the year of Christ's Crucifixion.

The Apostles Peter and Paul were both imprisoned in Caesarea, and the great Rabbi Akiba, supporter of Simon Bar Kochba whom he proclaimed the Messiah, was brought to Caesarea, kept there for a time and then executed after the failure of this last revolt against the Romans.

Christians as well as Jews were executed in the arena at Caesarea until the acceptance by Rome of Christianity in the fourth century A.D. Struggles between the Greek majority and large Jewish minority in the city led to rioting and an appeal to the Emperor Nero, whose decision in favor of the Greeks brought on violent disturbances, followed by the Roman order for a massacre of the Jewish population of Caesarea. Thus began the Jewish War against the Romans in 66 A.D. when Caesarea was used as a base by Vespasian. He was there declared emperor by his troops, and his son Titus then carried on the struggle until Jerusalem was destroyed four years later.

Caesarea continued to be connected intimately with the history of the early Christian Church. Peter converted the Roman centurion Cornelius here, baptizing him with his family and friends after they had experienced the first such manifestation of the Holy Spirit known to Gentiles. (Before then, this revelation of the Holy Spirit celebrated in the Christian Pentecost had been known only to the Jews who became Christians.) Caesarea became the seat of the Metropolitan Bishop of Palestine, and many of the early Church Fathers wrote and taught here.

By the mid-sixth century, local Christians were massacred by Jews and Samaritans. During Islam's phenomenal expansion in the seventh century, Caesarea surrendered to the Moslems. It was retaken in 1102 by Baldwin I, king of Jerusalem, who massacred its Moslem inhabitants in its mosque, which had once been the Christian cathedral. Among the loot seized by the Genoese Crusaders was a green crystal chalice alleged to be the Holy Grail from which Christ had taken the Last Supper and which received some of the blood of Christ at the Crucifixion, preserved by Joseph of Arimathea and his family, and later to turn up in the stories of King Arthur, Galahad and the other Knights of the Round Table, who spent a good deal of time in quest of this miraculous vessel.

Saladin captured Caesarea in 1187, only to have it recaptured by Richard I in 1192. Louis IX fortified it strongly in 1251. The town by now covered no more than one-tenth of the city of Herod. When stormed and devastated fourteen years later by Sultan Bibars, that was the end until present-day excavations and restorations and the establishment of the golf links. The Sultan destroyed the Christian fort and broke the aqueduct, whose water converted the land about into a malarial marsh. And so it remained until the late nineteenth century, when the Turkish government settled there in the ruins of the Crusader city, a village of immigrants from Bosnia, a far-flung part of the Ottoman Empire which now finds itself in Yugoslavia. The Bosnians fled during Israel's 1948 War of Independence, but their presence there raises a question which has always bothered me.

The burden of much, if not most, of the grievance of the Arab states which I've read or listened to against the State of Israel, or Zionism, or, at its most forthright, against the settlement of any Jews at all in this region, seems to rest on the conviction that the Jews have been absent so many hundreds of years that they have become foreigners in what was once their land. The Arabs who were in the majority from the seventh until the twentieth century except for the brief Crusader Kingdom are seen as having established themselves over a period so long that any other people, any other government, is the vilest injustice.

I suppose it is unfair to attempt to introduce logic or the historical facts of life into what is essentially a violent exercise in propaganda, but aside from the fact that the Jews founded their State with the blessing of the United Nations, when this was contested by force, they established themselves by right of conquest, as had been done before them by the Turks, the Crusaders, the Arabs, the Romans, the Greeks, the Egyptians, the Hebrews, the Canaanites, the Syrians, the Babylonians and the others going back to the dawn of history and probably before.

With all of the migrations, the conquests and the colonies which have accompanied them, there are as many pockets of people, different races, religions and varieties of origin very much alive in Israel today as one could possibly imagine. Even with the departure of the Bosnians there are some twenty-six hundred Circassians, a handsome people from the Caucasus once famous in the Middle Eastern slave markets, who remain in Israel and ten thousand of whose fellows live across the way in Jordan, serving as the traditional bodyguard for King Hussein as they did for his grandfather King Abdullah.

Jews have lived uninterruptedly in Israel since they returned from Egypt to the Promised Land more than two thousand years ago, in spite of the wars and dispersion, sometimes many, sometimes few, sometimes banned from Jerusalem, sometimes masters there, but

94

always living in this land. There are Catholic and Protestant sects without reckoning, and there are some schismatic Moslem sects, too, like the six hundred Ahmadia in Galilee. There are two hundred members of the Bahai faith, a universalist religion which was founded in Persia and with many members living in the United States and England, but whose center is in Haifa. There are Turcoman villages, settled by Uzbek and Kazakh Moslems from what is now Soviet Central Asia, and in the south of Israel there are Negro Bedouin, descendants of the Africans brought from Nubia and East Africa by Arab slave traders.

Wandering through the ruins of Caesarea, I feel the place is full of ghosts. The centuries have become one and the ancient allies and the adversaries are all there. They have become part of the present. Pablo Casals visiting Israel has played in the ancient Roman amphitheater. The archways of a Crusaders' citadel remain, soaring into nothingness like the ribs of a stone skeleton. The stones were taken from Herod's city, just as were the columns used in building the Crusaders' walls and their breakwater, the old rose granite from Egypt and the marble from Italy. Parts of the Roman statues, too, were used to reinforce the Crusaders' buildings, but even with this strengthening the massive constructions have not survived. Most not covered by the drifting sands have been toppled by earthquakes into the sea.

Excavations have uncovered two armless, legless and headless statues, one of red porphyry, and the other of white marble. There are also the remains of a synagogue nearby and those of a large church.

One moment which never failed to seize me with a sense of time past and present is late afternoon with the light nearly horizontal from the setting sun, striking through the archways carrying the high aqueduct built by the Roman legions, its weathered stone now softened by erosion, moss and lichens, sprouting grasses and desert bushes. The light is a dark-lemon sometimes, making the sand rippled by the tide stand out in sharp relief. The piers up-holding the arches cast long, bluish purple shadows. Beneath lies what is left of the cities through the centuries, waiting to be returned to the world above.

95

Driving along the roads of Israel, one occasionally comes across the carcass of a jackal, usually the lesser or Indian jackal (*Canis aureus*) which ranges all the way from here to Burma, or, less frequently, the wolf-like Egyptian jackal (*Canis lupaster*)—reminders that we are already in Asia and not far from Africa just across from Sinai and the Suez Canal. There is also a striped hyena (*Hyaena hyaena*), the kind known in Nairobi as the "Dust Bin Patrol," who in my experience is equaled for persistence and noisiness while marauding garbage cans only by our American raccoons, and for maniacal midnight laughter only by our loons. There are also African monitors (*Varanus niloticus*), lizards which commonly grow to a length of three feet but may reach seven.

Nahal Tanninim, or Crocodile River as it was called by Pliny, just a little to the north of Caesarea, is another link with the south, for until the end of the nineteenth century and the settlers' draining of the swamps surrounding the river, it was a breeding ground for crocodiles (*Crocodilus vulgaris*) well known to the Crusaders and to the Arabs of the neighborhood. Crocodile eggs were sold in Jerusalem in the latter half of the last century, and crocodiles were reported from the river as late as 1920 or so, but it seems likely now that the beast has gone to join those former inhabitants of Palestine such as the lion, whom the Crusaders also encountered, the leopard, the Barbary wild sheep, the Syrian bear, the ibex, the hippopotamus and the ostrich (though the Fauna Preservation Society of London reports the sighting of an ostrich in Jordan within the last couple of years).

Almost anyone would agree with the advice of David Catarivas that "It is with Bible in hand that tourists should visit Israel, it is with Bible in hand that archeologists survey the country to excavate, it is with Bible in hand that the high-ranking officers of the Israeli Army learn strategy, as it is with Bible in hand that members of parliament prepare their speeches and the geologists prospect for oil." Still, I think one might be wary about natural history. The exhaustive and almost always trustworthy *Dictionary of the Bible* edited by James Hastings notes that both the Revised Standard Version and the Revised Version of the Bible render *tannim* (crocodiles) as "jackals," while the King James Version calls them "dragons." The Biblical dictionary also reports of the crocodile,

"It is supposed to have been brought there by some Egyptian settlers," a proposition which seems a touch unlikely, even if it was a minor deity along the Nile.

Perhaps this is not too exceptional, as I see in another list of translations that the King James Version calls the Nile monitor a "mole," the stork an "ostrich," the ostrich in one place an "owl," and eagle owls "doleful creatures."

Two more reminders that Israel is a continental bridge for all of the animal kingdom and not just man are the Egyptian vulture and the cattle egret. The former, also known as *Neophron percnopterus* and as "Pharaoh's Hen," is by Israel law protected as a scavenger as are the four other species of vulture and all birds of prey. There is something about this squat, dingy-white bird with black wingtips and tail feathers, naked, ketchup-red skin around its face, forehead and throat, and an untidy spray of whitish hair which gives the impression of an unsuccessful confidence man six months in need of a haircut. The Pharaoh's Hen can often be seen waddling clumsily at the seashore, eating small crabs and dead fish, but aloft he is superb. And also large enough so that the Israeli ornithologist Paula Arnold reports that in wartime she has seen him shot at by anti-aircraft gunners mistaking him for an enemy plane.

The egret (*Ardeola ibis*), which used to be a winter visitor, has been a resident of Israel since just after the War of Independence in 1948, not long after it had made its way from its home in West Africa, across the Guianas and, more recently, from there north to the United States. At the same time, it has turned up in India where it follows farmers plowing and forages for ticks on the backs of water buffalo just as it does on cattle in Israel and the southern United States.

One of the pleasures of traveling in Israel is watching its water birds, on the beach or over the sea, in the carp ponds or along the river banks. On both the Mediterranean and the Red Sea coasts there are great flocks of the lesser black-backed gulls (*Larus fuscus*), one of Israel's ten species of gull. In the spring and fall, there are flocks of white storks (*Ciconia ciconia*) and black storks (*Ciconia nigra*) on their way north to nest in Europe; the elegant but determined-looking purple heron (*Ardea purpurea*); on the telephone wires can be seen the Smyrna kingfisher (*Halcyon smyrnensis*), with a large chocolate head and breast and azure wing and tail feathers.

Twelve miles to the south of Haifa is Atlit, the last stronghold of the Crusaders in the Holy Land. This is the Château Pelerin or Castellum Peregrinorum of ancient maps, built by the Knights Templars over a number of ancient Phoenician tombs. It was never conquered by the invading Mamelukes, but rather evacuated quietly in 1291 by the order which had built it ninety-three years earlier for the protection of pilgrims, a few weeks after the fall and sack of Acre to the north.

Close by the massive ruins of the Crusaders' castle was the Jewish Agricultural Experiment Station, established two years before the First World War and abandoned in 1917 when the Turkish government learned that it had been used for some years for Allied intelligence. It was run by a remarkable family named Aaronsohn, fervent Zionist immigrants from Rumania who believed that the future of the Jewish State lay with America and England, and in particular with the liberation of Palestine from the Turks by the British. All six of the Aaronsohn children worked with the espionage network called NILI, together with their friends and colleagues, and one brother named Alexander ended as a captain on General Allenby's Headquarters Staff. In the end, many of the NILI group were caught and many, including Alex and the seventy-year-old father Ephraim, were tortured and some executed. But none talked. The leaders were Aaron Aaronsohn, the eldest son, and his sister Sarah, who was only twenty-four when she left a comfortable life as the wife of a prosperous merchant in Constantinople to return to Palestine and join the fight. Sarah, who was described by her biographer Anita Engle in her book *The NILI Spies* as "a fine-looking young woman, tall, full-bosomed, straight-backed, with . . . pleasant face and wide-set blue eyes," was in effective charge of the operation during her brother Aaron's absence, in Cairo or elsewhere, feeding to the Allies a steady stream of detailed information on the disposition of Turkish and German forces in Palestine —going down to the beach at night and there in the shadow of the Crusaders' castle dispatching her information via a small French warship out of Cairo which put a boat ashore to meet her.

Aaron was very largely self-taught, but a brilliant scholar, an incisive thinker with a clear and prophetic view of the dangers likely to threaten the Jews in the Diaspora, looked on with suspicion and unease by many of his fellow settlers who, in the tradition which had enabled them to survive under alien and often violently hostile governments for many generations, were far more inclined to accept the ill usage of the Turkish authorities than to challenge them by aiding the Allies, as did Aaron. Describing Aaron as a "tall, sinewy young man with blazing eyes and wide sensitive mouth," Miss Engle goes on to describe his protean career in which as a very young man he traveled throughout Palestine systematically collecting plants and minerals, identifying them and giving them Hebrew names. In 1906 he found himself world famous by discovering in northern Galilee and on the slopes of Mount Hermon a truly wild wheat, something for which botanists had been searching for years, and which, it turned out, prehistoric cave dwellers at Mount Carmel had probably domesticated eight thousand years before. Exploring the possibilities of dry farming, Aaron Aaronsohn wrote in December, 1907, to the U.S. Department of Agriculture suggesting that a plant, *Atriplex leucoclada,* which grew in the desert and to which camels and goats were partial, might be useful for cattle ranching in the Negev, and in arid zones in the United States; this was fifty years, exactly, before the Israel Ministry of Agriculture announced that it was establishing an experimental plot of this plant for the same purpose.

Aaron spent two years in the United States at the invitation of the Department of Agriculture, which was taken by the idea of using strains of the wild wheat he was growing in Palestine for arid zones. In America, he refused all offers, including that of a Chair at the University of California. Aaron remained intent on agricultural research and its application in Palestine, and the settlement of the Jewish people there; then, with the outbreak of war, working to help the British and their Allies frustrate the Turks and the Germans. These he saw with almost uncanny prescience as the approaching danger to the Jews—this at a time when the world's Zionist headquarters was still in Berlin, German anti-Semitism had been moderate in contrast to the government-inspired slaughter in Russia, the worst the modern world had yet seen, and when the Jews of Germany prided themselves on being patriotic citizens and were proud of their impressive contribution to the Kaiser's war effort. But Sarah, in Constantinople and on her return after two years to Palestine, had seen something of the Turks' best efforts to annihilate the Armenians: the wounded and maimed begging for bread, vultures circling over children who had been shot and were lying beside the road, families being clubbed by Turkish soldiers into the Syrian desert to perish there. Aaron Aaronsohn became convinced that the Germans were using the Turks to test growing ideas of racial ideology at the same time Henry Morgenthau, American Ambassador to Turkey during this period and deeply distressed with the Armenian massacres, himself came to this conclusion, that the Turks were employing methods of genocide quite new to them in all their long ill-treatment of the subject peoples of their empire, specifically "the idea of deporting people *en masse*, which is in modern times exclusively Germanic," as he wrote in a book called *The Secret of the Bosphorus*. Now it appeared that the Turks were about to use the same techniques in Palestine. The governor, Djemal Pasha, ordered all Jews expelled from Jaffa and Tel Aviv. The State Department and the British Embassy in Washington began a propaganda barrage recalling the Armenian massacres, suggesting the same fate awaited the Jews in Palestine, while Reuters sent the story around the world. The German government cautioned the Turks to be careful, and an order arrived in Palestine just in time to stop the Jews, who were being rounded up, from being driven into the Transjordanian Desert.

Meanwhile, at the request of Henrietta Szold as Secretary of the American Jewish Committee, Aaron was forwarding from Cairo long reports on the progress of the Agricultural Experiment Station, political analyses of Palestine and the region, and news of the precarious position of the Jewish communities there. It was the first such report to reach America, where the Supreme Court Justice Louis Brandeis called it "one of the most excellent and most important documents that I have ever read in my life."

This ability to excite interest and enthusiasm in those close to the center of power, in whatever sphere, was to remain Aaron Aaronsohn's to the end of his short life. Ambassador William C. Bullitt who knew him in Washington and then again at the Peace Conference in Paris, where Bullitt was a member of President Wilson's delegation and Aaron Aaronsohn assistant to Dr. Chaim

Weizmann, began a most moving appreciation of Aaron with the statement, "He was, I believe, the greatest man I have known."

When finally captured by Turkish counter-intelligence, Sarah Aaronsohn was tortured more brutally than any of the others of the NILI ring who had been caught. After four days of torture, she managed to commit suicide lest she inform on her companions.

Aaron Aaronsohn, who had gone to London to prepare a report on Palestine's boundaries, left by RAF to return to Paris. His plane disappeared in the mists over the English Channel and was never seen again.

If the Bay of Haifa is a crescent moon, Acre is its upper tip and Haifa the lower. Haifa itself climbs nearly a thousand feet up the slopes of Mount Carmel, green and wooded and with many parks and gardens. At night, when the lights wink like fireflies on the heights, cars with luminous eyes move along the twisting mountain roads. There are more lights and horns echoing eerily from the vessels riding at anchor in the harbor; visitors are reminded of Naples and San Francisco and Rio de Janeiro.

By day, shining from the midst of the mountain greenery, are the Persian gardens surrounding the classical Greek building which shelters the Bahai Archives and the Bahai Temple's golden dome, ornamented with white-marble icing like a confectioner's delight.

Mount Carmel has always attracted shrines and worshippers. To the Greeks it was sacred to the god Zeus. The Roman Vespasian offered sacrifices to the god of Carmel and received auspicious omens concerning his ambition to become emperor. At the north-western slope of the mountain lies Elijah's Cave, holy to Jews, Christians and Moslems, all of whom make pilgrimages. To Christians, Elijah's Cave sheltered Mary and Joseph returning from Egypt. To Jews and Christians alike, it offered refuge to the Prophet Elijah hiding from the men of King Ahab whose wife Jezebel—now a household word—had introduced from her home-land Phoenicia the priests of Baal and Ashtoreth (the goddess of love and procreation, known elsewhere as Ishtar and Aphrodite), dieties whom the Hebrews considered sinfully idolatrous. Into the bellies of brazen images of Baal, infants were thrust for sacrifice by burning. Self-mutilation by the priests, and male and female prostitution were a part of the worship of the fertility gods. Many local Baals worshipped at altars in the groves and high places. One of them was Beelzebub, Lord of the Flies, who survives in Milton's *Paradise Lost* as a fallen angel, second only to Satan, and is now another name for the Devil himself.

At Mount Carmel, Elijah challenged four hundred and fifty priests of Baal to a contest by prayer, asking them to call forth fire and ignite a sacrificial pyre. When the priests of Baal had cried out ecstatically, danced and cut themselves from morning until afternoon without results, Elijah first drenched the pyre with water, then prayed to the Lord his God, whereupon the pyre and its sacrifice were immediately consumed with fire. He then ordered the great crowd which had assembled to put to death the priests of Baal.

This first of the prophets since Moses, a strange figure in woven haircloth robe, appearing from nowhere and without antecedents—unlike the later prophets, relying on the sword as well as the word—Elijah became a favorite among Jews, certainly for his defense of the God of Israel against all idolators, and perhaps also for the many stories associated with him, such as his hiding in the wilderness where he was fed by the ravens and his ascent to Heaven, not by death, but through a whirlwind in a chariot of fire.

Mary Ellen Chase in her book *The Prophets for the Common Reader* comments that the "mistaken idea of prediction by the prophets, of foretelling the future, existed early in the Christian church and is by no means absent from it today." She goes on to mention another misconception, that the prophets were "little more than eager and active social reformers," explaining that "the prophets were, of course, concerned deeply with the injustices of their day. They could hardly fail to fight against such sins since all such wrongdoing was directly opposed to the commands of God whose spokesmen they were. Yet to see them only, or even largely, as social reformers is to obscure their real meaning and to dim their chief and dominant concern: *the spiritual relationship of a man and of a people to God Himself.*" Putting it most simply and clearly, Miss Chase has written "The Hebrew prophet was . . . a spokesman; and he spoke in place of God." She adds, "That prophecy was an institution *unique* to ancient Israel has been, and still is, held by many scholars to be entirely true; that just as Rome produced

her statesmen and Greece gave to the world her philosophers, so
Israel alone gave rise to her prophets."

Mount Carmel and its environs have been hospitable to religions.
The followers of the original god Carmel, according to Tacitus,
wanted neither a Temple nor an image, just an altar and worshippers. Over the supposed cave where taught Elijah and his
successor, the prophet Elisha, there is now a small mosque with
inscriptions by pilgrims in Arabic and Greek and Latin and other
tongues. The Carmelite mendicant order of friars and nuns, founded
here in mid-twelfth century and since spread throughout the
Christian world, has a monastery and a convent, and a church on
the mountain top where they believe Elijah's cave to have been.
The followers of the Bahai faith, who, like the Druzes, believe
that prophets have appeared at intervals to guide mankind, count
among these Moses, Zoroaster, Buddha, Christ, Mohammed, and
their own Baha-u-llah.

Descending the other side of Mount Carmel is the Arab village
of Kebabir, inhabited by the eight hundred members of the
Ahmadia, an offshoot from Islam founded in the late nineteenth
century by Ahmed al Kadiyani who proclaimed himself the Messiah
and who did not believe in the jihad, or holy war, against unbelievers; an emissary sent specially from India is responsible for
the spiritual welfare of the villagers, and since 1935 the official
religious publication of the sect has been edited and printed here.

Down at the water's edge overlooking the harbor, sheltered by
long breakwaters, is the Dagon Silo, a two-hundred-and-ninety-one-
foot grain elevator of handsome, spare, rectangular design, with some
Biblical ornaments, but nevertheless named after a pre-Hebrew
fertility deity associated with wheat and the invention of the plow.
Not far from here is the lower station of the Carmelit, an electric
subway which climbs the mountain. It is a green and tidy mountain,
nicely landscaped and prosperous-looking, with Druze villages in
the heights and villas of the rich at the summit. At the middle
and upper levels, conservative communities of Russians, Germans
and Poles, whose older members cling to the ways of Europe and
have not bothered much with Hebrew, all may give a misleading
impression of Haifa. For this, the third city of the country in

area and population, is basically an industrial, a manufacturing town, a town for immigrants, and one of Israel's Arab centers. The great stacks down at the bay mark an oil refinery which was the largest in West Asia at the beginning of the War of Independence when the Arab states cut off its supply overnight. Since then, pumping of more than two hundred thousand tons of oil a year from the thirty-eight wells now producing in Israel and supplying eight per cent of that country's needs, and with Iranian oil pumped up from Eilat, the refineries can serve Israel and export a small surplus. Around the bay there are foundries, textile and glass factories, and plants manufacturing and assembling cars. Renault abandoned its plant here under threat of the Arab blockade, a move which it is said to have regretted since the promised Arab market dangled before its sales managers' eyes never materialized. Ford moved in place of Renault, much to the annoyance of the boycotters, and a pick-up truck called the Susita (Horse) and a Fiberglas sports car called the Sabra is made here. There are also cement and structural steel plants, and factories making metal and concrete piping. The Haifa works of Chemicals and Phosphates, Ltd. alone produces from the raw material it brings up from the Negev ammonia, sulphuric and nitric acids, calcium-ammonium nitrates, fluorides, ammonium sulphate, detergents and potassium silicate and, just to vary the shopping list, dry ice, licorice and plaster of Paris.

Backing up all of this is the Technion, the Israel Institute of Technology, which occupies a wooded three-hundred-acre campus on Mount Carmel, has a student body of more than five thousand graduates and undergraduates, as well as a technical high school of twelve hundred, and seven thousand six hundred enrolled in extension courses. The elegant, lightly curved roof over the Technion's auditorium named for Winston Churchill, and a credit to the architectural department, is not unlike the carapace of a turtle about to soar gently off the mountain into space. To catch up with Harvard and its endowment, the Technion, which was founded in 1912, needs two hundred and eighty-five years, but there are many benefactors in America, Britain, Canada, South Africa and Singapore who have been most generous; Gerard Swope, for long the president of General Electric, left a bequest of seven million dollars.

Until the war of 1948, Haifa's population of one hundred and
fifty thousand was nearly evenly divided between Jew and Arab.
Before and during the battle between Jewish and Arab forces
which ended with the capture of Haifa by the Haganah on the
twenty-second of April, 1948, an impassioned effort was made by the
mayor, Shabtai Levy, to persuade the Arabs to stay, as did many
of their Jewish neighbors and British inhabitants of Haifa. When
the four Christian Arab and the two Moslem Arab members of
their delegation replied they must consult their superiors and returned with word they had been ordered to leave by the Grand
Mufti, Mayor Levy wept, and the British Major General Stockwell
presiding at the meeting appeared shocked. A year later, the Arab
National Committee announced that the exodus of what must have
been about forty thousand Arabs was organized by them, stating
that they had "proudly asked for the evacuation of the Arabs and
their removal to the neighboring Arab countries. We are very glad
to state that the Arabs guarded their honor and traditions with
pride and greatness." Three years after that, the Arab Higher
Committee in Cairo in a memorandum on "The Problem of the
Palestine Arab Refugees" placed the blame on unspecified "Arab
leaders and ministers in Arab capitals" who had encouraged the
evacuation of Palestinian Arab refugees. Undoubtedly, fear played
a part in the flight. The departure of the Arabs from Haifa came
exactly two weeks after the massacre of the Arab village of Dir
Yassin by Irgun and Stern terrorists. Dir Yassin was a village said
to be neutral and to have refused the Mufti's guerrillas but it
possibly on this day had been seized as headquarters by a group
of the local Arab commander Abd el Kader Husseini's terrorists
for an attack on Jerusalem. Jacques de Reynier, chief Red Cross
representative during the conflict, made four visits to the village
in which he counted the corpses of two hundred and fifty-four men,
women and children. There were a few survivors.

Then, three days later, a convoy traveling to Hadassah Hospital
on Mount Scopus was ambushed, with a loss of the seventy-seven
doctors, nurses, university students and professors some two hundred
yards from the British military post which was responsible for the
safety of the road. But the Jewish propagandists, experienced in
psychological warfare, did not stress atrocities, nor their own losses,
dwelling instead on their strength and on their successes, whereas

the Arabs played up stories of atrocity, exaggerating them and making them as horrible as possible, with a view to inflaming the Arab populace with hatred toward the Jews and action against them; instead, many of the Arabs were terrorized and fled.

The Arab population of Haifa has grown again, but the Arabs who arrive in numbers each day from Nazareth and elsewhere in the Galilee to work still face the dilemma of all the Arab minorities in the country. In the aftermath of the Six Day War of 1967, when all final adjustments have been made and boundaries and populations sorted out, whatever number may have been added to the approximately three hundred thousand Arab citizens of Israel—a figure which includes the Druzes, Arab Christians and members of the small local sects which are offshoots of Islam—they still will be in a minority. What is more, a minority which until recently was used to being a majority, and which will live still surrounded by a great majority of Arabs who can be expected to be hostile in varying degrees to Israel, and to work for her destruction, meanwhile continuing to warn their fellow Arabs within Israel of dire consequences if they coöperate with the Jews.

The Israeli government prides itself that eighty-five to ninety per cent of the Arab electorate votes and is represented in the present Knesset by three Moslems, three Christians and one Druze. Arabic is used in the legislature, and in courts, is on the bank notes and the coins and the road signs of the country. The death rate among Israeli Arabs has fallen from twenty per thousand in 1947 to fewer than six. Infant mortality had dropped from over sixty-seven per thousand to less than forty, the lowest in the Arab world. The U.N. reports close to two hundred in Egypt.

The proportion of Arab farmland now irrigated has increased more than fifteenfold since independence to upward of seventy-five hundred acres. Eighty per cent of the Arab farmers own their own land. Crops have increased more than sixfold, and the number of cattle has more than trebled.

The General Federation of Labor in Israel, called Histadrut, has been active organizing Arab workers, training them and looking out for their rights as employees, as well as setting up clinics in a number of Arab villages. Israeli Arab women were the first, and still almost the only ones in the Moslem world, to vote, and their lot has been improved by the abolition of polygamy, no matter what the Koran says, and of child marriage.

More than three-quarters of all of Israel's Arabs live in Haifa and other parts of Galilee to the east where are the ninety-nine Arab villages in which the majority live, and the two Arab towns of Nazareth and Shfar'am.

Except for the Bedouin in the south, most of the rest live in towns and cities of mixed but predominantly Jewish populations: Haifa and Acre, Jaffa, Lod, Ramle and Jerusalem. In addition to supporting vocational training, agricultural training, land reclamation, irrigation and the introduction of mechanized farming in the Arab areas, the Israeli government has seen to it that many of the outlying, mountainous villages now have decent access roads, running water, electricity and schools. This is a paraphrase of the latest official report I can find: one would hope that by this time all the Arab villages within the 1948 boundaries might be served.

All this is fine. But there is a single inescapable fact which surely takes away from the material progress that Arabs have found in the State of Israel. By some of the laws of the land, by a good many of the officials, and many if not most of the Jewish population, the Arabs have been treated as second-class citizens. They are keenly aware of this without exception and they resent it bitterly, whether loyal to the government, politically indifferent or hostile. Most resented were the restrictions of military government affecting frontier areas until late 1966. Among them were bans on Arabs moving between cities after dark, or leaving their place of domicile without special permission—restrictions which did not apply to Jews.

Looking at a page of letters from Arab students in their late teens published by *The Jerusalem Post* in the first days of 1967, and most of these are persuasive, moderate and in excellent English, I find the recurring themes are a strong feeling of discrimination and intense dislike of military government, a feeling that Arab employment and education are unfairly limited ("University doors are very narrow"), and a desire for closer relations between Arab and Jewish young people. The wording and general tone of the letters strike me as sincere.

One recurring protest is against the use of curses like "dirty

Arab" and *"hatichat Aravi!"* which obviously have the power to wound. That this sort of blanket disparagement or ridicule, which members of a majority are apt to shrug off, can be seriously damaging we have seen in the United States in the series of riots in the long summer of 1967, when police in Harlem were specifically warned not to use names like "spic" and "nigger."

Robert St. John has written in his Life World Library book *Israel* that it is only normal that the Israeli Arabs would resent having to become citizens of a state whose way of life was foreign to their own. It is curious to reflect that most of this is also true of the "Oriental" Jews who have come in numbers to Haifa and there live in the old, abandoned Arab quarters.

In their own way, these Jews from the Middle East and North Africa, although they now account for sixty-five per cent of Israel's Jewish population, are themselves slightly second-class citizens. There are many publicized worries that their relative lack of schooling and unfamiliarity with European ways will lead to the State's becoming "Levantinized." Among themselves, the loss of patriarchal authority by the father in the new Israeli society and the rebelliousness and eagerness to adopt new ways by the children has led to all sorts of family stresses and to an unexpectedly high incidence of mental disorder. It is ironic that the reverse happened in the United States where the Sephardim were the first among the Jews to arrive, with something of the aura of the Golden Age of Spain still clinging to them; they looked down on the uncouth German Jews who came later and had not learned the ways of the new land; and the Germans in turn scorned the barbaric Jewish immigration from Russia and Eastern Europe.

In Haifa, something is being done to bring the Jews and Arabs, particularly the young ones, together again. There is a Jewish-Arab school, and a large youth center which attracts both Arab and Jewish young people for athletics, exhibitions and lectures on both Jewish and Arab subjects, which has facilities for refreshments and social gatherings and which, in a relaxed and apparently successful way, does everything it can to bring the young people of both sides together. The center's director, Baheej Khleif, is a young and personable Israeli Arab graduate of the Hebrew University who has studied at the Hague Institute of Social Studies and has represented Israel at at least two international conferences where he identified himself as an "Israeli Arab" when other Arab delegates insisted that he call himself a Palestinian, and who is coördinator for Arab student affairs for Histadrut. He makes several points forcefully: while the Israeli government ministries employ Arabs, it is Khleif's contention that they tend to remain in the lower echelons, it is difficult to get into high school and more difficult to go on to the university (schooling is free in Israel only through the elementary grades, and many Arabs just can't afford further education). It is often hard for a trained Arab to find work, and when jobs are scarce for Jews, they are scarcer for Arabs.

Improvement in the Arab standard of living since the independence of the State is far less important to Arab students, Khleif argues convincingly, than psychological and emotional difficulties. And whatever material advantages the Arabs of Israel may enjoy, until they become and feel themselves to be full citizens in every way, it is his firm belief, and that of many others, that the problems will persist.

Robert St. John continues that "despite the fact that Israeli Arabs were always free to leave, few departed after the initial flight of 1948–1949. The Arabs stayed for a variety of reasons—an attachment to the land which was their home, business interests, family associations, a lack of funds for transportation, a wish to avoid becoming refugees, the unwillingness of most Arab countries to admit them and, in some cases, because they were content with life in Israel."

The reasonably large number of Arabs in Haifa and its surroundings, reinforced by the Sephardic community there, give the town many Arab touches. Buses run here on the Jewish Sabbath to carry Arabs in and out of town. There are a good number of Arab restaurants, patronized by both Arabs and Sephardim and featuring a selection of kebabs and other boiled meats, *humus* and *tehina,* patés of chick peas and sesame seeds, pickled green chilis, and the flat unleavened Arab bread which seems to be called *pita* in Arabic, Hebrew, Greek and most of the languages of the region. Pork is not usually available since most of the customers are Moslem or Jewish. Nor is pork permitted in Israeli institutions or government premises. It is available in Christian areas of the country. It always interested me when going to a non-kosher restaurant with Jewish friends to watch them tuck into the pork, while I, following the instructions of my doctor who was an anticholesterol crusader, contented myself with chicken.

Haifa has received so many refugees now, legally from the moment the State of Israel was declared and ships waiting offshore were berthed immediately, that it has become a familiar routine. Immigrant ships usually dock at about six in the morning and by ten o'clock they have landed all their passengers. Now, instead of first being quartered in temporary villages called *ma'abarot* (singular, *ma'abara*)—anything from tents, with duckboards across the mud, to reasonably habitable, simple but decent small houses—newcomers are sent directly to the settlements where they will live. Incentives are offered to encourage settlers to stay where they are sent—jobs, clinics, shops and the amenities of a small community—but there is nothing to stop them from drifting to Tel Aviv and the other centers where the bright lights are. Many of them do.

In Haifa's harbor are the ships of many nations, among them Ghana's Black Star Line which Israel helped create for that West African nation, just as it worked with Ethiopia to create the line with the heraldic gold conquering Lions of Judah on their stacks, manned by mixed Ethiopian and Israeli crews, which ply between Eilat and the Ethiopian port of Massawa in Eritrea.

From Mount Carmel north through Acre and what is now Lebanon and a good stretch of Syria was in Biblical times the home of the Phoenicians. This was the Greek name for them, a bit confusing since they called their land Canaan, a term which originally applied to all of that which became Syria and Palestine, but which we think of simply as the Promised Land of the Hebrews. The word "Phoenician" is thought to mean a reddish purple, after a famous and costly dye obtained from a whelk called the murex (*Murex brandaris* or *trunculus*). The Roman emperor customarily wore a toga of this color and its usage is still preserved in the phrase "the royal purple."

North of Acre, the Phoenicians living in their principal city-states of Tyre, Sidon and Biblos inhabited a rocky coastal strip hemmed in by the mountains of Lebanon, but rich in splendid forests of cedar. They had little taste for agriculture, and, with the collapse of the sea power of Crete in the middle of the second millennium B.C., pushed further and further abroad as traders until they had established colonies throughout the Mediterranean and the Red Sea. They brought home gold and silver from Spain, copper from Cyprus, and probably gold from Ireland and iron and tin from England. A partnership with Solomon brought their cedar of Lebanon and skilled artificers of wood and metal for the construction of the Temple in Jerusalem; it sent their ships from Ezion-geber, the ancient port at the tip of the Negev, with copper from Solomon's mines at Timna nearby to trade for gold in the land of Ophir. The rate of exchange was supposed to be not less than two bars of gold for one of copper.

The location of Ophir is uncertain, though south Arabia and Somaliland across the way, known to the Egyptians as a source of gold, have been suggested. The ships of Tharshih, which brought back precious metals to Solomon and to his Phoenician craftsmen, are mentioned in the First Book of Kings: "Once in three years came the navy of Tharshih, bringing gold, and silver, ivory and apes and peacocks"—a passage which inspired the rousing first verse of Masefield's poem "Cargoes," and was also echoed in Kipling's "The Merchantmen." The apes and the ivory suggest Africa or perhaps the Far East. The Phoenicians are known to have brought pearls from the East, and the skins of lions from Africa, but the word here used for "ape" is derived from the Sanskrit. The only trouble in carrying this too far is that we stumble again on translations: In the English translations other than the King James Version, "peacocks" is translated as "baboons."

Wherever Ophir and their gold mines in the East may have been, the Phoenicians in their day were mariners without rival. The Admiral Hanno from the North African Phoenician colony of Carthage was commissioned by the Egyptian Pharaoh Necho to circumnavigate Africa. Phoenician inscriptions have been found in Marseilles and Avignon, Malta, Sicily, Sardinia, Greece, Spain and a great many other places.

With the Phoenicians went their alphabet, and this is believed to be the first developed, the direct ancestor of every alphabet yet discovered, in use or abandoned. The Phoenician language itself in one form or another was spoken for well over two thousand years, among the Carthaginian peasantry until the Moslem conquest of the seventh century A.D. It survives in Maltese, which is its only living descendant.

10/ ACRE AND THE CRUSADES

Proceeding north from Haifa, through the industrial outskirts which are about as interesting as industrial outskirts anywhere, one comes before long to the massive walls of the city built by the Crusaders, later reinforced by their Moslem conquerors. Acre, or Akko in Hebrew, was named after St. Jean d'Acre—that is, Saint John the Baptist—when the Crusaders were driven from Jerusalem and this became their capital in the Holy Land. The city had also been known as Acca, Ace, Ptolemais and the Colony of Claudius Caesar. It has had the usual number of conquerors for these parts, among them Assyrians, Egyptians, Alexander the Great, the Crusaders, the Persians and finally, in 1293, the Mamelukes, a dynasty of former slaves, young Circassians and Georgians, originally Christians but captured or bought and converted to Islam. The Mamelukes became famed as administrators and warriors for the Egyptians. In the end, their skill enabled them to supplant their masters.

Two and a half centuries of Mameluke rule came to an end with their defeat and the capture of Jerusalem by the Ottoman Sultan Selim the First's far-better-disciplined Turkish Janissaries. It is estimated by Dr. James Parkes that the population of the territory ruled by the Mamelukes had been reduced to one-third of what it was when they came to power. Along the coast, they systematically destroyed each city which they overcame.

Acre is mentioned in the manuscripts of the Canaanites, as well as the Egyptians and the Assyrians, and by Shakespeare in *Henry IV*. Jonathan, the Maccabean warrior and high priest, was assassinated in 142 B.C. in Acre. Here the great rabbi, Moses ben Maimon, or Maimonides, lived for a time in the twelfth century, writing in Arabic the first systematic exposition of Judaism, influencing both Moslem and Christian thinkers, including Thomas Aquinas. Maimonides made medical observations far in advance of his time on the nervous system, epilepsy, allergies and psychosomatic disorders.

The Franciscans are proud of having at Acre a convent established by the founder of their order, Saint Francis of Assisi, who landed here some seven hundred years ago.

Acre surrendered to Saladin after his great victory at the Horns of Hittin in Galilee in 1187. Then, in a two-year seige between 1189 and 1191, eight thousand Crusaders were killed before Acre finally capitulated.

After a successful campaign in Italy in the spring of the year before, Napoleon had embarked on the conquest of Britain's eastern empire in Egypt and Syria. This had begun well enough with control of Egypt assured by the end of July with the Battle of the Pyramids, but a week later his plans were frustrated by the destruction of his entire fleet by Lord Nelson during the Battle of the Nile. With return to Europe now not possible, Napoleon was obliged to spend the winter in Egypt, where he began reformation of the Mameluke government and launched a great series of archeological and scientific projects in the region which were to bear fruit for years to come. One of these was discovery of the Rosetta Stone, a trilingual inscription on a battered slab of black basalt, now in the British Museum, on which was inscribed the same passage in hieroglyphic Egyptian, demotic Egyptian and Greek, giving Jean François Champollion and others the clue to Egyptian writings. This led directly to knowledge of the great part played by Egypt in the ancient world, including the four centuries of Hebrew captivity in Egypt.

Less weighty than the studies in Egyptology initiated by Napoleon, but also the result of his winter in the Middle East, was the vogue for all things Egyptian, real or imitated, which swept France and which can still be seen in the carved sphinxes on Empire furniture and those made of stone which decorated the gardens of châteaux.

Acre is an old town, and that is saying a good deal in latitudes where such things are measured in millennia. It has an antique patina. There are memories of other rulers, its besiegers and defenders of many days, much like Caesarea. But whereas at Caesarea the arches of the aqueducts and the other ruins look like a theatrical set, perhaps a ballet just before the dancers enter, Acre is very much alive. The Mosque of Jezzar Pasha, after the Dome of the Rock the richest and largest in the Holy Land, is ornamented with marble and columns brought from Ashkelon and Caesarea and Tyre, and is busy with the coming and going of worshippers through the lovely gardens which surround it and in which are a sun dial and a fountain for ablutions which looks like a small shrine in itself. Nearby is the Khan al Umdan, the Inn of the Pillars, a caravansary built by Jezzar Pasha with more granite columns from Caesarea used by bygone merchants to hitch their camels to, and upstairs, in the gallery running around the courtyard, small rooms for the travelers.

Acre to me is the most Arab in feeling of all of the towns this side of the Old City of Jerusalem, including Nazareth and Beersheba. Dark little shops in a maze of narrow alleyways sell spices and yard goods, fish and second-hand shoes. Moslem women may wear beneath their long skirts pleated bloomers of blue or yellow or red. There are also Moslem and Druze and Greek Orthodox and Maronite holy men in the crowd, Israeli Jews of every description and tourists armed with cameras stalking local color. The municipal museum of Acre, which contains Phoenician glass, is in Jezzar Pasha's old Turkish bath house. There is another caravansary, the Shahwarda, in which can be seen the cannon used by the Pasha in his battle, aided by his Albanian mercenaries and a strong British squadron commanded by Sir Sidney Smith, in which the thirty-year-old Napoleon was repulsed, marking the end in the last year of the eighteenth century of his dream of subjugating Syria, the closest he came to that province's ancient city of Jerusalem.

The fortress built in the mid-eighteenth century by Jezzar Pasha on a street along the shore, now known as Haganah Road, was used as a central prison by the British Mandatory government. Together with the prison in Atlit, it housed terrorists from the Stern Gang and Irgun, captured underground members of Haganah, and even senior officers of the Jewish Agency.

One of these involuntary guests of the government was Moshe Dayan, who had worked with the underground Haganah for eight years by 1937 when he became second in command to the brilliant, iconoclastic, religious and deeply Zionist, British captain Orde Wingate, who had been given permission to form Jewish commando companies known as Special Night Squads. These were to protect the oil pipeline from Iraq to Haifa, tracking down and exterminating pro-Axis, Arab marauders and saboteurs. Two years later, it occurred to the British authorities that the commando tactics being taught might well be used against the government, and so Wingate was removed and sent to Ethiopia to organize more Night Squads, and then to Burma where, now a general, he died in 1946, leading one of his unorthodox reconnaissance patrols far behind the Japanese lines. The Special Night Squads were declared illegal in Palestine, and Dayan given five years in the central prison in Acre (he and others had already been teaching Wingate's tactics to Haganah), but after serving two years was released, disguised as an Arab and sent out to reconnoiter for Allied forces from Palestine moving against the Vichy French in Syria. A similar job in the Lebanon scouting for the Australians cost him his left eye, when a bullet hit his binoculars, and so he acquired his famous eye patch.

Also incarcerated in the Acre prison were Baha-u-llah, imprisoned by the Turks until his old age when he was permitted to move to a house in a village a little to the north, now surrounded by more Persian gardens, and the holiest of all Bahai shrines.

The fortress used by the Mandatory government as a prison was also the place of execution, the condemned men dressed in scarlet after the British tradition. In 1947, Stern and Irgun raiders attacked the prison, breached the wall and helped a number of prisoners to escape, many of whom were recaptured. The room at the prison used for executions has been preserved as a sort of grisly historical exhibit, while visitors now tramp up the outside stairs of the fortress to the crenelated city walls and to the roof where they inspect the eighteenth-century cannon mounted against Bonaparte.

When, on the eighteenth of May in 1291, Acre fell to the Mamelukes and its defendants were slaughtered, the remaining Crusader settlements quietly evacuated all those for whom ships could be found. The last of the Europeans were driven from a little island named Ruad, south of Latakia in Syria, in 1303. Thus ended ingloriously two centuries during which the Christian West had tried to reopen and secure the pilgrims' path to Jerusalem, to establish itself by armed force in the Holy Land.

The neatly labeled eight Crusades were a complex, confused and almost continuous movement from Europe to the Holy Land during these years, when each decade saw at least an expedition or two. We are familiar to a degree with the madness and the follies of our own times, in that we live among them, but it is difficult at first to credit the Crusades' medieval mixture of religious exaltation, superstition, brutality, chivalry and honor, deep faith, avarice and perfidy, treachery, cruelty in this world and real fear of hell-fire in the world to come. Charles W. Ferguson, reviewing Zoé Oldenbourg's *The Crusades* in *The New York Times* quotes Mrs. Oldenbourg's emphasis on "the real and obsessional horror of cowardice" of the age and its "utter disregard for death elevated to a point of dogma." Mr. Ferguson goes on, "We are forewarned of what was to happen in Jerusalem when we witness an example of the mixed morality of the period: a knight burning a convent with all the nuns inside and then refusing to eat meat afterwards because he is reminded that it is Good Friday."

It had all begun when the relatively tolerant Omayyad and Abbasid caliphates, under which Harun al Rashid had recognized the Emperor Charlemagne and his successors as protectors of the Christian holy places in Palestine, were succeeded by Caliph Hakim, who destroyed all synagogues and churches including that of the Holy Sepulchre, and spared only the Church of the Nativity in Bethlehem. The caliph, who appears to have been a madman, further forbade all pilgrimage. Word spread in Europe that somehow this was all the work of the Jews. The Fatimid dynasty of Hakim, descended from the daughter of Mohammed, was succeeded shortly by that of the Seljuk Turks, who were even harsher in their treatment of pilgrims. Reaction to this was one of the immediate causes of the Crusades.

Peter the Hermit, a man who had been a soldier before he became a monk, had been to Jerusalem where he saw the plight of pilgrims. Peter received a vision in which he believed that Christ had appeared to him and promised him aid and protection in rescuing Christians and the Holy Sepulchre from the hands of unbelievers. Obtaining the ear of Pope Urban II who accepted his mission with great enthusiasm, Peter was empowered to preach a holy crusade to the masses throughout Europe while the Pope addressed himself to the princes and the potentates who were to lead it. Both were men of great eloquence. Crossing Europe in his undyed woolen tunic and a dark mantle which fell to his heels, arms and feet bare, taking only a little fish and wine and eating neither meat nor bread, Peter was looked upon as someone of almost supernatural sanctity, and, as he spoke, fired tens upon tens of thousands with the crusading fever. Palestine, that land flowing with milk and honey, would be divided among the Crusaders, who would receive full pardon for all of their sins against God and man, the Pope promised. "Go, then," the Pope exhorted, "in expiation of your sins; and go assured that after this world shall have passed away, imperishable glories shall be yours in the world which is to come."

The times were propitious for these words. At the end of the tenth and the beginning of the eleventh centuries, it was widely believed in Christendom that the thousand years of the Apocalypse were drawing to an end. Jesus Christ would descend to Jerusalem to judge all mankind. There were meteors in these times, great earthquakes and hurricanes which uprooted the forests. An aurora borealis of great brilliancy was seen, increasing the apprehension in Europe to panic. Many thousands set out for Jerusalem.

Those who survived the journey found that the days of the earlier, milder Saracens—as the Arab rulers and later all Moslems, particularly those in opposition to the Crusaders, were called—who got along tolerably with the Christian West and thrived on the pilgrim trade, had changed and the pilgrims who continued to crowd Jerusalem waiting for the end of the world were beaten, plundered and persecuted unmercifully by the Turks. It was word of this, spread by the Pope and Peter the Hermit and many who had returned, which helped kindle the fervor in Europe which led to the Crusades. Fervor grew to frenzy. Farmers sold their plows, craftsmen their tools, women their jewelry, and noblemen mortgaged their estates to buy swords with which to deliver the Holy Land.

The inflamed Crusaders, when they gave the poor Jews a chance, demanded that they embrace the Cross or die, and so while a few were protected, some were able to flee, and many chose baptism, the greater number elected death, whole communities committing suicide. There is a prayer for Yom Kippur composed at this time which reaffirms in the face of destruction Jews' belief in their God: "Though maimed and shattered, yet we are Thine."

Those of the First Crusade were not helped by the fact that the swarms following Peter the Hermit who had preceded them in Constantinople had stripped the lead from the roofs of the churches and then sold it on the outskirts of town. Nor were they helped by the excommunication half a century before by Pope Leo IX of all the Eastern churches, including those of Greece, Byzantium, with its Ecumenical Patriarchate of Constantinople, and the Patriarchates of Alexandria, Jerusalem and Antioch, among others. There was no love lost between the East and the West, and successive waves of Crusaders sometimes found themselves fighting in Cairo or Constantinople instead of securing Jerusalem and the holy places as was their mission. As for the Crusaders, they liked to say that the Byzantine Emperor Alexius and the Greeks were greater enemies than the Turks and the Saracens. The rupture was long and bitter, lasting until our own times when the present Patriarch of Constantinople, which is now Istanbul, met Pope Paul VI twice, once on the Mount of Olives and once in Istanbul, in an effort to begin to heal the breach.

Half a million to six hundred thousand foot soldiers and a hundred thousand cavalry took part in the First Crusade, not counting the women and children and priests who accompanied them. Far fewer reached Jerusalem when it was finally taken in 1099.

Crusaders at first were unfamilar with the poisoned arrows used by the Turks. Decimated by famine and thirst and pestilence, in extremity abandoning their helmets and chain mail in the desert, they were rent by dissension among themselves. Horses were slain and eaten, dogs, cats and rats in lean times sold for high prices.

The Crusaders' trading colonies and the military orders could negotiate with the infidel Moslem enemy, make war or peace without consulting the King. The word "crusade" acquired increasing elasticity. Popes and princes were ready to use the word to describe their attacks on rival Christian sects, to put down public protest, to raise money for the Church. (A special yearly tithe levied in Europe after Saladin had captured Jerusalem is considered by some economists to be the origin of modern taxation.)

Charles Mackay, from whose book of 1841, *Extraordinary Popular Delusions and the Madness of Crowds*, I have taken some of the more fevered examples of Crusader behavior, sums it all up with the lines: "Now what was the grand result of all these struggles? Europe expended millions of her treasures, and the blood of two millions of her children; and a handful of quarrelsome knights retained possession of Palestine for about one hundred years."

James Parkes has explained the superiority of the Moslem civilization which the Crusaders encountered in the East as the "inheritance of the Greek, Roman, Hebrew and Persian civilizations which were far older than that of Europe. . . . In the end the Latins took back with them to Europe the philosophical, medical, mathematical and other knowledge which they had acquired in Syria, together with many pleasant plants and stuffs." Among these were cotton and sugar.

One curious aspect of the Crusades, as it seems looking back now, was the wild enthusiasm they aroused among women. At the time of the preaching of Urban II and Peter the Hermit, women branded themselves with the sign of the cross on breasts and arms, dyeing red the wounds, and sometimes doing as much to their children. Husbands, suitors, every male within reach, whether capable of bearing arms or not, was urged to put all behind him and to hasten to the Holy Land. Many women accompanied them. The leader of a female troop from Germany, all in armor, wore half-boots and gilded spurs and was known as the Golden-Footed Lady.

Regulations for the Third Crusade drawn up by Richard Coeur de Lion specifically forbade young girls following the Crusaders, admitting in women's clothes only laundresses at least fifty years old, or others the same age. It didn't work; women continued to change into battle dress. "Many high-minded and affectionate maidens and matrons," wrote Charles Mackay in his chronicles, "bearing the sword or the spear, followed their husbands and lovers to war in spite of King Richard, and in defiance of danger."

Almost all is gone now. Some of the battlements can be identified as Crusader; most of the walls and earthworks around the city of Acre were rebuilt by the Turks, a fine example of late-eighteenth-century fortification. Under the citadel which was the prison is a great ribbed and vaulted crypt built by the Knights Hospitalers of St. John. Prisoners attempting to dig their way to freedom in the last days of the Mandate tunneled through into a series of underground halls also built by the Crusaders. There have been a number of projects suggested in recent years to make use of the great wall of Acre, the Crusaders' crypts and their surroundings as a museum, an art gallery, or for entertainment. One about which I have somewhat mixed feelings was reported some time ago by *The Jerusalem Post* when a New York art gallery announced "plans to develop part of the historic wall of Acre" . . . which turned out to be a "supper club surround by a wall of live torches, lighting up groups of Crusader tents housing the diners." The *Post*'s New York correspondent, Jesse Zel Lurie, wrote that when an intense Israeli girl, drink in hand, asked the art director and promoter of the proposed supper club whether his designer's sketches of all this would harmonize with the ancient city, she was reassured, "Everything will be built in *modern crusader style*." Whereupon the Israeli girl choked on her gin and tonic.

11/ THE GALILEE:

TABOR, NAZARETH, CANA, SAFED AND TIBERIUS

N orthernmost in Israel is the Galilee, running sixty miles from the northern and eastern borders to include Megiddo, Nazareth and Mount Tabor, overlooking the fertile valley of Jezreel where Zionist pioneers who had come to the Holy Land in the latter part of the nineteenth century established many of their first communal farming settlements. Just to the south of Mount Tabor is the village of Ein Dor, in one of whose caves lived the Witch of Endor, consulted by King Saul, and who prophesied the deaths of Saul and his sons fighting the Philistines on Mount Gilboa nearby.

The eastern boundary here is the Sea of Galilee and south of it the Jordan River flowing down to the Dead Sea. To the west are the ports of Acre and Haifa, with the Carmel range forming the Galilee's southwestern boundary.

In this thirsty land, Galilee is verdant, with many woods, the waters of the Jordan and of the Sea of Galilee itself. Rainfall is more abundant here than elsewhere. There are more springs and brooks. Moisture comes from Mount Hermon a little to the north, whose snowy peak rises to more than nine thousand feet. The highest peak in Israel is Mount Meiron, about six miles to the west of Safed and a little over four thousand feet. The mountains of upper Galilee average about two thousand feet, a continuation of the limestone Lebanon range, their westerly slopes descending gently to the sea, but on the east plunging from nearly three thousand feet at Safed down to the Sea of Galilee at seven hundred and thirty feet below sea level.

Travel writers are in the habit of referring to the valley of Jezreel as smiling and I can see why they do so, for traveling inland from the Mediterranean to the Sea of Galilee or up to Nazareth, this of all the valleys of Israel seems smiling and peaceful. There are cypresses planted along the roads, and everywhere there are wild-flowers. There are orchards, and fields which are patches of viridian, with the dark grey-green olive groves on the hillsides, dappled with the delicate lighter green of new leaves. From the highway, farm equipment clanks into the fields along country roads of dark reddish brown. Climbing the hills toward Nazareth, one comes across more Arabs and Druzes, for this is the land of their villages. Along the road, they are waiting for buses, driving tractors, herding sheep and tending vineyards and fields of wheat and barley; working as masons or shopkeepers or in a hundred other pursuits in the villages. Women may be tattooed below the lower lip and elsewhere on the face, and wear long, full, dark-blue robes and headdress. Men wear the Arab *keffieh* or just a head cloth with black or grey-pencil-striped, ankle-length robes, corded at the waist and hanging just above an indifferent, scuffed pair of black or brown oxfords. It's common to wear the Arab headdress with a business suit, often with an ill-fitting double-breasted jacket and a sweater. Many of the Arabs and Druzes claim to be descended from the Crusaders, and many have gingery or lightish hair, derived from them perhaps or from any of the many peoples who have traveled this highway between the continents.

A town of something more than thirty thousand souls living thirteen hundred feet or so above the plain, Nazareth is the home of nearly half of the Christians in Israel, now over sixty thousand and largely Arab and divided among most of the twenty-four denominations. Many of the Christian orders maintain churches, shrines, monasteries, convents, schools, hospitals, clinics and dispensaries in Nazareth.

Just as there are elsewhere two Gardens of Gethsemane, two places where occurred the Transfiguration, two Mounts of Temptation and two each of other rival shrines, usually one Roman Catholic and one Orthodox, here there are two different churches marking the spot where the Archangel Gabriel appeared to Mary to tell her that she would give birth to the Messiah: at both the Greek Orthodox Church of the Archangel Gabriel, north of Nazareth's Old City, and the Roman Catholic Church of the Annunciation near the center of town. The newly completed Basilica of the Annunciation is now the largest church in the Middle East, and one of the ten largest in the world. The Israeli contractors who built it, Solel-Boneh, as a gesture of good will, contributed the twenty-foot copper cross which crowns the church while the Franciscan Custodian of the Holy Land, responsible for all the Roman Catholic sacred places here, did his part at the church's completion by flying the flags of the Vatican, of the Franciscans and of Israel.

Jewish Israeli guides, who must know their country well, and prove it in stiff examinations to get their licenses, defer when they reach Nazareth, and turn their visitors over to the local Arab tourist guides, duly licensed and with little buttons in their lapels to prove it. They have the exclusive franchise for this area. The guides of Nazareth have for their visitors a great store of shrines which over the years have become associated with the family of Jesus, his childhood, and the beginnings of his ministry. Among the two dozen and more churches and monasteries are those places now believed to have been the home and carpenter's shop of Joseph, the well where it is presumed Mary went to draw water and the Church of the Rock, where is exhibited a great limestone slab on which, tradition has it, Jesus and his disciples ate together after the Resurrection. The Greek Orthodox Church of the Synagogue commemorates the place where Jesus may have taught and worshipped. Another ancient Jewish synagogue in the Franciscan monastery does likewise.

There is also, about a mile from town, the Mount of Precipitation, where the congregation at the synagogue attended by Jesus was so angered by his words in speaking to them that they rose up and hurried him out of Nazareth to a hill from which they prepared to hurl him, when somehow, mysteriously, he passed through their midst and went his way, down to Capernaum where he continued his ministry around the Sea of Galilee.

What had roused the congregation was the reading by Jesus of a passage of the Prophet Isaiah which declares, "The Spirit of the Lord is upon me, because he hath anointed me to preach the gospel to the poor; he hath sent me to heal the broken-hearted, to preach deliverance to the captive, and recovering of sight to the blind, to set at liberty them that are bruised." Jesus had told the congregation, "This day is this scripture fulfilled in your ears." He had also said, "Ye will surely say unto me this proverb, Physician, heal thyself: whatsoever we have heard done in Capernaum, do also here in thy country," adding, "Verily I say unto you, No prophet is accepted in his own country."

So little is known of Nazareth in the time of Jesus or of his own life there that it has been difficult to identify the places of the gospel stories. Nazareth was mentioned neither in the Old Testament nor in the Talmud.

Nazareth was a village with a population of a very few hundred, looked on with some ridicule by the inhabitants of Jerusalem. As Robert Aron has emphasized, there are only two references in all the New Testament to the life of Jesus between his birth and his baptism by John the Baptist. One is: "And the child grew, and waxed strong in spirit, filled with wisdom: and the grace of God was upon him." The other is the story which follows this passage from Luke, of his being presented at the Temple in Jerusalem at the age of twelve.

In the gospel according to St. John, the doubtful Nathanael of Cana, who later became a disciple, expressed what appears to be the general opinion of the rustic village which was the home of Jesus when told the Messiah had appeared there, "Can there any good thing come out of Nazareth?"

A great deal can be inferred reasonably from Aron's brilliant reconstruction of Jewish family life, the synagogue, and the influences which Jesus must have encountered during his formative years and his young manhood; and from the scholarship of the Rev. William P. Paterson and the Rev. S. MacLean Gilmour, writing in *The Dic-*

tionary of the Bible in an article which assumes that the home of Jesus in Nazareth was one of "orthodox Jewish piety." Paterson and Gilmour go on, "Jesus, furthermore, was no 'unlettered Galilean peasant.' In His home and in the synagogue school He would have been thoroughly grounded in the Jewish Scriptures, and His recorded sayings show that He had caught not only the literary charm of the Old Testament, but also an understanding of its highest religion."

The authors commend Luke's straightforward telling of the visit of Jesus to the Temple in Jerusalem: "The point of the story is that even as a boy Jesus thought of God as Father and of God's House as His true sphere of work. Luke's narrative was originally independent of the virgin-birth cycle, for it speaks of Joseph and Mary as Jesus's parents. It is in sharp contrast to the revolting tales of Jesus the boy wonder and magician that fill the later so-called 'Infancy Gospels,' and its very naturalness vouches for its authenticity." They also note that it is only in the gospel according to St. Matthew that the doctrine of the virgin birth is basic to the proclamation of Jesus as the Messiah, and that Matthew's authority for this comes from "a narrative that had no messianic connotations for Isaiah and that loses all relevance when it is observed that the Greek word for 'virgin,' which Matthew took over from the Septuagint text, is a mistranslation of a Hebrew noun meaning nothing more specific than 'young woman.' "

In Nazareth, in the last days of 1620, the Franciscan Father Custodian Thomas of Novara obtained from the powerful Druze Emir Fakr ed-Din Maan permission to safeguard the remains of the Basilica of the Annunciation, a great Byzantine stone church built over the grotto of the Annunciation, rebuilt by the Norman Crusader Tancred, Prince of Galilee, after its mid-thirteenth-century destruction by the Sultan Bibars, who is reported to have razed the church completely except for the grotto and its small antechamber.

(The antechamber was believed to have been carried miraculously by angels first to the coast of Dalmatia and then to Loretto in southeast Italy where it became a goal of pilgrimage, the sacred shrine now enclosed in another great church, adorned with treasure brought by pilgrims. It is now the subject of the Roman Catholic Litany of Loretto in honor of the Virgin and this shrine.)

The unquenchable enthusiasm for relics, real or manufactured, has been described by the Rev. James Parkes in his *History of Palestine*:

> The Church of the first three centuries grew up in the Jewish belief that a dead body was unclean; and there is little trace of any veneration being paid to bodies, even the bodies of saints and martyrs, until the fourth century. The remains of martyrs were collected and reverently buried where they had died; to do so was indeed a pious duty linked to the belief in a bodily resurrection; but that their bodies should be divided into bits in order to give special sanctity to other places, this was the distortion of a later age, but a distortion that, once admitted, spread like fire. By the eighth century, it was impossible to consecrate an altar which did not contain the relics of a saint, and the collection of heads, arms, legs and other single bones became the natural ambition of a pious prince or churchman.

In the end, I suppose, in spite of the eagerness to find a miracle on every hilltop and behind every bush, the commercialization of holy places and the mulcting of the credulous by salesmen of sacred souvenirs, what counts is the devotion of the numbers who come on pilgrimage to any holy place and there receive the reassurance of their faith.

Writing of a visit to the grotto below the Basilica of the Annunciation, the Israeli historian Pinchas Lapide reflected that "without this place there would have been no Bethlehem, no Calvary, no Pentecost —none of the milestones of the revolution which has changed the face of Western civilization."

Noting that, when the Franciscan Fathers in 1957 began work on the new basilica replacing their seventeenth-century church, excavations for the foundation led to discovery of an earlier Crusader church, and below that a Byzantine church, and, still lower, vestiges of the village of Nazareth of the time of Herod the Great, the Roman census and the Annunciation, Lapide wrote, "Next to the grotto the fathers also discovered a small Judeo-Christian sanctuary dating back to the second half of the first century—proving that a few decades after the birth of Jesus, the faithful had already gathered here for worship."

For my part, I liked on occasion to go to visit the Salesian Fathers, whose Italianate building stretches along the brow of a high hill overlooking the town and where they maintain a church, an orphanage and a vocational-training school which has a CARE program including, appropriately, a carpenter shop. A long balcony on one side of the Salesian school looks over all of the little town of Nazareth, gentle hills on the other side not far away. Almost directly below the Salesians and a little to the left as one looks down are the orphanage, the girls' school and dispensary of the French teaching order Les Dames de Nazareth. There the Mother Superior of the convent Mère Gigues, a merry, sweet-faced and highly organized soul, took greatest pleasure—once inspection of sewing and knitting classes had been completed—in showing guests her catacombs.

A wondrous discovery has been made under the Convent of the Nuns of Nazareth. In 1884, a clumsy workman trying to repair their cistern dropped a heavy stone which fell through the surface below him, disclosing a large chamber surmounted by a groined, Roman vault supported by pilasters. This led to a catacomb containing many tombs, in one of which was a seated skeleton with a ring on its finger, apparently that of an early bishop. Through a deep archway to the north of the vaulted chamber was a well, now dry, but with grooves deeply cut in its side by ropes used in drawing water.

Also discovered were the remains of a small Jewish house, and a round cave containing a stone altar surrounded by clay lamps, the chains of other lamps and censers, and, fixed to the rock beside the altar, a pair of knight's spurs. When two flagstones were lifted from the small aperture over this cave at the time of its discovery, those present reported the strong odor of incense.

Then, next to the cave of the stone altar was found a fine burial chamber with the great, thick and rounded rolling stone traditionally used to close Jewish tombs.

It was now remembered that when the nuns had bought the land for their convent in 1881, the owners had demanded an unusually high price, insisting that it was "holy ground" since it contained "the tomb of the saint," as well as the house in which he had lived. Also, that here had stood "the great church of Nazareth," which had drawn its water from its own well. No trace of any of this had been seen within living memory; there were no local records of another great church in the center of Nazareth close to the Basilica of the Annunciation, whose history was known. It was strange that pilgrims would not have mentioned another church of such importance. It seemed that all there was to go on was another exasperatingly vague local legend in an area already overstocked with them.

Now began an exercise in historical detection. It turned out that, while many pilgrims described their visits to Bethlehem, there were far fewer accounts of Nazareth. Of those mentioned by other authors, numbers had disappeared from all libraries. The sixth-century map of colored mosaic of Palestine and Egypt, now found in the Greek Orthodox Church of Madeba in Jordan and which shows the buildings of Jerusalem in some detail, was missing the portion where Nazareth would have appeared.

Then some texts were found confirming that, before the Moslem conquest, indeed there had been two great churches in Nazareth. The most convincing account was that given by a French Bishop Arculfe, quoted by the Venerable Bede among others, who stated that in Nazareth there were two great churches, one built over the spot where the Archangel Gabriel appeared to the Virgin Mary, the Church of the Annunciation, and the other built "at the place where the Lord, Our Saviour, was reared," specifically mentioning that it was built on pilastered arches and that "It has a well of very clear water. . . . The water can also be obtained from inside the church built above the well, by drawing it up in small vessels by means of pulleys." This last detail is confirmed by the stones of the archway above the convent's well which also show deep scoring, presumably by the same ropes used to raise buckets. A seventeenth-century engraving, Terre-Sainte—1634 by Eugène Roger from the Bibliothèque Nationale in Paris, shows the Virgin Mary's house, the Virgin's Well close by, buildings of a monastery, and a lonely mosque tower—all of which bears out what can be pieced together: that in earliest Christian times this cave may have been used as a sanctuary and a catacomb, as were others; in the Byzantine era the great basilica was built above the cave, as described by Arculfe; under Moslem rule, the basilica must have been destroyed and a mosque built to replace it, as can be seen in several other seventeenth-century pictures; by the late seventeenth century, the mosque had disappeared; the same was the fate of a Benedictine monastery meanwhile erected here.

This still leaves the Church of Joseph, built later by the Franciscan Fathers some two hundred yards north of the Basilica of the Annunciation, but which lacks the specific details given in Arculfe's description. The traditional Fountain of Mary is very probably too far to the north of the ancient settlement of the time of Jesus, according to *The Dictionary of the Bible*. There the matter rests.

The Nuns of Nazareth are convincing, and remain convinced. A pamphlet, "Excavations at Nazareth," which the Mother Superior offers her visitors ends its summation of the evidence with: "As for the tomb, could it not be that of Saint Joseph, 'the Saint of Nazareth'? No text so far enables anyone to affirm or to deny this."

Nazareth remains strongly Arab in character, even though there are few of the narrow, tortuous cobbled lanes and the mazes of dark little shops selling everything under the sun that mark the bazaars of Jaffa, Acre and particularly the Old City of Jerusalem. Occasionally, someone will cry hopefully, "Arab headdress, lady? Arab headdress, lady?" There are small boys who qualify in the Victorian sense as street Arabs and who have been known to throw stones at tourists who did not want to engage their services, or whose looks they didn't like. Government of Israel statistics show the annual income of the average family in Nazareth as the equivalent of $2,333 as opposed to that of the average urban Jewish family in the country as $2,453, but there is evident unemployment and underemployment among Nazareth's Arab population, and when the country as a whole suffers an economic recession, it is worse in Arab Nazareth.

Another marked characteristic of the town is the presence of so many foreign missions, here over so many generations that they have greatly influenced the population and, inevitably, found themselves sharing some of their parishioners' views of the world around them, including their grievances and their prejudices. Most depressing has been an occasional unholy alliance between some of the Christian churches in Nazareth and the local Arab Communists. The death of an Israeli Arab youth killed by the border patrol, perhaps a terrorist, a dangerous dissident, a rebellious schoolboy, or just plain adventurer, would be used as a splendid opportunity to create a martyr to further the cause, with the body being paraded through the streets by the Comrades while at the same time church bells tolled and the sponsors circulated denunciatory leaflets, on occasion printed on missionary presses.

At its best, this closeness between the different groups has led to understanding. George Hakim, Greek Catholic Archbishop and the highest-ranking church dignitary in Israel and a zealous defender of Israeli Arab rights, was one of the staunchest supporters of the 1964 Ecumenical Council's overwhelming approval (a vote of 91 per cent) of the Vatican's specific exoneration of the Jewish people from the ancient charge of deicide, and its condemnation of anti-Jewish teachings in any form. "The Jewish Schema is an act of historic redress," said Archbishop Hakim on his way back to Nazareth from Rome after attending the Council.

It was significant that at the Council only two among the more than half a hundred bishops expressed any concern over possible anti-Catholic repercussions from absolution of the Jewish people from guilt of the death of Christ, while the thirty-three other speakers at the convention, including seven Cardinals, spoke in favor of Cardinal Brea's draft, or recommended even stronger rejection of anti-Semitism.

Equally interesting was the expression just after the Vatican vote by the four Kadis of Israel, Moslem religious leaders and magistrates, endorsing absolution of the Jews for the Crucifixion, and pointing out that the Koran in Verse 156 of the Chapter of Women teaches that this is not the true story, that the Jews did not kill Christ, but that he was taken by God into Heaven.

Arab League offices and the Arab embassies in Rome had lobbied against this decision of the Vatican, but now Arab commentators in Cairo and Beirut press and radio followed with more reminders of the Koran's assertion of the innocence of the Jews, and argued strongly that anti-Jewish bigotry served as only an aid to Zionism.

Apart from Arab Nazareth, there is also a nearly all-Jewish Upper Nazareth, Nazerat Illit, on the town's heights, inhabited by immigrants largely from Eastern Europe, neat, rather like some of the better of the new towns elsewhere in the country. This with a large, airy and attractive union rest home and with a large industrial zone in the same area, with plants employing up to eight hundred people manufacturing chocolate and textiles, and smaller factories making carpets and clothes, biscuits and razor blades. But this is a zone for Jews. What it amounts to is de facto segregation of the Arab and Jewish communities in housing, even as most education is segregated up to the university level (due to differing religious and cultural needs, according to the government).

There are many differences in the difficulties faced by the two minorities, but just as the frustration and resentment of the American Negro has become real bitterness and anger no longer masked, and with an increasing readiness to lash out against the barriers which confine him, or even at that which he sees as symbolic of his second-class estate, so the Israeli Arab may feel many of these same inequities of schooling and housing and the chance to earn a decent living. The Israeli Arab, no doubt, has many imaginary woes, or at least distorted out of all perspective and fanned by hostile propaganda from the surrounding Arab states. But many of the problems faced by Israeli Arabs are real enough, particularly land tenure. The government is certainly aware of this, and has consistently maintained its position ever since the founding of the country that without peace between Israel and her neighbors there can be no satisfactory solution to persistent problems, such as repatriation or compensation for the Arab refugees who fled Palestine and, generally, the establishment of a *modus vivendi* between Israel and the Arab lands. (It's curious that, with all the agitation calling for immediate reparation to Arab refugees without considering other allied issues at stake, few people have mentioned the property of which about a million Jewish refugees were relieved before being permitted to leave their Arab homelands, before they came to Israel.)

The Israeli government says truthfully that its own Arab population enjoys a standard of living higher than that of any other Arab population in the Middle East. I doubt that any responsible observer would question this, nor the sincerity of the Israeli government in its plan steadily to improve the lot of its Arab minority, nor doubt that this is being done. Yet it is worth remembering that in our own time the American Negro community of over twenty millions, with all the deprivations which it suffers, has been described ruefully by some of its friends as enjoying the highest material standard of any large minority in the world—and this is clearly seen as by no means good enough.

The Israeli Arabs do have a number of both reputable and thoughtful friends to speak on their behalf, including an association called IHUD (Union), founded in 1943 by Jews in Jerusalem and elsewhere in Palestine, and which has published since then a bi-monthly journal, *Ner*, which is devoted to "political and social problems and for Jewish-Arab rapprochment." In what strikes me as an even-tempered yet forceful manner, *Ner* has printed news good and bad from the Israeli Arab world and the Arab world around it: articles on expropriation of Arab lands; provisions of the military government which the editors have considered unjust; filthy and overpriced slum accommodation for migrant workers in Tel Aviv suburbs when they can find no other; notes on progress in Arab agriculture, bank loans, new night-school courses; the failure of ninety-two per cent of Arab high school seniors to pass their final examinations; the failure of Israeli government officials working with Arabs and Druzes to learn their language; encouraging developments such as the joint Jewish and Arab community centers in Haifa, a summer camp in Acre, and joint publication projects in both Arabic and Hebrew.

Among other stalwart friends and a champion of Arab rights was Martin Buber, to whom the magazine devoted a memorial issue, the simple, profound and greatly loved Jewish religious philosopher, author of *I and Thou* and *Good and Evil* who influenced the Christian theologians, Reinhold Niebuhr, Paul Tillich and Karl Barth. At the time of his death in Jerusalem in 1965, Martin Buber had been a Zionist for more than sixty years, and also a friend of the Arabs.

People working for Arab-Jewish friendship, or at least coöperation, can be found in all sorts of places. Each in his own way. The flamboyant Tel Aviv proprietor of the California restaurant and bar, Abbie Nathan, was off again in his plane *Shalom* as soon as the Six Day War was over, flying from Cyprus to Port Said, once again intent on seeing Colonel Nasser with personal proposals for peace, once again turned back by the Egyptian officer in charge, who commented only, "You're a little late."

In the meantime, however, Nathan, who had garnered front-page publicity around the world, had solicited support for a common Jewish and Arab training school in northern Israel.

In our own small way, we have been instrumental in launching a vocational training workshop at Tamara, which is the center of a group of Arab villages in the Jezreel valley, supplying some $7,400 worth of electrical and automechanics training equipment, donated by the Fraternal Order of Eagles through CARE, being used by eighty students in a school named for the humorist Harry Hershfield in a new building provided by the Israeli government, their share being $10,000. In the same program, vocational training kits have been supplied to classes throughout the country serving newcomers from Iraq, Morocco, Yemen and other countries of the Middle East.

There is a long way to go. But there is hope. A fair start has been made. An example of what can be done with a bit of vision, good sense and a feeling for coöperation was given by Nazareth during the War of Independence when its Arab mayor did not panic and refused to be intimidated, keeping his people together so that they are now the largest and most prosperous of the Arab communities in the country.

It may also help in the future that the Arab population of Israel during the Six Day War and the agonizing weeks before it while the country awaited its outbreak, the Israeli Arabs did not become a fifth column, as had been widely feared.

Looking ahead, I still find exciting and not in the least far-fetched the idea which I heard Baheej Khleif express: that the day will come when trained Israeli Arabs will take their places beside their Jewish compatriots in Israel's extensive program of aid to the new countries of Africa and Asia—an idea which might shake people up a little, but which should be of real help all the way around.

One note which I found encouraging was the comment of Archbishop Hakim at a meeting of the Israel Press Club: "I am going to say things here you may not like to hear, but at least I can say them; I could not make such a speech in the neighboring countries."

Nazareth has led a checkered life since it emerged in history as a provincial Jewish village at the time of the Roman occupation. It was too insignificant a settlement to be greatly bothered by the conquerors, not seeing a great deal of them though much of Galilee was in a ferment of rebelliousness and messianic expectation. The Romans were succeeded in turn by the Christian Byzantine Empire, the Arab dynasties, the Seljuk Turks and by the Mameluke kings under whom the region declined sadly. These were followed by the Druze Emir Fakr ed-Din Maan, and he by Dahir al-Umar, the greatest of the local rulers in the long Turkish period. Al-Umar raided and sacked Safed and Tiberius, and made Acre his capital in the latter seventeenth century, but he did give peasants security from raids by other tribes and afforded equal justice to Moslem, Christian and Jew. He managed to attract many Greek Christian settlers and others to the country around Acre, and to Tiberius which was settled and rebuilt by a rabbi and his congregation from Smyrna. At the end of rule by Turkey, "The Sick Man of Europe," Nazareth was headquarters for Turkish and German military commands until the town capitulated to Allenby in 1918. During Israel's War of Independence, Nazareth was the base for the commander of the northern Arab forces, the Lebanese freebooter Fawzi al Kawkji who began operations with three thousand troops including Pakistanis, Saudi Arabians, Yemenites, Turks, Germans and Yugoslavs, and ended up with eight hundred. Nazareth was taken by Israeli forces in July, 1948.

About a quarter of an hour from Nazareth on the road to Tiberius is Cana of Galilee, where the government road sign announces in English that this is the place where Christ performed his first miracle, changing water into wine. Our Biblical dictionary says not so, that it was in Khirbet Qāna, mentioned in the history of Josephus and which lies in an entirely different place. There is also a warning not to confuse this Cana of the Galilee with the other Cana near Tyre. The touring maps in our *New Israel Guide* by Efrayim and Menahem Talmi have it confused with a Circassian village named Kafr Kama. At any rate, this Cana, a little northeast of Nazareth, has been accorded the honor perhaps because of its original name Kufr Kenna (the fact that there are no vowels in Hebrew makes for untold confusion in translation).

Cana of Galilee is an attractive Arab village, now a home of many churches, two of which claim to be the exact place where Jesus performed his miracle. That of the Roman Catholics was consecrated in 1906 by an Italian bishop accompanied by a secretary named Angelo Roncalli, later Pope John XXIII.

The second chapter of the gospels according to Saint John tells the story of how Jesus, accompanied by his mother and his disciples, was invited to a wedding in Cana. There, when he learned there was no more wine, he asked that six large vessels be filled with water and carried to the man in charge of the feast, who discovered them to be full of excellent wine. Whereupon the latter called for the bridegroom and, in what sounds to me like a complaint, announced that it was the custom first to serve good wine and then, after all the guests had drunk well, to serve poorer wine, asking the bridegroom how it was that the inferior wine had been served first at this festivity.

At the Greek Orthodox Church of Cana in Galilee there are now two conical stone basins which are exhibited as the vessels which contained the miraculous wine, but which look remarkably like baptismal fonts. Cana's Catholic Church exhibits a plaster replica of a jar with a handle in the form of a snake, all painted to represent alabaster, explaining that the original is in the treasury of the Dome in Cologne. For refreshment in Cana now, there is only a small inn which sells bottled beer in the shade of its pomegranate trees.

The road from Nazareth and Cana down to Tiberius now leads past the turn-off to the Horns of Hittin and, just a little further, the path which leads to the Tomb of Jethro. The Horns of Hittin are the upturned ends of a long hill, seen in the imagination as an Arabian saddle. This was the scene of the decisive defeat by the forces of Saladin of the Crusaders of Guy de Lusignan, the young king of Jerusalem who was foolish enough to march his men in armor and chain mail a good distance across a hot plain before the battle, so that some dropped along the way, and others, close to exhaustion, were cut down by the waiting Saracens. Twenty thousand of the Crusaders were killed, and thirty thousand were captured, including Guy, though he was later released. Saladin sent to Damascus as souvenirs the pieces of the "True Cross" which the Crusaders had carried, for although he himself placed little value in them, the caliph knew how precious they were to the Crusaders.

From the Arab village of Kfar Hittim a path leads up to a medieval shrine with shallow domes and pointed archways, visited on pilgrimage in the spring each year as the Tomb of Yethro-Shueib, the Jethro of the Bible and the Midianite priest who was the father-in-law of Moses.

The number of Druzes is uncertain, but there are probably upward of a hundred and fifty thousand living in the Lebanon, Syria, Jordan, and in Israel, where there are about thirty thousand. A warlike people, the Druzes have rebelled against their former rulers, the Egyptians and the Turks, and the French as late as 1925. In his history, *The Faithful City; The Siege of Jerusalem, 1948,* Dov Joseph who was Military Governor there at that time, wrote that a battle at Ramat Johnana "eliminated the Druze mercenaries who had been hired by Kawkji; ever since that time, the Druzes have been the most loyal of all of Israel's minorities." Male Druzes, at their own request, are drafted into the Israeli Army together with Jewish fellow citizens of their own age. "In the War of 1948 they were conspicuous for their bravery," Robert St. John has reported, also commenting, "They appear the most content of any minority in the country."

Almost all Israeli Druze villages are in this northern part of the country, just a little above and to the west of the Sea of Galilee. Other Druze villagers live just across the border in Syria on the heights which served as an emplacement for Syrian artillery commanding the water and the fields fifteen hundred feet below, and which were taken by Israeli forces in June of 1967. The occupying Israelis were immediately approached by local Syrian Druzes who professed friendship and asked for permission to live there—something which might help solve the local security problem since Druzes and Jewish Israelis enjoy mutual respect.

The Druzes call themselves "Muwahhidin," which means Unitarians, and practice a religion which they are sworn not to reveal to outsiders, but which is known to be a monotheism incorporating the teachings of the Pentateuch, the gospels of the New Testament, the Koran and the Persian Sufi allegories and perhaps also some Hindu elements. They also believe in the transmigration of souls, and in the end of the world preceded by an Armageddon between Islam and Christianity. They believe that God has manifested Himself on earth in no fewer than ten occasions, including the Fatimid Caliph Hakim, but not including Mohammed. The most renowned of the Druzes remains the seventeenth-century Emir Fakr ed-Din Maan II, who conquered Sidon and Beirut, threatened Damascus, and was a great success at the court of the Medicis for several years before he returned home and was executed by the Turks in mid-century.

Of the four cities holy to the Jews, two of them are in the Galilee. Besides Tiberius and Safed, there are Jerusalem, and Hebron, two hundred miles to its south, the site of the coronation of David and of the tombs of the Hebrew Patriarchs in a cave bought by Abraham. Following their capture by Israeli troops of this part of the Jordanian West Bank during the Six Day War, they are once again open to visits by Israelis.

Safed sits toward the top of an old volcano hopefully described as extinct. (The last great earthquake to shake Galilee took between four and five thousand lives here.) The town's many levels, crooked, cobbled alleys and the rooftops mounting one above the other, rise from twenty-four hundred to twenty-nine hundred feet. It is popular with vacationers, who are enchanted by its twists and turns, and who find its mountain coolness agreeable in summer, as in winter they do the sub-tropical warmth of Tiberius on the Sea of Galilee thirty-six hundred feet below. The lanes, the streets of stairs, the old houses, the panorama over Galilee past Mount Tabor and Mount Meiron as far as Mount Hermon, have given birth to an artist's colony of sculptors, painters and poets.

There are also people deeply interested in the fine handicrafts of the region, in particular our friend Miriam Mirvish, also known as Mirvish the Dervish, who thunders over Galilean hills with Vespa and crash helmet, gathering giant Yemenite baskets, the shining red-brown terra cotta bowls now found only in Safed and Tiberius, painted Hessian hangings brought from Roumania, and bright-scarlet Moroccan handwoven covers, all to go with old Safed work in copper, ceramics and wrought iron, Jewish ritual objects, Arab copper bowls and trays and gleaming leatherwork, blue-green plates from Iran, and the many other things for sale in the shop, also called Dervish, which she keeps with her sister Doreen, in the middle of Safed's Old City.

Safed is particularly famous for its Cabbalists, the Jewish mystics whose center this has been for the last four hundred years. Also for the simple, very devout who have come to Safed to live out their years. While we lived in Israel, the housing authorities had difficulty with an old lady in a tumble-down house at the lower entry to the city from which they wanted to move her to better quarters. She refused, explaining that she was absolutely convinced that one day the Messiah would come along the winding road leading up the mountain into town, riding his white donkey as prophesied, and that she intended to be the first to welcome him. The old lady won.

During the War of Independence, about fifteen hundred elderly

Orthodox Jews in Safed were cut off by twelve thousand Arabs holding the strategic heights above them as well as the only entrance to the town below. In what seemed a miracle to some, the fifteen hundred were saved from the twelve thousand by two hundred members of the Haganah in several fierce engagements, and with the help of the Israelis' new secret weapon, the Davidka, the invention of a young Jewish engineer, David Leibovitch. It was made of a length of six-inch drain pipe used as a mortar to fire a bomb of nails and scrap metal and whatever else was handy, inflicting some damage, but mainly—following an ancient Chinese principle of warfare—causing an horrendous noise to frighten the enemy. Through the night, the Haganah raced from one position to another, firing their few Davidkas with fearful bangs that echoed through the valley. Convinced that they were outnumbered, and prey to a rumor that the Jews now were possessed of an atomic cannon, the Arabs fled.

Jews had been spared during the Safed massacre by the Mameluke Bibars, and in the early years of Turkish domination beginning in 1517, the Jews here entered into a sort of Golden Age in which Safed for a time became the center of Jewry.

By the sixteenth century, Safed was a center of commerce, manufacturing woolens to be exported along the trade route between Sidon and Damascus. "Safad was rich in merchants, it was even richer in scholars of the Cabbala," Dr. James Parkes has written. "The Jewish population . . . rose to something like 15,000 by the middle of the century, possibly the most extraordinary community in Jewish history, as it passed its time in almost continuous religious excitement, dancing and ceremonial."

Safed became and remained the center for Jewish religious mystics, searching for knowledge of the eternal mysteries of God and creation, of man and his soul and its destiny, the nature of evil and the meaning of the Torah, but approaching this by a search "for hidden wisdom" in the sacred writings, juggling and rearranging numbers and letters of the Biblical texts in geometric and magical forms, and other occult approaches instead of the rational inquiry of the Talmud and the commentaries which follow it. Nathan Ausubel's *Pictorial History of the Jewish People* describes the Cabbala as "an intoxicated mystical brew which combined Jewish ethics with primitive occultism, Zoroastrian dualism and Pythagorean numerology, and neo-Platonic emanations with just ordinary mystification."

Two positive aims of the Cabbalists were redemption of the Jews from their unhappy lot through spiritual purification. This they hoped to do through the use of "practical magic." They believed in the transmigration of souls (the famous Dybbuks), the evil eye, ghouls, specters and a host of supernatural apparatus going back to the Babylonian and ancient Canaanites.

The leader, Isaac Luria, known as The Ari, is said to have learned Cabbala from the prophet Elijah, who, it was prophesied, would announce the Messiah. Ari, whose own Cabbalistic writing has been described as "an odd blend of fervent piety and poetic superstition," settled in Safed in 1569 where his ascetic life induced visions and trances, and he came to look upon himself as the Messiah's herald. The Ari had obtained one of the first printed copies of the *Zohar* (Splendor), a thirteenth-century occult encyclopedia incorporating astronomy and the creation of the world, physiognomy, angels and demons, and numerology. The *Zohar* was allegedly compiled by a Spanish mystic named Moses Shem-Tov de Leon, but, in a confusing move, attributed to Simeon ben Yohai who commanded a greater following.

Isaac Luria, or The Ari, had only a small following, but a disciple named Haym Vital popularized his teaching and told stories of the miracles his master had performed. The recent invention of printing, and the establishment at Safed in 1538 of the first printing press in West Asia provided the tool for rapid dissemination of these doctrines to an enthusiastic public, reaching a great many Jewish villages in Europe.

One of the most influential Cabbalist works was the medieval *Book of Creation*, which is the oldest philosophical work in Hebrew and one which has had, according to an unnamed modern Jewish theologian quoted by Brandeis University's President Abram Leon Sachar, "a greater influence on the development of the Jewish mind than almost any book after the completion of the Talmud." The best of Cabbalist literature and theological speculation intrigued Christian as well as Jewish thinkers of the time. But for the most part it was embraced with a fervor amounting to frenzy, by the poor and disinherited, by the miserable and persecuted of the ghettos who hoped that here was the magical solution to their woes. All of this came at a time of messianic expectation. There had been plagues, fires and floods, and the sacking of Rome, the fall of Jerusalem, the advance of Islam, pogroms, famine and a thousand portents. Messianic prophets arose to warn of the approaching and terrible End of the Days, the Day of Wrath, the Day of Woe.

In the Jewish world, the sixteenth and seventeenth centuries were the time of the religious charlatans, the professional mystics and the false Messiahs.

The strain of mysticism which had always run through Jewish theology and philosophy was given great impetus by the Cabbalists. That life was so wretched for so many of the medieval Jewish communities, the unhappiness of each day so real, despair of release from suffering and the apparent hopelessness of ever escaping from the ghettos in which they were confined, and with no rational solution of their infinity of woes, led hundreds of communities to embrace the magical, mystical solution to all of their troubles preached by the self-proclaimed Cabbalists and Messiahs, the charlatans who called themselves wonder-workers, and who battened on the mass hysteria. A careful Ukranian Christian writer who was witness to the frenzy in his region, which was particularly distressed and particularly susceptible, is quoted as saying of the Jews: "Some abandoned their houses and property. They refused to do any work whatsoever, claiming that the Messiah would soon arrive and would carry them off in a cloud to Jerusalem. Others fasted for days, denying food even to their little ones. During that severe winter they bathed in ice holes, at the same time reciting a recently composed prayer."

In the early sixteenth century, a Cabbalist named Asher Lämmlein assumed the mantle of Elijah and announced that he was the forerunner of the Messiah who was to arrive in 1502, which would be a Year of Penitence. Thousands of Jews followed him, giving away all their belongings, praying without cease, keeping long vigils and mortifying the flesh. When the end of the year appeared and there was no Messiah, many of them abandoned Judaism as false and were converted to Christianity.

Abram Leon Sachar has written in his *History of the Jews*: "The living world was full of sorrow; there seemed to be no hope for a better day except through the miracles of God's own messengers. Whole communities were carried away. . . ." In the first quarter of the sixteenth century, the Turks had reached Yugoslavia, taken

Malta, and seemed likely to sweep through Europe. The Catholic Church struggled with the Protestant heresy. At this point a self-created nobleman called Prince David Reubeni rode into Saint Peter's square on a white charger. It was an effective entrance. Swarthy, dwarfed, and speaking a Hebrew dialect which most Jews found difficult to understand, he announced that he came as ambassador for his brother, Joseph, king of the Lost Tribe of Reuben, who lived in the wilderness of Khaibar, far off in the interior of Arabia. To the Pope, Clement VII, to Charles V of Spain and to King John of Portugal, Reubeni proposed an alliance with the Jews of Khaibar. It was most tempting. The Pope's astrologers reported that omens were favorable. Clement considered a new crusade.

Reubeni was cautious enough to deny that he considered himself the Messiah, or even the herald of such a one, but he aroused the enthusiasm of a young Marrano nobleman named Diego Pires, who reverted to Judaism, took the name of Solomon Molcho, had himself circumcised, received visions which commanded him to preach the coming of the Messiah and traveled secretly to Palestine where his charm and great Cabbalist learning created a most favorable impression upon the scholars there. Molcho also somehow won the confidence of the Pope, and lived outside Rome, dressed in rags and suffering self-inflicted privations, preaching fearlessly the Jewish religion and prophesying imminent doom, assisted by further floods, a fearful comet, and an earthquake which all but destroyed Lisbon in 1531. Meanwhile, Reubeni had been sent by the Pope to King John of Portugal in a vessel flying at its masthead a flag with the Star of David. Reubeni and John had serious discussions about the number of men and quantity of supplies to be furnished the mythical Jewish warrior tribe in Khaibar. In the end, Molcho was delivered up to the Inquisition and burned at the stake, while, after a number of other picaresque adventures, Reubeni was cast into prison where he died in obscurity.

In Europe, things were going from bad to worse for the Jews, and even Poland, which had provided a refuge of a sort, by mid-seventeenth century had become a place of fear. In 1848 there was an uprising of Cossacks along the Dnieper River against their avariciously oppressive Polish overlords and especially against the large numbers of Jews acting for the Polish nobility as financiers, estate managers and tax collectors. Urged on by the successes of the

141

rebellious Cossack chieftain, Bogdan Chmielnicki, whose hay ricks had been stolen and his small son flogged to death by the Polish owner of the estate on which he lived, and led by him, serfs rose against their masters in almost unprecedented fury. According to Abram Leon Sachar, "The Polish gentry were hunted down, burnt, flayed alive, sawed asunder. Catholic priests were hanged to trees together with dogs and Jews. The Jews died in their tens of thousands after suffering cruelties which have rarely been equaled. Their infants were slit like fishes, their women were ripped open, live cats were let into their bowels, and then they were sown up again. . . . It is impossible to estimate accurately the toll of these awful years, perhaps the worst in Jewish history since the destruction of national life . . . the darkness seemed never to lift and Jews turned more and more to the comfort of the Talmud, to the promises of the Cabala and above all to the pseudo-Messiahs who continued to bring emollient messages from heaven."

It was in these days and in this climate that a Cabbalist scholar, Shabbatai Zevi, son of a wealthy merchant of Smyrna, at the age of twenty-one in 1648, the same year as the Dnieper massacres, declared himself the Messiah, promising to depose the Turkish Sultan, then ruler of the Holy Land, and then personally to lead the remnants of Israel back to Jerusalem and life eternal. Shabbatai Zevi was taken seriously in both Europe and the Middle East. He had married twice, but refused to live with his wives, and was twice divorced. Later in a mystical ceremony, he publicly took the Torah as his bride. Then he married a vivacious and beautiful Polish adventuress named Sarah, who had been sheltered in a convent when her parents were massacred by the Cossacks of Chmielnicki, who had led a rather fast and loose life and who announced in Amsterdam that she was the intended of the new Messiah. He immediately sent for her to come to Cairo, fell in love with her on the spot and married her.

Nothing seemed to shake the faith of Shabbatai's followers. They justified the propriety of his last marriage, to a woman considered unchaste, by pointing out that the Prophet Hosea had married the harlot Gomer at divine command.

Crowds followed him crying, "Long live the Messiah!" In Smyrna, twelve hundred children of ten to twelve years old were married in haste so that their own children to come would now be united and thus share in the Redemption which was at hand. The presses became a fountain of new prayer books with special prayers for Shabbatai Zevi. His progress was of interest to the European stock exchanges. All were greatly stirred, those who were considered wise as well as those who were known to be ignorant. *Pepys Diary* noted that some Jews of London would wager one hundred pounds against ten that Shabbatai would be acknowledged by all Eastern princes as the king of Jerusalem within two years. Samuel Pepys added, "And certainly this year of 1666 will be a great year of action; but what the consequences of it will be, God knows."

In the end, Shabbatai was invited by the Turkish Sultan to Constantinople, and there he proceeded with a train of twenty-six disciples for whom he created kingdoms and principalities and in whom he invested mystical Cabbalist titles. At a loss to know what to do with this remarkable man, whether to execute him and thus make a martyr of him, or to free him and thus add to his prestige and his power, the Sultan found an answer when Shabbatai was denounced by a rival Messiah as an enemy of the Turkish state. He was offered Islam or death. It was all over quickly. Shabbatai embraced Islam at once, took the name of Mehamed Effendi, was awarded the post of royal doorkeeper and given the assignment of turning Jews into Moslems. At length, as a punishment for continuing his Cabbalistic agitations, he was banished to Albania, where he died.

After Shabbatai Zevi's death in Albania in 1676, the next messianic mountebank did not appear until well into the eighteenth century, this a Polish Jew named Jacob Frank, who preached the usual doctrine that all Messiahs were incarnations, each of the preceding, David, Elijah, Jesus, Mohammed, Shabbatai and, now, Frank. He added that, according to his mystical calculations, he had become the second figure in the Trinity. The alarmed rabbis of Poland excommunicated Frank and his followers, also forbidding any student under thirty to study the Cabbala. In 1759, the Messiah Frank was baptized into the Roman Catholic Church, taking with him several thousand of his followers. A backslider like Shabbatai, he was discovered continuing to forward his claims as the Messiah, arrested and jailed for thirteen years. Undaunted, after his release he styled himself Baron von Frank and carried on his religious confidence game for another two decades. Upon his death in 1791, his plump and pretty daughter Eva took over as leader of the family sect and, as Ausubel has it, "artfully combined licentiousness with mysticism to preserve her hold on the minds of her emotionally unstable followers." She lasted until 1817.

A relative of Cabbalism is Hassidism, which was born in eighteenth-century Poland of the teachings of Israel ben Eliezer, known with love as Israel Baal Shem Tob, Israel of the Good Name.

The Cossack massacres of the preceding century had left the people of the countryside impoverished spiritually. They were demoralized, their ecstatic dreams fled with the shattering of the messianic movement. In contrast to the Biblical tradition that every man should perform some sort of work, usually with his hands (the tradition was inherited by Jesus who fashioned wooden yokes and plows, and Saint Paul as Saul of Tarsus was a tentmaker), now the scholars of the Talmudic academies were contemptuous of working people, and spent their own time in the intricate sort of theological debate which the Baal Shem called hair-splitting. Israel ben Eliezer traveled from village to village teaching that simple faith and prayer are more than learning, a belief which did not endear him to the academicians but which was received with joy by the majority, humble people who were enslaved by poverty and by the ignorance into which the ghettos of Eastern Europe had sunk. They were unable to understand the prayers they had been taught to recite, unable to find encouragement in the arid, legalistic pronouncements to the scholars.

Himself the poorest of the poor, yet he was possessed of a happiness, a kindness and a kind of radiance which made him all but worshipped by his followers, who were called "the Hassidim" (the Pious). To them he taught that man is good, the world and the universe beautiful and blessed; that worshipping the Lord calls for joy and optimism rather than affliction with fasting and mortification. Deep and joyous love of God was more important than ritual or even the study of the Torah. Laughter, singing and dancing offered as praise of God were the highest form of prayer. This warm, personal and mystical approach to God as opposed to the dryly rational, formal and scholastic approach of the learned élite was denounced by the Talmudic and rabbinic authorities, but it conquered Eastern Europe.

"It is one of the melancholy facts of history," writes Abram Leon Sachar, "that nearly every faith suffers most from its own followers; too often they misunderstand and distort a great teacher's words and ruin the good which he creates. Israel's ideals did not long survive his death. The fervent devotion for which he appealed degenerated into hysterical prayer and vulgar spiritual antics. His subordination of learning to faith was taken to imply contempt for learning. The ignorant masses prided themselves upon their ignorance. It became dogma in Hassidic circles that 'where there is much learning, there is little piety.'"

Toward the end of the eighteenth century there appeared the institution of the *rebbe* known as the *tzaddik* (righteous one), a rabbi who would undertake to intercede with God for something urgently desired by a Hassid among his congregation, usually a blessing on his wife that she might bear children, the curing of illness, or guidance in business matters. This would seem a circumvention of the nature of Jewish prayer as described by Robert Aron: "Jewish prayer is not a petition addressed to God, it is man's support of the action of his Creator. Every prayer based on purely personal motives is habitually repressed."

In addition, the *rebbe* provided amulets with Cabbalistic incantations for the sick or as protection against Satan, demons or evil spirits. For his part, the Hassid was expected to give the *tzaddik* "free-will offerings" at least three times a year, and no doubt a little extra something at times when special requests were made. Moreover, the office of *tzaddik* became hereditary, the eldest son inheriting not only his father's prominence but the handsome income provided by his followers. Hundreds of these *tzaddikim* dynasties were founded in Eastern Europe, some of them maintained with the opulence of a minor court.

They did give much in exchange to their congregations, with scores of Hassidim coming to eat with them, sometimes staying for weeks at a time, listening with awe to the *tzaddik*'s Cabbalistic interpretations of the Torah, worshipping with song and dance in the mystic circle, and carried to states of transcendent rapture.

"Whatever its backwardness and other undeniable retrogressive features," says Ausubel, "Hassidism as an historic movement created a necessary religious revolution in Jewish religious life in its time. It revitalized the Jewish spirit, gave it emotional warmth and hope in the future, set for it a practical pattern of ethical group living and, above all, provided it with the inner strength to endure the many ordeals it had to undergo."

With the nineteenth-century emigration to Palestine and America came the same Hassidic dynasties of *tzaddikim*. There has been a revival of interest in Hassidism, both by those like Martin Buber, who was taken with the idea of applying the essence and the beauty of original Hassidic teaching to contemporary Jewish thought, and also by the tens of thousands of students flocking to the Hassidic schools in New York as well as Israel. Part of this is the dizzying increase in religious schooling as well as other forms of education. In Israel there are now well over fifteen thousand students at Talmudic colleges and high schools, with many hundreds turned away each year.

New York has become a flourishing Hassidic center with a number of *tzaddik* dynasties represented, the most influential of which are the Lubavich, the Satmar and the Skvir. The Skvirer *rebbe*, who belongs to the Twersky dynasty, has founded near Spring Valley, a quiet little suburb of New York, a Hassidic community complete with a synagogue bus so that members may pray on their way to the city.

The neighborhoods inhabited by the other two sects, both living in Brooklyn, are reminiscent of Meah Shearim in Jerusalem, with bearded men wearing long coats of rusty black and uncreased, wide-brimmed black hats, communities scrupulous in their observance of the Torah, the Law given in the five Books of Moses. Streets are closed on the Hebrew Sabbath.

To an outsider, it is curious that little or no time is given to the Bible itself. With this the student is supposed to be familiar. Study is concentrated on Talmudic exposition of the Bible, study which is demanding and which can be without end. In these communities, it is not uncommon for a wife to work supporting her husband during his four or five years of Talmudic college study, and perhaps for the rest of his life, should he decide that scholarship is his vocation.

The Lubavicher congregation, considered more rational and liberal and less traditionalist than the other two, supervises fifteen *yeshivot* for rabbinical studies in the United States, with a further ninety-six boys' schools and thirty-five girls' schools, an adult-education program, a labor exchange, agricultural society, summer camp, broadcasts, bulletins, posters, a stand at the New York World's Fair, six million books and pamphlets distributed in the past two decades, and maintains institutions in Israel, Great Britain, France and Morocco. The rabbi at the center of this network, Menahem Mendel Schneersohn, has publicly advised a follower that he need not trouble himself about the Darwinian theory of natural selection, "because it has not a shred of evidence to support it," going back to the arguments used at the Scopes Monkey Trial in Tennessee in the twenties, holding firmly to the Biblical date for the Creation of 3,762 B.C., or, as Israel and the United Nations sensibly put it, B.C.E., which is to say Before the Common Era. As to the argument that fossils found would have taken much longer than this length of time to fossilize, Reb Schneersohn has used the rebuttal, time-worn itself, that there was no reason why God could not have created fossils within the earth at the same time he created the earth.

If the Lubavicher Hassidim and their teachers can be considered liberal, then the Satmarer congregation with its Reb Yoel Teitelbaum is far to the Hassidic right and as unyielding in the minutiae of worship as was the fossilized rabbinical establishment from which the forebears of the present Hassidim escaped. There are ties between some members of the ultra-Orthodox Hassidic communities in New York and Jerusalem, specifically the Natorei Karta, a violently holy group from Meah Shearim who specialize in attaining merit by encouraging children to spend their Sabbath throwing rocks at people traveling on wheels.

Natorei Karta's finest hour came with the kidnapping of a small boy named Yossele Schuhmacher. When the boy's grandfather, Reb Nahman Shtarkes, became fearful that, although the boy was receiving an Orthodox religious education, it was not Orthodox enough, he conspired with some others to have the child dressed in girl's clothing and, with falsified credentials, spirited out of the country via England and hidden in the Williamsburg section of Brooklyn with a family of disciples of the anti-Zionist Satmarer *rebbe.*

A handsome forty-five-year-old French divorcée and former underground fighter had become converted to Judaism and taken the name Ruth Ben-David. Through arrangements made by another rabbi named Dov Sokolowsky she had married the octogenarian and fiery former leader of the Natorei Karta, Reb Amram Blau, whom she had never met before their betrothal ceremony. She revealed unabashedly to *Newsweek*'s Jerusalem correspondent, Richard Chesnoff, that just before the wedding it was she who had smuggled the boy to New York.

A few families living together with the artists' colony in the lower town of Safed claim to be descended from the Cabbalists who made the city famous when they settled there in the conviction that the establishment of a religious center in Galilee was a portent of redemption by the Messiah. Some claim to be descendants of the disciples of Israel Ben Eliezer, the Baal Shem, who founded Hassidism after he had begun life as a Cabbalist, and whose followers came to Safed in the second half of the eighteenth century after the town had been afflicted by "numerous natural calamities, such as epidemics, locusts and earthquakes," according to the Talmi guide, and when there were only fifty families left in all the town.

The strength of the Hassidim lies now in communities in Jerusalem, in Bnei Brak next to Tel Aviv, and in Brooklyn. The Cabbalists are remembered by the tomb in the Safed cemetery of The Holy Ari and by two synagogues bearing his name, one Ashkenazi and the other Sephardi. The Sephardic synagogue of the Ari is the oldest building in town and one of the few to survive the earthquake of the eighteenth century. It sits on a ledge high above the cemetery where lie The Ari and the other mystics who keep him company. There is among the synagogue's Scrolls of the Law one kept in a case of ivory ornamented with mystical calligraphy by The Ari himself. The Ari liked to travel from Safed to the hamlet of Peki'in not far away, and there pray and meditate in the cave in which the second-century sage Simeon ben Yohai had taken refuge with his son after the crushing of the Jews' last revolt under Bar Kochba and Rabbi Akiva, who was Simeon's teacher. Reportedly, the two had lived in the cave for thirteen years subsisting on carobs and water while Simeon wrote the Cabbalists' mystical and allegorical *Zohar* (that is, if it weren't written by Moses de Leon, and so the debate goes on).

About three thousand feet below Safed the road comes to a sign which says, in English, SEA LEVEL. But don't stop. Just keep on going down for another seven hundred and thirty feet and you will come to the Sea of Galilee. The word Galilee in Hebrew and Canaanitic means "a ring, or circuit." The Sea of Galilee, also known as the Sea of Chinnereth, or Chinneroth, or the Sea of Tiberius, the Lake of Gennesaret, or Bahr Tabariyeh, is thirteen miles long from north to south and eight miles across at its widest, and about a hundred and fifty feet deep. In modern Hebrew it is called Lake Kinneret because it is supposed to resemble a harp though I can't get over the idea that it looks like an avocado with the narrow end downward. It is a lovely lake. The western descent to Tiberius is steep and swift, through the hills of the Galilean range. Across the changing greys and blues and greens of the water, a thirty-five-foot ribbon of Israeli land follows the northeastern shoreline. Then comes the former Syrian frontier and, abruptly, a high dull-grey bluff—great folds at its base, occasionally relieved with a little brown or green—rises sharply from the level of the lake to the Trans-jordanian plateau some fifteen hundred feet above. The mountains all around and the great difference in altitude make for abrupt changes in the weather, with great winds and violent storms sweeping the lake with little warning.

After once seeing the sky darken, feeling the swift wind and watching the pleasant ripples lashed into whitecaps, it is not difficult to imagine the fears of the disciples crossing the lake with Jesus before Jesus "arose, and rebuked the wind and the raging of the water: and they ceased, and there was a calm." The storms are soon over and the sun shining again on the hillside and the lake, the cypresses, pomegranates and locust trees, and, down at the grove of palms at the southern end of the lake, on the papyrus and bull rushes and iris growing at the water's edge.

When the sun shines, small boats put out from the docks along the waterfront of Tiberius and from the kibbutz of Ein Gev on the other side of the lake, here about five miles across. There are sailboats, launches towing water skiers, and some in bathing suits resolutely pumping away at cycles on pontoons. Sitting on the water-front in a folding chair is an old salt looking a bit like Barnacle Bill, tattooed and wearing a blue yachting cap, with a tray of post-cards slung around his neck and hanging over his Falstaffian belly. Restaurants along the waterfront specialize in seafood, in particular a tilapia called Saint Peter's fish, which is appropriate since one of the most plentiful carries the specific name of *Simonis* after the original name of the Apostle. Whenever we had a couple of honored guests touring the country and stopping for lunch at Tiberius, it was the custom of Noah Klivitsky, the best of all of the Israel guides whom I had encountered, to arrange to have placed an Israeli coin in the fish's mouth when it was served for two, claiming that this was the shekel which would pay their Temple tax. Noah, a tall, rangy, sandy type who looked as if he might be on leave from a western movie except for his moustache, which retained a distinctly British Army character, left over, I suppose, from the days when he, as did so many others, joined the services with one eye on training for the future fight for Palestine.

The tilapia which we used to eat is common but curious, belonging to a family of fish named *Cichlidae* in which the mother carries her eggs in her mouth until they are hatched. Because of the shape of their dorsal fins, the group in English are known as combs, while the Arabs call them *Musht* which is even worse.

Fishing for tourists is an important occupation in this town of twenty thousand since it can offer more than a thousand badly needed jobs in hotels, cafés, transportation and other services for visitors. It is especially popular in winter, when there may be heavy snows on the peaks of Galilee. I can remember driving through sleet on my way down, only to find it nice and warm by the lake, with steam rising from the water. I have also seen a little snow on the prickly pears in Tiberius, but this is only momentary and is soon removed by the sun. As with every place in the Holy Land which I can think of, Tiberius has had a tumultuous history, yet, like Nazareth, it begins with the Christian era, in this case because it was built by Herod Antipas between 16 and 22 A.D., and named after his emperor, Tiberius Caesar Augustus. According to the history of Josephus, the place had originally been a burial ground and hence was ritually unclean for Jews who were unwilling to settle there, and who had to be dragooned by Herod in order to provide a population. By a quirk of fate, this same city, after the fall of Jerusalem, became the center of rabbinic learning. In addition, in this once unhallowed ground were now installed the tombs of two of the greatest rabbis, Maimonides and Akiva.

The Sanhedrin was moved here, and here the authoritative compilation of Hebrew Oral Law called the Mishnah was completed by Rabbi Judah the Prince about 210 A.D. The Jerusalem Talmud, as it is called, largely an expansion of and commentary on the Mishnah, was completed in Tiberius about the year 400. Among the other works completed in Tiberius was the Masoretic text of the Old Testament which definitively fixed for the Hebrew Bible orthography, pronunciation and vowel sounds by means of diacritical marks.

On the authority of the Emperor Constantine, who gave him the title of prince, the converted Jew Joseph of Tiberius in the fourth century built a number of churches there, and it became an Episcopal see. The Jews of Tiberius, however, were so wretched under rule from Constantinople that they joined with enthusiasm the invading Persians who occupied the country in 618. When the Persians were driven out eighteen years later by the Arabs, Tiberius continued to wax strong as a Jewish religious and cultural center.

Taken by the Crusaders in 1099, Tiberius became the fief of Tancred, capital of the Galilee, and seat of a Roman Catholic bishopric subordinate to Nazareth, and more churches and monasteries were built. But for over nearly a century, until it fell to Saladin in 1187, Christianity never seemed to take permanent root. Later Crusaders made the mistake of allying themselves with the Sultan of Damascus, and were massacred by his enemy, the Sultan of Egypt, in mid-thirteenth century. The Christian population was never replaced. When a traveler named Quaresmius visited Tiberius in 1620, nearly four centuries later, the last Jewish inhabitant had just died, and Moslems were the only survivors.

The Bedouin Emir Dahir Al-Umar in the eighteenth century helped Jewish colonies to reëstablish themselves, restoring the walls of the town and building a fortress which, though badly shaken in the earthquake on January first, 1837, can still be seen. Tiberius lost seven hundred of its population of twenty-five hundred in that quake, just as Safed lost half of its population of ten thousand.

A most colorful chapter in the history of Tiberius was begun but never quite finished during the reign of Suleiman the Magnificent at whose court was one of the most influential, wealthy and remarkable of the Jewish refugees from Spain, a woman known as Doña Gracia who was much taken with the hot springs of Tiberius, long used as medicinal waters. Doña Gracia established a settlement and a college in Tiberius and promised to retire there, at the same time persuading Suleiman to give her nephew and son-in-law Don Joseph Nasi the title Duke of Naxos and charter to Tiberius and seven villages around. He did his best, rebuilding the city wall, planting mulberry trees in anticipation of a silk industry, importing fine Spanish wool for weaving, and planning to establish a fishing industry.

The Duke of Naxos invited Jews anxious to leave Italy in the intolerant times of the Popes Paul IV and Pius V to come and settle, supplying his own ships for transportation, but few appeared able to accept the invitation, and some who did were captured at sea by the Knights Hospitalers and sold as slaves. It is possible that Doña Gracia lived for a year or so in Tiberius before her death in 1569, but the Duke found himself unable to leave Constantinople where he was kept busy with court intrigue, and he never visited his Tiberius estate, gradually undermined by the Franciscan Custodian for the Holy Land, working through the French Ambassador, helped along by the raids of local Arab tribes. Another influential refugee Jewish courtier named Alvaro Mendes, or Solomon ibn Ayesh, became the Duke of Mitylene, taking the same concession for his son Jacob who was already resident in Tiberius. But Jacob was interested in scholarship and had no head for commerce and administration, and at his death in 1603 it had become necessary for Safed to save the scholars of Tiberius from starvation. And so the dream died.

There is a little bit of everything along the lake. On the way to the Tiberius baths, tourists are shown a spot where "Miriam's Well disappeared." The well, according to the tale, accompanied the Children of Israel on their exodus from Egypt, touring with them in their forty years wandering in the wilderness, and disappearing only after they crossed the frontier into the Promised Land. Now it is supposed to rise in the middle of the lake and in it the great Cabbalist, Rabbi Isaac Luria, The Ari, immersed his disciple Haym Vital before teaching him the deepest secrets of the Cabbala.

At the southwestern corner of the lake is Beit Yerah, which in Hebrew means "House of the New Moon," probably from worship of the moon goddess by the Canaanites at the time they held sway here. The ruins are extensive, not yet fully excavated, but those of a city of importance even in the Bronze Age, between 4500 and 5000 B.C., and perhaps before.

At the time of the ministry of Jesus around the Sea of Galilee, there were along its shores and overlooking the water ten cities, some

of them large and, except for Tiberius, far more populous than anything seen since then. They were supported by a fertile and well-
tended countryside, with vineyards and olive trees and many crops, a
prosperity which was to disappear, the land cut over and neglected
until its resurrection began with the arrival of the Zionist pioneers
at the turn of the century.

Following the shore north from Tiberius, beyond the Minus 206
Club with its water-ski rental service and occasional nightclub,
passing a small Russian Orthodox church dependent on the patriarchate of Moscow, and near quarters for a U.N. team of truce observers,
comes Magdala, known in the Talmud as Migdal Nuneya which
means "Tower of the Fishes," and in Greek as Tarichea which means
"Salted Fish," a Hellenized town of four thousand, which had a
fishing fleet of two hundred and thirty boats. This was the home of
Mary Magdalene for whom, Saint Luke tells, Jesus cast out seven
devils. Probably because of the juxtaposition of the two stories,
with only a few paragraphs between them, tradition has identified
Mary Magdalene with the unnamed woman in Luke's next chapter,
described only as "a sinner," who kissed and anointed the feet of
Jesus and washed them with her tears, forgiven for her sins because
of her love and her faith.

Without any particular evidence, tradition has also come to the
conclusion that "sinner" means that Mary Magdalene was a fallen
woman, or as my old headmaster used to say in chapel, "a woman
who was no better than she should be."

At the northwestern rim of the lake, between Magdala Capernaum, are the two underground hydraulic stations which pump
water eight hundred and forty-five feet up and over the Galilean
mountainside into a wide, concrete-based canal, and the hundred-
and-fifty-four-mile system of tunnels, pipelines, siphons and the nine-
foot concrete pipes which carry it all the way down to the Negev
Desert for irrigation there and points in between.

Capernaum lies at the foot of the Mount of Beatitudes and just
a little before the upper Jordan, a stream really, here at the head of
the lake as it comes down along the Syrian border. Jesus made his
home there after he left Nazareth. In Capernaum, Jesus preached in
the synagogue, and there he performed many miracles.

Not far from the Franciscan chapel which encloses the rock traditionally used by Christ and his disciples for their meal after the

second miraculous draught of fishes is the Church of the Multipli-
cation of the Loaves and Fishes, also just outside Capernaum. The
place is called Tabagha after the Greek Heptapegon which means
"Seven Springs."

Basilicas built on the spot in the first and fourth centuries were
destroyed, and even the site itself forgotten until excavations in the
nineteen thirties which uncovered some of the handsomest mosaics
yet to be found in the Middle East. They are protected now by a
simple structure erected by the Lazarist Fathers of Cologne.

Chief interest, of course, is drawn to the simple, stylized and most
effective representation of two fishes standing on their tails and
flanking a tall, striped basket holding round loaves. Other scenes
are of a variety of water birds, one with a snake in its beak, and
growing among the reeds, lotuses, which were not known here in
the north, leading some to believe that the mosaics were probably the
work of Egyptian craftsmen.

Israeli love for all things ancient has led to the enthusiastic adop-
tion of a style which can only be called mosaic-type. Not only is the
great mosaic at Beit Alpha depicting the zodiac, with Apollo the
Sun God driving his chariot through the skies and surrounded by
the symbols of the Bull, the Crab, the Scales and all the rest—
certainly a very non-Hebraic concept—reproduced as a jumbo postage
stamp which divides into four sections, but the individual signs of
the zodiac have been reproduced on a series of small stamps, each
carefully painted to look as if it had been a mosaic, but in fact the
creation of the artist. This has been extended to what are ostensibly
reproductions of mosaics, but advertising wines, tourism or whatever
else seems appropriate. There is also a series of postage stamps, and
extremely well done, too, as was the zodiac, illustrating David and
Saul and other heroes, all looking as though they had been taken
from stained-glass windows instead of the artist's drawing board.
There is a splendidly special name for this process, called skeuo-
morphism, which Professor William Foxwell Albright, in his work
*From the Stone Age to Christianity: Monotheism and the Historical
Process*, defines as a change of material accompanied by a minimal
change of form, giving among his examples the Egyptian columns
and capitals carved to look like the bundles of papyrus or lotus stalks
or palm trunks from which they once were carved.

It was at Capernaum, returning to speak in the synagogue there after the miracle of the loaves and fishes, that Jesus preached the miracle of the Eucharist which was to be his message again at the Last Supper and which became Holy Communion: "I am the bread of life: he that cometh to me shall never hunger; and he that believeth in me shall never thirst." A toll collector named Levi, while sitting in his customs house at Capernaum heard Jesus call, "Follow me," and did so, becoming the evangelist and Apostle Matthew. In Capernaum Jesus healed the servant, near death, of a centurion who, himself a pagan, was a friend to the Jews and had built them a synagogue there.

Ever since the teaching of Moses, Hebrew priests had been responsible for public health, carrying out injunctions governing food and drink, personal hygiene, health of the community, contagion, isolation and disinfection—a great deal of it still demonstrably rational as well as ritual. In the time of Jesus, the rabbi was the physician. As Matthew put it: "And Jesus went about all of Galilee, teaching in their synagogues, and preaching the gospel of the kingdom, and healing all manner of sickness and all manner of disease among the people . . . people that were taken with diverse disease and torments, and those which were possessed with devils, and those which were lunaticks, and those which had the palsy. . . ."

So much happened to so many in the Holy Land, and so much of it is still a part of our lives, that it seems a great world to itself. Yet the Galilee and the country round about was not large, and the longest distances traveled by Jesus—though we don't know what roads he may have taken—were no more than a hundred or a hundred and twenty miles from Capernaum to Jerusalem and perhaps another thirty miles from Caesarea Philippi whence Jesus was called at the time of the Crucifixion.

Jesus upbraided the nearby cities of Choarazin and Bethsaida, the home of Peter, Andrew and Philip: "Woe unto thee, Choarazin! Woe unto thee, Bethsaida!" Jesus also avoided visiting Tiberius, whose founder, Herod Antipas, the Tetrarch of Galilee, he referred to as "That fox."

Robert Aron maintains that, when Jesus admitted in Jerusalem to being King of the Jews, this would have sounded to his Roman judges to be revolutionary.

To Robert Aron, the words of Jesus were not political defiance (after all, Jesus had advised "render unto Caesar"), but an echo of the teachings of the Hebrew Scriptures.

Aron points out that "son of God" and "son of Man" in Jewish tradition meant a spiritual sonship credited both to the angels and the Kings of Israel, especially David, and that in all these uses it should be taken as allegorical. Aron quotes from the book *Jésus et Israël* by Jules Isaac: "It is certain that the idea of an actual divine sonship was unknown in Jesus's time and would have been inconceivable to him; it was utterly alien to the rigidity of his monotheistic faith and its notion of divine transcendence."

From Capernaum, a path leads up the Mount of Beatitudes, in truth more of a hill, and just after a little grove of pine trees, there is the church looking out over the waters, utterly peaceful. Around the inside of the dome of the small church are the Beatitudes: "Blessed are the poor in spirit; for theirs is the kingdom of heaven," and so on through the eight who are blessed.

Rabbi Elias Soloweyczk in his study of the Beatitudes and the Sermon on the Mount has found in the Talmud closely equivalent passages, sometimes using the same words. The Vatican Press has published a compilation by the Reverend Joseph Bonsirven of several thousand extracts from Jewish commentaries during the first two Christian centuries which the Vatican feels helpful to understanding the New Testament.

The commentaries of the Talmud as well as the Law as given in the five books of Moses and the rest of the Old Testament permeate the teaching of Jesus. In Matthew's rendering of the Sermon on the Mount just following the Beatitudes is the famous "Think not that I am come to destroy the Law, or the prophets: I am not come to destroy, but to fulfill." When asked by a scribe which was the First Commandment, Jesus answered him, according to Mark in his twelfth chapter, with the basic Jewish prayer, the Shema Israel, which states unequivocally its monotheism: "Hear, O Israel; the Lord Our God is one Lord." Jesus continues, "Thou shalt love thy neighbor as thyself. There is none other commandment greater than these." The second commandment given is much like that of the great Rabbi Hillel who was a contemporary of Jesus and who replied to a would-be convert who said he was willing to become a Jew if he could be taught the whole of the Law while he was standing on one foot: "Do not unto others what you would not they do unto you.

That is the whole of the Law; the rest is only commentary. Go, and learn this." Also quoted by the Talmud and even closer to the wording of Jesus is that of Rabbi Akiva: "Love your neighbor as yourself; that is the great principle of the Law."

The number of believers in Christianity grew in Capernaum and the other nearby cities, then throughout the land and overseas as the disciples traveled. The fame of the miracles wrought by Jesus, of his teaching and of his message spread with almost incredible rapidity. In the first century, Capernaum was known for its community of *minim*, which is variously translated as "heretics" or "sectaries" or "Judeo-Christians." There is still on the map a Mount Minim a few miles southwest along the lake from Capernaum. It is fair to remember that with the destruction of the Second Temple, Jews once again were scattered, clustered around their local synagogues which kept the faith, and it seems likely that times were not propitious for radical reform within the faith whose adherents now were scattered through a good part of the world.

There was a resurgence of Judaism in Capernaum during the second and third centuries, as can be seen in the remainder of the magnificent synagogue built there during the third century to replace that of the Roman centurion, but by the fourth century and the conversion of the Roman Emperor Constantine to Christianity, uncounted numbers of citizens and just the populations of the lands ruled by Rome predictably adopted the new state religion.

With the passage of time the originally narrow difference between Judaism and Christianity widened until at last it became a gulf. Meanwhile, the pious among the Jews preserved their own faith, kept their Covenant, no matter what the cost.

At the foot of the Mount of Beatitudes is a Franciscan monastery and on its grounds is the splendid third-century monastery, long ago tumbled by an earthquake, but recently excavated and partially restored by the Fathers. It is typical of the scrambled history of the Holy Land that what is probably the finest ancient synagogue in Israel should belong to a Roman Catholic order. A thirteenth-century pilgrim called Rabbi Jacob of Paris reported, without seeming especially disturbed by it, that the Moslems had seized so many shrines, tombs and other holy places from Christians and Jews that the only originally Moslem holy place he was able to find at that time was the mythical tomb of Moses on the road between

Jerusalem and Jericho, built to honor the patriarch who had been brought there by angels because he felt lonely on Mount Nebo.

At Capernaum, a colonnade with Corinthean capitals was surmounted by an architrave which supported the Doric columns of an upper gallery. Throughout the synagogue, whose décor is a fine example of late Hellenist Jewish symbolism, there are the Star of David and the Ark of the Covenant, olive branches and a palm tree, bunches of grapes and pomegranates. If they are not already aware of this, and if the Franciscan guide book is correct, any archeological museums within reach will be unhappy to learn that a number of "pagan motives" were later chiseled off, such as winged genii and "the unicorn or sea-horse with a horn on its forehead and a beard on its chin, ending in a spirally, curled fish-tail."

In 1906, the year that Tel Aviv was founded, the Jewish National Fund which had been created five years earlier at the Fifth Zionist Congress began to buy land for settlement in Palestine, in great part what was then marsh or rocky and eroded hillside. In 1909, a band of twelve teenagers, most of them students, were allocated a plot of seven hundred and fifty swampy acres. The local Bedouin and the absentee Persian landowners called it "The Spot of Death" because of the fever there, but the colonists called it Degania after the seven kinds of corn—which is to say grain in this sense—in the Bible. The seven shacks in which they lived were called *deganim* after the corn flower. The new settlers were deeply imbued with the ideas of Aaron David Gordon who, after serving as a functionary in the Russian lands administration, had come to Palestine a few years before to work as a manual laborer and help with the setting up of the first agricultural settlements, preaching the gospel of back to the land, writing about it in his book *The Religion of Labor* and other works, and living this in his own life. The first settlers at Degania cleared the undergrowth, rocks and boulders, dug drainage ditches and planted the Australian eucalyptus, to this day much favored in Israel as a thirsty sort of tree which is of great help in reclaiming bog land. Supplies for the settlers at Degania all had to be brought in by donkey. At any one time, about a third of the settlers were bedridden from malaria. At the end of two years, one member of the group had been killed and two had died of malaria, yet they had cleared and cultivated several hundred acres of land. By now, the community had increased, there were marriages and children, and with the mothers working beside their men, community nurseries were established.

From the beginning all agreed to work without personal gain, coöperatively purchasing food, clothing, farm equipment, fertilizer, building materials and other needs. The land belonged to the Jewish National Fund and the Jewish people. If a member chose to leave, he took, in effect, the clothes on his back. What each member needed was supplied to him within the capacity of the community.

This was the first kibbutz. It was to become the pattern for future communal settlements in Israel.

Membership in all kibbutzim is voluntary and everyone above the age of eighteen is an equal partner. Anyone may apply for membership, and of those who are accepted, most are on probation for a year to see whether they fit the community and vice versa. All decisions of importance are taken by majority vote, though there are committees for schooling, adult education, defense, finance, culture, health and the work of the kibbutz, with officers responsible for the general management, finances and assignment of work tasks. What creature comforts a kibbutz can offer depends directly on the efforts of its members and their success. Even before the *deganim*, which were shacks, the settlers lived in tents and then adobe huts before permitting themselves the luxury of wooden structures. Now at Degania they live in houses of stone, with flower gardens, a museum called Gordon House, pleasant lawns, a school and a children's home where all youngsters live, visiting their parents on their return from work for two hours each afternoon. On their way to the community dining hall, a device which saves the women for more than housewifery, parents return their young ones to the Children's Home.

The kibbutz of Degania is surrounded by woods, and beyond them fields and orchards, date palms and citrus groves, and a dairy farm of repute. Other kibbutzim have taken up light industry, canning food, breeding carp, manufacturing plywood and motor scooters, and a variety of other things. Ein Gev, just a little north along the lake from Degania, does quite well with tourists, receiving visitors who cross the lake by boat or arrive by car, and offering them a café and restaurant with a most agreeable terrace looking out over the water.

The tendency of a kibbutz, when it grows large enough, is to hive off and for some members to establish another kibbutz of their own. This happened at Degania after about a decade, when Degania B was founded nearby. At about the same time, other members became dissatisfied with the lack of privacy on the kibbutz and formed a new sort of community known as the moshav, where members farmed their own land with the exception of certain crops calling for large fields and better handled collectively. Members earned their own money, and owned their own homes. They retained coöperative marketing and purchasing, but each family ate and slept in its own house and brought up its children with the family. The first moshav, Nahalal, a little west of Nazareth, was begun in 1921 when its founders got together and drained another swamp (it seems extraordinary, considering how arid most of the land of Israel is, that communal pioneers should keep ending up in swamps).

In time, particularly with mass immigration after the War of Independence, the moshav type of small holders' settlement, with greater emphasis on family life and greater flexibility of coöperation, became the more popular of the communal settlements. There were, at last count, three hundred and eighty-four moshavim and two hundred and forty-three kibbutzim, with populations ranging from sixty to two thousand.

Perhaps it was in part a reaction to the cramped life of the ghetto, to the peddling and the shopkeeping which inculcated in the founders of the first kibbutzim the almost mystical ardor with which they viewed the return to living by tilling the soil, by the sweat of their brows. It has affected the philosophy of the entire country.

Doing their own work has also enabled these newer communal settlements to avoid some of the difficulties inherent in the earlier settlements, so generously supported by Baron Edmond de Rothschild during the last two decades of the nineteenth century. Some of Rothschild's settlements have grown into quite large communities like Petah Tikvah, a suburb of Tel Aviv, and Rishon-le-

Zion in whose wineries Ben-Gurion worked in 1914. But in general, the Baron's administrators looked on colonizing as the white man's burden, and discouraged those sent out from Europe to settle from doing their own plowing and digging and building, reserving this for the Arab "natives" who as a matter of policy were to be hired by the settlers. In spite of the fifty million dollars which Baron de Rothschild contributed to the settlements to keep them going, they were not really successful, though their benefactor was loved for all he had tried to do.

The cultural level at contemporary kibbutzim is surprisingly high for an agricultural or village population. They have libraries and collections of classical records, often their own orchestras, choirs or chamber-music groups, discussion groups, galleries and some good museums. The kibbutzim have provided much of the leadership of the country, first in the Haganah as the forerunner of the Israeli Army, and then of the Army itself; both before and after independence providing those who came to positions of power and decision in agriculture, trade unions and industry, in government and its foreign service. Moshe Dayan, twice Commander-in-Chief of the Army, was born in Degania, while President Levi Ishkol and Kadish Luz, Speaker of the Knesset, are also from that kibbutz, and David Ben-Gurion has long been famous for his sheepshearing at his kibbutz Sde Boker in the Negev.

Another large city among those clustered around the Sea of Galilee was that next to the present Ein Gev, on a flat-topped mountain called Hippos in Greek, or Susita in Hebrew, both meaning "horse," and presumably so called because of the horse-breeding practiced somewhat north of here in Syria. Hippos was one of the Decopolis, a league of ten cities with Greek populations, allied for mutual protection against the Hebrew tribes. They included Damascus, the Scythopolis that now is the Beit Shean in Israel a little below the Sea of Galilee, and Philadelphia which is now called Amman, the capital of Jordan. Worship of the Mediterranean fertility goddess under her various names and guises remained popular throughout this part of the world for a time, even in the Hebrew cities until the end of the Judean dynasty. At Hippos were found vessels for offering libations and incense, apparently to the Queen of Heaven who is identified with Isis and Astarte, the custom denounced by the Prophet Jeremiah, himself from a village named after the allied fertility goddess Anath, as incurring the particular wrath of Yaweh. Another find of the Israel Department of Antiquities at Hippos was a large jar with the inscription *leshakya*, written in a rare Hebrew-Phoenician script and apparently meaning in Aramaic "belonging to the wine steward." Excavations at Hippos, which straddled the Inland Sea road which ran from Egypt to Assyria, have just been begun, and in the five cities built one on the other here, and in all the country around this remarkable lake, there is enough work, there are enough wonders, to occupy an army of archeologists.

A botanical gardens at Degania A exhibits the flora of the region and the museum offers a sampling of the extremely varied fauna of the country. Israel is especially rich in birds, with some four hundred species which can be seen in the course of the year, as against about eight hundred in all of the Indian subcontinent, including Pakistan, India, Ceylon and Burma. On the flyway from Southern Asia to Northern Europe, the Sea of Galilee is a convenient place for birds to break their journey and a fine place to watch them. There are pelicans (*Pelecanus onocropalus*), spoonbills (*Platalea leucorodia*), and besides the Smyrna kingfishers also the shaggy-crested pied kingfisher (*Ceryle rudis*), which is a resident, and the European kingfisher (*Alcedo atthis*), which is a winter visitor. There is the avocet (*Recurvirostra avosetta*), Siberian ringed plovers (*Charadrius tundrae*), the Far Eastern cormorants (*Phalacrocorax sinensis*), though no one has ringed their necks and taught them to catch fish here, the graceful demoiselle cranes (*Anthropoides virgo*) with their handsome crest, and the purple gallinule (*Porphyrio caeruleus*). There is also the great crested grebe (*Podiceps cristatus*), a large and comical bird with mutton-chop whiskers and two clumps of brushy, dark feathers growing a bit to the right and left of its forehead, looking like a bad Chinese haircut. The passage of the migratory birds from Southern India through Galilee on their way to Siberia and other parts of Northern Europe, coupled with the availability of competent Israelis such as scouts, kibbutzniks, scientists and others who might be induced to aid with bird banding, would be a most useful thing, especially now that it has been conclusively proven that migratory birds carry diseases such as encephalitis which may be passed on to man as well as to livestock.

Members of the kibbutzim around the Sea of Galilee have had to learn to defend themselves. In 1948, the men and women of Degania, armed with Molotov cocktails, rifles and machine guns, withstood an attack by Syrian tanks, leaving as a war memorial one which had penetrated their fence in the middle of the kibbutz.

Kibbutzim are located near the country's frontiers as a security measure. In particularly difficult and dangerous areas, young men and women who have reached eighteen and volunteer to spend their military service in Nahal, the Israeli name for Pioneering Fighting Youth, are assigned to these posts after combined military and agricultural training. Nahal has hoped that many of these volunteers would elect to stay on. Many have, taken by the idea of continuing their own kibbutz in company with the friends and comrades with whom they saw service.

Since Israel's Operation Sinai in 1956, which effectively put an end to the frontier sabotage, assassination and ambush in which Israel had lost nearly fourteen hundred of her frontier settlers in her first eight years to the raids of especially trained Arab terrorists known as *fedayin*, the Egyptian and Gaza frontier had been relatively quiet. But the same rabble rouser and hate monger who had incited the *fedayin*, a man from Acre named Ahmed Shukeiry, in succeeding years organized the Palestine Liberation Organization, based in Gaza, and trained its military arm, the Palestine Liberation Army. The new generation of terrorists is known as El Fatah (The Conqueror). Shukeiry is a man of many portfolios. Formerly Ambassador to the United Nations for Saudi Arabia and then for Syria, he has, with President Nasser's blessing, kept up a screaming campaign of vilification against Israel with announcements of her horrible and imminent end, sometimes varying this with calls to the Palestinian refugees in Jordan to do away with King Hussein, calling him a prostitute of the United States—the sort of thing which has on occasion caused Shukeiry to be persona non grata in the kingdom where he formerly maintained an office in the Old City of Jerusalem, handy for sabotage and subversion, against both

Jordan and Israel. He is likely to turn up anywhere and with varying credentials, as he did at the United Nations Security Council debate on the Six Day War, and again in Khartoum at the later summit conference there—always urging the most violent and extreme action possible against the Israelis and his Arab opponents of the moment.

Fatah terrorists now operated out of Syria rather than Gaza or sometimes from Syria through Lebanon or Jordan, steadily stepping up their attacks, and in the latter months before the Six Day War, joined by the regular Syrian Army, either as saboteurs, or with artillery, tanks or air force. It became alarmingly reminiscent of the days preceding the Sinai War of 1956, and was precipitated for many of the same reasons: increasing and deadly harassment by saboteurs along Israel's border; the massing of great numbers of troops along the frontiers of Israel together with the accumulation of vast stocks of weapons and ammunition; and, finally, the closing of the Gulf of Aqaba and the Straits of Tiran.

Saboteurs attempted to blow up an apartment house in the Jerusalem suburb of Romema, but did not do a very good job and only injured slightly the nineteen persons who had gathered on a Sabbath for a *bar mitzvah* celebration. Three men on a border patrol in the Negev near the Dead Sea were killed by a land mine. A boy lost his life stepping on one of a number of mines planted in a football field. A retaliatory commando raid was made on the village of Samua in Jordan, first evacuating the population and then blowing up forty houses which the Israeli authorities were convinced had been used to give aid to the Syrian-trained saboteurs responsible for the border-patrol killing and thirteen other minings within the past six weeks. A quick retaliatory raid was made by the Israeli Air Force, knocking out Syrian engineering installations and earth-moving equipment engaged in diverting the sources of the Jordan River and thus denying Israel so much water for irrigation. The idea was to hit civilian targets comparable to those attacked by the Syrian infiltrators, and also to show that the air force would be used where considered necessary.

Infiltration and sabotage continued. When winds were favorable, fires were set in Syrian territory to burn Israeli crops. Life was particularly dangerous along Israel's shortest frontier, the forty-seven miles it shares with Syria. In the Almagor area just north of the Sea of Galilee, more than a dozen people were kidnapped or murdered, including the wife of a British Air Attaché, found shot dead with the flowers which she had been picking scattered near her.

Three Belgians and three Israelis, on an outing caught by sudden high winds on the Sea of Galilee, made for the eastern shore where they were abducted by Syrian soldiers who hurried them all across the frontier. The Belgians were released immediately, but the Israelis only after five months of intensive negotiations by the United Nations, when they were returned with eight other Israelis for whose release their government had been working nearly fourteen years. None except the three excursionists was still capable of expressing himself coherently.

At four o'clock in the morning of August fifteenth, 1966, an Israeli police patrol-boat protecting fisherman at the northeastern end of the Sea of Galilee ran aground in shallow waters and called for help. A second police boat sent to its rescue was unable to dislodge it, whereupon Syrian positions across the border about a hundred yards away began intensive fire. Two Israeli reporters and a press photographer hurried to the scene and got their story, with the Syrian positions opening up against their speedboat with machine guns and a mortar while a recoilless cannon engaged the police boat. At this point, the reporters and photographer jumped overboard, ducking whenever they heard machine-gun fire. Four Syrian MIG 17s and two MIG 21s joined the fight, armed with machine guns and rockets. Planes from the Israeli Air Force broke it up, downing one MIG 17 which dove into the lake and another MIG 21 which crashed in Syria. There were some injuries but, amazingly, no fatalities aboard the police boats, and the reporters and the photographer returned to Tiberius, shaken and dripping. The Syrian press and radio announced that they had sunk fifteen "Israeli gunboats." If there is anything of that size on the lake, it must be so cleverly camouflaged that no one has ever been able to see it.

At Kibbutz Tel Katzir, at the southeastern corner of the Sea of Galilee, in the first armored battle in the area, Israeli tanks destroyed two German-built Panzers and disabled a Russian T-34 in an hour and a half's duel with the Syrians one day in January of 1967, not a bad feat considering the Israelis were returning the fire of the well-dug-in Syrian positions on the heights far above them. Another T-34 was destroyed two days later.

Some weeks after and just two months before the Six Day War, Syrian fire against an unarmored tractor cultivating the land of Kibbutz Ha'on just to the north on the way to Ein Gev turned into another artillery duel, with the Syrians first using the guns of their tanks against armored tractors which had been brought in to continue the cultivation, then calling in heavy artillery while Israeli forces returned fire. The Israeli tractors continued plowing, and when one was hit in its engine, it was replaced by another machine. Syrian positions had fired on Tel Katzir, Ha'on, and Ein Gev on the eastern shore of the Sea of Galilee, and on Gadot to the north in the Hula Valley, when, at 1:35 P.M., after the Syrians had ignored a cease-fire arranged by U.N. observers, as they had in the earlier battle over the stranded boat on the lake, the Israeli Air Force silenced the Syrian positions. This brought out Syrian MIGs which were taken on by Israeli Mirages as they appeared. By five in the afternoon it was over, six MIGs were down and six Israeli tractors continued plowing.

Working under attack which is sometimes almost continuous, peering dead ahead through a narrow slit in the steel box that is the cab of the lumbering tractor while Syrian fire ricochets off the metal, is conceded to be more than the usual agricultural strain. But the work goes on.

Day by day, life on the frontier kibbutzim, fortunately, is less exciting. Still, when the night watchman at a border kibbutz greets the visitor with "Shalom," he is cradling a submachine gun.

12/ WEIZMANN AND
THE INSTITUTE

From Tel Aviv and Jaffa along the coast endless sand dunes begin, stretching all the way to Cairo and beyond. A little beyond the sister cities, at Nahal Sorek, is the nuclear reactor whose stubby, severely handsome tower of sweeping curved surfaces as they rise look like an exercise in solid geometry, but which is irreverently known as The Swimming Pool. This is an installation of Israel's Atomic Energy Commission which is also responsible for the Negev Nuclear Research Center. And there is an Institute of Nuclear Science at the Weizmann Institute in Rehovot.

The highway which leads from Tel Aviv down to the Negev passes through Rehovot, which means "Broad Acres." There is on one side of the road Israel's Institute of Agriculture, studying soils, animal husbandry, biochemistry and nutrition, plant physiology and protection, deciduous fruit trees and agricultural economics, with a thousand-acre experimental farm at Beit Dagon, not far away, two more experimental farms in the north and the south of the country, and a network of experimental field-crop stations.

The Weizmann Institute on the other side of the road has a staff of some three hundred scientists, about three-quarters of whom were either born in Israel or came to the country in their youth. There are about as many graduate students and working scientific visitors, such as Professor Manoj K. Bannerjee (from the Saha Institute of Nuclear Physics in Calcutta, studying nuclear physics), John Valdemar Braemer Petersen (from Copenhagen, a guest of the Organic Chemistry Department), Dr. Mark Schleyer (biophysics, from the Max Planck Institute in Munich), Dr. A. U. Ogan (organic chemistry, from the University of Ibadan, Nigeria), Dr. Nobuhisa Imai (physics, from the University of Nagoya in Japan), a Thai couple who were married at the Weizmann Institute, Puttipongse Varavudhi and Miss Sudjit Suwannarat (he working in biodynamics and his bride in experimental physics, both from Chulalongkorn University in Bangkok).

Both of the institutes in Rehovot are part of a group of exceptionally good, inter-connected institutions doing work of highest caliber which has won an international reputation, or, to put it most simply, has enabled Israel to thrive and flourish.

In all of Weizmann's long and single-minded struggle to establish a Jewish State, education was central to his plans. With his friend Martin Buber he published a pamphlet in 1903 which said plainly that to make cultural Zionism a reality would call for a Hebrew University in the Holy Land. In 1918, with Turkish troops retreating in the distance and British artillery pounding away from the outskirts of Jerusalem, Weizmann laid the foundation stone of the Hebrew University on Mount Scopus. Now, the new Hebrew University at Givat Ram in Jerusalem works together with its medical faculty at the Hadassah University Medical Centre at the Jerusalem suburb of Ein Kerem and the original Mount Scopus campus recovered in 1967, which is the site of the Harry S. Truman Peace Memorial. The university also maintains branch institutes in Haifa and Beersheba as well as the agricultural faculty at Rehovot.

The University Authority for Research and Development spends over three million dollars a year in about three hundred research projects, the majority of them in science, medicine, agriculture and the social sciences. Many of the projects are complementary to the ones at the Weizmann Institute, such as geological surveys and exploration for underground water, and for mineral deposits like the extremely successful find of phosphates in the Negev. Other related work is being done throughout Israel by the Technion in Haifa; the Israel Institute for Biological Research working mostly in preventive medicine, epidemiology and public health; the Geological Institute surveying natural resources; the Geophysical Institute, which makes seismographic, gravimetric and other surveys, looking particularly for oil; a Fibres and Forest Products Institute; the National Physical Laboratory, which is responsible for national standards and applied research in such fields as solar energy, power units and the invention of new medical instruments; and the Negev Institute for Arid Zone Research. All of these scientific institutions are coördinated by the National Council for Research and Development in the Prime Minister's Office—between them a formidable array of scientific talent which has proved of great value to Israel and to the world.

Chaim Weizmann, who was to become the first President of Israel and who was for many years president of the World Zionist Organization and the Jewish Agency for Israel, was very likely the most influential of that disparate collection of extraordinary talents known as Zionists. Deeply influenced by Asher Ginzberg whose pen name was Ahad Ha'am, a Russian-born philosopher and major writer in modern Hebrew who taught that Jewish culture rather than economic, political or military power was the base of the unprecedented survival of this people, Weizmann agreed with this conclusion, adding science to the humanities as part of this Jewish cultural inheritance.

Arguing at the Eleventh Zionist Congress in Vienna in 1913 for his dream of a Hebrew University, Weizmann said: "Although we have at present an ardent desire to see our people plow the fields and to make it faithful to its soil, we know that we are and shall always be the People of the Book. Our strongest weapon is the spirit, and it is our duty to cultivate this spirit, to sharpen the weapons with which we must fight for a better existence. The university will be our spiritual dreadnought; it will be of greater value to us than armies and navies are to other nations."

Isaiah Berlin, Chichele Professor of Social and Political Theory and Fellow of All Souls College at Oxford, has said in his brief, beautifully written biographical essay *Chaim Weizmann*: "As he reflected on the poverty of the land and its lack of natural resources, he placed his hope upon turning the one kind of capital that the Jews did seem to possess—technical skills, ingenuity, energy, desperation—to the production of miracles in scientific technology."

Abba Eban, between his ten years' assignment as Israel's Ambassador to the United States and Permanent Representative to the United Nations, and his return as Foreign Minister and Chief of Israel's U.N. Delegation at the time of his eloquent exposition at the Security Council of his country's position before and after the Six Day War, had in the interim served as Minister of Education and president of the Weizmann Institute. In an appreciation called "Israel's Most Modern Statesman," Abba Eban wrote, "Weizmann's disciples had learned from him that the driving force of Israel's history was the need to transcend her smallness by attaining a vision of excellence in the spiritual and intellectual domains.

"But it is doubtful if even they grasped the full extent of Weizmann's prescience in requiring a scientific tradition to be built into the very foundations of a hard-pressed pioneering society."

The Weizmann Institute has eighteen specialized Departments working on everything from isotope research for use in exploration for underground reservoirs, to experimental biology concerned with the origins of leukemia and breast cancer, to research on polymers, the long, threadlike molecules whose forms differ from one substance to another and which may provide the clue to the transmission of inherited characteristics. The Institute studies ways to desalt water, to help transform desert into arable soil, or to the making of polyester resins to be used in manufacturing plastic car bodies.

There is also work in the Department of Biodynamics, under Professor M. C. Shelesnyak, concerned with the physiology of reproduction, on a simple contraceptive pill to be taken three days after sexual intercourse, instead of a regimen of twenty-one pills per month. A building for biodynamics is being contributed by the Population Council of New York.

In the Department of Applied Mathematics, prospecting for water and oil by geophysical methods is helped by computers made within the Institute, the WEIZAC and the GOLEM, the latter named for the legendary figure of clay brought to life by the Cabbalist Rabbi Judah Löw in order to protect the sixteenth-century Jews of Prague against their persecutors.

"Dr. Weizmann," announces the guide book to the Institute which bears his name, "always believed that congenial surround- ings promoted fruitful scientific activity." The four hundred acres of the Weizmann Institute and Memorial, bosky and tranquil, with terraced gardens, quiet, dappled with sunlight, the simple, clean lines of the buildings, the flowering creepers, all seem an ideal place to work. I could believe it when Nechemia Meyers, the Public Affairs Officer for the Institute, said, "Israel is a reservoir of scientific talent, and not too well paid, which makes Israeli projects attractive to the United States and other outside donors. There are some four hundred research projects under way, with emphasis on molecular biology and nuclear physics. Israel is a natural place for the manufacture of science-based industry, for which we don't have the raw material." The Yeda Research and Development Company affiliated with the Institute is now applying laboratory and research discoveries to the manufacture of heavy oxygen, fine chemicals, precision instruments, plastics and, on a commercial basis, helping industry in the fields of plant genetics, biophysics and medical electronics.

In memory of John Fitzgerald Kennedy, forty-eight scholarships at the Institute are being awarded, one for each year of the President's life.

All this was made possible by a man born in 1874 in the village of Motol near Pinsk in the Pale of Settlement where Jews were permitted to live in western Russia. In a compendium called *Chaim Weizmann, A Biography by Several Hands* published in 1963, Maurice Samuel in his chapter, "The Road from Motol," describes the typical Eastern European village called the *shtetl* as a mass of contradictions, "Forlorn little settlements in a vast, hostile and primitive environment, isolated alike from the centres of Jewish and non-Jewish civilization, their tenure precarious, their structure ramshackle, their existence a prolonged squalor to the outer view," and yet, "Half the time the *shtetl* just wasn't there; it was in the Holy Land and it was in the remote past or the remote future, in the company of the Patriarchs and Prophets or of the Messiah. Its festivals were geared to the Palestinian climate and calendar; it celebrated regularly the harvests its forefathers had gathered in a hundred generations ago; it prayed for the . . . subtropical . . . rains, indifferent to the needs of its neighbors, whose prayers had a practical local schedule in view." This was the world into which Chaim Weizmann was born, the sort of little Eastern European Jewish village described by almost every Yiddish writer, and familiar throughout a great part of the West in the days when that language was spoken by twelve millions, now known to us best through the stories of Sholom Aleichem and the musical *Fiddler on the Roof* taken from one of his stories.

It was a tightly knit society, poor, warm, quirky, sometimes persecuted, living a life very much of its own. "We were separated from the peasants by a whole inner world of memories and experiences," Weizmann wrote in his autobiography, *Trial and Error*. "My father was not yet a Zionist, but the house was steeped in rich Jewish tradition, and Palestine was at the centre of the ritual . . . the Return was in the air, a vague, deep-rooted Messianism, a hope which would not die."

As Isaiah Berlin put it, there was no insurmountable social problem for the Jews of Eastern Europe "so long as rigid religious orthodoxy insulated them from the external world. Until then, poor, downtrodden and oppressed as they might be, and clinging to each other for warmth and shelter, the Jews of Eastern Europe put all their faith in God and concentrated all their hope either upon individual salvation—immortality in the sight of God—or upon the coming of the Messiah. . . . Once the enlightenment—secular learning and the possibility of a freer mode of life—began at first to seep, and then to flood, into the Jewish townlets and villages of the Pale, that a generation grew up, no longer content to sit by the waters of Babylon and sing the songs of Zion in Exile."

The winds of change carried the ideas of such men as Leo Pinsker, a Polish physician whose work during a cholera epidemic had been cited by the Russian government, and who himself had been an assimilationist, but who was so shaken by the government-inspired pogroms of 1881 following the assassination of Czar Alexander II that the following year he published his historic "Auto-Emancipation," calling for Jewish self-rule in the ancient homeland. Pinsker's pamphlet attracted wide attention among Eastern European Jewry, and he joined Ahad Ha'am's Lovers of Zion movement which led to the agricultural settlements supported by the Baron de Rothschild in Palestine.

The Jews, said Pinsker in Berlin's paraphrase of his message, "were but the spectre of a murdered nation, haunting the living, causing everywhere uneasiness, fear and hatred; it would not be laid until the homeless wanderers acquired a land of their own. . . ."

The family of Ezer Weizmann was not untouched by these new currents. Before his twelfth birthday his son Chaim had written in a letter to a friend, "Let us carry our banner to Zion and return to our original Mother upon whose knees we were reared. For why should we expect mercy from the Kings of Europe that they should in their pity for us give us a resting place—in vain!" In a line that foreshadowed his deep attachment to Britain which was to sustain him for most of his life, the boy added, "All have decided that the Jew is doomed to death, but England will have mercy on us nonetheless."

At his secondary school in Pinsk, Chaim was helped by a science master who encouraged him to specialize in chemistry. Upon graduation, he took one of his father's rafts of logs down the Vistula to East Prussia where he enrolled as a student in the local polytechnical school in Darmstadt, then moved in 1893 to Berlin, where he pursued biochemistry at the Technische Hochschule in Charlottenburg. Three years later, Theodor Herzl, the Vienna *Neue Freie Presse* correspondent in Paris, after the despicable condemnation of Dreyfus and the furor which followed it, revealing the extent and depth of anti-Jewish feeling in Europe, published his scorching pamphlet, "The Jewish State," calling for the establishment of a Jewish nation and giving organized political form to Pinsker's and Ahad Ha'am's philosophy of a Jewish national revival.

By the time that Weizmann had moved on from Berlin to the University of Fribourg in Switzerland, he was a follower of Herzl, though he and his Zionist friends among the Russian intellectual community of Berlin did not share Herzl's optimism about the durability of any charter for settlement in the Holy Land which might be obtained from the Sultan of Turkey or with the blessing of Kaiser Wilhelm II or the Pope or any of the others whom Herzl solicited; and certainly not the proposal, which Herzl in desperation later supported, for five thousand square miles of territory near Uganda which Joseph Chamberlain as British Colonial Secretary had offered; nor earlier British consideration of the idea of Jewish settlement in Cyprus or at El-Arish in the Sinai Peninsula. Nothing would do but the Holy Land, and then only if the Jewish settlers secured it with their own work. "If the governments gave us a Charter today," Weizmann wrote in 1907, "it would be no more than a piece of paper. It would be a different thing if we were working in the Land of Israel; then the Charter would be written and sealed in blood and sweat, which would have it in their power to secure an everlasting possession."

When he was thirty, a post in biochemistry became available at Manchester University and Weizmann took it, a most propitious move which affected his whole life and, in the course of time, the birth of Israel.

In Manchester, Weizmann met C. P. Scott, the editor of the Liberal daily, *The Manchester Guardian*, a man of great political influence whose words were listened to in the British Cabinet. Scott became a convert to Zionism, and in turn introduced Weizmann to Lloyd George who was to become Prime Minister in 1916, and to Herbert Samuel who was later the first Governor-General of Palestine and who earlier had held a number of Cabinet and other posts in the Asquith administration. Samuel was himself an ardent Zionist and a member of the Anglo-Jewish élite, which as a group was by no means so favorably disposed.

All accounts agree that Weizmann personally was a man of great charm and persuasion, tactful, unruffled, quietly sure of himself and, from the beginning, with an understanding and love of things English which helped him to attract and bring to his side many Englishmen in positions of real power. In some of his portraits he looks, surprisingly and disconcertingly, a little like Lenin.

In 1914, Winston Churchill as First Lord of the Admiralty asked Weizmann if he could create a process for the manufacture of acetone needed as a solvent in making naval and other ammunition. There is a story attributed to Lloyd George, perhaps apocryphal, which relates how, when asked what honor he wished as a reward for his extremely valuable scientific service, Weizmann replied that he asked nothing more than a country for his people. This and other evidence, however, does suggest how well Weizmann succeeded in establishing himself with the Establishment.

Another tale grew out of the 1922 White Paper in which Churchill as Colonial Secretary, though strongly in favor of Jewish settlement in Palestine and most friendly to Weizmann, decreed that Jewish immigration should be limited by "economic absorptive capacity," an argument which in the difficult days to come was increasingly employed by those in the British government to a greater or lesser degree opposed to Jewish immigration, or on occasion to try to still the Arab outcry against Jews being permitted in the land. Another story describes an eminent Briton visiting Weizmann in his laboratory, asking him what he was doing with his chemical apparatus, and receiving the reply, "Manufacturing absorptive capacity."

As a matter of fact, on the seventeenth of December in 1939, Weizmann went to call on Winston Churchill, thanking him for his increasing interest in Zionist progress, and saying that after the war the Zionists would want a state of three to four million Jews in Palestine. Churchill replied, "Yes, indeed, I quite agree with that." In 1944, Dr. Walter C. Lowdermilk, an American authority on soil, irrigation and reclamation, estimated in his book, *Palestine, Land of Promise*, that by using the methods which had proved successful with the Tennessee Valley Authority, Palestine could support a population of approximately six million—a number which might well be increased with techniques for more effective utilization of land developed over the subsequent decades. With the present Jewish population of Israel at about two and a half million, the Arab population of the area, if one includes the Gaza Strip and the West Bank of the Jordan occupied by Israel during the war of 1967, could be estimated at about a million and a half.

Weizmann's work before, after and during the two World Wars continued to be a mixture of chemistry and Zionist diplomacy. In contrast to Theodor Herzl who came from the West almost like a Messiah, with his gleaming silk hat and glossy, long, square-cut black beard, neither understanding the language of the Eastern Europeans nor familiar with their intense preoccupation with the Bible and their own traditional, distinctive life within the rural settlements and the ghettos of the Pale of Imperial Russia, Weizmann was a man of these people.

Herzl had once considered mass conversion as a possible answer to the afflictions of the Jews. Weizmann's whole being was deeply imbued with traditional Jewish scholarship and piety. He commanded admiration in Western halls of learning and had access to the mighty of the world, but to his own people he remained the son of Ezer Weizmann, the lumber merchant. The way he walked and talked, the images he chose and his language (of the seven tongues he spoke well—and the snide comment has been made that he spoke English almost too well—Yiddish was the one in which he best expressed himself) were those of the people he came from. His looks, his voice, his humor was their own. He was one whom they could understand.

Herzl fired the imagination of Jews throughout Eastern Europe when he visited them, even if they did not always understand. For, at last, he seemed to be pointing the way.

Weizmann was not essentially an innovator: he was an empiricist, working to give practical expression to the ideas of his time. And in the ancient Jewish view of things, the practical and the spiritual were parts of the whole. Early in Weizmann's life, Isaiah Berlin has written in his biography, "He accepted the proposition that the ills of the Jews were caused principally by the abnormality of their social situation. . . . Weizmann and his generation assumed without question that if Jews were to be emancipated, they must live in freedom in their own land, that there alone they would no longer be compelled to extort elementary human rights by that repellent mixture of constant cunning, obsequiousness and occasional arrogance which is forced on all dependents and clients and slaves; and finally that this land must—could only—be Palestine." In his contribution as one of the Several Hands, Berlin adds of Weizmann's philosophy, "He distrusted any political shortcut which omitted or played down the need for a mass movement from below, and insisted on the need for the growth, necessarily gradual, of a widespread consciousness among the Jewish masses of their needs and capacities for collective action, in the first place for practical work for creating an agricultural and industrial base in Palestine itself."

Throughout all the troubled years, Weizmann remained president of the World Zionist Organization and the Jewish Agency, with the exception of the years from 1931 to 1935, when he was replaced because of his coöperation with the British, a position at that time discredited by Zionists who had become increasingly anti-English; and again, briefly in 1930, when he resigned following Lord Passfield's British Labour government's White Paper on vicious anti-Jewish riots in Safed and Hebron and elsewhere in Palestine in which many Jews were massacred, and only a few Arabs killed, mostly in combating the police trying to restore order. The British government, while deploring the riots, explained their cause as the Arabs' natural reaction to the dangers of Jewish immigration, calling for further restrictions on the numbers of Jews to be accepted. Following a storm of protest by the Conservative, Liberal and, in part, Labour Parties, and a letter in *The Times* signed by most prominent Britishers, the Prime Minister, Ramsay MacDonald, relented and sent Weizmann a more liberal interpretation of the regulations, and these enabled Weizmann to resume office.

There was a great deal to do. With Hitler and his fanatical followers gaining strength in Germany, the noose tightening there and in the countries over which she was gaining control, it became a race against time to try to save those Jews who could be rescued from the Continent.

The war clouds had already gathered. The day after the Munich agreement, when Britain, France, Italy, and Germany agreed to dismember Czechoslovakia, Jan Masaryk in despair had called on Weizmann in London, predicting a series of Munichs in which the smaller and weaker countries would be abandoned by the greater, as had been Manchuria, Ethiopia and now his own Czechoslovakia.

The 1939 British White Paper restricted Jewish immigration to Palestine to a total of seventy-five thousand over the next five years, just at the time when it was most desperately needed. There was to be no further Jewish immigration permitted without Arab permission, and this was to be accompanied by severe restrictions on Jewish purchase of land.

Weizmann had come out of the house of the Colonial Secretary Malcolm MacDonald livid and shaking with anger when he was given this news in advance. But he was still capable of saying to Prime Minister Churchill, with his usual forthrightness, later in the war, "Remember, sir, our enemies are also yours."

"Infamous" was the kindest word applied by the Jews to the new British White Paper, and even the Philadelphian editor of the *Palestine Post*, Gershon Agron, a man known for his moderation, called it "the perfidy of the monstrous White Paper, a creature of funk spawned by a government dominated by a passion for appeasement."

On the eve of the war in which she was to fight for her own survival, Britain had decided to appease the Arabs, inclined to be friendly to the Nazis. From their land came a great part of the oil on which Britain depended, and they lay near the Russian oil fields in the Caucasus. Britain hoped to keep the Arabs quiet at the expense of the Jews.

Christopher Sykes, who explains in some detail the reasons for this 1939 White Paper, comments, "To have opened a major quarrel with Arab states when Europe was moving toward war would have been an act of folly by Great Britain without precedent." He still concludes that "Nothing can disguise the fact that there was an odious moral cruelty in inflicting so heavy a disappointment on millions of people to whom Palestine was the only hope left on this earth. . . ."

Nevertheless, after presiding over the 21st Zionist Conference at Geneva in the week before the outbreak of hostilities, in an atmosphere of foreboding of what was to come (most of the Eastern European delegates were never to return from the Nazi death camps), Dr. Weizmann was still able to carry to Neville Chamberlain their decision to stand by Great Britain and to fight on the side of the democracies. As was said by the Jewish leaders many times later, "We shall fight the war as if there were no White Paper, but we shall fight the White Paper as if there were no war."

There was an almost superhuman amount of work to be done. The road ahead was to be agonizing for Weizmann and his people. Perhaps throughout the years no one had seen more clearly than he just what might come.

In 1903 he had said, "The Jewish people are sitting on a volcano, and this position will continue to exist until an appalling disaster takes place."

Speaking of Central and Eastern Europe, in 1936 he said, "There are in this part of the world six million people doomed to be pent up where they are not wanted, and for whom the world is divided into places where they cannot live, and places to which they cannot enter."

At the end of the war, speaking of the death camps, he said, "There is one thing I know: if we can prevent it, it will never happen again. That is what the Jewish people have set out to do."

Weizmann's health was frail at best, but he threw himself into his work relentlessly, calling on all his reserves. Immediately following the declaration of war by Britain and France he offered his scientific services to the British government, proposing to the French Ambassador the recruiting of a Jewish Legion in France and continuing to press for one in Britain, working desperately to rescue every Jew marked for destruction in Europe, getting them to Britain or the United States or other havens, and, if possible, to Palestine. Using all of his powers of persuasion, he expounded his position to every diplomat, editor and member of government he could reach, even catching up with the Egyptian Ambassador to arrange for further meetings, at the Ambassador's suggestion, at regular intervals.

It was not always enough. Malcolm MacDonald categorically refused Weizmann's plea for visas to enter Palestine for twenty thousand Jewish children for whom exit from Poland had been arranged. He authorized only visas for one hundred and sixty-nine Zionist leaders who had already received their Palestinian permits before the war. The Colonial Secretary remarked piously to the Jewish Agency delegation come to see him that he "fully realized the tragic consequences of his refusal for those involved."

On one occasion Weizmann was successful in using his personal influence to gain special admittance for a group of Jews to Palestine, but in general, as the war continued and the remaining years of British administration in Palestine wore on to their increasingly confused and finally chaotic end, as the British authorities became less and less sympathetic to the Zionists and more and more partial to the Arabs, the 1939 White Paper's restrictions against the Jews were enforced as though they were provisions of the Mandate, which they were not. No one will ever know how many leaky tubs manned by underaged Zionists in attempting to run the blockade went to the bottom, but behavior of the British Colonial authorities toward those who did manage to get through to Palestine was so obdurate and unimaginative, and on occasion inhumane, that reaction through much of the world, well used by the Zionists to help their own cause, was one of revulsion and anger, and of sympathy for the refugees. On the eleventh of November, 1940, the British Navy intercepted and brought to Haifa two broken-down antiques called *The Pacific* and *The Milos*, which were carrying between them more than seventeen hundred refugees. A French ship called *La Patria* was requisitioned to carry the refugees in internment on the British island of Mauritius off the east coast of Africa when the Stern Gang, in an attempt to disable the ship's engines and so keep the refugees in Palestine, miscalculated their explosion and sank the ship, with the loss of two hundred and forty refugees and about a dozen Palestine police officers. This was represented as a deliberate attempt at suicide on the part of the refugees rather than be turned away from Palestine, a story which was widely credited.

Another hulk called *The Struma*, which had been a cattle boat and should have been beached long before, carried seven hundred and sixty-nine Balkan refugees, reaching Istanbul in December of 1941 and remaining there for two months while the Jewish Agency pleaded for visas so that the passengers might enter Palestine. When at last the Palestine government gave way sufficiently to agree to visas for the children on board between the ages of eleven and sixteen, Turkish authorities had already ordered *The Struma* out of her waters. She was towed into the Black Sea where there was an explosion aboard the ship. She swiftly sank. There was one survivor.

Running the blockade at any cost continued throughout the Mandate. With tension mounting almost daily, the voices of moderation were stilled by those of the extremists calling for ever more violent action. To keep his leadership, Ben-Gurion himself was obliged to speak the language of extremism, and in April of 1947, while addressing the Jewish National Council, Va'ad Leumi, he went so far as to declare that British policy was "to liquidate the Jews as a people, and to recognize only the existence of individual Jews who could serve as objects either of pogroms or of pity." Not to be outdone, the official information services of the British government released unsubstantiated stories about Zionist recruiting in Europe of Gentile gangsters to work as terrorists in Palestine, and about the "strikingly inhuman kidnapping rings" organized in Hungary to abduct Jewish children from their families in order to increase the number of illegal immigrants.

The British government took no exception to the opinion frequently voiced in the British press that the whole Zionist movement was a plot, a creature of the Kremlin, and there is some evidence that the Foreign Secretary Ernest Bevin actually believed this.

It was in this superheated atmosphere that the British Navy escorted into Haifa the old *President Garfield*, now renamed *Exodus 1947* and jammed with some forty-five hundred refugees. Instead of making an exception and permitting the refugees to land as a concession to the United Nations Special Committee on Palestine, known as UNSCOP, which was then visiting the country and would have provided the British authorities with an acceptable reason, or follow their routine of interning the refugees in Cyprus until visas became available, Bevin, who had become increasingly vexed with the Palestine problem and noticeably anti-Semitic, flew into a rage and ordered the *Exodus* back to its port of embarkation near Marseilles in order "to teach the Jews a lesson." Haganah activists encouraged the refugees to refuse to be landed anywhere else than in Palestine. When the British government persuaded the French to accept the refugees, the latter did so with the stipulation that no one be obliged to land who didn't want to. In actuality, the French government and press, which still smarted from differences with the British over Lebanon and Syria, made common cause with the Haganah and the refugees. The three ships to which the refugees had been transferred from the *Exodus* were finally shipped back to the British zone of Germany. (The British explanation was that, after Jewish terrorists had executed two British sergeants and carried out other acts of reprisal, the refugees would be unsafe in a Britain where popular opinion was highly aroused.) And so the few thousand refugees ended back at the German camps where they had started. World opinion was outraged.

The result of all of this was Leon Uris's novel *Exodus* which sold more than five million copies. Whatever the arguments about the literary merits or demerits of his book, it seems to me that the story of the refugees and the blockade and the fight for survival in the new land is in itself so intensely dramatic that the reader is swept along with it. There followed a picture book with the title of *Exodus Revisited*, with striking photographs of Israel by the Greek photographer Dimitrios Harissiadis. Then there was a film made of *Exodus* which reached even larger audiences. The characters may have been pasteboard and the romance celluloid, but the kernel of truth was there and the hearts of millions were moved. Altogether it was a propaganda triumph.

One earlier hope of Chaim Weizmann, that of offering refuge at Rehovot to endangered scientists in Germany and elsewhere in Europe, never materialized. Richard Willstätter, who won the Nobel Prize for chemistry in 1915 for his work on the coloring matter of plants, especially chlorophyll, did attend the opening of the Institute in 1934, but declined the post of Director, and remained in Germany despite all humiliation until 1939 when he was expelled and found sanctuary in Switzerland. Fritz Haber, who won the Nobel Prize for chemistry in 1918 for his conversion of the nitrogen in the air into ammonia and nitric acid, the two chemicals necessary for the manufacture both of explosives and artificial fertilizer, had been converted to Christianity, but still was stripped by the Nazis of all his honors, his academic position and his fortune. He died in Basle on his way to Palestine, but left his library to the Institute. Many who managed to escape from Europe went, like Einstein, to the West, though Einstein did teach briefly at the old Hebrew University in Jerusalem where he didn't get along too well with Weizmann.

No opportunity to save some or any at all of those destined for the Nazi death camps was dismissed by Weizmann and his fellows, no matter how slight or implausible the possibility. In July of 1944, a Hungarian Jew named Joel Brand brought to Jewish Agency representatives in Istanbul an offer from Hungary that the hundreds of thousands of Jews still alive there could be saved, although Eichmann, who was charged with their extermination, had already begun shipping them to Auschwitz. In the presence of a Dr. Kastner, representative of the Jewish Rescue Committee in Budapest, Eichmann had purportedly made the offer to spare the remaining Jews if ten thousand trucks were made available to Himmler by the Allies. Brand swore that, if he could return to Budapest with the answer that this offer was being considered seriously, "the mills of death would stop grinding."

There were many possible considerations in this extraordinary and ghoulish offer. Allied armies were closing in on Germany, and it was just conceivable that Himmler was taking out insurance against the defeat of the Nazis which now seemed certain. Weizmann, joined by Moshe Sharett, went to see the Foreign Secretary, Anthony Eden. As Weizmann agreed, "The Gestapo offer must have ulterior motives. It is not impossible, however, that in the false hope of achieving their ends they would be prepared to let out a certain number of Jews, large or small. The whole thing may boil down to a question of money and the ransom should be paid."

Eden argued that "There must be no negotiation with the enemy," and in spite of Eden's assurance to Weizmann that there would be no objection to Brand's return to Budapest, the whole proposal, or opportunity if it was that, was allowed to trail off into nothingness. There is still controversy as to whether the thousands of Jews, or even some Jews, might have been ransomed in return for the trucks.

The day after the interview with Eden, Weizmann again called at the Foreign Office, this time to urge that the Royal Air Force be directed to bomb Auschwitz. It was Weizmann's conviction that this would at least delay the extermination of those who were to be sent to their death there, that it would demonstrate direct action by the Allies to obliterate the machinery of the death mill—and, in a consideration with grim overtones, "It would give the lie to the oft-repeated assertions of Nazi spokesmen that the Allies were not really so displeased with the action of the Nazis in ridding Europe of Jews." Several weeks later, the Foreign Office replied that the recommendation of bombing the death camps could not be carried out by the RAF "for technical reasons."

There were more setbacks, and some successes. After traveling to Switzerland to interview refugee scientists about the plans of their German colleagues for support of Hitler's war effort, Weizmann was able to bring news of these developments to the then Foreign Secretary, Lord Halifax. Halifax reciprocated by agreeing with Weizmann that the new White Paper land restrictions should not be enforced, creating further friction in wartime: "It is impossible to have these things cropping up now." In addition, Weizmann had managed to get through to the military. In that November of 1939, the Chief of the Imperial General Staff, General Sir Edmund Ironside, announced his decision to release forty-three young Jews to whom the Palestine government had given long sentences for "indulging" in military training. General Ironside commented, "Fancy, they have condemned one of Wingate's lads to life imprisonment: he ought to have been given the Distinguished Service Order." When Weizmann reported that Malcolm MacDonald was opposed to the Jewish Army project, Ironside commented: "Oh, I see. But the Jewish Army will come all the same. Besides, if it is to be a better world after the war, the Jews must get Palestine." The continuing effort to see an Allied Jewish Force fighting under its own flag finally bore fruit in September of 1941 during a meeting at the War Office presided over by Eden as Secretary for War and with Lloyd George present. Eden confirmed that "the government have decided to proceed with the organization of a Jewish Army, on the same basis as the Czech and Polish Army." Blanche Dugdale, a niece of Balfour, wrote in her diary: "Walls of Jericho have fallen, fallen. I looked in at the Dorchester about 5 pm and found Chaim just back from the interview elated and solemn. He said, 'It was almost as great a day as the Balfour Declaration.' Orde Wingate was also there, radiant."

Throughout the Second World War and during the First, Weizmann continued his scientific contributions. Weizmann was successful in producing a butyl alcohol for the manufacture of synthetic rubber which in wartime was in critically short supply—this, according to Abba Eban and to Ritchie Calder, in spite of the opposition of American oil interests who controlled the sources of the raw materials.

Perhaps the least known publicly of Weizmann's contributions was his part in the invention of a concoction known as "Blitz Broth," protein used to help sustain air-raid-shelter populations in Britain when the country was short of meat, milk and eggs. Since these proteins are ultimately derived from vegetables which the human digestive system cannot cope with so effectively as sources of protein without an intermediary, Weizmann found this intermediary in the yeast cell, which could be fed on vegetable matter and then plasmolysed, or milked, of the liquid contents of its cell so as to provide the missing protein. Blitz Broth with brown bread kept Britain's city workers going when they returned to their shelters at night, and

1   EUROPE: Nazi roundup in the Warsaw Ghetto

2 ISRAEL: Policemen are here to help

ISRAEL GOVERNMENT PRESS OFFICE

3 Boy and girl paratroopers

ISRAEL GOVERNMENT PRESS OFFICE

4 Bokharans dancing with the Torah ISRAEL GOVERNMENT PRESS OFFICE

5 Divinity students celebrate in Jerusalem MAGNUM PHOTOS

6　Israeli soldiers reach the Wailing Wall

7 Damascus Gate to Jerusalem's Old City

8 Prayer at the
Moslem cemetery
before Gethsemane

9 Fragile façade of
the Holy Sepulchre

10 Israelis visit the
Dome of the Rock, site
of Solomon's Temple
WIDE WORLD PHOTOS

11 Allenby Bridge
after the Six Day War
WIDE WORLD PHOTOS

12   Roman columns in the surf at Caesarea

13   Haifa from Mount Carmel

14   Crusader wall at Acre

ISRAEL INFORMATION SERVICES

15 Old Nazareth

16 Mount of Beatitudes
overlooking
Sea of Galilee

17 Kibbutz Ein Gev on the shore
under the Syrian heights

18 The River Jordan

19   Egyptian tank at the Israel frontier, Six Day War.

20   Masada at the Dead Sea, symbol of freedom, where nearly a thousand Jews chose death over captivity

21   Young camel at Negev water hole

ISRAEL GOVERNMENT PRESS OFFICE

22   Israel of the future: Reactor south of Tel Aviv,
     for the study of the peaceful use of atomic energy
     ISRAEL GOVERNMENT PRESS OFFICE

was used as a paratroopers' iron ration when they were dropped at the time of the invasion of the Continent.

Chaim Weizmann died on the ninth of November of 1952, a week and a day before his seventy-eighth birthday. It is doubtful whether in all these years working for the return of his people he accomplished more than in the days of October and November of 1947 when he joined the great United Nations Palestine debate on whether to accept the report of their own fifteen-nation committee submitted the previous month after painstaking work in the field. It recommended, yet once again, partition of Palestine into Jewish and Arab states, thus giving the Jews their home, and—by an extraordinary combination of persuasion, coincidence, timing and luck—the assurance by President Truman of American recognition of the State of Israel upon its establishment.

Abba Eban was in New York acting as aide to Dr. Weizmann and in his diary has given us a picture, with his customary intelligence, of those times when, quite literally, the birth of the new nation hung in the balance.

Dr. Weizmann was growing blind, suffered from a bad heart, had a chronic infection of the lung and had been seriously ill for many months. Eban tells of their working steadily for four hours on a draft of Weizmann's speech: "After each sentence was written in huge letters and agreed, he would go to the lampstand and bring the text right to his eyes, endeavouring to learn it by heart. By the end of the session his eyes were watering . . . finally he said: 'We'll make this do—but how about a posuk (Biblical verse) for the ending?' We looked for a Bible and eventually found one supplied by the hotel in the bedside table." Presumably this was a Gideon Bible. "Spent half an hour on Isaiah looking for 'return to Zion' passages. Finally his mind was caught by the prophecy of 'an ensign for the nations.' As I left he said: 'Well, this is it. Over the top for the last time!' "

The delegations of the fifty-seven members of the United Nations listened intently to Dr. Weizmann. Of the contention of some Arab delegates that the Jews returning to Palestine under the Mandate were not really descendants of the inhabitants of the kingdoms of Judah and Israel at all, but in fact were descendants of the kingdom of the Khazars, a confederation of warlike Mongol tribesmen who had embraced Judaism and held sway over parts of southern Russia from the eighth to tenth centuries, Dr. Weizmann said only: "It is very strange—all my life I have been a Jew, felt like a Jew—and now I learn that I am a Khazar." He spoke paternally, personally, recalling his feeling twenty-five years before when the Mandate for Palestine was ratified in the council room of the League of Nations that the "ideals of our own history had been sanctioned by the conscience of all mankind." He ended with the Biblical verse of the Prophet Isaiah: "The Lord shall set his hand the second time to recover the remnants of his people. And he shall set up an ensign for the nations and shall assemble the outcasts of Israel and gather together the dispersed of Judah from the four corners of the earth."

On this note, the United Nations General Assembly by a vote of thirty-three to thirteen with ten abstentions approved the special committee's report with its recommendation of partition of Palestine into Jewish and Arab States.

All was not over. With the establishment of a Jewish State now authorized by the United Nations, the Arabs concentrated on detaching as much territory as possible, in particular the southern desert region of the Negev, from the area to be authorized. The State Department was persuaded that all the Negev should be a part of the proposed Arab state. Weizmann rose from his hotel sickbed and went to see President Truman. It was a race against the clock. Moshe Sharett, who was to become Israel's Foreign Minister, and briefly Prime Minister, was called with other Jewish Agency representatives to the United Nations lounge in New York to meet the American Ambassador Herschel Johnson and hear his announcement that the United States would insist on exclusion of the Negev from the Jewish State. At the same time, Weizmann was captivating President Truman with the importance of the southern Negev, of King Solomon's mines and the trade of the Hebrew kingdom through the Red Sea with the lands of Arabia, Africa and Asia, the importance of retaining for the Jewish State this outlet to the Indian Ocean, India, the Orient, and Australia and New Zealand, the importance of the Negev itself for industry and in settling the immigrants who were to come from Europe and elsewhere in the world. Soon the telephone rang in the United Nations lounge and Ambassador Johnson, about to announce United States support for incorporation of the Negev into the Arab state-to-be, told the messenger he was not to be disturbed and dispatched his deputy, General Hildring, to take the message. Hildring returned to say that President Truman was waiting at the other end in Washington, whereupon Ambassador Johnson "leapt to the telephone booth like a startled and portly reindeer." He returned twenty minutes later to explain to Sharett and the delegation that the American government really had no changes to recommend in their proposal to include the Negev within the boundaries of the new Jewish State.

The political victory at the United Nations in late November was unrecognizable by early 1948. Weizmann in London on his way back to Rehovot was called again to New York and found there that the Five Power Commission which was to carry out partition of the Holy Land and which was known as the "Five Lonely Pilgrims" was still marking time. A number of supporters of an independent Jewish State had changed their minds and were now calling at the U.N. for trusteeship.

"The United States was in full flight from partition," wrote Abba Eban, and "was having every sort of nightmare—from Soviet military intervention, to the massive influx of Communist agents in the guise of refugee immigrants to Palestine."

On Weizmann's return to New York, he found that Jewish Agency representatives and others had been exerting such pressure on President Truman that the President had refused to see any of them since November. Truman wrote in his memoirs, *Years of Trial and Hope*: "I do not think I ever had as much pressure and propaganda aimed at the White House. . . . The persistence of a few of the extreme Zionist leaders—actuated by political motives and engaging in political threats—disturbed and annoyed me. . . . Individuals and groups asked me, usually in rather quarrelsome and emotional ways, to stop the Arabs, to keep the British from supporting the Arabs, to furnish American soldiers to do this, that and the other. . . . As the pressure mounted, I found it necessary to give instructions that I did not want to be approached by any more spokesmen for the extreme Zionist case. I was even so disturbed that I put off seeing Dr. Chaim Weizmann. . . ."

Enter Eddie Jacobson of Kansas City, an old friend of President Truman, who during the nineteen twenties had been his partner in an unsuccessful haberdashery.

Eddie Jacobson was not a Zionist. He had never met Weizmann. But Dr. Weizmann was a hero to him, and he sent a telegram to President Truman urging another meeting.

When he received a polite but vague reply from the President, Eddie Jacobson flew to Washington and made his way into the White House, pleading personal business. President Truman was not pleased when he learned the real reason for the visit, saying with some chilliness that he respected Dr. Weizmann, but that a further meeting "would only result in more wrong interpretation." At that moment, Eddie Jacobson had an inspiration. He noticed on President Truman's desk a bust of Andrew Jackson, and said:

"He's been your hero all your life, hasn't he? You've probably read every book there is on Jackson. I remember when we had the store that you were always reading books and pamphlets, and a lot of them were about Jackson. You put this statue in front of the Jackson County Court House in Kansas City when you built it. I have never met the man who has been my hero all my life, but I have studied his past like you have studied Jackson's. He is the greatest Jew alive, perhaps the greatest Jew who ever lived. You yourself have told me that he is a great statesman and a fine gentleman. I am talking about Dr. Chaim Weizmann. He is an old man and a very sick man. He has traveled thousands of miles to see you, and now you put off seeing him. That isn't like you."

They were in the Oval Room of the White House, and the President turned to look out over the rose garden. Eddie Jacobson expected an angry reply. Instead the President said, "All right, you bald-headed son-of-a-bitch, you win," asking that the Appointments Secretary arrange for the reception of Dr. Weizmann.

Eddie Jacobson continued on to New York where he brought the news to Dr. Weizmann, meeting him for the first time. Again Weizmann rose from his sickbed and returned to Washington.

President Truman wrote:

> Dr. Weizmann, by my specific instruction, was to be brought in through the East Gate. There was to be no public announcement. . . . We talked for almost three-quarters of an hour.
>
> Dr. Weizmann was a man of remarkable achievements and personality. His life had been dedicated to two ideals, that of science and that of the Zionist movement. He was past seventy

now and in ill health. He had known many disappointments and
had grown patient and wise in them.

I told him as plainly as I could, why I had at first put off
seeing him. He understood. I explained to him what the basis
of my interest in the Jewish problem was and that my primary
concern was to see justice done without bloodshed. And when he
left my office, I felt that he had reached a full understanding of
my policy and that I knew what it was he wanted.

During their talk, President Truman made a promise to Dr.
Weizmann, that he would work for the establishment and recognition of a Jewish State, and that the Negev should be a part of this.

But the following day, Warren Austin, who was now the American
Ambassador to the United Nations, addressed the Security Council,
requesting that plans for partition be suspended, and pressing for a
special session to work out trusteeship under the U.N. There was
consternation at the Jewish Agency and among Jewry in Palestine
and throughout the world at the apparent abandonment by its fore-
most proponent at the United Nations of the plan for partition
together with a Jewish State. Only Weizmann kept faith, and he
telephoned Eddie Jacobson. He believed that Truman would keep
his promise. According to his own memoirs and Jonathan Daniels's
biography, *The Man of Independence*, the President asked his administrative assistant, Clark Clifford, "How could this have happened? I assured Chaim Weizmann that we were for partition and
would stick to it. He must think I am a plain liar." Truman was as
deeply upset as his assistant had ever seen him. According to
Christopher Sykes, Truman for some time had chaffed at the
"Eastern-oil-dominated policy of his State Department and the
American armed services," and he did not propose to accept this.

Now began another race against time. Weizmann, who had always
been known as a moderate and a conciliator, was inexorable in his
pursuit of the final goal. When Meyer Weisgal telephoned from
Nice at the request of Ben-Gurion to seek Weizmann's views in New
York, Weizmann said shortly, "Proclaim the State no matter what
ensues."

General Marshall, the Secretary of State, a man friendly to the
Jews but concerned that they might not be able to hold out against
the overwhelming Arab superiority, warned against proclamation

now of a Jewish State. The advice was politely rejected, and as Moshe Sharett prepared to take off for Palestine with this news, he was followed to the airport by Weizmann with the plea, "Don't let them weaken, Moshe, it is now or never." On May thirteenth, Dr. Weizmann wrote a letter for delivery by hand next morning asking President Truman for recognition of the Jewish State. The White House asked that the petition be in the name of the representative of the Jewish State, rather than of the Agency, as had been done. A new letter was quickly drafted in Washington by Eliahu Elath in Dr. Weizmann's name as representative of the Jewish State, and sent to the White House in a taxi. While the taxi was on its way, there came news that in Tel Aviv the State of Israel had been proclaimed. At the White House, protocol was in order; Israel was recognized at 5:16 P.M. by President Truman.

He had the last word, which was: "The old Doctor will believe me now."

13/ TO THE SOUTH:

LACHISH AND
THE NEW TOWNS

Rehovot is only about a dozen miles or so south of Tel Aviv, but in 1934 when Weizmann chose it as the site for a scientific institute in memory of his former student David Sieff, it was described as a desolate wasteland without grass or trees. It was then the Gateway to the Negev, the southern desert. Now that Rehovot is watered and blooming and landscaped, the Gateway to the Negev has been moved another fifty miles south to Beersheba, where only a very obstinate man would argue that he was not sitting on the edge of a desert, if not actually in one.

About halfway between Rehovot and Beersheba is Lachish, site of the great walled city which was the southern bastion of the kingdom of Judah and which was taken by the Syrian king Sennacherib after a terrible battle in 701 B.C. Again in 586 B.C., Lachish was besieged and conquered by King Nebuchadnezzar of Babylonia. Now, around archeological excavations known to scholars and museums throughout the world for the picture they give of life and war two and a half millennia ago are fifty-six villages farming a quarter of a million acres in an area that is still known as Lachish.

It is a most successful experiment in comprehensive regional planning. Earlier experiments in mass settlement in Israel had run into difficulty when immigrants from far-flung parts of the world with varied customs and languages found themselves flung together (a hurdle for the older people in spite of crash courses in Hebrew available everywhere). At close quarters, tension and hostility between some of the groups inevitably began to emerge. In the Lachish region, four or five villages, tightly knit communities each sharing a common background and—if from a patriarchal society—perhaps kinship, are grouped around a somewhat larger rural center providing them with an elementary school, a clinic, and with agricultural services including plowing and aerial spraying, crop marketing, a youth club and a cultural center. Each village itself has a kindergarten, a synagogue, a first-aid clinic, the village office and a shop. This means that for the thirty-two private smallholders' moshavim and the sixteen jointly owned communal kibbutzim, purchasing as well as marketing is done coöperatively, with savings on food, feed, fertilizer, water and rural credit available to members of these communities, to the nine educational institutions and farming estates in the area, and to their regional center, the town of Kiryat Gat, the original home of the Philistine giant, Goliath of Gath.

Kiryat Gat, which now has a population of over twenty thousand, expects perhaps forty thousand in the nineteen seventies, and eventually between seventy and eighty thousand. There is a secondary school in the town with a library open to everyone, a large beet-sugar refinery, a cotton gin, five yarn spinning and three weaving mills, furniture and concrete-products factories, a central packing and refrigerating plant for vegetables, and a few small clothing manufacturers. The population of the villages is nearing twenty thousand, growing cotton, sugar beets, sorghum, flower bulbs and a variety of vegetables. There is also dairy farming and the raising of beef cattle with the help of some of the cowhands trained under U.S.

AID's Operation Cowboy. In addition to extensive pasture lands, about seventy thousand acres are under cultivation.

A great advantage of a group of individual differing villages clustered around a rural center is that their inhabitants come to know one another gradually, their children go to school together and integration is simpler this way.

About sixty per cent of the inhabitants of the Lachish area came from Moslem countries, and they have brought with them the—again different but deeply ingrained—ways of life of their homes. But they are proud of the fact that, among them, there is only twenty-five per cent illiteracy, which gives an idea of the problems faced by others of some of the new frontier towns having a more difficult time of it than Lachish.

As elsewhere in the country, almost none of the settlers at Lachish had had any previous experience in farming. A technique called "managed farming" evolved. Each family on arrival was provided with a modest house and its first acre of land so it might grow its own vegetables. Work at fixed wages was provided, helping to cultivate the arable land of the village. At the end of the first year, the settler's individual holding was increased to a bit more than three acres, from which he earned half his income. Wages still accounted for the other half. By the fourth year, the settler had taken over all of his allotment of ten acres, half of it now irrigated. From these he earned all his living. The farm remained under the general direction of the settlement authority.

Thanks to this gradual approach, learning from the mistakes made by other new communities, the regions are able to plan on a large scale because land reserves and funds for development are under national control, put to use through the coördinated efforts of the Jewish Agency Settlement Department, the Ministry of Agriculture and other authorities working through the local center.

The problems solved largely or in part by Kiryat Gat and the Lachish region which it serves are faced by the score of other communities described without mincing words in *21 Frontier Towns* issued by the United Jewish Appeal and The Jewish Agency for Israel, whose pictures and text give a pretty good idea of what life is like in most of the new settlements. First of all, about seventy-five per cent of the people in the new towns and villages come from Moslem countries in North Africa and Asia, some of them "from the most primitive Jewish communities in the world." The Yemenites, who came from one of the most feudal and savagely intolerant states in all the East, are looked upon as attractive, hard-working, highly adaptable and, in general, the exceptions, the pets of Israeli society to which they have contributed much in handicrafts, dance and song. The Yemenites seem to have escaped the faint disrepute with which the majority of Eastern Jews are regarded by the Westerners, but most of the half-million Sephardim whom the Western Jews call "Orientals" labor under this disadvantage, including the majority of the inhabitants of the new settlements. There is not a great deal of mixing between the two groups. Illiteracy ranges from twenty per cent in a new Negev town called Dimona, which is considered very good, through fifty per cent in Safed, to seventy per cent or more in a couple of other towns. Young Nahal members from the more dangerous border settlements are helping by coming into the new villages and towns to teach whole families at a time, in addition to those of school age. And anyone doing military service emerges literate in Hebrew and with a basic grip of his country's and people's history, no matter how little he started with.

The most difficult time comes between the ages of fourteen, with the end of compulsory schooling, and eighteen, when military service begins, years in which there may be casual employment, if any, in some areas. There is often little incentive to take whatever vocational courses may be available, and there are insufficient youth clubs or such tried and true builders of community spirit as young people's bands.

"Most of the towns are drab and dreary to look at and live in," says the UJA and Agency description. "They have a 'frontier-town' look—no public buildings of distinction, no parks, few trees, no gardens. Central shopping centers look crude and shabby. Residential quarters often look like slums, or are slums."

They are also cramped, with not enough space available for the prolific Oriental families who number upwards of six persons to a family in contrast to the national average of 3.7. The non-productive portion of the community may be as high as one-fourth, depending on direct relief and public work projects to create jobs. Tuberculosis, malnutrition, trachoma and skin diseases from Moslem countries where they are endemic were a problem on arrival, and, among the Bnei Israeli, even some elephantiasis from southern India. The incidence of blindness is high. In some communities, the hardier, the more energetic and the skillful citizens tend to leave, so that there have been places with a turnover of more than fifty per cent or occasionally one hundred per cent since 1948—instead of the settlers putting down roots as had been hoped.

When all this is said, the lot of the two hundred thousand who live in the new towns and villages continues to improve, and there is great hope in the approach to development through regional planning now beginning to bear fruit in Lachish and elsewhere, places where immigrants want to settle, ask to be sent, instead of trying to leave.

It is said that the ancient city-state of Lachish gave aid to the Hebrew tribes, known as Habiru, on their trek north to the Promised Land. In the last year of the seventh century B.C., the new king of Assyria, Sennacherib, following the assassination of his father, Sargon, moved against Judah under King Hezekiah. Among the frontier fortresses, only Lachish resisted and the story of its destruction is told in detail by the massive bas-reliefs, executed by the artists of Sennacherib at his command after the descriptions of eyewitnesses, found years later by Sir Henry Layard in his excavations at Tel Nimrud, and now to be seen at the British Museum: siege-engines with battering rams are being pushed up great earthen ramps built against the city's walls while tunnels are being burrowed under the fortifications. Bricks and stones and fire bombs are falling and being hurled from the wall. The air is full of arrows. Impaled bodies are hanging from stakes as the first men and women are being led away captive.

Lachish was the last defense before Jerusalem, which Sennacherib now attacked. But then an extraordinary thing happened. The Prophet Isaiah had predicted that Assyria's armies would march against Jerusalem, but that they would be destroyed by the hand of God. Sennacherib's contemporary account which he had written in cuneiform at Nineveh, his capital, of all his triumphs and victories in this campaign inexplicably announces, not the fall of Jerusalem, but only that the city had paid tribute, "And Hezekiah of Judah . . . him I shut up in Jerusalem his royal city like a caged bird." This is not the record of a conqueror. The clue to what happened was provided by Herodotus of Halicarnassus, among the greatest travelers of the ancient world and a friend of Pericles and Sophocles, who in the fourth century B.C. picked up a strange story from a Temple priest in Egypt: While the army of Sennacherib slumbered, "An army of field mice . . . gnawed through their quivers and their bows, and the handles of their shields, so that on the following day they fled minus their arms and a great number of them fell." Hence a statue of the Egyptian priest-king who also marched against Sennacherib at this time "still stands in Hephaestus' Temple with a mouse in his hand and with the following inscription: 'Look on me and live in safety.'"

Interpreted, this means plague. At the edge of the city of Lachish, the British archeologist James Lesley Starkey found confirmation of this during his excavations in 1938—a mass grave with two thousand human skeletons of besiegers, obviously buried in the greatest haste. The pestilence had overcome a great part of the army before it even reached Jerusalem. The Bible in the Second Book of Kings says only of the delivery of Jerusalem: "And it came to pass that night, that the angel of the Lord went out and smote in the camp of the Assyrians an hundred fourscore and five thousand: and when they arose early in the morning, behold they were all dead corpses. So Sennacherib, King of Assyria, departed, and went and returned and dwelt in Nineveh."

Starkey's excavations of the stratum recording the fall of Lachish to Nebuchadnezzar reveal a surprisingly different technique of siege. What Starkey found were ashes, several yards deep and, after twenty-five hundred years, in places higher than the remains of the fortress walls. According to Werner Keller in *The Bible as History*, Nebuchadnezzar's engineers were without peers in the art of arson. Clearing miles around the fortress of its trees and bushes and anything which would burn, they made a monstrous conflagration. All the olive groves in sight were cut down, and in the ashes are countless charred olive pits. A ring of intense fire must have been kept going for days, until at last the white-hot stones burst and the walls collapsed. Now, only Jerusalem remained. There was famine in the city, the wall was breached and King Zedekiah, who had rebelled against his Babylonian overlords, the successors of Assyria, by Babylo-Assyrian law was forced to watch his children murdered before he himself was blinded and led off into captivity in the second deportation. The royal house of David had come to an end after reigning for four hundred years.

As for the archeologist James Lesley Starkey, he was shot by Arabs at the age of forty-three while traveling from Lachish to Jerusalem, and Keller records this in a curious way: "His death was a tragic case of mistaken identity. In the course of the protracted excavations he had grown a beard and the Arabs took him for a Jew."

14/ BEERSHEBA

Although the 1947 United Nations plan for partition of Palestine
had awarded all of the Negev to Israel, fifteen thousand
Egyptian troops still held large parts of it, including the desert
capital of Beersheba.

Following an Egyptian truce violation, Israel launched Operation
Ten Plagues which cleared the Negev of Egyptian forces except for
a group of two thousand five hundred who were completely surrounded in the north at a place called Faluja, who held out for
some months until repatriated through the good offices of the U.N.
One of the officers negotiating with the Israelis was the young
Egyptian captain, Gamal Abdel Nasser.

It was in this operation that the Israelis moved swiftly all the way south to the small Arab police station and collection of mud huts at a place called Umm Rash Rash on the Gulf of Aqaba, and there raised their flag with the Star of David. They rechristened the place Eilat after a Biblical town with a similar name through which the Israelites had passed in their earliest wanderings. Later, with the copper mines at Timna and the smelters at Ezion-geber, it had become a flourishing city busy with Solomon's trade with Africa and the East.

Writing of the partition of Palestine in 1948, Robert St. John notes that guidebooks of the time gave the population of Beersheba as three thousand, commenting, "The census—if there ever was one—must have been taken on market day when the Bedouins were in town to do a little camel trading and buy an ounce or two of tobacco before vanishing again into the desert heat and dust." Fewer than half that number of inhabitants would be a more likely estimate. Nelson Glueck estimates four hundred.

Beersheba was taken at dawn on the twenty-first of October, 1948. It was a dusty, raggletaggle Arab town of no surpassing interest, though of great antiquity, chiefly important as a provincial administrative center during the days of the Mandate, and earlier as an Ottoman administrative and trading center for the Negev's Bedouin tribes.

Now it is a boom town. The population is nearing seventy thousand. There are a couple of dozen new factories producing potash from the desert, asphalt from the deposits around the Dead Sea, bricks, fertilizers, a plant making fine ceramics from the Negev clays, and a score of other manufactures. Instead of a single comfortable place to stay, HIAS House, built a few years ago by this American philanthropic organization especially to provide a shelter at the edge of the desert where scientists could live and work on the arid-zone projects which had brought them here, there are now four new hotels, including one called the Desert Inn which has a Nabataean Room named after the ancient Negev civilization, and which launched itself on a public in search of desert glamour with a much-ballyhooed camel race in which the beasts did get from one side of the field to the other, but seemed a little confused as to what they were supposed to do.

There is also in this boom town a night club called The Last Chance which has been described as "existentialist." There is a grain elevator, a cultural center and an archeological museum, a new synagogue towering over the desert with emphasis on vertical louvers acting as sun-breaks against the glare.

A photograph of the entire Jewish population of Beersheba in 1923 shows three young men and four young women, all apparently in their twenties or perhaps early thirties, all four women with their hair bobbed after the fashion of the period. Another picture of the Palestine police's three-man Jewish Security Force for the area that same year reveals the uniform for this hot though dry post was a long-skirted tunic with cummerbund and bandoleer, jodhpurs, puttees and boots, and the tall black astrakhan military headgear inherited from the Turks and called a *kalpak*. Within three years after Israeli forces had taken Beersheba, the first fifteen thousand Jewish settlers had arrived. Many of them were immigrants from the Arab countries, the Orientals who were to play such a large part in the colonization of the Negev, for which the Prime Minister David Ben-Gurion foresaw in those years, and still predicts, a population for the Negev of two million. A Tournalayer machine, which looks like a monster piece of yellow earth-moving equipment with a great snout, was brought to Beersheba to fabricate concrete dwellings. By the time the new Beersheba was five years old, there were three thousand and six hundred new apartments and six hundred new businesses. Thirty thousand trees and two hundred thousand saplings had been planted in a green belt ringing the city to protect it against the hot desert wind often accompanied by a driving storm of fine sand, known as the *sharav* in Hebrew, or more usually by the Arabic name of *khamsin*.

The burly and bustling mayor, David Toviahu, pressed for planting and building, building and planting. Times had changed since the Turks cut down everything in sight to fuel their wood-burning locomotives and once built a special spur of their Damascus-to-Hejaz railway to take out a great stand of oak and beech.

By the time the new Beersheba was ten years old, it was acquiring a reputation for bragging about its population of forty thousand and for predicting a hundred thousand. Ninety-eight per cent of the citizens now had permanent housing and ninety-five per cent of them had permanent employment.

Americans contributed their share to this repopulation of the desert, something which began as an effort to make use of that sixty per cent of the country which lies in the south and whose greatest resource seemed to be sand. Israel had to find room for the immigrants pouring into the country with the Ingathering of the Exiles and the Negev was part of the answer. It also turned into a sort of Alaskan Gold Rush at 120° Farenheit.

HIAS House, built for the scientists come to make the desert bloom again and to discover how man can most effectively live and work here, was the contribution of the Hebrew Sheltering and Immigrant Aid Society, organized in 1884 on Ellis Island in New York Harbor to help the stream of refugees coming to the New World to escape persecution and poverty in Europe.

Another American contribution in Beersheba was the district hospital donated by the AFL-CIO's International Ladies Garment Workers Union in honor of its president, David Dubinsky. The hospital is a big one, light and airy, surrounded by lawns, date palms, carefully nurtured shrubs and saplings, and with the larger buildings connected with pavilions, labs, sleeping quarters and other outbuildings by long walks open at the sides but covered against the sun, and the rain in case there should be any, down which ride the nurses on their white bicycles. The nurses school at this central Negev Hospital, according to the matron, Arima Cohen Litman, has about a hundred students, of whom five per cent are men, and most of these from North Africa, where there is less disinclination to accept a job as a male nurse. Two Bedouin brothers were trained as nurses, one working with Dr. B. J. Ben-Assa, head of Medical Services for Bedouin, and one serving in the operating theater here in the hospital. Among the nomadic tribes, the hospital was winning acceptance and persuading an increasing number of Bedouin mothers to come in to be delivered of their children. The twice-weekly Bedouin clinic run by Dr. Ben-Assa and his colleagues on camel-market days was doing a land-office business.

All nurses must be at least seventeen years old, with a minimum of eight years of elementary school demanded of the practical nurses, who account for sixty per cent of the students, and ten years of schooling preferred, before they begin their eighteen months of training. Here again, most of the students come from North African or Middle Eastern countries, with anywhere from eight to twelve children in the family who may find it not always easy to make a decent living. In nursing school, all necessities, even pocket money, are supplied. Qualified nurses working for their R.N. must have at least eleven years' schooling, though graduation from high school is preferred. Some of the girls from kibbutzim may be thirty or so, and even the newcomers a little older than expected, for ten years in a North African school may be the equivalent of eight years in Israel. Most of the nursing students, women and men, would like to take medical studies, but of the six hundred who apply only seventy or eighty are admitted each year. Similar nursing and medical courses for African and Asian students are given, with the assistance of the World Health Organization of the U.N. at Asaf Harofeh Hospital near Ramle and at the Hadassah-Hebrew University Hospital in Jerusalem. Nurses are required to do only a single year of military service, though some elect to go into army training and join the paratroopers' nursing corps.

Anything from Beersheba south, or north, east or west, for that matter, is training grounds for archeologists. In the never-ending studies of the supposed "absorptive capacity" of Palestine for settlers —to use the wretched official phrase inherited by Israeli English from the Mandatory government—it was described by a succession of specialists and commissions as approximately nil. Probably no single man has done more to controvert this assessment than the American rabbi, scholar and archeologist, Nelson Glueck. His four decades of exploration in this desert that even Deuteronomy calls a "howling wilderness" has shown that it was populous and cultivated in the past. At intervals, invading armies destroyed, slaughtered, burned and carried all they could away with them, leaving a once-prosperous land to the encroachment of the desert and the nomads. Then there would be long breaks in settlement and civilization until new peoples, new cultures could establish themselves.

The Negev, from the pre-Bronze Age known as Chalcolithic some five thousand years B.C. down through the decline of the flourishing Byzantine cities of the mid-seventh century A.D., had known towns protected by fortresses and with large populations, villages culti- vating thousands of acres of farmland, intricate, and so far unsur- passed, systems of water conservation and irrigation. Highways running through the desert connected the continents. All this was in a land which in latter centuries was known chiefly for its desolation. And all this could be done again.

Nelson Glueck, whose work among the sands of the Negev and Transjordania, whose probing of the past has helped throw much light on the exciting possibilities of Israel's future in her southland, was the rabbi to deliver the inaugural benediction, partly in Hebrew, for President Kennedy that snowy day in 1961: "May the Lord be gracious unto thee." As president of the Hebrew Union College-Jewish Institute of Religion in Cincinnati, Rabbi Glueck is a spiritual leader of Reformed Judaism in the United States, and has seen to it that the archeological school in Jerusalem with which he is associated has a small Reformed synagogue. At last count, this was only the third such congregation in the country permitted by the Rabbinate, which is Orthodox and theoretically does not recognize Conservative or Reform Jewish marriages or divorces, governing the majority of their co-religionists in the United States, Canada and Britain.

To his archeological work when he arrived in Palestine in 1927, Glueck brought an array of talents. Entering Hebrew Union College himself at the age of fourteen, he had taken his bachelor's degree there and another at the University of Cincinnati, enrolled at Heidelberg and Berlin where he took his doctorate, then studied Assyrian and Ethiopic before going on to work for three years under Professor William Foxwell Albright who was Director of the American School of Oriental Research in Palestine. The science of pottery identification, a technique available only in cruder forms to the earlier great archeologists, had attained a degree of great accuracy in the second quarter of this century, and now, working with Professor Albright for three years, Glueck perfected his own knowledge of these sherds of the civilizations which had gone before. "Wood disappears, stone crumbles, glass decays, metal corrodes," Glueck has said. "Only pottery lasts forever. . . . Man's discovery of how to make and bake earthenware vessels in which water could be carried and food prepared and stored ranks in importance not far behind his learning the kindly uses of fire."

A good reporter as well as a good student, Glueck's admiration for the precision of Albright's work was great. He describes Albright's conclusion from some sherd found at the site of the Biblical Dedir in southwestern Palestine that this community had been inhabited from 2000 B.C. to 600 B.C., only to make the careful correction of his dates after four years and many thousands of sherds more; the inhabitants had really lived there from 2200 to 586 B.C.

"I have gathered fragments of pottery from the surfaces of one or another ancient site which fairly shout out the periods of history they belong to," Glueck has written in his *Rivers in the Desert*. "It is as if they had been waiting for ages for someone to come along and notice them and pick them up, so that they could describe with eloquent pride the time and quality of their kingdoms. I can assure you that the archeologist regards each artifact with feelings akin to personal affection."

Pottery may be fragile and easily shattered, but pieces will remain, seemingly almost imperishable. From them, and using a brilliantly inductive imagination, Glueck recreated the life of the Negev, of that portion of it just across the way in Transjordan which the Jordanians also call the Negev, and of the Sinai Peninsula which shares a greal deal in common with them both. In the greater Negev, Glueck has found more than fifteen hundred sites which once were inhabited.

The Bible was his guide and his principle tool. Of inestimable importance was the location of water holes, wells, springs and ancient cisterns and oases. "It is axiomatic that wherever there is or once was water in the Negev or elsewhere in the Fertile Crescent," wrote Glueck, "it is possible to find remains of ancient settlements."

Glueck reasoned that the travels through the Negev of the Patriarch Abraham and his family as briefly told in Genesis must have taken place between the twenty-first and nineteenth centuries B.C., for his would have been a slowly moving caravan dependent on the peaceful villages throughout the country at that time. Later, it was ravished by the kings of the East, leaving it a devastated and uncultivated wasteland from the eighteenth to the eleventh centuries B.C., inhabitated only by the predatory nomads who "were always the only ultimate victors, who had only to bide their time in order to win every war." Also, it was clear to Glueck that the Exodus of the Children of Israel from Egypt led by Moses could not have taken place before the thirteenth century B.C. since it was then that the strong, fortified kingdoms of Edom to the south of the Dead Sea and Moab to the east arose. Both denied passage along the King's

Highway through the Transjordan to the weaker Israelites, though these explicitly promised to turn neither to the right nor to the left of the path, nor to enter the fields of the overlords of these lands. And so the Israelites must take a long, a circuitous route in their forty years' wandering through the wilderness, skirting Edom and Moab to the east, and finally entering the Promised Land through Gigal and Jericho.

Negev means "south land" or "arid land," a long triangle shaped rather like a flint arrowhead pointing downward. It is about seventy miles at its widest and a hundred and twenty to its tip on the Gulf of Aqaba where lie the modern ports of Eilat and Aqaba and Solomon's ancient port of Ezion-geber.

What Dr. Glueck has called "the amazing accuracy of the historical memory of the Bible" led him from the puzzling description in Deuteronomy of the Promised Land as a place "whose stones are iron and out of whose hills thou canst dig brass" to the correct supposition that this last was probably a mistranslation for copper. Coupling this with his confidence in the reliability of the Biblical location of Solomon's port of Ezion-geber given in the Book of Kings as "beside Eloth, on the shore of the Red Sea, in the land of Edom," he systematically explored the shoreline of the Gulf of Aqaba, the eastern arm of the Red Sea known in the Bible by the same name. There in the Wadi Arabah at a spot known to the Arabs as Khirbet Nahas, or "Copper Ruin," which may well be the City of Copper mentioned in the Bible, Glueck some two thousand five hundred years later rediscovered Solomon's great port, the smelters, copper and iron mines which were a major source of his legendary wealth—"not only Israel's only seaport, but also, for its day and age, one of the largest, if not the largest, of metallurgical centers in existence."

Nelson Glueck, whose meticulous studies and findings in the Negev have literally changed both the face of Israel and our knowledge of her history, writes: "Those people are essentially of little faith who seek through archeological corroboration of historical source material in the Bible to validate its religious teachings and spiritual insights. The archeological explorer in Bible lands must be aware of the fact that as important as the Bible is for historical information, it is definitely not primarily a chronicle of history, as we understand that term today. It is above all concerned with true religion and only secondarily with illustrative records. Even if the latter had suffered through faulty transmission or embellishments, the purity and primacy of the Bible's innermost message would not thereby be diminished."

"As a matter of fact, however, it may be stated categorically that no archeological discovery has ever controverted a Biblical reference."

North from the Gulf of Aqaba, or south from Jerusalem, west from the Dead Sea, east from the Mediterranean ports, or almost anywhere across the country and from other lands, the old Biblical roads, the caravan routes and nomad trails, the modern Israeli roads converge on Beersheba. If HIAS House and the Desert Inn and the other caravansaries are not full of archeologists, they are sheltering arid-zone specialists working on a score of other problems.

Working in a group of Chalcolithic suburbs around Beersheba, of the period when bronze and copper were used as well as stone, but before the use of iron, Jean Perrot and other French and Israeli archeologists excavating these, in particular one called Tel Abu Matar, uncovered large underground villages with rooms ten or fifteen by twenty feet carved from the tawny loess soil, entered by vertical shafts six feet deep with handholds and footholds, or by tunnels in the side of the hill on which the village was built. Ceilings were so low that the inhabitants must have been either very short or moved about crouching. They were a civilized people allied to other agricultural communities found from the Israeli highlands down to Egypt. They cultivated wheat, barley and lentils, had domesticated sheep, goats and oxen, worshipped a fertility goddess and practiced some form of magic.

They made distinctive earthenware, using a simple potter's wheel to produce elegant chalices and bowls of basalt, which is a difficult stone to manage yet which was smoothly cut and as little as two-fifths of an inch thick. They wore mother-of-pearl pendants, amulets, rings of copper and bracelets of ivory and stone. They made little clay figures of sheep, apparently intended as prayers to multiply their flocks. Child sacrifice was practiced to propitiate the gods and bring abundance. Perforated, pear-shaped clubheads designed for cracking skulls were made by village smiths of a very pure copper probably taken from the mines of the great trough called the Wadi Arabah leading southward to Solomon's smelters.

The villagers of Tel Abu Matar made statuettes of bone and ivory, too. A toggle pin well carved in the form of a pelican has been found and carvings of men and women of attenuated form and great circular sunken eyes high in the head, the men's faces framed with holes in which hair might be stuffed to make a beard.

While archeologists have been learning how man used to live in Israel, from the Late Mesolithic Natufian cave dwellers of Mount Carmel, whose ancestors more than ten thousand years ago had already tamed the dog and learned to harvest seed grasses, through their relatives living west of Lake Hula, whose "burial of decapitated bodies in a walled pit showed an unexpected degree of organized ritual," according to Dr. Shimshon Applebaum's pamphlet "Archeology in Israel" in the *Israel Today* government series, down to the Chalcolithic civilization, which was apparently overrun in the thirty-second century B.C., through the Bronze Age walled cities of the Canaanites, to the Age of Abraham, seeking what lessons of conservation, irrigation and cultivation can be learned from the past, still other scientists are at work in Beersheba at the Negev Institute for Arid Zone Research, seeking contemporary solutions to many of the same problems. At any one time there are at the Arid Zone Research Institute between sixty and eighty engineers, physiologists, physicians, biologists, agronomists, architects, meteorologists, climatologists, geologists, experts on soils, on desalination and other fields applicable to the Negev. Solution of common problems will help not only Israel, and enable her to give the technical assistance to neighboring Arab countries which she has so often offered, but will be applicable to other arid zones, which cover a large part of the world's surface. In 1956, for example, UNESCO, the United Nations Educational, Scientific and Cultural Organization, launched as a major project support for arid-zone research and experimental work in Israel, Egypt, India and Pakistan. Now, at the Institute in Beersheba, there is a sixteen-acre Ecological Desert Garden with plants from the Australian Out Back, the American prairie, the Soviet steppes and Central Asian deserts, the South African veldt, Israel's own Negev and other arid zones whose flora has either shown or proven to be of potential economic value, supplying food and fodder, fibers, oils and resins, essential oils, medicines, cover for growing dune and desert in cut-over lands, or simply for aesthetic reasons, ornamental and shade plants for desert towns.

At the Institute in Beersheba they are off to a good start, with much of the guidance, as usual, coming from the Bible. Dr. Joseph Witz, an Israeli authority on forestry, has explained: "The first tree which Abraham planted in the soil of Beersheba was a tamarisk. Following his example we have planted two million of them in this area. Abraham did absolutely the right thing. For the tamarisk is one of the few trees . . . that will flourish at all in the south where the annual rainfall is under six inches."

In addition to research on indigenous plants, introduction and acclimatizing of exotic plants is an important part of the Beersheba Institute's work. Work in collaboration with Hebrew University's Agricultural Research Station at Rehovot on best agricultural techniques in the Negev using the available supplies of water, usually highly brackish or saline, have produced some answers: groves of date palms, highly resistant to salinity, planted around each salty spring or well in places like the Wadi Arabah are a good investment economically. The reed *Juncus*, which flourishes in brackish and saline waters, can be used for the manufacture of paper. Saline water irrigates fruit trees, sugar beets and other commercial crops, and the Institute is proud of growing roses with extremely salty water.

Ritchie Calder, in his brief, lucid report on the importance of the sciences and their application in this same *Israel Today* series, describes other coöperative efforts with the research station, such as the anchoring of the roving sand dunes which had laid waste a quarter of a million acres in Israel and threatened many more. Not only were tamarisks, eucalyptus and acacia planted, but so were pulses, hay and vegetables. With sufficient irrigation and a little fertilizer, the dunes became productive in three or four years. Even sea water, it was found, could be used to irrigate the dunes, passing through them and flushing out the poisonously concentrated salts which had collected with the passing of time.

Prime Minister Ben-Gurion had asked his scientists to "Harness the sun and sweeten the sea." Israel is one of the four countries where this harnessing of the sun is a major project, the others being the United States, the Soviet Union and France. The two thousand kilowatts of heat falling every year on every square mile of Israel have given rise to the tantalizing thought that the sunshine striking the Negev alone furnishes as much heat as all Israel imports annually in the form of fuel. Simple, darkened flat-plate collectors such as are seen now in Israel have long been manufactured commercially in California and Florida, and under suitable conditions can supply enough heat to serve a family's needs for hot water. The problem has been more efficient collection and storage, and the Arid Zone Institute has been pursuing methods devised by Dr. Henry Tabor of Israel's National Physical Laboratory whereby solar energy can be used to operate refrigerators and air conditioners; also, by providing far larger collectors of solar energy in the form of shallow solar ponds whose bottoms are painted black. A pilot plant producing a ton of steam daily has been at work for some time at the Institute, using parabolic mirrors following the sun and intensifying its rays, while a Beersheba factory using this principle in the manufacture of insecticides and fertilizers is, according to UNESCO, the world's first sun-operated industry.

A permanent center for the study of environmental physiology has been established at the Negev Institute, concerned with the influence of climate, and especially heat, on man and beast, and the adaptations which we and the other species can make to cope with this. What we call climate is the combination of temperature, radiation, humidity, air pressure and air movement, and, in the case of the desert, sand and dust. In man, as a warm-blooded animal, compensation for changes in climate is made largely through his body's complex heat-regulating mechanisms. Just how this happens is of special importance in Israel, settling large numbers of immigrants from lands with a variety of dissimilar climates in the Negev with its own peculiar extremes.

The maintenance of the body's equilibrium, called homeostatis, in the intense heat, and sometimes at night the intense cold, of the desert is the subject of much research at the Negev Institute. The results of heat are tested on volunteers from the armed forces, the Institute's own staff, pregnant women mainly from the southern port of Eilat, the Bedouin of the desert, and laborers at the Dead Sea Works in Sodom, one thousand two hundred and eighty-six feet below sea level. It was discovered that living in a desert climate changes the acid-base balance in man's body fluids. Sweat, whose evaporation is a key factor in maintaining man's bodily temperature under extreme heat, is found to lose in sodium and gain in potassium as the individual becomes accustomed to the desert climate, even though there is great variation among individuals, whether acclimated or not. Those acclimated have shown higher levels of the hormone aldosterone. It has been discovered that a protein called fibrin, which is formed in blood coagulation, is destroyed to a markedly greater degree under heat stroke, heat prostration, exercise, emotional stress or surgical operations, and this may cause severe hemorrhaging and prolonged coagulation, with a possible depletion in the body's supply of the parent enzyme of fibrinogen. Most or all of these studies will have a bearing on settlement in the Negev.

For long, an article of faith in the Israeli Army was something known as Water Discipline, in which a soldier was taught to drink little, given two canteens daily, one of which he must use to wash and shave. This dogma was thrown out the window after a controlled experiment in the late fifties by Dr. Ezra Zohar of the same climatic research unit who marched twenty soldiers in three groups from one end of Israel to the other, from Metula at the extreme northern border with Lebanon down to Eilat on the Gulf of Aqaba, doing twenty-five kilometres a day for six hours daily. One group was given the regular ration of a single canteen to drink, another group all the water it wanted, and the third group obliged to take more water than the men wanted. Further, drink was restricted to a single kind for each soldier, water, pop, cool, hot, cold, fizzy and alcoholic. Kidney and lung functions were tested carefully and perspiration was measured, an average of 10.5 litres daily in the desert. At the end of the march, doctors concluded that light, cool but not cold drinks, slightly sweetened and with lemon juice added, won hands down. And the men had performed far more efficiently with all the water they wanted instead of being rationed.

The desert from Beersheba south abounds with a great variety of animals which have evolved individual adaptations to this barren land. Where by day there is apparently no life or even shadow under the pitiless sun, the desert comes alive at night with fireflies and fire-beetles, leopard moths, white with black dots, and the hawk moths which hover like humingbirds, pipistrel bats (*Pipistrellus nathusii*) and the larger horshoe bat (*Rhinolophus ferrumequineum*). Among the nocturnal rodents are the gerbils, one of whom was named for Lord Allenby (*Gerbillus Allenbyi*) and all of which are stocky with long hairy tails, short necks and heads, large ears and saucer-like eyes; the whiskery, fat, red-brown sand rats (*Psammomys obesus*), popping out of their burrows, and the leaping jerboa, the commonest species of which bears the fine name of *Jaculus jaculus*— all coming out in their countless thousands searching for food in the nighttime desert. The snakes also usually sleep during the hot desert days, emerging at night to hunt for small rodents or birds, lizards or other prey. Of the thiry-four species of snakes known in Israel, seven are venomous, not counting the Egyptian cobra (*Naja have*) which is common enough in its home territory and may be assumed to slip occasionally across the border. It is extremely poisonous, and sometimes thought to be the asp that killed Cleopatra. A more likely candidate, according to Dr. Heinrich Mendelssohn, Professor of the Hebrew University's Department of Zoölogy in Tel Aviv where he maintains a collection of Israeli fauna, would be the horned viper (*Aspis cerastes*), a sidewinder widespread through North Africa and Arabia and in Israel in the Arabah depression, which can sink swiftly out of sight by flattening its sides and throwing sand over its back with a lateral motion of its ribs. It is about two feet long, yellowish brown, with largish brown spots almost converging into bands on its back, and horns over its eyes, as have some of our rattlesnakes, which give it a distinctly malevolent expression. It is difficult to imagine Cleopatra applying one to her bosom.

Only one poisonous snake is common, the Palestine viper (*Vipera xanthina palaestinae*), which bites only if trodden on or touched by accident, and which is seldom fatal.

On a wall of one of the Negev Institute's buildings is a plaque commemorating the donation in 1959 "in token of cultural brotherhood" by the American Special Cultural Program for Israel of a water-desalination pilot plant. This works by a process known as electrodialysis which interposes in either salt or brackish water a series of special membranes through which the saline solution must pass. Two electrodes immersed in the water trap the salts it carries in the form of electrically charged particles called ions and the water emerges salt-free on the far side. After a series of experiments and test runs, it was considered feasible to construct a compact desalination apparatus "only a little larger than a large radio cabinet" which would supply a household with a thousand litres or one thousand and fifty-six quarts of drinking water daily, using an ordinary electrical outlet as its source of power. A pilot desalination plant was built at Eilat using Israel's own Zarchin modification of transforming salt water into sweet water through distillation by freezing the residual brine which yields substantially salt-free ice. In the next step, after negotiations between Israel and the United States—conducted in part by the indefatigable, meticulous and quietly imaginative Ambassador Ellsworth Bunker, in between his sure-footed progress toward a solution of the Dominican crisis and his appointment as American Ambassador to Saigon—the United States agreed to assist Israel in the establishment of a desalination plant using nuclear power which by the early nineteen seventies will provide Israel with substantial quantities of fresh water while producing power at the same time.

The Israelis have overlooked no possible means of augmenting their water supply. To them, water literally is life for the nation.

In 1943, the Jewish Agency for Palestine had set up Negev outposts, called Guvlot, Revivin and Beit Eshel, where three hardy, sceptical bands of pioneers were given the job of experimenting with wet and dry farming in the desert and drilling for water. They found the water, too brackish to drink, but adequate for irrigation. They relearned the ancient lesson of conserving some of the torrential rains which fell sporadically during three months of the year. Their conclusion was that settlements like theirs could cultivate the Negev.

Three years later—under the old Ottoman law which provided in effect that the authorities might not tear down a man's house if it were completed and the roof already in place—eleven Tower and Stockade Settlements were constructed during a single night along Negev frontiers and in other strategic spots. Convoys of trucks moved out carrying skeletons of wooden stockades, pre-assembled watch towers, lumber, bricks, cement, hardware and tools to be used by volunteers from the nearest Jewish settlements, working through the night and the following day, repelling Arab attacks if necessary and, by the next evening, moving off with the trucks and leaving a reasonably completed village, a powerful light atop the watchtower illuminating the new settlement, now inhabited by a number of determined young men and women. An old photograph of such a settlement shows a rectangular wooden watch tower which looks to be twenty-five to thirty feet tall, rather like an old U.S. Army fort in Indian country, with an overhanging observation platform, one-storey buildings around it, the first saplings planted and a couple of playpens with infants in front of the tower. Sufficient water was supplied so that each of the eleven instant settlements could irrigate fifty acres of land, supplied through one hundred and five miles of six-inch piping which had originally been used in London for fire-fighting during the Nazi blitz.

Anything which shows any promise of producing water is tried. An Australian pilot was hired to seed clouds with silver dioxide in an effort to produce rain, inconclusive so far as I know. Tel Aviv sewage waters are being treated for irrigation further south. Through an ingenious process worked out by the national water-planning board TAHAL and the Weizmann Institute, even the source of the sixteen-mile Yarkon River, a spring no bigger than a swimming hole, is tapped during the winter rainy season, stored and released for irrigation during drier times.

The greatest addition in recent years to the country's water supply was made at the very end of the Six Day War when Israeli troops occupied the Golan Heights from whose deep bunkers Syrian artillery had shelled the Israeli settlements below them intermittently for the past nineteen years. Here, near the village of Baniyas in Syria and unscathed by the fighting, is Tapline Pumping Station 530, part of the one-thousand-forty-mile Trans-Arabian pipeline owned by Aramco, the Arabian American Oil Company's pipeline running from its fields in Saudi Arabia to the Lebanese port of Sidon on the Mediterranean, capable of carrying three hundred and sixty thousand barrels of oil daily. The Israelis did not cut the pipeline, but after the Syrians got around to shutting it off some time after the fighting stopped, they began to lose transit revenues amounting to some millions of dollars. More important to the Israelis than the oil was the water here. At the edge of this sparsely cultivated Syrian plateau, almost all of whose inhabitants had fled before the advancing Israeli columns, where an occasional extinct volcano looking like part of a moonscape only serves to accentuate the desolation, the village of Baniyas lies on a flank of Mount Hermon on the border of Syria and Lebanon. Fifty yards away, the River Banias flows cold and clear from the cliff face before plunging to join the Jordan River and on for fifteen miles into the Sea of Galilee two thousand feet below. Both the river and the village were named after the god Pan to whom there was once a shrine here.

Other tributaries of the Jordan are the Hasbani River whose flow is seasonal, carrying the melted snows of Mount Hermon to the Kibbutz Dan in Israel three miles west of the village of Hasbani, and the little Dan River itself, fed by springs. Altogether, it is believed that control of these new sources of water should add another third to the eighty-five-billion gallons pumped annually from the Sea of Galilee, and should reduce the salinity of that lake's waters, fed by hot springs.

Also, for the first time in two decades, the upper Jordan could now be dredged along its four-mile course between the Daughters of Jacob Bridge and the Sea of Galilee. One bank had always been in Israeli territory, but it was impossible to bring in heavy equipment under the guns of Syrian fortifications two hundred yards away. Five great bulldozers and a crane scooping thick black clay from the river bank uncovered new springs whose waters were added to those of the Jordan.

Beersheba is scantily endowed with Biblical landmarks, but the municipality, or at any rate tourist guides, have done what they could to make up for this deficiency. Visitors are taken to inspect a rather decrepit hole known as Abraham's Well, thoughtfully dug by the Turks during their administration. There is a great variety of tamarisk trees planted by Abraham to show credulous visitors, though no one has explained the survival of such a tree for nearly four thousand years. I personally prefer to single out a large one just opposite Abraham's Well since this is the most convenient.

For those who have had their fill of the archeological museum and the Ecological Desert Garden, the tourist brochures offer the Monday and Thursday Bedouin camel market where you can "surprise your friends by buying them a baby camel," or, in the words of the Sonol touring guide, "We could stop at SHEIKH SULEIMAN'S Tent-Village, the largest colony of settled Beduin in the country, something like 'Israel's Red Indian Reservation,' where the tourist is sure to get some really swanky desert-romance snaps to take home." I don't recall having seen a baby camel for sale, but the last time we visited the market, a grown-up camel cost the equivalent of fifty to seventy dollars, a donkey about seventeen dollars, a fat sheep thirty-three dollars and a goat a little less than two dollars. The Bedouin who brought their camels and other livestock to the market were without exception wearing the traditional Arab headdress, usually a white *keffieh* bound with the simple black cord called an *egal* and, often, the full camel's hair mantle called an *abayeh*. Women wore ample dark-blue robes covering their heads and drawn across their faces, already half hidden by festoons of silver coins. Some of the Sons of the Desert were drinking orange pop and listening to transistor radios. Everyone exchanged gossip and news of the tribes, as important a function of the market as trading.

Another good reason for coming to town on market days was to call at the Bedouin clinics run by Dr. B. J. Ben-Assa, who has published in the journal of the Israel Medical Association a summary of his and his colleagues' findings during seven years' service in the Negev. All of them worked easily in Bedouin Arabic. In this time, reported the doctor, he had yet to see a single case of breast cancer. Venereal diseases were close to non-existent in his survey of twenty-one-hundred Bedouin ambulatory patients. Tuberculosis was most common, with other respiratory troubles accounting for 13.2 per cent of the diseases encountered. Skin diseases, especially impetigo, followed with 9.8 per cent. Diseases of the heart and blood vessels were relatively rare. Contagious diseases and diseases caused by parasites together accounted for another 14.5 per cent. Mental illness was surprisingly low, at two per cent, but the survey reported that the only patients who came to the clinic were those who had "failed to get a remedy from the dervishes," and that the true incidence was undoubtedly far higher. The symptoms of nineteen per cent of the twenty-one hundred patients were classified as undefined. Most Bedouin patients, the survey reported, refused to give blood for tests and, when they did so, complained for years of pain and weakness at the spot where they had been punctured.

Sterility among Bedouin women was only 3.6 per cent, but fear of sterility was great, including that of mothers of eight children who were deeply worried, and of a fifteen-year-old wife who had been married for two months and came to the clinic to complain. Many women patients were reluctant to take off their clothes, and even if they agreed time often prevented complete undressing and examination because they wore so many garments, often sewed together at the neck and ankles. Other difficulties encountered included the four separate names of each Bedouin patient, pronounced differently

and written differently on different occasions. Age had to be estimated. Descriptions of complaints were sometimes mysterious: "a
rocking liver" or a "completely open back" or "My womb has
moved."

Some of the Bedouin who come to the camel market in Beersheba
are Negro, descendants of slaves originally brought up from Arabia,
the Sudan or perhaps Somalia by their Arab masters. Interested to
learn more about these Negro Israelis, I called on Eleanor and
Mordechai Arzielli, he being the Negev correspondent for the largest
of the Israeli Hebrew morning newspapers, *Haaretz*, with stringers
throughout his sizable territory and who knows as much about the
comings and goings in this sandy triangle as anyone I have met.
Mordechai, a shortish but trim type, merry and energetic, who
seemed to be all over the Negev at the same time, told me of the
Negro Bedouin tribe of Abu Blal who had roamed this area for
the past hundred years, and whose Sheikh Salman had died the
previous Friday. He was about seventy. None of the non-Negro
Bedouin leaders had gone to his funeral, according to Arzielli, because of an Arab proverb which says that a slave shall never become
a sheikh.

There were something like twenty thousand Bedouin in Israel
after the partition, and later perhaps another hundred thousand
across the borders in Jordan, Egypt, Saudi Arabia and the other
neighboring states. The previous year, a delegation of African Moslem Ministers from the government of the Republic of Chad visiting
Sheikh Salman asked him, with the independence of the African
countries, if there had been any change in his position as a Negro
leader. He replied no, things were much as before except the bride
price was a little higher.

Many of the Israeli black Bedouin bear the name of Abd or Abed
or Abdo, all meaning "slave," as in the name of the former king of
Jordan, Abdullah, or "slave of God." The last Israeli born a slave
was Chard el Rijilat, who died in the Negev in 1964, at the age of
eighty-one or eighty-two, with an X branded on his right cheek, the
mark of his bondage.

It seems hard to remember now that the ancient Hebrews were
slaveholders, even as were their neighbors and the Greeks and
Romans and early Christians. In Israel and Judah the economy

favored hiring day labor rather than maintaining slaves except for those relatively few in domestic or Temple service, or those sent to join the gangs of forced laborers in the great public works like Solomon's mines. It seemed equally strange to be sitting with Eleanor and Mordechai Arzielli in their attractive house in a new suburb of Beersheba, walls hung with the work of good modern Israeli and European painters including two by Rouault and Raoul Dufy, and all the while discussing the continuing of chattel slavery just across the border.

There had been a continuing protest, first by France and Britain as African Colonial powers and then by the succeeding independent African states, against slave dealers from Saudi Arabia abducting their citizens or enticing them through African agents posing as Moslem missionaries and offering pilgrimage to Mecca and Medina, or simply buying servants or children from impoverished pilgrims. "These unfortunate children are thus converted into living traveler cheques by callous pilgrims," said the Lagos *Morning Post* for November 4, 1961, in its demand that the Nigerian government do something about Nigerian children who were reported variously to be enslaved, or, on the other hand, only to be "stranded" and working under "hard conditions." The newspaper recalled a decree by the late King Ibn Saud, then unrepealed, entitled, "Instructions Concerning Traffic in Slaves," quoting the query in a book on slavery by C. W. W. Greenidge: "Is it conceivable that any government would legislate in such detail to protect slaves if there were no slaves in the country to protect?"

Slavery was officially abolished in Saudi Arabia not long after this, but reports continued to reach the United Nations and the outside world of continuing, if somewhat diminished, traffic there. According to the British Anti-Slavery Society's reports in 1967, traffic in slaves out of West Africa had actually increased, and there were an estimated two million slaves throughout the world.

Hashish, not people, according to Mordechai Arzielli, was the most profitable item of contraband now being run through Israel. In the bootleg business, razor blades were still a hot item, but the real money in the Holy Land, as everywhere, lay in narcotics. This was a service largely conducted by the Bedouin who had cousins and uncles and family on either side of every frontier. Hashish, which comes from the same plant *Sativa* as the American marijuana or the Indian hemp, is brought by camel caravan from Lebanon down through Jordan and Israel to Egypt, the best customer in the area, though a little was sold in Israel itself, where young sports, including visiting Americans, smoking marijuana in Jaffa or Haifa were occasionally picked up by the Israeli police. The best seller at the time we talked was Lucky Horseshoe, a green package of hashish-and-tobacco cigarettes wrapped in waterproof tar paper convenient for submerging by the sackful in the sea off Aqaba until collected by a smuggling craft. Amounts are small by the standards of the Latin Americas supplying the United States, or of the Far Eastern countries exporting opium. Sixty-six pounds of hashish valued at twenty-six and a half thousand dollars is the most I have heard of in Israel, that recovered in 1966 by Detective Shalom Portal of the Ramle-Rehovot police disguised as a drug peddler and assisted by a "hashish dog" who proved his training by sniffing out the forty-eight pounds of the lot which were buried.

Before traveling from Beersheba down to the Dead Sea, I always made it a point to stop and call on Dita Natzor at Beit Ha'am, or People's House, a community center where she kept her offices. I don't believe I know to this day what her official title was. She was everywhere simultaneously, efficiently organizing everything, taking on every job in sight. She may have been mayor for all I know, except there were Toviahu and others who were called by that name, and I expect were doing well in their posts. But if Bertie and I went down to Eilat on business, there was Dita with the Prime Minister of Denmark or other dignitaries, seeing that they got exactly what they wanted from the Gulf of Aqaba and coming away with a clear idea of Israel's progress there. Dita was small, dark-haired, puckish, intense and like a hummingbird, a high-speed, perpetual-motion public relations magician for Beersheba, all the Negev and all of the State of Israel. It was her habit to work to the point of collapse, pick herself up and start all over again. She was reliable and could get almost anything done in a hurry. Her answers to questions were absolutely straight. Once, when we were talking about immigration and refugees, and before we knew her very well, she looked at us and said evenly, "Nobody else wanted us, so we came here."

15/ THE DEAD SEA

F rom Beersheba to the Dead Sea is only about forty-five miles on
a road that leaves the city at an altitude of about five hundred
feet, climbs eastward over bluffs at eighteen hundred and then
descends abruptly to thirteen hundred feet below sea level, the
lowest spot on the earth's surface. There is a place called Badwater,
California, in Death Valley at two hundred and eighty feet below
sea level, which is the lowest in the Western Hemisphere, but that
is comparatively so high in the air that people at the Dead Sea
Works don't even bother to pooh-pooh it. The route to Sodom,
secured by Israeli forces in November, 1948, in Operation Lot, winds
from the Negev plateau and the Judean Wilderness through the
desolate, crazily eroded cliffs and canyons, fissures and outcroppings

of salt down to the water's edge where the branches and trunks of dead trees, heavily coated with minerals, rise from the receding shoreline like arms and hands clutching at the heat. On the other side of the reeking waters, to the northeast, the mountains of Moab rise precipitously, among them Mount Nebo where Moses before his death was permitted his only view of the Promised Land. Describing this infernal scene, Joseph Wechsberg commented in *The New Yorker*, "It struck me that Moses must have suffered a slight sinking feeling."

The Dead Sea is fifty-three miles long from north to south, about ten miles wide between the drear mountains which surround it, and another thirteen hundred feet deep from the surface to the hot springs bubbling below. There is no outlet to the Dead Sea. It is replenished by the Jordan River, rising at the foot of Mount Hermon, picking up more salts in the Sea of Galilee and twisting in great loops down through a great jungly gorge before it enters the Dead Sea, which is also fed by four small salty streams, all of these waters flowing through highly nitrous soil. Beginning at the ancient shrine to Pan in the Syrian heights and continuing through the Sea of Galilee, the Dead Sea and the lower Negev Desert, this widening depression is all part of the African Rift, a long crack in the earth's crust caused by two massive geological faults. It keeps on going right under the Red Sea and emerges in East Africa, continuing as far as the great African Lakes.

The Dead Sea, also known as the Salt Sea, the Sea of Arabah, Asphalt Lake, the Sea of the Plain, and Mare Mortuum, is divided between Israel and Jordan, with a wavy frontier running north from the southern shore and then turning abruptly west about halfway, after the snack bars, the Dead Sea Works, the bathing establishments with pebbly beaches, and a couple of youth hostels near Herod's fortress and the Zealots' stronghold at Masada and the oasis of Ein Gedi, the Spring of the Kid, just below the border with springs, caves, luxuriant tropical greenery and a waterfall cascading a hundred feet to the pools which served camel caravans making their way from Mesopotamia and Jerusalem down to Egypt. At Ein Gedi, David sought sanctuary from the wrath of Saul, and here the priests of the Temple came each year for grapes from which to make their ritual wine.

To the existing Dead Sea tourist attractions, the stalagmites and stalactites of Lot's official cave, buoyant bathing and the extraordinary ruins of Masada, there was added in 1967 when Israelis captured the West Bank, the mouth of the River Jordan there and the Dead Sea Casino. The Jordanian Royal Racing and Hunt Club had taken over the Dead Sea Hotel in 1965 and installed an Italian dance band and a Turkish belly-dancer, roulette and baccarat in a gambling casino in competition to those in Beirut and Cairo. Bedouin tribesmen offered coffee outside in what was described as a desert tent, there was a swimming pool, and a track marked with oil drums was laid out on the sand for races between Arab stallions and thoroughbred dromedaries, their jockeys wearing the owners' silks. Travelers were reported more interested in Jordan's holy places and ancient ruins, while the Jordanians concentrated on gambling. Tourism, helped by a well-executed series of advertisements in *The New Yorker* and elsewhere, full-page and illustrated with beguiling photographs in color, had become an important source of revenue to the kingdom. Now, still remaining to Jordan were the desert, the spectacular Roman ruins at Jerash, and Petra, the "rose-red city half as old as time" which the travel people maintained Antony had given Cleopatra, but in the Six Day War the Casino had gone to the Israelis, along with the Mount of Olives, the Garden of Gethsemane and the Old City of Jerusalem with the Via Dolorosa, the Holy Sepulchre, the Wailing Wall and all the other shrines.

The most exciting way that I know of approaching the Dead Sea is by light plane. One flies over the darker soil of the northern desert, wanting only water to bring it to life. In the Negev there are estimated to be nearly four hundred thousand miles of arable land, about half of the country's total but with first priority in the irrigation projects, for this is where a great many Israelis will live, it is extremely fertile and its tableland makes it suitable for mechanized cultivation, for the laying of the great water conduits and for the building of roads. A great part of the land is loess, a soil whose mechanics are not yet fully known, but which crumbles differently from others and which forms a crust tending to keep water from seeping through.

Flying over the desert, it looks simply sandy, in long waves. Its color changes from nougat to mocha to black-brown, to taupe, then oyster. One passes over tan bluffs, many-layered like millefeuille.

Light and shade play on the deeply eroded wadis winding through the desert, dry now and with the land they traverse cut in curious arabesques. Toy camels and burros and people with little black tents of the Bedouin cluster about caved-in Nabataean cisterns here and there. Occasionally a Bedouin school appears in the midst of nowhere. Roads snake through canyons in the badlands. Winding along the hills east of the Dead Sea is the road where a few years ago a bus with some thirty passengers was ambushed by marauders. The road to Eilat was then moved inland.

The seemingly sterile desert leading to the Dead Sea holds much of Israel's mineral wealth. In addition to the copper and manganese found at Timna by the southern port of Eilat, there are here huge phosphate deposits, feldspar, mica, glass, sand, granite, marble, fine gypsum, fluorite, bitumen-bearing rock, and chrome. There are oil wells near Ashkelon, and natural gas wells at Zohar near the Dead Sea which supply the Oron phosphate factory, the Dead Sea Works, plants in Dimona and domestic consumers in Arad.

A Biblical city whose king was slain by Joshua and where the metal-working ancient Kenites lived, Arad is being repopulated. One of the first settlers was an octogenarian named Yehiel Adler, who had come to Palestine in 1919 and had been chef to three British High Commissioners. Arad is the site of a new chemical-manufacturing complex whose initial cost of fifty million dollars is expected to yield more than seven million annually in exports. There are five million tons of iron ore in proven reserves suitable for open-cast mining, though of poor quality, and deposits of kaolin, a clay which was used for the finest porcelains in China, an ingredient making medicines soothing to the alimentary tract, and from which can be manufactured ceramics withstanding extreme heat.

Just over the edge of the Negev's forbidding plateau is the Dead Sea, shimmering in the heat, sometimes a bright-blue, sometimes dark, with a rim of orange-brown and emerald streaks along the bluffs leading to the water.

On the northeastern Jordanian shore, a red, grey and violet rock formation rises from the blue, the weathered remains of a fortress called Machaerus, one of the palaces built by Herod Antipas. Here, according to the historian Josephus and to Saint Mark, John the Baptist was imprisoned until beheaded at the request of the nineteen-year-old Salome.

There is now an air strip on the other shore, near the Dead Sea Works which I visited one day, the pilot announcing happily as we came in for a landing, "Now we're flying below sea level." At the plant, I found Dita's husband, Israel Natzor.

Israel Natzor, a barrel-chested, tanned, grey-haired and distinguished man who looked as though he might recently have given up a career as a financier, was smiling warmly. He showed us through a compact plant occupying a square kilometer. Part of a new plant being built was still a skeleton of bright-orange girders. That already working produced a half-million tons of potash annually, an export second only to citrus and expected to double.

In the sea are milliards of tons of common salt, magnesium chloride, potassium chloride, magnesium bromide and calcium chloride. It all began in 1910 when a mining engineer from Russia, Moshe Novemissky, obtained the franchise to extract potash from the waters for fertilizer and built plants for the extraction of chemicals at both the northern and southern ends of the Dead Sea. That in the north was captured and destroyed by Arab forces, apparently not realizing its value, during the war of 1948, later put into production again under Jordanian management, and in the 1967 war captured once again by the Israelis.

At the Dead Sea Works, water is pumped into large, shallow evaporation pans where salt and bromide are allowed to crystalize. Taken from the water are fertilizer, insecticide ("No Silent Spring," said Israel Natzor), bromides used in photography and in medicine, and a number of industrial chemicals. There were twenty Americans living nearby with their families and engaged in construction of a new potash plant, as a group tending to be weathered, lanky, wearing crewcuts, with Midwestern accents, sports shirts and long cotton pants, whereas their Israeli colleagues were weathered and wearing short cotton shorts. The Americans came from a firm named Stearns Roger. "We've built just about all the potash plants in the Free World in the last twenty years," one of the Americans said, "and they are always in a hole. They find the most miserable places to work in."

The long, low mountain of salt over which we flew as it stretched northward from Sodom had been a basic factor in the settlement, commerce and prosperity of this region from before the Bronze Age.

It was the availability of mineral salt which made possible the populous civilizations of the Jordan valley including that of Jericho eight millennia ago, of the region between the Tigris and Euphrates Rivers, along the Yellow River in China, the Salt River in Arizona, the valleys of Peru and Mexico and of the Roman Empire. Under the Caesars, the salt pans of the Mediterranean yielded something like a million tons of salt annually for the Empire's population of about one hundred million. By contrast, the salt-poor continent of Africa could support only a meager population, with large areas beyond the North African salt caravan routes where the inhabitants were obliged to drink the urine and blood of livestock for its salt content, much as the Masai tribesmen around Mount Kilimanjaro in Kenya and Tanzania to this day subsist on a diet in great part of milk and blood from their herds of cattle. Until very recently, a caravan of two thousand camels was sent twice each year from Timbuktu in Mali to the Taodeni Salt Swamp in the Sahara four hundred and fifty miles away, bringing back on each trip three hundred tons of salt for trade and local use.

Hebrew priestly legislation called for a special chamber in Herod's Temple in which was kept the salt used in all sacrifices, echoed by Matthew, Mark and Luke in the New Testament when referring to the loaves to be set forth before the Lord.

16/ MASADA

F lying north along the western shore of the Dead Sea, one comes to Masada, a rugged mesa which is part of the range which runs along the coast, but stands alone, its seaward side falling almost thirteen hundred feet to the water, and in Roman times accessible from this side only by a narrow, tortuous trail called the Snake Path winding back upon itself for three and a half miles until it reached the summit and so perilous that only the very sure of foot could negotiate it; one other path led up from the other side, a little better, but not much. On the tableland at the summit of Masada, which means "Fortress," Jonathan Maccabeus built just that. Here Herod the Great fled in 42 B.C. when Parthian invaders from Persia took Jerusalem, and eight years later the king strengthened Masada's defenses until it was almost impregnable. A limestone wall eighteen feet tall and twelve feet wide with thirty-seven towers, each seventy-five feet high, enclosed the plateau whose rich soil could be culti-vated, while at the northeastern corner was built an immense three-storey palace, strongly constructed with ninety-foot towers at each of the four corners, floors of mosaic, apartments, bathrooms, halls, colonnades whose pillars were each cut from a single block of stone, large reservoirs and cisterns supplied by an aqueduct which brought waters from a nearby wadi during the rainy season, storerooms hewn from the rock for storing oil, wines, peas, beans and lentils, grapes, pomegranates and dates. After nineteen hundred years, the smooth plaster walls of the cisterns and vaults are still uncracked.

Flying around the mesa in a light plane, we could see in stereopti-con detail the work of the archeologist Yigael Yadin and his corps of volunteers. Pink-grey rock marked the chambers and defenses of Herod's citadel at one end of the mountain top. Next to it was a large circular spot where a Roman garrison had camped after the Tenth Legion under Titus's general, Flavius Silva, had breached the fortifications following a siege of three years.

In the end and in their own way, it was the nine hundred and sixty-seven defenders of Masada who defeated the six thousand men of the Tenth Legion.

The story is well told in *The Jewish War* by Josephus Flavius, to use the full name he took as an "honorary Roman," a man who has been called "a bad Jew, but a good historian," or, by the eminent jurist and historian, Dr. Cecil Roth, "the traitor of Jerusalem." Josephus was a Jewish hereditary priest, descended on his mother's side from the Hebrew kings. He was born in 37 A.D., the year of the accession of the mad emperor Caligula, and at the age of twenty-six was in Rome negotiating for the release of three Jewish priests held on trivial charges at the time the new emperor Nero watched the city burn. At thirty, Josephus was governor of the Galilee and general of the Jewish forces there charged with resisting the advance of the Romans under Vespasian. After supervising the mutual suicide of his fellow survivors during the destruction and massacre at the city of Jotapata in Galilee, Josephus joined the Romans, attempted to persuade his fellow countrymen to surrender at the siege of Jeru-salem and ended living in Rome as an imperial pensioner in an apartment given him in the emperor's house. Josephus's ability to change masters smoothly in times of great difficulty and danger was equalled only by Herod the Great.

On the defenses of Masada, Josephus wrote that Herod the Great had stored weapons sufficient for ten thousand men, silver, wrought iron and bronze and lead, and provisions sufficient to withstand a siege of any length.

"It is believed that Herod equipped this fortress as a refuge for himself, suspecting a double danger," wrote Josephus, "the danger from the Jewish masses who might push him off his throne and restore to power the royal house that had preceded him, and the greater and more terrible danger from the Egyptian queen, Cleopatra. She did not conceal her intentions, but constantly appealed to Antony, begging him to destroy Herod, and requesting the transfer to herself of the kingdom of Judaea. The surprising thing is . . . that he did not yield to her demands, hopelessly enslaved as he was by his passion for her."

Writing of the long siege of Masada, Josephus described in detail the techniques used by the besiegers and the defenders.

A group of Jewish patriots called Zealots, including the terrorists known as Sicarii or Dagger Men, led by Menahem ben Judah, had captured Masada by a ruse in 66 A.D. at the beginning of the Jewish War. Menahem was killed, but after the fall of Jerusalem in 70 A.D., his nephew, Eleazar ben Yair, made his way from that city to Masada with reinforcements and took command. For another three years, until April fifteenth, 73 A.D., they held out against the seasoned, disciplined and expertly led troops of the Tenth Legion. First, the Roman general had his troops build on a long rocky projection known as the White Cliff, at the western side of Masada but still four hundred and fifty feet below the fortifications, a solid earthen platform rising another three hundred feet. On this was built a pier of large stones seventy-five feet wide and seventy-five feet high. A siege-tower another ninety feet high and protected with iron plates was raised above this and, on it, mounted catapults and a great battering-ram. When finally the ram battered through the Zealots' wall and a small section of it collapsed, the Romans found themselves confronted with a second wall constructed of two parallel rows of great beams, tied at the ends and secured with cross-pieces. The space between the rows, the width of a normal fortification wall, was filled with earth so that blows from the siege-engines only made it more solid.

At length, Flavius Silva decided upon fire. Burning torches were thrown against the wall, whose sides were of wood, and the Zealots' defenses became a mass of blazing flame.

The Romans retired for the night, and when they entered the gutted and still-burning city in the morning, they were greeted by a deathly silence. Two old women and five frightened children found hiding in a conduit were the only survivors. The remaining nine hundred and sixty-seven had elected death rather than bondage and prohibition of their religion. Each man lay down with his family, taking them in his arms until all were dispatched by ten executioners chosen by lot. Again by lot, all were killed by the last executioner, who fell upon his sword.

Determined to leave no victory to the enemy, Eleazar had persuaded his followers to burn everything within their citadel except for their large store of food, which would "bear witness when we are dead to the fact that we perished, not through want, but because, as we resolved at the beginning, we chose death rather than slavery."

Masada stands alone and eerie, its heights rearing from the Dead Sea and accessible by the Snake Path as it follows its narrow, convoluted way up to the summit. The reminder that here in this stillness nearly a thousand chose suicide rather than submission is omnipresent at the graduation each year of the cadets from Israel's military academy. They take the oath: "Masada shall not fall again!"

It is entirely Israeli that the person in charge of excavation and restoration at Masada should be both a passionate archeologist and a military man who at the age of thirty had been Chief of Staff of the Israeli Army in the War of Independence.

Dr. Nelson Glueck, returning to his presidency of Hebrew Union College in Cincinnati in late August of 1967, after visiting the territories in Jordan and Egypt newly occupied by Israeli forces, aroused some interest with an article appearing in *The New York Times*: ARCHEOLOGY WINS ISRAEL'S WARS, SAYS A SCHOLAR and with the subhead: Digging Called Way to Find Roots for Conquest.

"If you want to win a war in Israel, you become an archeological explorer, an archeologist or a student of the Bible. That's my recipe," said Dr. Glueck at a press conference at Hebrew Union.

He declared that General Yigael Yadin's victory against Arab forces in 1947 and 1948 "was based on the fact that he knew every roadway, as any archeologist does, leading through the Negev into Egypt." General Moshe Dayan, the Commander-in-Chief who led Israel's victorious forces against the Arabs in the 1956 Sinai Campaign and again in the Six Day War of 1967, is "for all practical purposes a professional archeologist," said Dr. Glueck. He recalled that Viscount Edmund Allenby who commanded British forces in Egypt and Palestine against the Turks in 1917 and 1918 had been a great student of the Bible. "He knew the routes that went from Sinai to southern Palestine and the Negev, up to Meggido, the Armageddon of the New Testament." He mentioned that Lawrence of Arabia, the T. E. Lawrence who wrote *The Seven Pillars of Wisdom*, was another Biblical scholar. He might have added that Lawrence, before embarking on his successful career as a Lieutenant-Colonel attached to Allenby's staff, working with the desert raiders of Feisal and other insurgents blowing up Turkish trains on the Hejaz Railway, had begun after his graduation from Oxford as an archeologist working for the highly respectable Palestine Exploration Fund, founded in 1863. *The Times* noted that Dr. Glueck himself, the Biblical scholar and archeologist, was from 1942 through 1947 a field agent in the Transjordan for the Central Intelligence Agency's wartime predecessor, the Office of Strategic Services. According to a cover story in *Time* about him, Glueck had been called by General Wild Bill Donovan a few months after Pearl Harbor, brought to Washington where he took a short course in codes and went back to Transjordan where, as he said, "I had the best cover of any spy. . . . I went on doing what I had always done. . . . I was supposed to play some sort of Lawrence of Arabia role. I knew all about the country, so I would have been invaluable if we had landed troops there. But we did not."

The London *Observer* helped to finance, publicize and recruit the small army of volunteers who worked under Yadin's direction between 1963 and 1965, excavating ninety-seven per cent of the summit at Masada, leaving three per cent in ruins as originally discovered. The job took eleven months of intermittent labor, suspended in summer when the temperature was over 120 degrees.

The *Observer* quoted the explanation of Dr. Yadin, now Professor of Archeology at Hebrew University in Jerusalem, of why he had resigned from the Israeli Army at the age of thirty-six after serving as its Commander-in-Chief: "I never liked soldiering very much."

During the Second World War, Yadin was ordered to remain out of sight, and on occasion drove a delivery truck while quietly making plans for the underground Haganah which was to become Israel's national army. Yet, as the *Observer* remarked, "he is a Jewish soldier and the epitome of the new sort of Israeli. . . . Yet, whatever clothes he wears, he looks as though he were relaxing out of uniform."

The newspaper emphasized that in Israel the military are not a caste apart and, in comparing Yadin with his successor Moshe Dayan, remarked that both were intellectuals, and both essentially gentle people, "two remarkable men—outstanding among the soldiers of the world—products of necessity in a small, brilliant and threatened country."

The brief biography of Yadin touched on that familiar phenomenon in Israel, the reliance for assistance in defense on good knowledge of archeology and history, particularly that of the Bible. Yadin chose as his field of study ancient Jewish military history, but he was so frequently called away from the university for underground Haganah duty, and for a period with Orde Wingate's Special Night Squads, where he became Jerusalem district platoon commander, that it took him ten years to complete the four-year college course. He had just begun work on the thesis for his Ph.D. when Ben-Gurion asked him to take charge of the armed forces. "It was a terrible blow, archeologically speaking," said Yadin.

Knowledge of Biblical battles combined with studies of modern military critiques such as Lidell Hart's *Strategy of Indirect Approach* enabled him to counter a massive Egyptian advance from the south in 1948, by recalling an old Roman road long since buried under the sand dunes and nowhere appearing on modern maps. He dispatched a light force by this route, taking a large number of Egyptians from the rear and capturing their brigadier in his pyjamas.

He may be deprecatory about matters military and his own rôle, but Yadin's attack on Masada was planned with both imagination and military precision. The original advertisements in British and Israeli newspapers were answered by more than five thousand volunteers who paid their own way from twenty-eight different countries and without whose help Yadin estimated the dig would have cost well over a million dollars and have taken twenty-five years to complete. Together they removed one hundred and fifty thousand cubic feet of earth and rock, sifting two-thirds of the dirt through five sieves. Enough was recovered to fill a museum built at the foot of the cliff, and to mount an exhibition called "Masada: A Struggle for Freedom," which in 1966, 1967 and 1968 was shown to crowds in London, New York and other large cities, garnering on the road the sort of enthusiastic reception usually reserved for hit plays or musical comedies.

The treasure of the show was a fragment of a scroll unearthed at Masada and identical with some of those found in 1947 at Qumran, a little further north along the same coast. There had been some argument about the date when the original Dead Sea Scrolls of Qumran had been written, but the duplicate found at Masada by Professor Yadin and effectively sealed with the destruction of that fortress was proof that the identical Qumran scrolls had been written no later than 73 A.D., and probably within the first half of that century. Discovery of the matching scrolls has also added more fuel to the continuing controversy over whether the caves at Qumran and nearby where the first Dead Sea Scrolls were found were indeed inhabited by ascetic, pacific Essenes. This is the judgment of the majority of scholars, led by Professor Yadin, who reasons that, in the end, even these peaceable people joined the common fight against the Romans, and that some of them had come south to join the Zealots at Masada, bringing with them some of their scrolls, including those using the special Essene calendar of twelve months of thirty days each, plus four intercalary days. Another theory, vigorously argued by the Oxford historian Cecil Roth, holds that the authors of the Dead Sea Scrolls at Qumran were not Essenes at all, but themselves members of the same fanatical Zealot sect as Masada's Sicarii or Dagger Men. The most that the people responsible for the Masada show would say was that there certainly seemed to be some connection between the bloodthirsty Zealots and the gentle Essenes.

In addition to the objects chosen for display, the legions of volunteers uncovered utensils, catapult balls, slingshots, arrowheads, a toga pin, a silver ring and a belt buckle, tunics, and the remnants of a prayer shawl with mauve threads woven through its pinkish gold cloth. Also, twenty-one Augustan pottery lamps, silver-plated scales from the armor of the sort worn by Roman officers of high rank, more than twenty-two hundred coins, including the twenty extremely rare Israeli silver shekels struck during the revolt of the Jews against the Romans, and some two hundred ostroka, inscriptions in ink on pieces of pottery, and the remains of the dates, grapes and pomegranates dried but still preserved. Before leaving the site at Masada, the volunteers could see the excavations of Herod's Roman baths, the largest yet found in this part of the world, and equipped with hot rooms, cold rooms, dressing rooms and a sit-down flush toilet which is the oldest example known, all converted by the luxury-despising Zealots and used as simple religious ritual baths until all of Masada was systematically destroyed by the Romans following its burning by its defenders.

17/ SCROLLS

A rt Buchwald's column for March 21, 1961, datelined THE DEAD
SEA, began: "The national sport of Israel is archeology and the
greatest living player is Prof. Yigael Yadin." Buchwald had just
returned from visiting Yadin at the spot south of the Jordanian
border where the year before in the three communicating cliffside
caverns known collectively as the Cave of the Letters, the archeologist had discovered fifteen dispatches to the garrison there from Bar
Kochba himself, thus dispelling lingering doubts about the authenticity of the rôle played by this last civil and military leader of the
Second Jewish Commonwealth, a national hero about whom very
little was known. To the Israelis, eager to learn as much about their

heritage as possible, this discovery, as Buchwald pointed out, was as important as that of the Dead Sea Scrolls.

The Israeli passion for archeology is not surprising when one considers the enthusiasm shown by the Israeli leaders who created the new State, their respect for the lessons of antiquity, and the accuracy of the Biblical account of their own history and that of their neighbors for the past four thousand years. As Yadin has remarked, whereas the Bible was above all a religious work during the dispersion of the Jews throughout the centuries, to those now born in Israel, to even the *Sabras* who may not be religious, the Bible remains the primary history and the source book of the land of their fathers, through which they can wander with the Old Testament as a sort of *Guide Michelin*.

It is entirely in keeping with the national character that, just after the new State was born and while its hold on life was still precarious, comparatively large sums were spent by the government for archeological study and exploration. Yadin's father, Professor Elazar Lippe Sukenik, then chief of the Department of Archeology at Hebrew University, after preliminary negotiations with an Armenian antiquities dealer from the Old City conducted across the barbed wire separating Arab and Jewish quarters of Jerusalem, accompanied this intermediary on the dangerous trip to Bethlehem, the professor disguised as an Arab. There, on the twenty-ninth of November, 1947, Dr. Sukenik bought from a Syrian Christian named Khalil Iskander Shahin, known as Kando, the first two of the Dead Sea Scrolls which the latter had acquired from the Ta'amireh tribe of semi-nomadic Bedouin who ranged the country between Bethlehem and the Dead Sea and with whom he did a regular business in whatever contraband they might bring in for the Bethlehem black market.

That night, as he began his examination of the first two scrolls, Dr. Sukenik heard over the radio news that the United Nations had voted by far more than the required two-thirds for the Palestine partition plan and the establishment of Arab and Jewish States.

Savage fighting broke out the following day, but in December Sukenik was able to buy a third scroll. During the months to come he became increasingly convinced that the scroll which he called *The War of the Children of Light Against the Children of Darkness* must have been lettered in the first or second century B.C. A scroll of Isaiah which he had bought turned out to be at least a thousand years older than any Biblical manuscript yet known. He supposed that the cave overlooking the Dead Sea had been used as a *Genizah*, the room in a synagogue in which discarded texts are customarily stored since Hebrew sacred writings may not be destroyed. It was a bad year for Sukenik, one in which his youngest son Mattatyahu had been killed as an air force pilot, bombing the Egyptian fleet from a Piper Cub, a year on whose last day Professor Sukenik wrote in his diary, "An historic year in our people's history has concluded. A painful year—Matti died, God bless him! Were it not for the *Genizah*, the year would have been intolerable for me."

Jerusalem was besieged, and with the fierce fighting between the invading Arab armies and the Israeli defenders, all contact with the source of the scrolls was severed.

"The excitement of discovering the scrolls had enabled him partly to forget the war," Edmund Wilson wrote in his book *The Scrolls from the Dead Sea*. "At a time when the Arab Legion had been shelling the offices of the Jewish Agency in the middle of New Jerusalem, between three and five every afternoon, he had not hesitated to call a press conference at this dangerous place and hour, promising important news. To attend it required some nerve. An American correspondent fainted in the street on the way, and had to be carried in by his colleagues. The reporters were flabbergasted when Sukenik, who seemed quite unperturbed by the flashing and banging about him, announced the discovery of the Dead Sea Scrolls. . . . The reporters had at first been rather peevish at having been asked to risk their skins for old manuscripts, but they ended by being impressed by the scholar's overmastering enthusiasm."

Professor Sukenik knew that in addition to the scrolls and a number of fragments which he had purchased, the Bedouin Dead Sea cave robbers and their fences in Bethlehem had sold to the Metropolitan of the Jacobite Syrian Monastery of Saint Mark in the Old City (held by their church to be the site of the Last Supper), Mar Athanasium Yeshue Samuel, another five scrolls and a number of fragments which the Metropolitan had lent to scholars at the American School of Oriental Research in Jerusalem. The American School had published them before the Metropolitan brought the scrolls to the United States in 1949 after his monastery, its back against the wall separating Jewish and Arab neighborhoods in the Old City, was severely damaged by Arab Legion shelling of the Jewish quarter.

Dr. Sukenik died in the spring of 1953, but the following year his son Yigael, while lecturing in the United States, was shown an ad carried by *The Wall Street Journal* the first three days of June under the heading MISCELLANEOUS FOR SALE:

THE FOUR DEAD SEA SCROLLS
Biblical Manuscripts Dating Back to at Least
200 B.C.
Are For Sale. This Would Be an Ideal Gift to
An Educational or Religious Institution by
An Individual or Group.

The air between New York and Tel Aviv crackled with cables in code. The price was a quarter of a million dollars, payable to a lawyer in New York not associated with business with Israel, a device the Syrian Church had hit upon.

A wealthy American paper manufacturer, D. Samuel Gottesman, presented the scrolls to Israel. They have become a national monument, on exhibition at the strikingly handsome Israel Museum for which the ebullient mayor of Jerusalem, the former kibbutznik and Haganah gunrunner Teddy Kollek, worked indefatigably for over two and a half decades. The scrolls are housed in a white Shrine of the Book whose shallow, circular dome is rather like the lid of a Chinese soup bowl though it takes its shape from the distinctive covers of the jars in which the scrolls were found. Its circular walls of black basalt rising to the white dome above contrast light and darkness.

When in 1947 the Dead Sea Scrolls first were offered for sale, there was guerrilla warfare, terrorism, reprisal and counter-reprisal throughout Israel and in the bitterly divided city of Jerusalem. There was even less communication than usual between the rival religious sects and schools of archeology. The Metropolitan found himself unable to get through to the Biblical scholars who might have helped him authenticate the manuscripts which he had come to believe were of great antiquity. Those few who did examine his scrolls almost without exception dismissed them as relatively recent work. Except for one or two fragments, there was no known text of the Bible in Hebrew before the Masorite version completed by the scholars at Tiberius in the ninth century A.D. Of the two ranking Biblical archeologists working in Jerusalem, Père Roland de Vaux, Director of the Dominican French School of Biblical and Archeological Studies at Jerusalem, was in Paris at the time. To use Edmund Wilson's words, the Metropolitan "did not succeed in gaining access" to Gerald Lankester Harding, responsible for archeological work in both what was then called Transjordan and in Arab Palestine. Father van der Ploeg, a Dutch scholar at the French Biblical School, identified one of the scrolls as Isaiah, but was dissuaded by colleagues at his institution to pursue this lead. A Syrian compatriot of the Metropolitan at the Department of Antiquities assured him that the scrolls were "not worth a shilling." The Syrian Patriarch of Antioch, to whom the Metropolitan took them himself, thought they were probably not more than three centuries old, but referred his caller to the American University in Beirut's Professor of Hebrew. He turned out to be away on vacation.

Unlike Dr. Sukenik, who was absent from Hebrew University at that time, no one to whom the Metropolitan showed the manuscripts was able to recognize their great age, or to believe that there could be in existence anything older than the Nash Papyrus, a small fragment sold some fifty years ago to a British traveler by an Egyptian dealer and which is now in the University Library at Cambridge, believed to have been written sometime between the earlier part of the second century B.C. and the latter part of the first century A.D.— until that day, recognized by Biblical scholars as the oldest Hebrew manuscript.

"Never during the past two centuries," wrote Professor Albright of Johns Hopkins when considering what Edmund Wilson called the "stubborn incredulity of scholars" mulling over the Dead Sea Scrolls, had there been "such a wide refusal on the part of scholars to accept clear-cut evidence." Professor Albright softened this somewhat by recalling that the discovery of Pompeii had been written off as fiction; that no one had really believed in the findings of the excavations of Troy; and that the deciphering of cuneiform was not credited by many well-informed scholars until the end of the nineteenth century. One might add that the world long refused to believe in the existence of such an animal as the okapi, and respectable zoölogists for long scoffed at descriptions of the gorilla as the invention of sensation-seeking adventurers.

At last, in 1948, the Metropolitan Samuel was able to show his manuscripts to the Acting Director of the American School of Oriental Research, Dr. John C. Trever, and to his colleague, Dr. William H. Brownlee. This was in the midst of the battle for Jerusalem. Electric current had been cut off, and Drs. Trever and Brownlee stayed up until midnight examining photographs of the Metropolitan's scrolls by kerosene lamp until they became absolutely sure that at least the Isaiah scroll was as old, and perhaps older, than the Nash Papyrus.

"Sleep came with greater difficulty," Dr. Trever wrote in the *Biblical Archeologist*. "The added evidence kept racing through my mind. It all seemed incredible. How could we be right?"

By the next morning, current was restored, they were able to photograph the fifty-four columns of the Isaiah scroll and sent prints to Dr. Albright at Johns Hopkins, who was an authority on the Nash Papyrus. An airmail letter from Albright written the same day he received the evidence said: "My heartiest congratulations on the greatest manuscript discovery of modern times! There is no doubt in my mind that the script is more archaic than that of the Nash Papyrus. . . . What an absolutely incredible find! And there can happily not be the slightest doubt in the world about the genuineness of the manuscript."

The scholars at the American School also explained to the Metropolitan something he did not know, that the antiquity law of Palestine under the Mandate required that any new discoveries be reported immediately to the Department of Archeology. This they did for the Metropolitan. For his part, he said he would now be sure to observe the regulations. The scholars at the American School of Oriental Research also urged the Metropolitan to leave the country in those troubled times, going to the United States if possible. Drs. Trever and Brownlee were relieved to hear that the monastery's Brother Butros Sowmy had left Palestine the same day, taking the manuscripts to a safe place outside the country.

The Metropolitan arrived in the United States with the scrolls in January, 1949, while Brother Butros returned to the monastery where he was killed in the crossfire between the two sides of the city.

The Great Scroll Search was on. "The Syrian Metropolitan was asking something like a million dollars for the scrolls in his possession in the United States," said John Marco Allegro, or so it was believed in Jordan and broadcast over the Jordanian radio.

The caves in the cliffs overlooking the Dead Sea were swarming with clandestine Bedouin archeologists eager to make a fortune. Of these, by far the best organized were the Ta'amireh tribes who had settled in this region in the seventeenth century and had since specialized in highway robbery until recent years when this had been brought under control by the Arab Legion. They still knew every crevice and cave, and it was one of their number, a boy called Mohammed the Wolf, belonging to a group of Ta'amireh contrabandists smuggling goats and anything profitable from Transjordan into Palestine, who discovered the original cache of scrolls in the cave at Khirbet Qumran in 1947. Now, every able-bodied member of the tribe was engaged in a business organized by the tribal elders. They worked in shifts, jealously guarding the location of the caves, using Kando as their agent, but themselves now taking a larger share, and steadily raising the price.

Before the Archeological Museum could get its own official expeditions into the field in early 1952, word came to de Vaux and Harding of the highly unofficial explorations of the Ta'amireh who were rifling caves in the Qumran area. Harding at once set out with the Bethlehem Chief of Police and two soldiers from the Arab Legion, guided by the clouds of dust which the cave robbers were raising as they worked. "The Bedouins," said Edmund Wilson, "upon their arrival came swarming out of these holes like chipmunks."

A few of the illegal diggers were given light sentences, and the rest hired to work with the archeologists. The maximum price set was a pound sterling, or two dollars and eighty cents, per square millimeter of scroll fragment. For substantial portions of the scrolls, the Bedouin and their agent Kando tried to force prices still higher by cutting up the scrolls, selling the first portion for a moderately high price, the second, needed to continue the manuscript, for quite a bit more, and the third at an even higher rate. And so it went.

This technique was countered by Harding, who offered a scale of prices which increased per square millimeter with the size of the manuscript offered.

The archeologists had to move quickly in order to prevent uncontrolled sale and scattering of fragments throughout the world instead of bringing together as many as possible for preservation and study by responsible scholars. Much damage had already been done and the dangers were great. The reader can almost feel the shudder in Allegro's explanation that "A small piece of Dead Sea Scroll may look very nice framed and hung over the mantelpiece, but it may well ruin the value of larger pieces, depending for their sense on the inscription on 'the souvenir,'" as he reported that irresponsible people were already finding their way into the market and that a famous museum, which he was discreet enough not to identify, was at one point willing to consider buying smuggled scroll fragments for the prestige of having a few in its cases.

Meanwhile, the ransacking of the caves by the Ta'amireh and others had hopelessly scrambled the remaining scrolls and fragments and other artifacts so that no stratographical studies could be made. Scroll jars were broken and, together with potsherds, linen coverings and other material of great value to the archeologists, were unceremoniously dumped as rubbish. Some of the largest fragments from Qumran were buried by Kando in the rich soil of his back garden and this change from the dry atmosphere of the caves left him with only undecipherable sticky lumps like glue when he went to retrieve them.

The search for more scrolls has never ended. Following the original discovery of seven scrolls at Khirbet Qumran, ten more caves were found in the vicinity. Another and unrelated collection of contracts, letters and some Biblical documents from the time of the Bar Kochba revolt was discovered in a cave in the neighborhood excavated by de Vaux and Harding. A third collection turned up in the ruins of a Byzantine monastery at a place nearby named Khirbet Mird.

All of the findings from the area are now known collectively as the Dead Sea Scrolls, with special interest centered on those from Qumran which contain all of the books of the Old Testament except for Esther, commentaries on Genesis, the Psalms and some of the Books of the Prophets, as well as books of the Apocrypha, and a Greek translation made of the Bible by Saint Jerome in the fourth century. This last has become the Roman Catholic Douay Version, which contains those portions not found in the original Hebrew, and so not accepted in the King James Version and the American and Revised Versions which followed. Also found at Qumran were portions not in the Biblical canon called Pseudepigrapha, elaborations now considered to contain a good measure of invention which lean heavily on angelology and demonology, with special importance given Satan or the Antichrist as the foe of God, and with most emphasis of all on the Day of Yahveh, the Day of Days, on which all mankind is to be judged, and which is expected momentarily. All of this in the eyes of Biblical scholars, in these days of late Judaism, shows a strong influence of early Christianity.

Most of the scrolls were written on parchment, a few on papyrus, and one on copper twelve inches by eight feet long, so badly oxidized when found that it first had to be cut into strips with greatest care by the College of Technology at Manchester before it could be deciphered by Allegro, who found it to be the inventory of a Temple treasure, possibly that of Herod the Great which had been looted, but most of whose great wealth had been hidden in secret treasuries whose locations the scroll disclosed in terms which could be understood only by the initiated.

The Hebrew or Aramaic writing on the copper scroll was deeply incised, but that of the other Dead Sea Scrolls was done with ink of carbon black used with a quill, much of it still fresh and clear today and inscribed with elegant calligraphy. The religiously unutterable Tetragrammaton of YHWH or its variations, the name of God, or Yahweh, from which the modern Jehovah is derived, but which might be pronounced only by the High Priest in the Holy of Holies on Yom Kippur, it otherwise always being pronounced as Adonai, or Lord, when read aloud in the temple, in the scrolls always was written in archaic or Phoenician Hebrew to lend it an air of greater sanctity.

General Yadin, as editor of *The War of the Children of Light Against the Children of Darkness,* described this apocalyptic struggle as a vision of the triumph of those of God against the hosts of Belial, but presented as a war with Hebrew arms, strategy and tactics. The Reverend Millar Burrows in his essay on the Dead Sea Scrolls in *The Dictionary of the Bible* says that weapons and tactics are plainly copied from those of the Romans, but there is no necessary contradiction here since each side borrowed from the other. Still different interpretations view the ascetic religious community at Qumran studying, performing their religious duties and preparing for the arrival of the Messiah, as picturing themselves as the Children of Light preserving the true religion in contrast to the Sadducees and Pharisees of the Temple in Jerusalem as the Children of Darkness who had lost the way. To the High Priest and those who supported him, those at Qumran and in many similar communities throughout Israel were guilty of "sectarianism," from which comes the English word "heresy."

The other scroll which excited particular attention, *The Manual of Discipline,* described the strict monastic life of these Jewish orders, some celibate and some permitting marriage, but all sharing their worldly goods, and fervently studying the Scriptures. It was a democratic and communal society, with no slaves and no masters, almost no rank, in many ways rather like the present kibbutzim, and with many similarities to the societies of early Christians, and to the teachings of St. Paul and of John the Baptist.

The several Dead Sea Scrolls were found largely intact and the remains of another four hundred scrolls represented by more than forty thousand surviving fragments, most of them written between the second century B.C. and the first half of the second century A.D. They are in Aramaic, Nabataean and Hebrew, both Biblical and secular works. They had been copied, revised, corrected and annotated by generations of scribes, with anything from words to passages to individual characters missing. These, if they can be recreated, become literally invaluable to the Biblical scholars anxious to recreate the late Hebrew and early Christian world. They throw great light on the years in which Jesus and the Apostles lived and taught.

18/ DAVID BEN-GURION

T he road from Beersheba running south through the Negev to end at Eilat about a hundred miles away passes the kibbutz of Sde Boker of which David Ben-Gurion is a member, and where he sometimes has had his picture taken shearing sheep, still sharing in the work of the kibbutz though he celebrated his eightieth birthday in the autumn of 1966. And, as was said by James Feron of *The New York Times* on that day, when several thousand Israelis made the pilgrimage to Sde Boker to honor the octogenarian: "He turned over the reins three years ago, but has continued to bark instructions."

I flew down to the kibbutz, admiring the crops of corn, tomatoes, peaches, olives, grapes, figs, watermelons and pomegranates which surrounded it as we came in over the windswept, yellow-gray table-lands not far from the Dead Sea, to touch down at Sde Boker's long loess air strip. Lunch with the kibbutzniks was simple, quite good and without ceremony. Women were not necessarily served first. Work was obviously quite hard on the kibbutz, where they raised cattle and sheep as well as vegetables, but its members, most of whom were young, perhaps in their early twenties, seemed to enjoy it.

There was still occasional danger: a girl and a boy out hiking with friends near Sde Boker had fallen behind the rest of the group not long before, and had been killed by Bedouin brigands for their few valuables.

Ben-Gurion was not there at this famous kibbutz—having gone off to run the country from some other command post—but I was able to catch up with him in the modest house he maintains in Tel Aviv. It was hard to tell whether there were more books in his cottage at the kibbutz or his house in Tel Aviv where three rooms were lined with volumes running right up to the ceiling.

The great flying tufts of white hair sprouted from either side of his head much as they appeared in all his photographs, and he was wearing his customary short-sleeved white shirt, open at the wide, stubby collar which has become his trademark. On this day, he was wearing a pair of citified trousers of some quiet, fine, light-gray material, secured by a black belt, and he received me while wearing a pair of green carpet slippers. He had a reddish nose with a pair of horn-rimmed spectacles perched on it, and a flatish, reddish face, with freckled, hairy forearms. For some reason, I suppose because he had shown such strength and been so prominent for so long, I was surprised to find him very short. But burly.

As an octogenarian, Ben-Gurion seemed to be as vigorous, as informal, as strongly opinionated, as encyclopedic, and with as in-quiring a mind as ever. He was also ubiquitous. I recalled seeing pictures of him dressed in Burmese costume with U Nu when he was in Rangoon for a time studying Buddhism, with General Moshe Dayan inspecting the Israeli guard after capturing the Egyptian position at Sharm el Sheikh during the Sinai campaign of 1956, with his wife Paula having breakfast with Dag Hammarskjöld at Sde Boker in 1959, and with President Eisenhower in Washington in 1960. An inmate of Bergen-Belsen, Josef Rosensaft, has described how Ben-Gurion arrived at the camp in November, 1945, after it had been liberated by the British that April, and in the course of an argument with the UNRRA officials who wanted to send the children among the Jewish survivors to England, when some among the Jews advised the others to "accept this offer with gratitude," Ben-Gurion concluded an impassioned oration by putting his hands on his head, exclaiming, "You see my grey hair, these grey hairs will live to see a Jewish State in Eretz Israel."

He was familiar with Russian, French, Turkish, German and Latin, had learned Greek in order to read Plato in the original, being dissatisfied with the translations, and Spanish so that he might read *Don Quixote*, but, interestingly, the language in which he found it easiest to express himself, next to Hebrew, was English. He was practicing Yoga.

Mostly we talked about the Negev, though I did want to learn what Ben-Gurion had to say about Israel's Arab neighbors and about the Arab refugees living in the neighboring countries—except that I discovered, with his enthusiasm for all things Biblical, whatever the subject we were likely to end up with a Biblical illustration.

"Five years ago, and again two years ago, there was no rain," said Ben-Gurion when I talked to him in the fall of 1965. "The Bedouin from the Negev came north where there was water and pasture. When I came to Eretz Israel nearly sixty years ago, the minimum amount of land necessary to sustain a peasant was sixty-two-and-one-half acres, but now with irrigation seven-and-one-half acres is sufficient. Within another ten years, more or less, we'll have desalinated water, and that means we can settle a minimum of two million people in the Negev. Israel can absorb five million, ten million people—the population depends on how many Jews have to or want to come.

"Aqaba has water, and that is where Eilat was in the days of King Solomon and King David, the godson of Yehoshaphat. King David was born in Bethlehem, you know. He and his six brothers and their grandfather were born there. And for six and a half years, David was king of Hebron," said his namesake, David Ben-Gurion, speaking now of the fourth Holy City of the Jews, later taken by by them in the course of the Six Day War.

"Agriculture is important, but I believe the main prospects for the Negev lie in industry," said Ben-Gurion. "I believe we can export

245

more to Asia and to Africa than we now do to Europe where most of our products go."

"I was in Aqaba in 1933 and 1934," Ben-Gurion said, "and there were only two police huts where our present Eilat now is. You know, the Bible says that the Jews in their wandering through Eilat and through the wilderness were expelled by the Amorites. That's not so. "It really was the Edomites."

Ben-Gurion remained intransigent about the possibility of accepting in the forseeable future any substantial number of Arab refugees, whom he continued to regard as a potential fifth column.

"We told the Arabs, you can stay if you give up your arms. In Haifa, the Mufti said No. We said the same thing two days before independence in Jaffa. You saw what happened." His opinion of the military prowess of the Arabs was low. "Of course there are some exceptions. The Sudanese would fight to the death. But there is no reason for most Egyptians to fight to the death."

It was wonderful how much Ben-Gurion knew about the religions of the world, Hinduism as well as Buddhism. In his memoirs, *Ben-Gurion Looks Back*, Moshe Pearlman recounts how Ed Murrow had arranged a three-way television interview between the Burmese Premier U Nu, who was in Hong Kong at the time, Ben-Gurion in Jerusalem, and Murrow in the United States. "One of the first questions he asked was the difference between Judaism and Buddhism," Ben-Gurion said of Murrow's conducting the discussion. "I answered that the essence of Judaism to my mind was contained in the first of the Ten Commandments: 'I am the Lord thy God,' and in the precept, 'Thou shalt love thy neighbor as thyself.' U Nu answered that Buddha was an atheist. He agreed with the Judaic precept and went even further by preaching not only love toward man, but also mercy toward all living creatures.

"In 1961, when I visited Burma as U Nu's guest, he gave a dinner in my honor and set before me was a dish of fish and meat. Remembering what he had said about mercy to all living creatures, I asked U Nu how he explained the food on the table. He reassured me. It was a Chinese dish with the look and something of the taste of fish and meat, but it was made entirely of vegetables!"

Ben-Gurion's biographers, and there have been numbers of them, tell of how he never let any work or appointments interfere with his Bible-study circle which used to meet twice a month when he lived in Jerusalem, and might include a couple of dozen philologists, archeologists, historians, President Ben-Zvi and other scholars interested in Bible studies, meeting to discuss a part of the Scriptures— Ben-Gurion usually arriving carrying two copies of the Bible, one the Hebrew and the other the Greek Septuagint.

The Bible, Ben-Gurion believed, that which has been called the "portable homeland of the Jews," is their single most precious possession. He felt that Jews, wherever they might live, should be bilingual, learning Hebrew as well as the language of their country. He seemed proud that the Irish Prime Minister de Valera, when he visited Ben-Gurion, had said the thing which impressed him more than anything else in Israel was the "miraculous revival of Hebrew," going on to describe the long, determined and unsuccessful efforts of the Irish patriots to bring their ancient Gaelic language Erse to life again.

"I believe that any Jew who lives in Israel, the land of Zion," Ben-Gurion was quoted by Moshe Pearlman as saying, "is more religious than the most religious Jew who can come to Israel and does not."

As Prime Minister of a coalition government for many years, and one which depended on the collaboration of the National Religious Party in Israel, a minority with very strict ideas of how the majority should live, Ben-Gurion even had a few kind words to say about the Natorei Karta, the ultra-Orthodox, stone-throwing inhabitants of Meah Shearim in Jerusalem. Talking with Pearlman about religion in general, his own beliefs and the place of religion in the State, Ben-Gurion had said, "I do believe that there must be a being, intangible, indefinable, even unimaginable, but something infinitely superior to all we know and are capable of conceiving. . . . I once talked about this to Einstein—even he, with his great formula about energy and mass, agreed that there must be something behind the energy. And when I spoke of this to Niels Bohr, he, too, agreed, and thought it was probably true of the entire cosmos that behind it there must be some superior being." Ben-Gurion did believe in a secular state but, because of the religious party alliance, had never been able to put this on the statute book.

"I am tolerant of any religious activity within the State which comes within the scope of legality," said Ben-Gurion. "I am adamantly opposed to any illegality even when performed by the most extreme of religious zealots, like Natorei Karta. Taking the law into their own hands and molesting people who fail to observe the Sabbath according to their traditions are the acts of a group which refuses to recognize the sovereignty of Israel. . . . I believe the Natorei Karta to be a thoroughly misguided group, but I also believe they are utterly sincere. It is a consolation they are so few."

He added, of the Zealots, that "They are not common law-breakers. They represent a world most of us came from, a world we knew as infants, the world of our grandfathers—they have the same beliefs, the same outlook, the same dress, the same beards; they *look* like our grandfathers. How can you slap your grandfather into jail, even if he throws stones at you?"

As I was leaving his small house, Ben-Gurion pointed to one of his Bibles and said, standing at the head of the stairs, "Everything that happens in the world is a miracle. . . . Until now, I have never been able to find a logical explanation for what is going on in the world."

19/ THE ROOTS OF
ANTI-SEMITISM

It seems hard for many of us—perhaps most of us who live in countries relatively peaceful, relatively prosperous, and where anti-Jewish feeling, if present, is discreetly muted—to comprehend the forces which have impelled Jews of more than a hundred countries in our time to return to a land of stony fields and of hills barren when they first saw them, of expanses of desert, and of marsh which until recently accounted for one of the highest malaria rates in the world; a country which, until 1917, was governed by a corrupt and discriminatory Colonial administration, and afterward found itself ringed with neighbors who, without exception, had sworn to destroy it.

For many from the Arab countries and Eastern Europe, the usual and straightforward answer to foreigners' questions as to the reason for the Israelis' formidable courage under fire and under the threat of annihilation, the answer is: *"Ein brera*—No alternative."

Many more have a nightmare memory of exactly what it meant to be a Jew throughout most of the world during most of the past two thousand years. Not just during the days of Hitler's terror. According to the Roman historian Tacitus, six hundred thousand Jews were killed or died from starvation and disease during the year and a half of the siege of Jerusalem, and nearly the same number, but mostly men, were led away as captives or slaves to Rome. Seventeen thousand of this miserable procession in chains died along the way through Syria. Everywhere the conquerer Titus stopped, he sent hundreds of his captives into the local arena to fight wild beasts or to kill one another as gladiators. At Caesarea Maritima, on the coast of Judea, he celebrated his brother Domitian's birthday by games in which twenty-five hundred Jewish youths were killed. Rome minted a coin showing a weeping woman kneeling under a date palm, labeled, "Iudaea Capta," while a relief on the Arch of Titus, near the Coliseum in Rome shows to this day Roman warriors carrying the spoils of the Temple of Jerusalem, including the great seven-branched candelabrum, or menorah.

With the fall of Jerusalem, the rebellion was not yet over. From 132 to 135 A.D., under Simon Bar Kochba and the Rabbi Akiba, who proclaimed Bar Kochba the Son of a Star and the Messiah, the Jews again rebelled, fighting so fiercely against their Roman conquerers that an estimated five hundred and eighty thousand were killed besides a greater number who died of pestilence and starvation. The writer Dio Cassius wrote, "All of Judea became almost a desert."

Yet Jewry was not extinguished. There were the survivors in Judea, many of them women, for it was the males who were transported by the Romans, as opposed to the whole families who were taken by the Syrians to Babylon. Also there were large settlements in Alexandria and elsewhere in Egypt and the Mediterranean world. It is ironical that, throughout the Middle Ages and until relatively recent years, Moslems have been comparatively hospitable to the Jews who lived among them. Jews occupied positions of great authority as viziers, ministers, advisers, warriors and financiers all through the upper strata of Moslem government. This was true until well into this century when their interests clashed, passions rose and a terrible, Semitic, family fight began. It is not yet over.

In medieval Europe, after the fourth century, the cry arose that the Jews were Christ-killers, that they stole the Host to profane it, that they slaughtered Christian children to use the blood in the making of matzoth for Passover. Jews were relegated to despised occupations: dealing in old clothes, huckstering, pawnbroking, money lending and money changing. Even though they were hated for usury, and even though the Merchant's Guild of Brindisi in 1409 A.D. petitioned the authorities to allow Jewish money lenders to return in order that the greed of the Christian usurers be checked (the Christians took thirty per cent as against the prescribed five per cent for Jews), this cherished belief in financial exploitation has clung to the Jews.

"Ghetto," it appears, is an Italian word. In Europe, for most of the first few centuries of the Christian era, there were no particular quarters in which the Jews were obliged to live, any more than there were restricted trades and professions which they were not permitted to follow. The first compulsory ghetto was probably Wroclaw in Poland, created during the thirteenth century. The first in Italy, from which all the other ghettos took their name, was that established in Venice in 1516. Typically, the European ghetto was surrounded by a high wall to seal it off from the rest of the town. It would be entered only by a massive gate, barred and bolted, and at night secured by great chains and locks. No Jew was allowed to leave the ghetto between dusk and daybreak. Ghetto streets were crooked, narrow, dark and mean. Houses were crumbling. All was overcrowded, and the stench of poverty was everywhere.

On occasion, the Jews were not only permitted but were required to leave the ghetto, as at the time of the coronation of a new Pope. The Jewish elders of Rome marched in procession through the ruined Gate of Octavian, carrying with them a *Torah*, and stationing themselves by the Arch of Titus, the reminder of the destruction of their Jerusalem. When the pontiff was carried by, he customarily paused before the Jewish elders, asking them sternly, "What are you doing here?" Vatican protocol prescribed the reply of the elders: "We solicit the grace of offering Your Holiness a copy of our *Torah*"; and also, the Pope's reply when he touched the *Torah* and said, "We praise and honor the Law, for it was given your fathers by Almighty God through Moses. But we condemn your religion, and your false interpretation of the Law, for you await the Messiah in vain. The apostolic faith teaches us that our Lord Jesus Christ has already come." Later Popes made a simpler reply: "Excellent Law—Detestable race."

For nearly a hundred years or so after the Crucifixion of Christ, the distinction was not entirely clear between Jew and Christian. Finally, the unbridgeable difference became very clear indeed to all: Christ was the Messiah to the Christians, but not to the Jews whose Messiah had not yet come.

With Jews dispersed throughout a great part of the world, the Judeo-Christians, to use this most general term, then, according to religious historians, most likely used the synagogues of which they were members as the best way to bring Jews into the Christian faith. For, after all, those Jews who had embraced the Christian faith were most likely to persuade their friends among the fellow Jews.

As the distinction between Jew and Gentile became clearer, then harder and harsher, so became the severity of the Christian attacks, and the firmness of the defenses of each side. A fearful mythology grew up about the Jews and their strange and un-Christian ways. Countless thousands of Jews were killed thanks to the libel that they used the blood of Christian children in their Passover rituals.

The first example I have been able to find is that of William of Norwich who in 1144 disappeared and then was found murdered. It was declared by a renegade Jew named Theobald of Cambridge that it was the custom of Jews to sacrifice a Christian child during Passover, and that William had been murdered for this purpose. The child was declared a martyr, made a saint, and a memorial chapel and shrine were erected in Norwich.

Far more terrible in its consequences was the ritual murder libel charged as the cause of the death of a small boy called Hugh of Lincoln. In 1255, an eight-year-old boy, according to the English chronicler Matthew Paris, was seized by Jews, fattened in a secret chamber, scourged with whips, then crowned with thorns and crucified.

The body of Hugh was found in the well of a Jew named Jopin, who confessed under torture everything he was asked to say. With Jopin, eighteen eminent Jews of Lincoln were tortured and they also were forced to confess before they were publicly hanged.

Twenty more were imprisoned in the Tower of London, but then freed by Henry III after a large ransom was paid for them by the Jewish community.

All the Jews of Lincoln had been arrested. Those who had been executed had their property confiscated by the Crown, and, oddly enough, they were among the richest Jews in the kingdom.

Hugh of Lincoln was buried in Lincoln Cathedral and shortly after canonized as St. Hugh. Many came to worship.

Pope Innocent IV in a Papal Bull of 1245 clearly denied the blood accusations against the Jews.

Other pontiffs in the long history of the papacy themselves persecuted the Jews, or at least tolerated this among their followers. Urban II in 1096, at a time when hatred of the Jews had been written into canon law, fanned the flames of religious enthusiasm for the Crusades which was to continue over the next three hundred years.

It was an attempt to secure the Holy Land for Christian pilgrims and for Christendom, to take and keep the city of Jerusalem. This was the mystical city for which not only the chivalry of Europe did battle against the infidel. Howling mobs led by Peter the Hermit and Walter the Penniless devastated Europe in their path, pillaging and murdering tens of thousands of Jews as an act of piety, as they marched. Pope Innocent III at the time of the Fourth Lateran Council in 1215 directed that Jews must wear prominently a yellow badge to identify them as social outcasts. Pope Gregory IX was persuaded by another apostate Jew, Nicholas Donin, to issue a Bull in 1240 calling for the burning of the *Talmud* everywhere, and establishing inquisitions and censors for all Jewish writings. In 1450, Pope Benedict issued a Bull which hit upon a new way of dealing with the Jews: the Conversionist Sermon. This would liberate the Jews from "the heresies, vanities and errors of the *Talmud*" which prevented them from knowing the truth, would convince them that "the true Messiah has already come," and emphasize "the destruction of the Temple and the city of Jerusalem

—all had been prophesied by Jesus." These Conversionist Sermons to captive audiences of Jews continued in Rome until early in the nineteenth century.

The Jew-baiting and the violence which became widespread throughout medieval Europe appealed alike to the fanatical church-men, to the rabble and to their rulers, often with an eye to the property of the perfidious Jews. Also, the Jews were wonderfully convenient scapegoats for everything from tyrannical government to natural catastrophe. When the Black Death killed at least a quarter of the population of Europe in 1348 and 1349, the Jews were blamed for it. German Christians were so incensed that they wiped out more than three hundred and fifty Jewish communities where, according to one contemporary chronicler, tens of thousands of Jews were "murdered, drowned, burned, broken on the wheel, hanged, exterminated, strangled, buried alive and tortured to death." A decade before, when the Host had allegedly been desecrated by Jews in a town called Deggensdorf on the Danube, the people of Deggensdorf believed that the Host, pierced by the Jews, had miraculously begun to bleed as though from the wounds of Christ crucified. The town synagogue was destroyed and in its place a chapel and shrine of the Holy Sepulchre were erected to celebrate the miracle. The ruling prince, Heinrich of Landshut, then per-formed a further miracle by declaring that no Christian need pay his debts to Jews. He congratulated his subjects for "burning and exterminating our Jews of Deggensdorf." The prince himself kept the property of the exterminated Jews.

Another example of the sort of mob violence which medieval Jewry learned to expect was that which originated in the German town of Rotingen in 1298, when a master builder there named Rindfleisch proclaimed that God had elected him to kill all the Jews. Rindfleisch led a mob through Germany and Austria, pillaging, burning, raping and murdering over one hundred thousand Jews in more than a hundred and forty-six different communities, all within six months. In the end, the authorities themselves became fearful of the growing power of this fanatic at the head of a great mob, and Rindfleisch was hanged.

Throughout these years, mobs roving Central and Western Eur-ope attacked the nearly defenseless Jews. Bands of Christian zealots called Flagellants roamed the land, lashing themselves with whips studded with nails, and calling on all devout Christians to the holy massacre of the Jews.

Pope Clement VI did what he could to calm the raging populace, and declared that the allegation that Jews had poisoned Christian wells was a falsehood and a calumny. This had little effect. The butchery continued.

Few in these terrible years, it seemed, were immune from the madness which had seized Europe. Even St. Thomas Aquinas, that "Angelic Doctor" who had learned so much from the great Jewish theologian, Maimonides, believed on both moral and religious grounds that the Jews should be kept in servitude. And so they were, literally chattels of the kings of England and of Saxony.

The worst was yet to come. There was a respite during the Jewish Golden Age in Spain following the conquest of the south of that country by the Moors, when Jewish and Arab intellectuals flourished and worked together in medicine, mathematics, astronomy, grammar, law and many other fields. There was at that time a free mingling and cross-fertilization in Arab lands of many cultures. Nathan Ausubel in his *Pictorial History of the Jewish People* says justly:

> When the Jews began to immigrate from Spain into southern France, Italy and other Mediterranean countries, they brought with them into those still backward Christian lands elements of the superior Greek-Arab-Hebrew culture. The historical fact seems somewhat paradoxical: the Jews and Arabs who were nurtured by the Orient were, in a cultural sense, the first Europeans. They planted the intellectual seed of Western civilization on the Continent.
>
> Undoubtedly, one of the great services the Jews rendered Western civilization was to make available, beginning with the Middle Ages, translations in Latin of important scholarly and scientific works of every variety that had originally been written in Hebrew, Greek and Arabic. This constituted the raw material out of which much of Christian culture, thought and knowledge was fashioned.

Meanwhile in Cairo, Maimonides was one of the greatest scholars in medieval medicine, and court physician to the Emperor Saladin. Maimonides was an Aristotelian thinker and interested in elaborating a practical framework of Jewish ethics in which the golden mean was the ultimate ideal. He developed the philosophy of reconciliation of religious faith with reason that so influenced Thomas Aquinas.

The Hebrew philosopher and poet, Solomon ibn Gabirol, who has his own street in Tel Aviv, was then, in the eleventh century, under the pen name of Avicebron, publishing his masterwork *The Fountain of Life*, which made a profound impression on much of the Christian world, including Duns Scotus, the founder of the Franciscan Order, and a Scottish philosopher who was probably unaware that the source of his ideas was this eminent rabbi.

The Golden Age of the Jews in southern Spain came to an end when the Christian kingdoms of the north united at the end of the eleventh century and drove back the Moors. The Moors then called on the far sterner Berber tribes of the Atlas Mountains. These new Moslem masters attempted to force the Jews at sword-point to accept Islam. Many chose death. Then, by 1411, a Dominican friar named Vincent Ferrer, at the head of a great mob of armed religious fanatics and looters, assaulted the synagogues of Castile, arriving during Sabbath services with a crucifix in one hand and a *Torah*, in the other, offering the choice, "Baptism or death!" Again, many thousands were killed, but Vincent Ferrer claimed that he had baptized thirty-five thousand Jews. About a hundred thousand Jews are supposed to have embraced Catholicism.

Then, in 1480, administered by the Dominicans, began the Spanish Inquisition, also called the Holy Office. Its purpose was to discover and punish heretics and infidels in general, but converted Jews suspected of practicing secretly their first religion were the most suspect. On February sixth, 1481, was held the first auto-da-fé. It reached Portugal in 1531, and for the next three hundred years in Spain and Portugal, in Goa in India and in the Iberian colonies in the New World, these burnings-alive continued. *The New Jewish Encyclopedia* counts some four hundred thousand martyrs tried for their loyalty to Judaism, and there were many Christian martyrs as well. The Grand Inquisitor of the Spanish Inquisition, Tomás de Torquemada, confessor to Queen Isabella of Spain, had obtained from the Spanish Court sanction for the expulsion of the Jews.

The grandson of a recently baptized Jewish grandmother, which some scholars feel helps to explain his ruthlessness toward Jews, Torquemada claimed to have burned two thousand heretics and to have imprisoned and ruined one hundred thousand others, most of them being Marranos. These Marranos were crypto-Jews, ostensibly Catholic, yet who throughout the years had preserved as much as they could of their Jewish faith. There are still some ten thousand families of Marranos in Spain alone, mostly in the Balearic Islands of Majorca and Minorca.

Jews were expelled from Spain in 1492, as Columbus noted in his journal. (There is, incidentally, a school, not necessarily Jewish, which believes that Columbus himself may have been a Marrano.)

Four years later, the Jews were expelled from Portugal.

In 1290, following a massacre of the Jews in England in 1189, they had been expelled from that country. They had already been expelled once from France by St. Louis in 1254. They had returned, but were banished again from France in 1394 by Charles VI. In 1421 they were expelled from Vienna, in 1495 from Lithuania, in 1670 for a second time from Vienna and in 1740 from Prague.

In his classic work *The Rise of the Dutch Republic,* the historian John Lothrop Motley wrote:

> The Inquisition was a bench of monks without appeal, having its familiars in every house . . . it arrested on suspicion, tortured till confession, and then punished by fire. . . .

In the specially constructed arenas where the autos-da-fé were conducted, great crowds of the people, the clergy, nobility and royalty assembled. Motley comments that they "regarded it as an inspiring and delightful recreation."

The Inquisition was not long in reaching the New World, where, to quote Motley again, it "taught the savages of . . . America to shudder at the name of Christianity." We have seen that there is some reason to believe that Christopher Columbus himself may have been a Marrano. Specifically, according to the Spanish historian Salvador de Madariaga, Columbus belonged to a Spanish Jewish family named Colón, itself a common Jewish name in Spain, which they had fled in 1390 to Genoa, where Columbus was born sixty years later. There was also his preoccupation with the fate of Spanish Jewry, the fact that he knew Spanish better than Italian, and his frequent mention of Hebrew Scriptures and Jewish history in his writings.

Many of the Spanish and Portuguese Marranos, or New Christians as they were also called, set sail for the Americas. But even there the Inquisition followed them. In Mexico, the first executions for Jewish heresy were held in 1528. The Mexican Holy Office was officially established in 1570, and not abolished until 1820. In 1596, Francisca de Carbajal and her four children were burned to death in an auto-da-fé in Mexico City, a few of the many who met their deaths at the hands of the Inquisition in the New World, or were returned to Portugal or Spain for trial and punishment there. As for the Indians, since the Spanish conquistadores were searching for gold and slaves and souls to save, those American Indians who fell into their hands were automatically baptized, and if they should revert to their own religions, it was the Inquisition again. The Spanish missionary and great friend of the Indians, Bartolomé de Las Casas, estimated that the number of Indians who perished at the hands of his countrymen through slaughter, death through overwork in the fields and in the mines, may have been about twenty million.

In that portion of the continent which is now the United States, there were estimated to be perhaps a million Indians at the time of Columbus's arrival. The U.S. Bureau of the Census in 1900 gave the Indian population as two hundred and thirty-seven thousand, one hundred and ninety-six. Meanwhile, the British, the French, the Spanish, the Africans and all the other groups had increased prodigiously. What happened to all the Indians? Surely, together with the Jews and the Armenians, this is one of the most terrible of all of the examples of genocide the world has known.

As England and Switzerland were later to become, the Netherlands was early a haven for those who could not find refuge elsewhere. Marranos expelled from Portugal and Spain settled there, as did Jews fleeing Poland after the uprising of the Cossacks in 1648, when the Cossacks slaughtered their Polish masters, and for good measure all of the Jews whom they could catch.

The newly Dutch Jews made their way to the overseas territories such as Recifé in northeast Brazil and Curaçao in the Carribean.

But in the mid-seventeenth century, the Portuguese conquered Recifé from the Dutch, and this thriving Jewish community, the first in the Western Hemisphere, was once again forced to flee the Inquisition. In September, 1654, a French naval barque, the *St. Charles*, brought twenty-three Jews to Nieuw Amsterdam, all former residents of Brazil, and once again fleeing the Inquisition. Robbed of almost all of their belongings on the way, two of the Jewish passengers, Abram Israel and Judic de Mereda, were held as hostages until sufficient funds could be raised from the auction of the little band's few remaining possessions to pay their passage.

Peter Stuyvesant, the choleric governor of Nieuw Amsterdam, testy as usual, reported to the Board of Directors of the Dutch West India Company, petitioning "of Your Worships that the deceitful race, such hateful enemies and blasphemers of the name of Christ, be not allowed to infest and trouble this new colony." In Amsterdam, the Directors of the Company which owned the colony, which had a number of Jewish officers and investors, and which was not unmindful of the patriotic service rendered by Netherlands Jews during the Thirty Years War in helping rid their country of the tyranny of Philip II of Spain, instructed the wrothful Governor Stuyvesant to let the Jews stay where they were, without, however, "exercising their religion in a synagogue or a gathering." These twenty-three passengers on the *St. Charles* and a single daring traveler named Jacob Barsimson, who had arrived a month before them on the Dutch West India Company ship, *The Pear Tree*, were the first Jews in the American colony, the two dozen forerunners of what was to become the largest Jewish community of any single nation.

The newcomers had to fight for their rights, the privilege of owning houses and property, of trading with the Indians, of commerce, and of erecting their own houses of worship. There was a small synagogue in New York, the first in the colonies, by 1730, in Old Mill Street which became known as Jews' Alley. Then in 1763, a second synagogue, and an outstandingly handsome example of New England Colonial architecture, was dedicated in Newport, Rhode Island, whose liberty-loving governor, Roger Williams, had declared in the charter for his colony that no one living there was to be in "any way molested, punished, disquieted or called in question for any difference in opinion"—a principle which was adopted one hundred and fifty years later as the First Amendment to the United States Constitution, that providing for separation of Church and State.

Jewish settlers in the Dutch, and then the British, American colonies suffered from some disabilities, it is true, and these were largely political, just as Jewish Americans still suffer from other disabilities, largely social. It took a number of years for the separate colonies and states, under the federal structure and each with the privilege of making many of its own laws, including who was eligible for office, before full civil rights were accorded all Jews as foreseen by President Washington in his letter to the Jewish congregation of Newport:

> The Citizens of the United States of America have a right to applaud themselves for having given to mankind examples of an enlarged and liberal policy: a policy worthy of imitation. All possess alike liberty of conscience and immunities of citizenship. It is now no more that toleration is spoken of as if it was by the indulgence of one class of people that another enjoyed the exercise of their inherent natural rights. For happily the government of the United States, which gives to bigotry no sanction, to persecution no assistance, requires only that those who live under its protection should demean themselves as good citizens in giving it on all occasions their effectual support.

It was some years even after the Constitution of 1776 that Jews were accorded full and equal civil rights, for this was a matter for state authority and not that of Congress. Still, the growing Jewish colonies flourished in the United States, in contrast to those in the Spanish and Portuguese lands or even in the French West Indies where Louis XIV had extended the Black Code of expulsion in which the Jesuits categorized all Jews "as declared enemies of the Christian faith." And from Colonial times on, the Jews of America were a part of every facet of the development of the new country. They were trappers and merchants and peddlers, seafarers trading with the Old World and with the Indies, shoemakers and saddlers, bakers and butchers, inventors of the whale-oil spermacetti candles and prominent in New England whaling. There were Jewish pioneers and Jewish cowboys. The levis made from the blue denim named after the town of Nîmes were invented by Levi Strauss of California.

There were a few Jewish planters in the southern colonies, though not many. After the great waves of Jewish immigration at the turn of the last century, Jewish leaders and workers played a prominent part in the establishment of American trade unions. There is almost no part of American life in which Jews have not played a part. There have been Jewish gangsters; Jewish privateers issued letters of marque by the American authorities, and preying on enemy shipping in Revolutionary times; and, I am sorry to say, Jews in the West African slave trade working with their Christian brethren in this unforgivable business which brought one-tenth of our citizens to this country, and which lost so many more lives in the terrible Middle Passage.

There were some five hundred and fifty thousand Jews serving in the Second World War and two hundred and fifty thousand in the First. A few were Tories during the American Revolution, most were Rebels, and many hundreds served with the Continental armies. A Jewish immigrant from Poland, Haym Salomon, who served as a broker negotiating bills of exchange and foreign loans for the "financier of the American Revolution," Robert Morris, was arrested in 1776 by the British and condemned to death as a spy. He escaped from prison, and advanced money to Jefferson, Madison, Monroe, Edmund Randolph and David Rittenhouse. Salomon died a few years later, a pauper, but a great patriot and one still respected.

Zionism and a deep belief that the Jews might one day return to their homeland was a part of the American credo from Colonial times. In 1818, forty years before Theodor Herzl was born, John Adams wrote, "I really wish the Jews again in Judea, an independent nation." In 1891, an Illinois minister named William E. Blackstone presented a memorial to President Harrison and James G. Blaine, the Secretary of State, asking them to call upon the European powers "to secure the holding, at an early date, of an international conference to consider the condition of the Israelites and their claims to Palestine as their ancient home." The Reverend Blackstone knew something of Palestine and had seen the misery of the Jews in Europe. His most Christian endorsement was signed by the mayors of the six largest cities, the editors of the principal newspapers there, leading clergymen of all faiths, jurists, educators and industrialists, among whom were J. Pierpont Morgan, John D. Rockefeller, Cyrus W. Field, Russell Sage, William E. Dodge and Philip D. Armour. There were in the nineteenth century colonies of Zionists from the United States who set out to till the soil of the Holy Land, some of them Jewish, some Christian, and some groups which were mixed.

An American passionately concerned was Emma Lazarus, who wrote the lines inscribed on the bronze tablet in the base of the statute at Liberty Island, concluding with:

> Give me your tired, your poor,
> Your huddled masses yearning to breathe free,
> The wretched refuse of your teeming shore,
> Send these, the homeless, tempest-tossed to me.
> I lift my lamp beside the golden door!

Things are still far from perfect in the United States, and that goes as well for the Jews in South Africa, in India, in Britain and in other countries where they have settled. In those countries which they have left or tried to leave, the statistics tell their own story: of perhaps three million two hundred thousand Jews in Poland before the Second World War, there are now thirty-five thousand; of perhaps half a million in Germany, there are about the same number left.

It is a most strange and curious and wonderful thing to ride from Tel Aviv to Haifa on a German train, given as part of German war-reparations to Israel. And to have friends whom one sees every day, who have received other restitution for members of their families killed in concentration camps, who yet display, at least outwardly, no anger against their former oppressors, nor vengeance; just Israeli citizens who want above all the world to be peaceful. A few have refused to receive the reparations; it must seem to them blood money.

There is some hope for a better world, it seems to me, in spite of all the carnage. It is coming now, but I remember the German exchange student, with a neat Nazi button in his lapel, with whom I went to secondary school, a nice fellow who came to visit my family in Chicago, yet who wrote just before the war to the school weekly newspaper with a picture of himself in German uniform, explaining that the whole Nazi military build-up was but a defense against the enemies who were about to descend upon them. I spent enough time in Chicago and in school with my schoolmate to know that he was honest. I used to argue with him about the Jews, but the idea of a holocaust seemed inconceivable. All I know, looking back at it, is that our friend was committed to exterminating a portion of the people of the world.

20/. . . AND THE WAGES

Bertie and I were surprised on our arrival in Israel, and through-out our stay there, to discover what struck us as an elusive but perceptible anti-Jewish bias on the part of a good many of the American staff at our Embassy. The atmosphere has since improved. But then, certainly, this could not help them do their jobs. Some-times it was only a turn of phrase, sometimes a more frankly admitted prejudice. Sometimes it took the form of being en-thusiastically pro-Arab on any given controversial issue. A couple of days after our arrival, at a lunch given for us to meet some of the Embassy and USAID people with whom I would be working, I was introduced to a very cheerful, smallish, plump older man with white hair, bright-blue eyes and a firm conviction that it was a mistake to admit Jews to country clubs, a thesis with which he regaled me for some twenty minutes. Out of respect for his seniority, and being very new on the ground, my rejoinders were mild; I'm not sure now that this was not a mistake.

It had been CARE's custom during the first years of Israel's independence to send Jewish Americans as their Chiefs of Mission, but in latter years they had restricted themselves to Gentiles, as had the American Embassy (though, after we left, there was a breakthrough with the posting of some Jewish secretaries). I wrote a memo pointing out that I did not really feel a Jewish American officer, if he were capable, should be unduly influenced by his co-religionists. I thought that President Kennedy had laid that ghost to rest, at least in the United States. And beginning with the first American Consul in this region, Major Mordecai Manuel Noah, American Consul in Tunis, where he had done an outstanding job liberating crews of a number of American ships captured by Barbary pirates, there had been both good Jewish and good Gentile American diplomats in this area. My trump card was that the present security officer for the Canadian Embassy in Israel, known to be an efficient post, happened to be a Hebrew-speaking Jewish officer in the Royal Canadian Mounted Police, dressed in scarlet tunic and all.

It is good news that the Catholic University in Louvain, following the Second Vatican Council's call for "mutual knowledge and respect between Catholics and Jews," is now methodically surveying schoolbooks, religious publications and other material in French to make sure that its contents do not include defamatory material.

But it is not surprising to learn that a Spanish schoolbook published about 1960 contains another account of the ritual-blood-sacrifice libel, complete with a picture in color of the martyred little Christian boy, or to learn from an article "Spanish Anti-Semitism Today" by Ray Alan in the magazine *Commentary* for August, 1964, that the ultra-right Catholic weekly *¿Qué Pasa?* in an article called "The Antichrist in Action" has discovered a "strictly secret" underground plot to wage "war to the death against the Christian world." It is finally revealed that this strictly secret revelation is the annual report of the American Jewish Committee. The chief religious commentator of *Radio Nacional de España*, Father Venancio Markos, says Ray Alan, has publicly regretted that "the times would not permit a revival of the Holy Inquisition," pointing out that "the Spanish Inquisition committed fewer crimes in its whole history than English Protestantism in one year." The enemies of Spain, he said, were Communists, Freemasons, Protestants and Jews. The former French Socialist Deputy and anti-Jewish writer, Paul Rassinier, was given interested press coverage in Spain, again according to Alan, when he denounced Jewish "lies" about the concentration camps: "It was the inmates themselves who ran the camps, under the supervision of German and Polish Communists, not the Nazis . . . the so-called gas chambers were a propagandist fiction. The one that is exhibited at Dachau was built after the war on the orders of the Allies . . . the Jews have made a fuss about these camps purely for financial reasons. German reparations are vital to Israel's economy. The more terrible the stories they can tell about Nazi persecution, the more reparations they can get. Hence the myth of the six million murdered Jews, hence the Eichmann trial." Alan also quotes President Nasser's statement: "The lie about the six million murdered Jews is no longer taken seriously by anyone, not even by the simplest man in our country." Apparently making the point that the six million, or whatever number, Jews just pretended to get themselves killed is now standard ammunition in the anti-Semitic armory around the world.

Now that the ecumenical breeze is blowing, there are straws of sanity in the wind. Yet it seems that one can never be entirely sure. We seem to have come a distance from those days five years before the Dreyfus trial when a certain A. Willette could run for the French Legislature as the Anti-Semitic Candidate for the Ninth Arrondissement of Paris, complete with a poster surmounted by the figure of Liberty blowing a bugle, female and nude to the waist of course, a patriotic song beginning, *"Gai! Gai!"* and including the admonition that "Jews are only strong because we are on our knees! . . . *Get up!*" A caricature of a little fleeing Jew with a battered top hat, umbrella over one shoulder and a very large hooked nose is being vanquished on the poster by four sturdy military and working types, one of whom is holding a pig's head and a double-bladed axe with which he has just broken a tablet labeled *The Talmud*.

In the United States of the thirties, there were a number of tinpot rabble rousers such as the Reverend Charles E. Coughlin of Royal Oak, Michigan, whose Christian Front's inflammatory publication with the happy title *Social Justice* printed *The Protocols of the Elders of Zion* in its first two issues, and whose own anti-Semitic radio diatribes were silenced by Cardinal Mundelein of Chicago; Joe McWilliams, leader of the Christian Mobilizers and the American Pioneer Party, for which he advocated, from the back of a covered wagon in Yorkville, violence and blood in the streets; Fritz Kuhn, Führer of the German American Bund, who was imprisoned on charges of embezzlement then deported to Germany after the Second World War; and a scattering of hate groups with titles like The Silver Shirts, The Black Legion, The Knights of the Camellia, The Christian Crusaders, The Defenders of the Christian Faith, The American Vigilantes, The Order of '76 and so on. They deluged second-class mail with vicious, libelous and often obscene anti-Jewish publications but in the end were rejected by the American people as the earlier anti-Semites had been by France. Justice Frank Murphy of the Supreme Court identified the campaign correctly with the warning to the public, "to recognize and combat hateful propaganda against American citizens of Jewish descent as a powerful secret Nazi weapon—powerful because it has been deliberately spread to this continent where no Nazi invading force has been able to set foot, and secret because victims so innoculated are often unconscious of the source from which it comes."

No nation or group of people, however moderate, seems entirely immune to a virus of this sort. When the Nazis appeared to many to be all powerful, the hate mongers' following increased sizably; with the defeat of the Axis, most of the membership crawled back into the woodwork.

The rising fever of intolerance in the United States in the nineteen thirties, aggravated by the frustrations and the miseries of the Depression, and then further inflamed as the native imitators and branch bundists of the Nazis began to make themselves heard, was foreshadowed by the fears and ugly striking out at minority groups during the early nineteen twenties when, as Frederick Lewis Allen wrote in *Only Yesterday*, "Intolerance became an American virtue."

The victims were the Koons, Kikes and Katholics, the targets of the Ku Klux Klan, which by 1924 had reached by careful estimate a national membership of nearly four and a half million. The way had been prepared following the Russian Revolution in 1917; it was seriously feared that the tramp of Bolshevik boots might next be heard in the land of the free. It was known that Trotsky, the head of the Red Army, was a Jew, as were many prominent members of the provisional Karensky and the succeeding Soviet governments. Karl Marx had been born a Jew, though he must have been a bad one, for his father had him baptized a Christian at the age of three in order to smooth his way in life, and Marx delivered himself of such nuggets as: "The basis of Judaism is selfishness. The only bond that ties Jews is the conservation of their property and their egotism."

What was not so well known in America was the long-standing Czarist anti-Semitism, and the credo of the Czarist White Guards still fighting the Reds that the Soviet government was a "Jewish government," set upon destroying "Holy Mother Russia." Also, that thousands of anti-Bolshevik Jews who had fled into still-anti-Soviet Siberia were butchered there by their protectors, the White Guard commanders, Admiral Kolchak and General Wrangel; and that about two hundred thousand of the million and a quarter Ukranian Jews had perished in the savage uprisings of the civil war.

What America did know was that Jews were associated with Bolshevism, syndicalism, anarchism and Communism. As Allen wrote, the American business man had come to believe that radicalism was the "spawn of long-haired Slavs and unwashed Eastside Jews," and that "the struggle of American laboring-men for better wages was the beginning of an armed rebellion directed by Lenin and Trotsky, and that behind every innocent professor who taught that there were arguments for as well as against socialism there was a bearded rascal from Eastern Europe with a money bag in one hand and a smoking bomb in the other."

At this point, Henry Ford discovered the International Jew, lending his name to a book with that title, which drew heavily on the repeatedly discredited Czarist forgery called *The Protocols of the Elders of Zion*, which purported to expose a world-wide Jewish conspiracy. From 1920 to 1927, scurrilous attacks on the Jews were run in Ford's widely circulated paper, *The Dearborn Independent*, which, to quote Frederick Lewis Allen again, "accused the unhappy race of plotting the subjugation of the whole world and (for good measure) of being the source of almost every American affliction including high rents, the shortage of farm labor, jazz, gambling, drunkenness, loose morals and even short skirts. The Ford attack, absurd as it was, was merely an exaggerated manifestation of a widespread anti-Semitism. Prejudice became as pervasive as the air. Landlords grew less disposed to rent to Jewish tenants, and schools to admit Jewish boys and girls; there was a public scandal at Annapolis over the hazing of a Jewish boy; Harvard College seriously debated limiting the number of Jewish students; and all over the country Jews felt that a barrier had fallen between them and the Gentiles."

Ford recanted, and before his death publicly apologized to Louis Marshall, president of the American Jewish Committee, begging the Jews to forgive him "as fellow men and brothers," and promising that "henceforth they may look to me for friendship and good will."

Yet damage was done. In 1921 and in 1924, Congress, with the help of the KKK, anti-Semitic legislators, protectionists, manufacturers, chauvinist labor unions and others, enacted stringent immigration regulations, discriminating heavily against Eastern Europeans and Asians among others. This virtually put an end to the great influx of Jews from Eastern Europe. A number of them went to Palestine.

As usual, the myths died hard. As recently as 1928, when a little girl was missing in the small town of Massena, New York (she turned up the next day, lost in the woods but well), the mayor dispatched a state trooper to bring in the local rabbi to ask if it were true that the Jews offered human sacrifice for Yom Kippur which was fast approaching.

Even after the Second World War, some New York newspapers were still running thinly disguised advertisements for resorts or hotels with "a Christian atmosphere." This venerable demonology is far from being exorcized. Within the last couple of years, my wife and I have been treated to a harangue by a British business man from Argentina, who commented on discrimination against the Jews with the simple logic: "Well, they killed Christ, didn't they?" This from a sojourner in a country whose Jewish population of half a million has been under attack by gangs of marauding hoodlums who call themselves after an old and supposedly ferocious Indian tribe. Next door in Chile, there is a Horst Wessel league of young men, uniformed, swastika arm-bands and all, named after the Nazi bully and street fighter who became a martyr and hero of the "Horst Wessel Lied," celebrating his refusal to accept help from a Jewish doctor as he lay bleeding to death on the pavement.

In addition to the groups in Argentina and Chile and some in Brazil, there are the neo-Nazis in Germany itself. An Associated Press story, datelined Bamberg, Germany, 16 June 1965, reported two visiting Americans discovering vandalism and desecration in the local Jewish cemetery with yard-high swastikas and such sentiments as "The six million Jews murdered during the Third Reich were six million Jews too few." The story also reported that in spite of official repentance by the city for the vandalism, rewards of three and a quarter million dollars offered for information leading to the arrest of the vandals, Catholic and Protestant clergymen as well as the editors of the city's two newspapers had been telephoned by an anonymous caller who said: "Croak the Kikes. We'll continue to fight. We'll continue to smear."

21/ THE DARK SIDE OF MAN

How to write about a memorial to the six million Jews who were killed in Europe? How does one feel in this quiet place, left alone with one's thoughts?

Our bookshelves at home are crowded with copies of the *Yad Vashem Bulletin* and the *Yad Washem Studies on the European Jewish Catastrophe and Resistance*, with their detailed accounts of the growth of anti-Semitic legislation in the Germany of the Third Reich and of the totalitarian Central and Eastern European states, legislation which prepared the grounds for the extermination that was to come.

These archives' document the multiple rôles played by the Gestapo in halting or sometimes even promoting Jewish emigration from countries in their power; the harassment and systematic looting of Jewish properties for the enrichment of the Reich; and the careful mechanics of extermination. The archives of Yad Vashem describe life in the ghettos with their Jewish self-governments used by the Nazis to control the inmates, Jews who sometimes worked—in vain— to save their own skins by selling those of their brothers; who also sometimes interposed themselves between the murder machine and their fellow Jews. There were the stories, step-by-step, of the survivors of the death marches, the daily life of the ghettos whose inhabitants, up to the moment of their annihilation, saw that schools and classes carried on, that there were lectures and there was music, that the synagogue was maintained, a lively underground press flourished. In Bialystok and elsewhere there were underground ghetto archives which have survived. There were chronicles of the lot of the remaining Jews in Italy and in France, Poland and the other European countries conquered by the Nazis.

There were reports on the fluctuating degree of liberalty or refusal to admit Jewish refugees by even such traditional havens as Switzerland, the United States and Britain. There were specialized studies like that of the Nazi vocabulary which followed the dictum of Talleyrand that *"La parole a été donnée à l'homme pour déguiser sa pensée,"* as shown in the great importance attached to words by Hitler and his followers. It was spelled out in *Mein Kampf,* where German sentimentality and love for high-flown phrases, and their respect for legal terminology were all put to use with the new meanings given to old expressions, leaning heavily when describing atrocity on words and phrases such as "uprightness," "readiness for self-sacrifice," "love," "faith," and "loyalty." Religious feeling was summoned up by this anti-religious state with such slogans as the twenty-foot banner over the doorway of Nazi headquarters in Nuremberg reading "By Resisting the Jews I Fight for the Lord," and by frequent use of such suggestively Christian turns of phrase as "Commandments for the Party Member," until at last Pope Pius XI was moved to warn the Nazi that "if he did not wish to be a Christian he must refrain at least from enriching the vocabulary of his heresy from out of Christian terminology."

On our bookshelves are documents of the Eichmann trial, stories of those few who fought in the forest with the partisans and survived, the handful who made their way out through the ghetto sewers, and eventually to freedom. There are passages from the diaries of more than one unyielding soul who kept a record of what happened to him and to his people until death came to claim him. There are novels like *The Wall* by John Hersey, made of the lives of human beings of the Warsaw Ghetto. Then there were the factual accounts such as the record of *European Jewry Ten Years After the War* published in 1956 in New York by the Institute of Jewish Affairs of The World Jewish Congress, telling of what had happened to the Jews of Europe, the pogroms, the escape of some and the fate of the remainder.

It bore out what I had learned in Jerusalem from Professor Arieh Tartakover, that of the three million two hundred thousand Jews in Poland before the war there were left some thirty-five thousand, with more than two and three-quarters of a million dead.

Popular magazines and scholarly monographs continue to be published with revelations of how our country and others, perhaps not through malice, sometimes with fatal indifference, sometimes moved by an official's dislike of Jews, had lent, through lethargy, their sanction to this openly advertised, greatest mass murder of our time.

As this is written, the floor around me is strewn with photographs taken in the days of Hitler: smiling, jolly-looking Wehrmacht noncoms are posing for a snapshot taken by a comrade. Against a winter landscape, the two subjects are smiling into the camera. In the background, two dead Jews dangle from a tree. I see an elderly Jew wearing prayer shawl and phylacteries, with a platoon of German soldiers in the background, at ease and smiling as though they were on a high school outing, giving him a few moments to pray for a row of dead Jews on the pavement in front of him before he is sent to his own death. There is a picture of an eleven-year-old inmate at Buchenwald, showing the American correspondent Martin Bursten the crematorium ovens which had consumed his parents. In a photograph taken by a German Army photographer of troops rounding up Warsaw Jews, there is a boy of perhaps six or seven in the foreground, hands raised high above his head, guns leveled against him; he is wearing a short overcoat and ankle socks, with a sensitive, intelligent face, but looking a little bewildered.

There is also a portfolio of water colors and drawings in pen and ink of the Kovno ghetto where the Palestinian artist Esther Lurie found herself trapped at the beginning of the Second World War and where she continued to paint and sketch through the years until the community with its several thousand survivors was liquidated. She was sent to a forced labor camp in East Germany. Her work, in which the ghetto dwellers had been intensely interested so that a record might survive, was hidden, then retrieved. Later, much of it was brought to Israel where it has become a part of the collections of Yad Vashem and a number of other museums, simple, moving, yet not seizing the obviously sentimental nor dramatic, neither cruel, nor heroic—just the daily lives of the beleaguered, persistent people of Kovno who did not give up until the very end.

Out of all of these I had thought to try to create some sort of description of what the Yad Vashem memorial is all about, what had happened, why it had happened. Its archivists had searched the world to find the records so many of the oppressors had tried to destroy. Israel tried to bring to life, to Jew and Gentile alike, the lesson of the Eichmann trial, that it really did happen and that it must never happen again. I had read the reports from the Nuremberg and other war-crime trials, and the testimony of doctors who had worked in the concentration camps and who had lived to answer the questions put to them by the judges. I had read accounts by American soldiers of their reactions as they walked into the death camps. I looked at pictures of bulky SS women guards being forced by British troops at Bergen-Belsen to bury tens of thousands of emaciated, naked bodies in a new mass grave.

It was a late afternoon in October, clear with a few clouds in the sky, as I climbed the few steps leading up a mountaintop on the outskirts of Jerusalem, bare, but surrounded with many newly planted saplings. There, at the southwest of the city, on what is now called the Mount of Remembrance, is the shrine, a low rectangular building, flat-roofed. Inside, it rises to a truncated peak, off-center. It is called in Hebrew the Tent of Remembrance. Outside were a few flower boxes and gnarled, transplanted olive trees.

Yad Vashem means "The Hand and the Name," or "Everlasting Memorial," words taken from a chapter in Isaiah.

The building is starkly simple—a weathered, horizontally striped, flat concrete box set on a foundation higher than a man, made of large, dark, iron-red boulders, volcanic and pitted, yet seemingly smooth to the touch, with a great double-gate set into the boulders. The doors of the gate are grey-black iron, embossed with slashed and jagged rough strokes of lightning. The immense boulders had been taken from the heights on one side of the Sea of Galilee.

Inside, it is twilight. There are no windows, and one's eyes gradually become accustomed to the dark. There is faint light which makes its way through narrow opening spaces running along each of the four walls of the building, between the concrete wall and the boulder foundation.

The floor is recessed below the catwalk which surrounds it. Here the visitor stands. At the center of the floor is a flame. There is no bravura here. Around the flame in raised letters in both Hebrew and Roman letters are the names of the twenty places where so many met their deaths: Bergen-Belsen, Dachau, Auschwitz, Treblinka, Babi-Yar and the others, all created for death.

In the flamelight at the center of this great cavern-like room, there is a common grave and in it lie ashes of the Jews from all of the twenty concentration camps.

There is a fearsome simplicity about this place. Tourists come, and why should they not? Also, the people who live here, who have made Israel, the people who would safeguard it and who want to remember. Chiefs of state come to Yad Vashem and lay their wreaths there. All I know of were visibly moved. But when the captains and the kings depart, still the people come.

I think, perhaps, not so much to see, as to feel what happened.

At Yad Vashem, I had the experience, on both my first and last visits, of being the only visitor. Outside, the sun was shining, an excavator had stopped gouging red earth from the hillside. It was deathly quiet inside and my leather heels clacked against the mosaic, echoing in the hallways.

There is an exhibition on the floor below, the studied horror of the killing of the Jews, and I went many times to spend some hours there. But on my first and last visits what I most wanted to do was to look at the flame, at the names on the floor, and to try to think a bit about how this all came to happen, how we came to do this to ourselves.

It is as clear as clear that if the Jews are to survive they must defend themselves.

It continued to be quiet in Yad Vashem, and I, as everyone must, wondered what my own part was in all of this. Long before I was old enough to vote, I had felt, as so many did, revulsion, and shame, the horror, the guilt, the waves of distaste against war and conquest of any kind, no matter how draped in splendid bunting. I don't think we understood all this, but there was then a vague pacifism in the air. Certainly, when I read about wars, I felt a kind of complicity through acquiesence.

This was fine as far as it went.

Gradually, many people became aware of the fact that there were no factories making soap out of Allied soldiers during the First World War. I do believe that this was a major factor in our discounting some of the earlier stories of the hell created by Hitler and his followers. They followed the same apparently fictitious pattern. Except that this time it was true.

Looking back, it is easy to see that there was ample warning in the book Hitler wrote in jail, *Mein Kampf*. We were all told clearly what was to happen, but perhaps in part because of the thoroughly discredited propaganda tales of the First World War, it was now hard to believe that people truly intended to try to make fertilizer and soap out of other people. This happened.

The spectre which haunts me is that which haunts millions of others: is there any way to stop this?

The last time I visited Yad Vashem, I asked myself questions which I could not answer. There was something hallucinatory about the place. Standing there in the half-light before the flame, I looked at the names of Bergen-Belsen, Buchenwald and the others, Theresienstadt and Ravensbrück, the women's camp to which our friend Bori and her sister had been sent: they were chosen to work, but their parents were murdered at Auschwitz. There was Dachau and Treblinka and all the rest in the terrible rollcall. Outside, a sparrow was singing in the trees.

I began to think of Poul Larsen, a laughing, barrel-shaped Dane with whom we had worked in India where he had represented the United Nations Children's Fund, who had been sent to Dachau because as an undergraduate he had understood that Hitler, even in his early years, was a monster, and had bicycled about Copenhagen in the night tacking up posters saying so. Poul was strong and lucky, and in the end it was he who won. Most didn't.

I thought of the rough reddish boulder just outside Copenhagen which was the simple, most eloquent memorial to those Danes, Jews and Christians who did what no other people did and closed ranks at only a few hours' warning of German plans to deport to their death the hitherto unmolested Jews of Denmark. Against the most fearful odds, the people of Denmark sought out, warned, hid, fed and smuggled through the strictest possible land and sea patrol, directed by Adolf Eichmann, to the safety of neutral Sweden all but a handful of their Jewish fellows.

Thoughts raced. From the bloody mists of prehistoric times, the history of man has been a record of slaughter, of cruelty. Now, here we find ourselves. Most of that which we should be ashamed of has been swept under the rug, what we, people, have done to other people: to the American Indians, the Armenians, the African slaves who made the Middle Passage and, recently, the ruthless extermination by the Chinese of the Tibetans and their way of life. We worry about refugees, while there are more refugees than there were at the end of the Second World War, and even more refugees now than when I began to write this account. I kept trying to remind myself that the Nazi policy of extermination was not directed only against the Jews, but against the Gypsies who were considered lower species, and against Negroes whom Hitler and his philosophers declared to be sub-human. It seemed to me that, even during the most terrible of the purges in Russia and in China in the last centuries as chronicled by their own historians and as judged by others, still these governments had at least made an obeisance to decency and to the feelings of the rest of the world by their insistence that there was no harm done, really, that most of the charges against them were false. This may seem a small excuse indeed for the great slave-labor camps which were long known, but at least it did reflect a vestigial feeling of guilt and conscience, some idea of right and wrong.

The Nazi government was the only one I knew in these centuries that made, as a matter of proud policy, persecution and extermination of groups which they declared to be sub-human, boasted of by the authorities through all the communications they could command. I tried hard to remember that this was over, or was supposed to be over.

I stood there for a long time in the quiet, large and lonely chamber of Yad Vashem.

The photographs and the documents which I had seen downstairs kept flickering through my mind's eye. I could see the lines in the books I had read, remember the pictures. There was one photograph of a group of middle-aged, naked men accompanied by a little boy wearing only a cap, all waiting in the winter woods to be shot by their warmly dressed German military captors.

What to make of all of this? Now, most of those who have heard of the killings act as though, Yes, that's true, perhaps it really happened, but then, the world must go about its own business. Some are anxious to dispute the record—which can never be an exact one—arguing that there were not really six million, but only three and a quarter, or four, or at the most five million Jews done to death.

The lesson I began to learn is that which Ben-Gurion was trying to teach through the Eichmann trial, easily understandable even to those North African and Middle Eastern immigrants called Orientals who European settlers seemed to believe, without the experience of the European holocaust, could not understand what was happening. Yet I saw Moroccan and Iraqi Jews day after day in the streets, transistor radios glued to their ears as if transfixed by the trial of the technician who said he was just carrying out orders in his enthusiastic direction of the killing of the Jewish people.

The message was: Do not forget. Never, never forget. This can happen again.

At Yad Vashem I felt that those people whose faces, whose photographs I had just seen were not really dead, not killed. How could they be dead? This couldn't happen. It was impossible to accept. Yet it did happen. In the outside world we did not, and many of us still do not, want to believe it, but it did happen.

This is what we have done to ourselves. When I left Yad Vashem that last time, I came away with a feeling of emptiness, a feeling, not that *They had done it*, but that *All of us had done it*.

I had a feeling alien to the Anglo-Saxon world in which I had been brought up, where men are not supposed to cry. I felt that I wanted to cry. But I could not cry.

On leaving Yad Vashem I bought all of the publications I could find on the Memorial Shrine itself, its archives and its publications, the many books and essays and pictures which these had inspired. Among them was a volume simply called *Belsen*, and in it was a poem by a girl twelve years old whose name was not known. Trans-

lated from the Yiddish, it began almost like a nursery rhyme with
the words:

> One, two, three
> When are we free?

ending with the lines:

> One, two, three
> We do believe in Thee
> And Israel's Eternity.

Then, after leaving Israel, I found a brightly colored album called
... *I never saw another butterfly* ..., children's poems and drawings
in pencil and big splashy paintings in happy poster colors and collages, all very, very much like the pictures I had seen in the children's
art classes in visits to Israeli primary schools as I made my rounds
making sure that the milk and school-lunch programs were running
smoothly.

The poems and paintings and collages in the album were all made
by child prisoners, none of whom was older than fifteen, at the
Terezín concentration camp, and while they drew and spoke of
flowers and princesses and wizards and cookies and candy and a little
mouse trying to catch a flea, of trees and beauty and home, and
smiling faces and children skipping rope, they also reflected the
world around them: the barbed wire, the bars, the uniformed prison-
camp guards. The children's poems speak of typhus and the dying
and the dead, of the filth in which they were forced to live, of the
piles of corpses and the camp's wagons and dirty hearse which came
to take them away.

Yet Terezín was supposed to be a model concentration camp, one
to which visitors were taken to show them how well the Nazi authorities were treating those interned, one in which the boys and girls
living in the "children's homes" were specifically encouraged to draw
and to paint, to recite poetry, to put on plays, to study. What the
visitors were not told was that the camp at Terezín, which the Nazis
referred to not as a concentration camp but as a ghetto, which
seemed to them to sound more attractive, was only a way station to
Oswiecim and the other extermination centers.

Fifteen thousand children passed through Terezín according to the records which the Nazis kept so meticulously. One hundred survived. Most of the children met their end in 1944, the year before the war ended.

The book of poems and drawings is a beautiful and heartbreaking volume, chosen in 1962 from the State Jewish Museum in Prague, printed in Czechoslovakia, and published in English, German, Yiddish, Spanish and Swedish. I only wish it could be translated into every language in the world.

Wherever the names and ages of the children and the dates of their deaths are known, these are given. Most are anonymous. These pictures and these poems are all that remain of them.

The poem from which the collection takes its name is called "The Butterfly," and reads:

> The last, the very last,
> So richly, brightly, dazzlingly yellow.
> Perhaps if the sun's tears would sing
> against a white stone. . . .
> Such, such a yellow
> Is carried lightly way up high.
> It went away I'm sure because it wished to
> kiss the world goodbye.
> For seven weeks I've lived in here,
> Penned up inside this ghetto
> But I have found my people here.
> The dandelions call to me
> And the white chestnut candles in the court.
> Only I never saw another butterfly.
> That butterfly was the last one.
> Butterflies don't live in here,
> In the ghetto.
>
> PAUL FRIEDMANN *4. 6. 1942*

22/ ISRAELIS AND AMERICANS

A nglo-Saxon newcomers, with the Americans leading the way, of course, are the subject of a predictable series of Israeli jests about the building by these frontiersmen of completely air-conditioned, pioneer kibbutzim.

It works both ways. One of the most successful of USAID's programs in Israel was Operation Cowboy, which did indeed teach the new and inexperienced Israelis how to be cowpunchers. Now, a very few years later, they have not only become seasoned wranglers on Israeli ranches, doing well with beef and milch cattle, but some of them have discovered the electronic guitar and launched them-selves as rock-'n'-roll combos, one such group, as this is written, successfully playing the U.S., billed as The Israeli Cowboys.

Tourists going to Israel spend at least one hundred and seventy million dollars annually—revenue now second only to that from the sale of citrus.

The Israelis take their tourist business seriously, and with good reason: it is a major source of revenue and, beyond that, they are intensely proud of their country and want to show it off. Results are varying, but on the balance good. It was found that Christian visitors to Israel now outnumber Jewish visitors by nearly ten per cent, that Christian visitors to Israel are younger, averaging about thirty-five years, as against forty-six for the Jews, and consequently far more of the Jewish visitors (sixty-two per cent) are married, whereas more than half of the young Christian tourists are still single, and it follows that the younger Christian tourists have less money to spend from their incomes, averaging seven thousand dollars a year, than the somewhat older Jewish tourists who make nearly fourteen thousand.

One curious sidelight which emerged from a survey made by the Israel Ministry of Tourism of the three hundred thousand visitors who came to the country in 1966 was that while, as might be expected, eighteen per cent of the foreign Jews were merchants, as opposed to eight per cent of the non-Jews, eleven per cent of the Christians visiting the country were teachers, as opposed to only six per cent of the Jews—remarkable when one considers the traditional Jewish respect for learning. In the United States, proportionately, about twice as many Jews as Christians go on to graduate school.

Five per cent of the Christian visitors to Israel were listed as clergymen whereas only six-tenths of one per cent of the Jewish tourists were such. This last may change now that the holy places barred to Jews for two decades are once again open to Jewish visitors, thronging to see the Wailing Wall, the great and ancient Jewish cemetery and the Tombs of the Kings on the Mount of Olives, Mount Scopus, and the Holy City of Bethlehem where David was born and which is doing a roaring business. Jewish, Christian, Moslem, Buddhist, animist and visitors of every other conceivable faith flock to the Church of the Nativity, which in spite of the neon cross and shooting Star of Bethlehem atop it, remains a fine specimen of Byzantine architecture and the one Christian house of worship still in use since the time of Constantine.

Ancillary benefits to all tourists visiting Old City hostelries such as the Intercontinental and the American Colony and the Israeli-occupied Arab territories in general are greater courtesy, perceptibly better service and a far more interesting, non-kosher cuisine.

Teddy Kollek, now the mayor of reunited Jerusalem, and more than any one man responsible for the flourishing of tourism in Israel, used to get off a well-merited blast about once a year against the Israeli hosteliers' and restaurateurs' delusion that they were offering international cuisine of high standard, and now the Tourist Administration, deadly serious, has summed up principal adverse reactions and tourist dissatisfactions over the past year or so. These add up to high and sometimes inflated hotel and restaurant prices, atrocious service and rude behavior. All of these I believe to be true. Tel Aviv seems far ruder than Jerusalem or Haifa or Beersheba, but what is called *hutzpah*, which might be translated as "brass" or "gall" or "cheek," has to be experienced to be believed, and it is endemic throughout the nation. I don't think it is personal. In many ways it reminds me of Manhattan, which I love, but which no one has yet complimented for its good manners, and where the denizens, Jew and Christian alike, are so intent on pushing through the crowds, so intent upon their own affairs, which are of course the most important in the world, that they jostle and tromp on you with fine impartiality.

Israelis will, however, once you get their attention, go miles out of their way to help a stranger find his destination or get anything which he may need.

Among the new inducements offered by the Ministry of Tourism to the visitors it woos are not only the fabulous, labyrinthine ways of what they now call East Jerusalem—but which the rest of us ignorant foreigners will probably continue to think of as the Old City—and the chance to visit the once-off-limits Jericho and the fourth Jewish Holy City, Hebron. Now also, from the port of Eilat on that finger of the Red Sea which is called the Gulf of Aqaba, there are visits in a glass-bottomed tourist boat to a "Romantic New Coral Island," which is about five and a half miles south of the Israeli port, and whose abrupt heights are capped by a fine, impregnable-looking Crusader castle, all part of what the tourist people now refer to as the Gulf of Aqaba Fjord Excursion.

Among the tourists, Americans seem to be all over the sidewalks and the sand. Still, not all of the tourists are Americans. For the past several years, Eilat itself has been a magnet for beatniks and/or hippies. (These seem to be the same people, depending on who is writing about them and in what year, with some minor variations in their guitar work, far-out makeup and costume or lack of it, and degree of emphasis on Oriental religions, of which they seem to know remarkably little.) As early as 1963, an enterprising young wanderer among the hundreds who had reached the beach managed to stake out squatter's rights to an Eilat municipal lifeboat to which he rented shelter for the night to fellow birds of passage. Many are from the United States, many from the Scandanavian countries, many from Germany. Quite a few of the young visitors go to work at the kibbutzim during their vacations. Two to three times as many young Danish Christians sign up for work on the kibbutzim each summer as do young American Jews.

The increasing number of young Germans visiting Israel presents a thornier problem. There have been heated and sometimes acrimonious exchanges in the Israeli press as to whether or not to receive them hospitably at all. These reached a boiling point when a students' association at Hebrew University, the scars of Hitler still too fresh, refused a meeting with a visiting group of interested, sincere and pro-Israeli German university students.

There was even greater bitterness at the arrival in 1965 of Dr. Rolf Pauls as the first Ambassador accredited to Israel from the German Federal Republic. Dr. Pauls, a trim and handsome, youngish man who had lost an arm in the German offensive against Russia as an officer in the Wermacht, though never a member of the Nazi Party and hence not carrying with him the guilt and the odium of the Third Reich, had, on the record, long before there was any possibility of diplomatic exchange between Israel and Western Germany, asked that he might be considered for work in Israel, should mood and feelings between the two countries ever permit the beginning of such a reconciliation. Dr. Pauls was particularly emphatic about the importance of exchange of students and visitors between Germany and Israel, the offering of scholarships, cultural exchanges and other fraternal overtures. But when I talked to him, just after his appointment and his arrival in Israel, he entertained no illusions about the difficulties, nor the road both countries would have to travel: he saw it as just the beginning of a very long job.

This seemed compassionate, humane and foresighted. It was at least a beginning in an extremely difficult position. It called for both wisdom and patience. Here was a man who was cool, clear-headed, willing to atone, and with a host of other virtues. But, to the survivors of the concentration camps, and many of the ultra-Orthodox Jews who might never have seen a camp, the Ambassador was a kind of personification of evil, the Devil incarnate, and they rioted with such violence at Pauls's presentation of his letters of credence to President Shazar that the new Ambassador was barely rescued by Israeli police from mayhem.

One Israeli diplomatic observer summed it up when he said, in effect, that, following this, if the government of Israel were able to extend the hand of friendship to the Germans, then the Arabs should be able to find a way to live with their Jewish neighbors.

At CARE in Israel, there were a great many subscriptions to vocational-training programs, self-help projects, refugee relief and school-feeding and all the other things with which CARE was customarily concerned, and I confess myself surprised at first, on arrival, to find how many of these—besides the expected large number from the United States—came from Western Germany. At first, I thought these must represent feelings of guilt, an anxiety to atone somehow for the horrors not so long ago. But gradually, as I looked at the names of the individual donors and the churches and associations and other groups in Germany who were subscribing, it seemed quite clear that many of them were inspired not so much by guilt but by curiosity and even enthusiasm for a pioneering society, a desire to share in making the desert bloom again and all the hard work in conquering this new frontier.

It seems that almost everybody has always wanted to visit the Holy Land, and still does. I remember a photograph of a very young Jack Kennedy, most likely then an undergraduate at Harvard, standing with the British Governor-General in front of Government House, which was to become U.N. Headquarters—later captured by the Jordanians and then by the Israelis successively in the Six Day War, again becoming United Nations Headquarters.

Haile Selassie, during one of his pilgrimages to the Holy Land, had his son and heir baptized in the River Jordan.

Kaiser Wilhelm II—the same Kaiser who was the "Willi" to the "Nicky" of Czar Nicholas II in the ineffectual flurry of cables and correspondence between them and their close relative King George V of England just before they found themselves swept, or swept themselves, into the First World War—made his own pilgrimage to Jerusalem in 1898, in a bid to increase Germany's influence within the Ottoman Empire and throughout the Middle East. The Kaiser, wearing a tropical white, spiked German helmet with a white cape flapping behind him, accompanied by the Kaiserin Augusta Victoria, in white sola topee, and his entourage, they also wearing the German *Pickelhauben,* saw to it that his entry was one befitting His Imperial Majesty, having a hole punched in the wall of the Old City by Damascus Gate so that he might ride in in regal style. Following the imperial visit, there was a noticeable spurt in German diplomacy, commerce and the building of churches, hospitals and other institutions throughout the Holy Land. The neo-Romanesque Church of the Dormition by a Cologne architect named Renard was built at this time, and placed under the care of the German Benedictines, with a white-marble image in the crypt of the Madonna uneasily reminiscent of some of the work at Madame Tussaud's. Also built then was the Lutheran Augusta Victoria Hospital on Mount Scopus, in which are paintings of a number of religious, rather Teutonic figures, one of them wearing a moustache said to resemble uncannily that of Wilhelm.

By contrast, when the victorious Allenby entered Jerusalem in 1917, he rode to Jaffa Gate, dismounted and entered the Holy City on foot like a simple pilgrim.

After capture of the Old City by Israeli troops in June of 1967 and some twenty-six hours of fierce fighting, even before sniper fire had ceased, officers and men, rabbis, paratroopers, infantrymen and commandos made straight for the Wailing Wall, and the photographs of them praying there are among the most moving I have ever seen.

All three of these entries were witnessed by Bertha Spafford Vester, that redoubtable *grande dame* of what was Jordanian Jerusalem, who takes after her mother before her, Anna Lawson Spafford, a resolute woman who refused during the First World War to obey the orders of the American Consul at that time, a Dr. Glazebrook, who announced that she, as an American, must leave Jerusalem. Mrs. Spafford felt that she had enough to do with her group of devout settlers at the American Colony running four military hospitals, helping

Turkish and German soldiers and British prisoners of war, hiding some of the Britons when they could, and seeing that those who died in her hospitals were given decent burials according to their various religions. She ran a soup kitchen in the olive grove adjoining the American Colony, feeding four thousand persons daily until it was closed by order of a German general on the ground that it constituted American propaganda. This seemed no reason to Mrs. Horatio Spafford to leave town, just because there was a war on.

Her daughter, now nearly ninety years old, defied instructions from the current American Consulate-General that she be evacuated with her fellow citizens from Jerusalem in June, 1967. There was too much work to be done at her Spafford Memorial Children's Hospital. There, among other things, she ran a Meals for Millions program, mixing a multi-purpose food sent by the voluntary philanthropic agency with vegetable or meat soup or stew for the Arab children in her charge. They didn't much like the taste of the patented, nutritious, scientifically prepared multi-purpose food all by itself. Bertha Vester also worked in collaboration with the St. John's Ophthalmic Hospital of the Old City which was the first in all the Arab world (plagued with eye afflictions since the dawn of time) to provide cornea transplants in a program supported by CARE and CARE/MEDICO donors, who also contributed to the Children's Hospital. Both programs were beautifully organized by an earlier CARE Jordan Chief of Mission, a beaming Mississippian, Bill Powell, who was the kingdom's most-sought-after foreign bachelor.

Mrs. Vester just stayed where she was and went about her work.

Most of her extraordinary story is told in a few of the publications of the American Colony Charities Association itself, in a *National Geographic* article called, "Jerusalem, My Home," published in December, 1964, and in her autobiography *Our Jerusalem: An American Family in the Holy City, 1881–1949*, which starts arrestingly with the Horatio Spafford family evacuating itself from the city to their suburban home at Lake View to the north on Lake Michigan during the Great Chicago Fire.

The uninterrupted continuity of Jewish settlement in Israel and throughout the Middle East for these thousands of years is well documented, and helpful these days when the more superheated among the latter-day Arab nationalists speak (there were no Arab nationalists until fairly recently). Perhaps they have convinced themselves that all the Jews left following the Roman victories over them in the first and second centuries A.D., and that the present Jewish inhabitants of the area are no more than interlopers, most of them from Eastern Europe and just off the boat, come to seize the rich lands of Palestine from their rightful Arab owners.

By the middle of the nineteenth century, the Department of State had appointed Warder Cresson as American Consul accredited to the Sublime Porte of the Turks for "All the Holy Land," an area which was left splendidly undefined and the jurisdiction of which presumably was at the discretion of Mr. Cresson.

Within a year of settling in Jerusalem, the new United States Consul became converted to Judaism and changed his name to Michael Boaz Israel, and in 1847 he established outside the Holy City a colony which he called God's Vineyard. As far as anyone knows, this was the first modern Jewish agricultural settlement. (Unfortunately, Major Noah's plans half a century before, to train Zionist agricultural pioneers on Grand Island in the Niagara River, an enterprise called The City of Refuge, came to naught, though its cornerstone was laid and survives, preserved by the Buffalo Historical Society.)

The new Michael Boaz Israel, while perhaps not quite so far ahead of his time, might reasonably be called a dreamer, though a practical one like William Burroughs or Johnny Appleseed, and he was duly denounced to the Secretary of State as a lunatic. Fortunately, diplomatic dispatches, recommendations and reprimands traveled a good deal more slowly in the epoch of steam and sail than contemporary communiqués via radio and cable. Michael Boaz Israel persisted, attracting two hundred American settlers within four years, about a fourth of them Jews and the rest divided between converts to Judaism, as he was, and Protestants who considered themselves just as ardent Zionists as any.

In 1871, the Holy Land Settlement Society was founded near Jaffa by a Polish American farmer named Simon Berman, straight out of the Wild West, who arrived wearing cowboy boots and carrying a six-shooter. By 1902, the number of United States citizens under the protection of the Jerusalem Consulate was over one thousand, and the Consul, who bore the good Biblical name of Selah Merill, reported to his superiors in Washington that, "Had it not been for Turkish immigration restrictions, their number would have soared to eight or ten thousand, assuredly."

Of all of the remarkable Americans who made their way back to Zion, probably none was more so than Henrietta Szold, born in 1860 in Baltimore, which she referred to as "a gilded ghetto," and where she had worked as a spinster school teacher, a woman of great warmth and compassion, yet strong-minded and endowed with indefatigable energy. In 1912, just three days after her return from a visit to Palestine, she founded the American Women's Zionist Organization, or Hadassah.

In Hebrew, Hadassah means "Myrtle," or, alternatively, "Esther," which is a form of Astarte, the pre-Hebrew Mediterranean goddess of love, though I doubt that this is precisely what Miss Szold and her eleven co-founders had in mind, or what the present three hundred and twenty thousand members in thirteen hundred chapters think of when they use the word.

By 1913, Hadassah had sent two nurses to Jerusalem, followed shortly by three doctors, including a surgeon. Before the war was over, forty-four Jewish American doctors, dentists, nurses and sanitarians were at work throughout Palestine, bringing succor to Jewish and Arab communities alike at a time when there was a nearly complete breakdown in medical supplies, starvation was widespread, hygiene primitive or non-existent, trachoma and malaria endemic, and when typhus and cholera were raging—all this when Palestine was under the authority of the Turkish government, with whom the United States was technically not at war, but which was fighting with the Germans and the Central Powers against the Allies, and when German authorities were very much on the scene and in control of their Ottoman allies' war effort and administration of their Syrian principality of Palestine.

Quantities of medical supplies were smuggled in, donated by American Jewry, and during the latter part of the war, the American Navy came to the aid of the distressed settlers, bringing in relief shipments of food and evacuating the aged and the disabled. It was extraordinarily fortunate that the girls, all of them registered nurses, and the American doctors with whom they worked got through and that this American Zionist Medical Unit of Miss Szold's was able to bring competent medical assistance to the area and restore public health under the most harrowing, chaotic wartime conditions, about half of the nurses staying on to help plan the Hadassah Hospital and clinics, setting up the working men's ubiquitous Histadrut Sick Fund.

There were other helping hands doing what they could in Palestine. As Lapide wrote, "Self-appointed Pimpernels bullied, bribed and threatened Turkish officials into more humane attitudes." The very fact that the Ottoman regime was almost unbelievably corrupt as well as hopelessly inept served in itself as an ameliorating factor helping to protect in some degree the miserable citzenry.

Still, there was real fear that the Ottoman governor of Palestine and leader of the Turkish forces against the British in the Eastern Mediterranean theater during the war, the Balkan, Jemal Pasha—whom Bertha Spafford Vester called "a strange man, and one to be feared," even though he had agreed to her American Colony's proposal to nurse wounded soldiers from both sides—had planned for the Jews in his domain a calculated policy of extermination, just as the Turks had already provided for the Armenians under their rule. Three years after the First World War was over, and the victorious Great Powers had solemnly agreed that Armenia was to be a republic, the state had been partitioned between Turkey and the Soviet Union, and half of all the Armenians in the world were dead.

Of the possible fate awaiting her people in Palestine, Henrietta Szold was already well aware from the detailed report, sent at her suggestion to her as Secretary of the American Committee, from Absalom Aaronsohn, describing conditions among the Jewish communities in Palestine, the problems facing them and their possible fate. Absalom was one of the NILI spy family then serving as their liaison man with the Allies through British Naval Intelligence at Port Said.

As if organization of the American Zionist Medical Unit and a hand in Jewish Palestinian assistance to Allied espionage in the Middle East were not enough, all of her share in these efforts being managed from Baltimore, Henrietta Szold was busy at the same time with Americanization classes for new Jewish immigrants to the United States, as editor at the Jewish Publication Society, also working as the publishers' secretary and translator, as editor of the *American Jewish Year Book,* and keeping up with a dizzying list of other activities.

She arrived in Palestine at the age of sixty, and promptly organized a system of care for immigrant mothers and infants there which grew to be the Women's International Zionist Organization, WIZO. She helped build the Hadassah Hospital and Medical School on Mount Scopus, and plunged into creation of school lunch programs, Palestine's first school for nurses, child-care centers, playgrounds and school hygiene services, vocational-training courses at two of Hadassah's Brandeis centers in Jerusalem, including one called the Fine Mechanics and Precision Instruments and Printing Workshop Program. She acted as the first Director of Hadassah Hospital's Nursing School, and she set up a research center for the study of social work among children and young people.

Photographs of Henrietta Szold in her later years show her with long hair coiled in a bun atop her head, warm brown eyes, a long bony face and an almost invincibly kindly expression.

Just after Hitler came to power in 1933, Recha Freier, the wife of a rabbi in Berlin, created a movement called Youth Aliyah. Within three years, this became organized rescue of Jewish children from Germany, with the indefatigable help of Henrietta Szold and Eleanor Roosevelt. They were none too soon. At least sixty-two thousand children were saved during the war years, most of them orphans. Some of them were the only surviving members of their families. They were taken to Yugoslavia, to northern China, to England, and to any place where refuge could be found.

Later they were sheltered by the kibbutzim in Palestine which became training centers for the surviving Jewish children. In time, the children grew up and became settlers, members of the defense forces, interwoven through all the fabric of the new nation.

These were the fortunate ones who escaped. Most did not.

Intending settlers who already had received their permits to come to Palestine, but who lived in safe countries such as Canada and the United States or Britain, were asked to make available their permits so that these might be allotted to children in places where they faced momentary danger of extinction. Most of those who were asked to wait for the children to make their escape did so.

After the Second World War, this mass migration of children and young people continued, with unpredictable numbers arriving at unpredictable times from the Arab lands and from behind the Iron Curtain. They might be allowed to leave at caprice of the government, with little notice or no notice at all.

By now, more than a hundred and twenty-five thousand children have reached Israel through Youth Aliyah.

There was a great deal in common between the two who had most to do with Youth Aliyah, Henrietta Szold and Eleanor Roosevelt. Both were endowed with tremendous warmth, with driving, fantastic energy, both homely and yet both beautiful.

We were privileged to meet Mrs. Roosevelt in February of the year she died, at a Youth Aliyah reception when she visited Jerusalem to see again her old friends in Israel, the country whose children she had done so much to help. Bertie and I drove up with Howard and Odessa Prunty, he then serving as CARE's Assistant Chief of Mission in Israel. Both he and Odessa had worked with Mrs. Roosevelt in New York when they had served as psychiatric social workers. Mrs. Roosevelt was seated, smiling, at one side of a large room, as guests were brought over to be introduced to her, charming everyone in sight. I believe that a hearing aid was concealed in her eyeglasses, which were suspended from a cord about her neck. I hope so, for this would have enabled her to turn on and off as the infinity of admirers came by, each trying to engage her attention. Mrs. Roosevelt looked her usual, cheerful self, quite well, and most interested in all the world around her.

The connection of both of those strong-minded women, Henrietta Szold and Eleanor Roosevelt, with Youth Aliyah and their collaboration in saving the lives of tens of thousands of children was a forceable reminder of the part played by women in achieving Israel's independence. There was, or so it seems to me, an analogy between Israel and India, either of which would have had a far more difficult time of it without the women who had joined in the struggle, no quarter asked, for independence.

In India, where we had lived for four years, Bertie and I had met dozens of doe-eyed women who had walked in their saris with Gandhi preaching the gospel of independence, who had gone to jail for non-violently trying to overthrow the Raj and who had lived to become administrators in a free nation. In Israel, women were administrators now by the dozens of dozens. We met women who were nuclear physicists and bridge-builders and ex-terrorists, who were statesmen, clearing agents and town planners. Golda Meir, then Israel's Minister for Foreign Affairs, a post she had held since she was fifty-eight, the only woman in the Western world to reach this level, had been born in Kiev in Russia under the name of Meyerson, then lived in Milwaukee until she was twenty-three and a schoolteacher and, of course, a formidable Zionist. She returned to Russia as the first Minister accredited to Moscow by the fledgling State of Israel, and was reported to have organized her Legation like a kibbutz, taking her turn at washing the dishes. Her appearance at the Moscow synagogue caused the emergence out of nowhere of some thirty thousand Jews, deeply excited, and many of them clamoring to go to Israel.

It was reported that, when Mrs. Meir was sent in 1947 to Cyprus to negotiate the release of a number of Jewish refugee children interned there as illegal immigrants by the British Mandatory authorities, the not-very-coöperative commandant of Great Britain's internment camps on the island received a rocket from his superiors, warning him to be most careful, to walk softly, for "She is a very forceful woman."

"We had never seen anyone like her, so plain, so strong, so old-fashioned—like a woman out of the Bible," said a member of an audience in Chicago listening to her speak on behalf of Israel. She stood up to John Foster Dulles at the State Department in Washington and commanded a respect not unmixed with awe from nearly everyone at the United Nations as she defended her country's position during the Suez crisis and Israel's Sinai campaign.

Women serving with the Israeli defense forces largely do clerical and administrative work in order to free men for combat duty. There are young women in the infantry, with the armored divisions, in the navy, in the air force where there are a few who themselves are paratroopers. They were with the occupation forces in the Old City of Jerusalem, stationed throughout the Jordanian West Bank after the Six Day War, and three girl sergeants were assigned to the small Israeli garrison posted at the formerly Egyptian position on the steep tropical height of Sharm el Sheikh by the blue-green waters just off the tip of the Sinai Peninsula. The guns of Sharm el Sheikh command the Straits of Tiran, and their threatened use to bar Israeli passage from this, her only outlet to the African, Asian and Pacific world, once the United Nations observers charged with ensuring the cease-fire here had been expelled by President Nasser, was a major factor in precipitating the war.

Sunbathing and swimming for the girl sergeants and the officers were reported to be excellent at Sharm el Sheikh, but duty there was said to be a trifle monotonous. (It might be noted that among the other curious creations of this lightning war was the decision of the Syrian government—by far the most inflammatory and intransigent of the enemies of Israel—to copy her lead in using women in the Syrians' own armed forces, announcing that Syrian girls were being trained in the new "People's Army." Syrian information services supplied photographs of a number of rather dowdy-looking young women wearing tunics reaching to the knees with pipestem trousers, belts with brass buckles at the waist, vaguely mannish shirts and ties, and caps which look as though they had been borrowed from the North Koreans. All of the new Syrian guerrilla girls, it was announced, know how to fire a rifle.)

Throughout the nineteenth century, families from Eastern European Jewish communities seeking refuge tended to go, some of them, to Palestine, while other members of the same family might travel on to the New World, especially to the United States. Then in 1882 the Sultan of Turkey forbade any further immigration of Jews into Palestine, or any other part of the Holy Land, all of which was included in the Ottoman province of Syria. Jewish pilgrims there simply melted into the landscape and remained as settlers. Moslems were permitted to immigrate from any part of the vast Ottoman Empire, and many did so. The Turkish prohibition against Jewish immigration to the Holy Land remained in effect until Allenby's victory in 1917. At about the same time as the Turkish action, the assassination of Czar Alexander II in 1881 was blamed, as usual, by the Russian government on the Jews, touching off a wave of frightful pogroms throughout Eastern Europe. Many of those who could escape and could find twelve dollars' steerage passage made their way to the United States, this at a time when the country's immigration regulations were still liberal. Until 1907, it was easy to acquire American citizenship. By this time, about two and a half million Jewish refugees, almost all of them from Eastern Europe, had reached America, and by far the greater number settled in New York's Lower East Side.

After 1870, Manhattan's Lower East Side had become a teeming, Yiddish-speaking ghetto characterized by the great Hester Street pushcart market and the sweatshops in which most of the work was done by women and children. There was a permissive municipal government in New York then, and there were avaricious slumlords— both earlier immigrants and old New Yorkers, who together conducted the single most profitable business of the era, extracting from their tenants the maximum possible rent with minimum possible accommodation.

The newcomers had the meanest jobs, yet still brought with them via the Yiddish-speaking neighborhoods of New York much which has become a part of the American national culture. Many of the battles which finally secured acceptance of the trade unions, the principle of collective bargaining, and decent working conditions for employees were fought in New York City. They were led by Samuel Gompers. Helped by Clarence Darrow, he saw the United Hebrew Trades grow from five thousand in 1909 to a quarter of a million members in one hundred and eleven affiliated unions by 1914.

Mostly in the needle trades, three hundred thousand employees worked in sweatshops, and about a million persons altogether were directly dependent on the fifteen to twenty thousand employers of New York's cloak industry, which supplied three-quarters of all America's women's clothes.

In a book called *The Promised City: New York's Jews, 1870–1914* by Moses Rischin, the author notes, "In 1909 reform became the order of the day." He describes a waistmakers' mass meeting at the Women's Trade Union League when "suddenly the audience was electrified by the impassioned Yiddish plea of Clara Lemlich, a slip of a teen-aged girl, for a general strike. At the chairman's call to take the Jewish oath, 'If I turn traitor to the cause I now pledge, may this hand wither from the arm I now raise,' 20,000 waistmakers went out in the first great strike of women in American history. *The American Hebrew,* generally silent on labor matters, printed Stephen Wise's salute to a new era in industrial relations."

The *New York Call* and the *New York Evening Journal* published special strike editions, while Women's Trade Union League members distributed thirty thousand postcards and raised a strike fund of one hundred thousand dollars.

Widespread publicity was assured by the many Yiddish monthly and weekly magazines and the Yiddish newspapers, including a trilingual journal in Yiddish, Italian and English, and the four leading Yiddish dailies: the *Forward*, with a circulation of 174,699; *Warheit*, 108,000; *Morgen Journal*, 106,258; and *Yiddishes Tageblatt*, 66,665.

In a day when this could mean a great deal, sympathetic support came from leading members of New York Society, among them Mrs. J. Borden Harriman, Mrs. O. H. P. Belmont and Miss Anne Morgan, who presided over a meeting at the Colony Club in support of the striking waistmakers. Emancipated college women of impeccable family, armed with aroused social consciences, took turns at strike duty, sometimes on foot and sometimes, rather daringly, behind the wheel of one of Mrs. Belmont's automobiles. The National Women's Suffrage Association denounced the employers, and Archbishop Farley blessed the strikers.

The nation was horrified on March 26, 1911, when the Triangle Waist factory near Washington Square, a non-union shop, whose eight hundred and thirty employees, mostly young girls, made it the largest single employer in the needle-trades industry, caught fire on a late Saturday afternoon, trapping the girls on an upper floor behind locked doors, and claiming one hundred and forty-six lives in ten minutes, with many more left maimed, crippled and disfigured.

Fifty thousand silent mourners marched from the Lower East Side, almost all of whose families had friends or relatives then working under similar circumstances. At Cooper Union, Morris Hillquit prayed that the girls should not have died in vain.

There were results. The next fall, a special State Factory Investigation Commission met at the City Hall. From the Commission's investigation into safety regulations, working conditions and hours of labor came recommendations which Governor Al Smith and Senator Robert Wagner, both themselves from the Lower East Side, were able to put through the New York State Legislature, where they became law.

Another contribution made by Jewish immigrants to the New World was the introduction of Yiddish. Before Hitler, twelve million Jews the world over read and spoke Yiddish, supported the Yiddish theater, and sent their children to Yiddish schools. The Yiddish which came to New York and to London and elsewhere in Europe is thought to have been based on the Middle High German, mingled with Hebrew phrases which comprise about twenty per cent of the vocabulary, together with elements from the languages of the other countries to which the Jews spread, particularly those of Hungary and the Slavic countries. Yiddish became a full-fledged language, and neither a dialect nor a jargon as is often supposed. It has a great literature—perhaps best known in the United States through the works of Sholem Aleichem and Isaac Bashevis Singer—and with widespread influence on colloquial British and American English, recognized by few of the people who use it daily.

American entertainment owes an incalculable debt to Jewish immigrants and their descendants. To take a few names at random, there are Yehudi Menuhin, Isaac Stern, Artur Rubinstein, Serge Koussevitzky, Leonard Bernstein, David Warfield, David Belasco, Oscar Hammerstein, George Gershwin, Irving Berlin, Alan Jay Lerner, Marcus Loew, Louis B. Mayer, Weber & Fields, Al Jolson, Eddie Cantor, Bert Lahr, Ed Wynn, Danny Kaye, the Marx Brothers, Melvyn Douglas, John Garfield, Sophie Tucker, Dinah Shore, Joan Blondell, Kitty Carlisle, Judy Holiday—and on through a roster as long as the Manhattan Telephone Directory. That includes Harry Houdini, Edward G. Robinson—who was born Emanuel Morgenstern—and Paul Muni, who began his career as Muni Weisenfreund, playing old men when he was about twelve years old, as was the custom in New York's Second Avenue Yiddish theater.

By a quirk of fate, the 1882 firman of the Sultan of Turkey closing the Holy Land to the Jews of Europe, which had sent them to the United States instead, now meant that, as United States citizens—and naturalized Americans were not penalized for living outside of the United States in those years—they and their children were now entitled to travel to Palestine as American nationals. Moreover, special consideration was given to American

Jewish citizens in the Holy Land by the Turkish government which was, for political reasons, most anxious then to please the United States. And so there was a great deal of intermigration, with a close sense of kinship and family feeling developing between members of these families with relatives in both countries, a transatlantic feeling which survives to this day.

American tourists, including the all-important fund raisers who return home to solicit support for the State of Israel, see modern Jerusalem against the background of their own individual histories and those of their families. They have grown up and lived all of their lives with the story of the destruction of the Temple and the exile of their people. Yet no matter how assimilated into non-Jewish society they might have become, they are somehow impelled to return. Now they are back. This most holy of cities is holy also to the Christians and to the Moslems, but the Jews bring with them the accumulated, pent-up emotion of two thousand years. I doubt if it can be surpassed, or even equaled. They have returned.

There was a revolutionary change immediately after the third round in Israel's struggle with the Arab states. Now Israel found herself blessed with a tourist boom, at the same time that her bad neighbors, the Egyptians, watched their own tourist industry disappear. Recently, there had been many thousands of money-bearing visitors shopping in the bazaars of Cairo, posing for snapshots against the background of the pyramids and the Sphinx at Gizeh just outside town, and skimming up the Nile on hydrofoils to Aswan to visit the monumental sculptures carved from the cliffs rising from the river just below the High Dam.

All this was lost by Egypt, at least for the moment. Both Iraq and Syria announced that they were by no means ready to welcome "imperialist tourists" again. This left in a difficult position the neighboring government of Lebanon which had been prudent enough to refrain from firing a shot during the hostilities, yet all the while swearing fealty to her fellow members of the Arab League and vigorously denouncing Israel.

Lebanon has traditionally been far more interested in trade than politics, and its twenty-million-dollar annual tourist revenue constituted a large source of the government's financial support. Yet now it found itself bounded by Syria, Israel, and Jordan whose Left

Bank was occupied by Israel. Lebanon had a good deal less to offer that flow of tourists who had habitually traveled on through Beirut to the Old City of Jerusalem, Jericho and Cairo through this convenient and pleasurable port of entry to tourist goals in the neighboring Arab states. Now these could not be reached except with considerable difficulty and perhaps a bit of maneuvering through Israel. Nevertheless, the Lebanese government at once announced her intention to revive her tourist industry in this Riviera-like Mediterranean playground, long a favorite of travelers headed for this region, half-Christian, half-Moslem in its population, rather French in its flavor, and traditionally a halfway house used in the white-slave traffic both for girls from Europe bound for the bagnios of the Middle East, and some, whose passports listed them as "entertainers," whose ultimate destiny was one of the remaining harems in Saudi Arabia and the neighboring oil-rich, princely states of the Arabian Peninsula. The Cabinet of the Lebanese government reassured the tourist world that "order and security are assured so that foreign visitors can come to Lebanon," and voted to share earnings of the gambling house and nightclub, Casino du Liban, at Beirut with hotels outside the capital in order to help them get started again—this giving Israel the only real tourist competition now in the immediate neighborhood.

Following the war Jordan suddenly found herself without the highly lucrative tourist attractions of the Old City of Jerusalem, with its Christian, Moslem and Jewish shrines and holy places, and bereft of Bethlehem and Jericho, Hebron and even Bethel, where the Hebrew monarchs of the northern kingdom of Israel had established a capital in rivalry with Jerusalem as the capital of the kingdom of Judah. The Dead Sea Scrolls caves at Qumran were now in Israel hands, leaving Jordan with a reduced list of attractions pretty well confined to the classical Greek ruins at Jerash in the north, the relatively uninteresting Jordanian capital of Amman (called Philadelphia in Biblical days when it was a member of the league known as Decapolis) and the fabulous Nabataean capital of Petra, the "rose red city half as old as time," carved from the cliffsides of a deep gorge in the Jordanian Negev Desert.

That left the Israeli government Ministry of Tourism offering Jericho, the Dead Sea Scrolls caves, Gaza, where the blinded Samson pulled down the Philistines' Temple upon himself and his enemies, the Syrian heights of Golan fifteen hundred feet above the Sea of Galilee from which the Syrians for so many years had shelled the Israeli settlements below, together with the previous Syrian officers' club with the clear, cold waters of the Banias River flowing beneath a glass floor in the main room, near the ancient shrine of the god Pan, before this tributary hurtles down the mountainside to join the Jordan.

Most important of all, Israel now held all of the capital of Jerusalem, where Teddy Kollek as mayor of the undivided city was planning, almost before the smoke had cleared, paving and other decoration in stone, following the Jewish tradition, at the site of the Wailing Wall; the creation of parks planted with olive and cypress trees in the acres which used to be the rubble-strewn No Man's Land; and around the wall of the Old City and on the slopes of the Mount of Olives evening displays providing a form of pageantry with lights, music and dramatic narration, following the French *son-et-lumière* technique which has proven extremely successful in Europe. All of this was backed by an intensified campaign prepared by Israel's advertising agency.

It would be rash to attempt to predict the ultimate disposition of those lands occupied by Israel in the spring of 1967, though it is worth noting that the argument over what to do about contested territories following the 1948 war lasted for nearly twenty years. I do think it safe to guess that Israel will do everything within her power, and that would mean committing all the resources of the nation, to retain sovereignty over all Jerusalem; and whatever agreement might be reached over the fate of the Holy City—even with the unlikely acceptance of the suggestion, made many times, that it be internationalized—Israel would insist on the honoring of the pledge of access by her Jewish citizens, and Jews everywhere, to the Wailing Wall and the other Jewish places of pilgrimage in the Old City and elsewhere on the West Bank of Jordan and in the neighboring territories such as Gaza.

Meanwhile, American Jewish tourists and the many who come who are not Jews are able to travel more freely in that area controlled by Israel than they have since the end of the First World War—from the Syrian Heights to the Old City, and holy places on the West Bank down to Gaza, and to the Monastery of St. Catherine at the foot of Mount Sinai, one of the fourteen completely self-governing bodies within the Greek Orthodox Church. St. Catherine's is the home of one of the richest collections of Biblical manuscripts in Greek, Hebrew and Aramaic extant, and of two thousand of the finest Byzantine icons known in the world, the one priceless collection to escape wholly the destruction of the "idol smashers" who, at one period in church history, made a point of destroying such things.

23/ JOHN FITZGERALD KENNEDY

A few seconds after nine o'clock in the evening, Israeli time, November 22, 1963, the news was broadcast by Kol Israel of the shooting of President Kennedy. First reactions, as almost everywhere, were of a terrible blankness. The world stood still.

Kol Israel newsmen ran to their small building near the ultra-Orthodox quarter called Meah Shearim, near No Man's Land and the ancient wall which then divided the city between Israel and Jordan.

It was the Hebrew Sabbath from sundown Friday to sundown Saturday, a time for prayer.

Now came the news that John Fitzgerald Kennedy was receiving Last Rites of the Roman Catholic Church at a hospital in Dallas.

In Hebrew and Hungarian, Yiddish, Spanish, French and the dozen languages that Kol Israel's announcers use, the news came to Israel. The voice of David Jacobs reading in English—he was normally the calmest of men—was trembling so that he could scarcely speak.

Near the house where Bertie and I lived in Nof Yam, there was a ma'abara camp for refugees: Moroccans and Egyptians, Turks and Poles, Mexicans and Brazilians, and the others who had come to live in Israel. A group of non-Orthodox young people in one of the small prefabricated shelters in this camp, where our friend and helper Zahava lived, was having a party. When the news came, they turned off the radio and the gramophone which they had been playing, put aside the food they had prepared and moved out on the dirt roads. There at the corners, little knots of people gathered, talking in whispers. Quietly, many people began to cry.

And when we told him about this, the Ghanaian Ambassador to Israel, Bediako Poku, said to us, "You people in America have many things which must be changed. But I cried, too."

A woman called at her neighborhood newsdealer to tell him she would not pick up her weekly copy of *Time*, explaining, "I just can't bear to read any more. . . ."

For the next two days and nights, scarcely sleeping, many of us spent most of our time listening to the radio: Kol Israel, the Voice of America, the BBC, Prague, Moscow. The news in English from Prague sounded like the Voice of America at its very best. That from Moscow, a citadel of organized anti-religious propaganda, was accompanied by Christian sacred music. The only voices which were silent were those of Peking, and of Radio Tirana in the capital of Albania.

Later, Kadish Luz, the Speaker of the Israeli legislature, the Knesset, gave a moving tribute in English, as well as in Hebrew, as did the Foreign Minister, Mrs. Golda Meir. At one o'clock on the day after the death of the President, and still on the Hebrew Sabbath, we heard a brilliant and almost unbearably moving program in memory of the President, his voice still alive in many of his most important declarations of policy and of faith—this prepared by Kol Israel's ex-Chicagoan Yehuda Lev.

The service ended with the Twenty-Third Psalm:

The Lord is my shepherd; I shall not want.
He maketh me to lie down in green pastures:
  he leadeth me beside the still waters.
He restoreth my soul: he leadeth me in the paths
  of righteousness for his name's sake.
Yea, though I walk through the valley of the shadow of death,
  I will fear no evil: for thou *art* with me; thy rod and thy staff
    they comfort me.
Thou preparest a table before me in the presence of mine enemies:
  thou anointest my head with oil; my cup runneth over.
Surely goodness and mercy shall follow me all the days of my life:
  and I will dwell in the house of the Lord for ever.

There was a Requiem Mass at eleven o'clock in the morning of Tuesday, November twenty-sixth, at St. Anthony's Church in Jaffa, and then a memorial service that evening at the Habimah theater, attended by the then Deputy Prime Minister, Abba Eban, and by the American Ambassador, Walworth Barbour.

In Jerusalem, there was a special memorial session of the Knesset on November twenty-fifth, and a service at St. Andrew's Scots Memorial Church in Jerusalem's New City at eleven o'clock the following morning.

There was something extraordinary and compelling hearing the Psalms and the prayers for Kennedy read there in Jerusalem. St. Andrew's was full, with U.S. Marine guards wearing black arm-bands acting as ushers.

The invocation at St. Andrew's was given by Rabbi Jacob Petuchowski, Director of the Theological Seminary of Hebrew Union College in Jerusalem. There were prayers by the Franciscan Reverend Father Patrick and the Presbyterian Minister Herbert Minard.

The Hundred and Twenty-First Psalm was read by William Hamilton, the American Consul-General in Jerusalem, accredited at that time both to Jordan and to Israel.

During the service at St. Andrew's, I was seated next to a tall, thin and very blond young American theological student who was wearing the traditional Jewish skullcap. Just before me were two Roman Catholic sisters in their black habits.

About half the congregation was weeping. But, again, there was almost utter stillness.

This was one day on which flags on both sides of this then divided city were at half-mast, and all of its people with all of their differences were at one.

24/ EICHMANN

D avid Ben-Gurion and those responsible for the government of
Israel were concerned, and deeply so, that the trial of Adolf
Eichmann in Jerusalem be, as much as anything else, a lesson to the
people of Israel, and to the world of what man can do to man, and
what truly did happen to the Jews of Europe.

It is a lesson which cannot be repeated too many times, and it
should be told as long as there are people to hear it.

There was also the worry that perhaps non-European Jews might
not comprehend the ghastly significance of this wretched little man
sitting in his bullet-proof glass dock at Beit Ha'am in Jerusalem,
looking like the most insignificant of clerks—the very ordinary sort
of person which in fact he insisted that he was—only one side of his

mouth, rather pursy, prissy and twitching spasmodically, betrayed any emotion. As the attorneys for the prosecution and the defense went through what British friends have called an example of English common law at its best and fairest—the fear evaporated that the half-million Israelis from North Africa and the Middle East who had no first-hand experience of the European slaughter might not be able to understand the enormity of what had happened. It was felt particularly important that they should know and should understand. Long before the monstrosity of this man, pictured as a petty functionary hardly to be held responsible in a bureaucracy for carrying out the orders he received, was documented by the mountain of evidence so meticulously gathered to be irrefutably, damningly presented, the Orientals from North Africa and the Middle East had understood, from the very beginning, without waiting. From the first day of the trial, one could see young people, perhaps from the Atlas Mountains of Morocco and not yet born when the war was over and the fires of the death camps extinguished—young people on the streets of Tel Aviv or outside Beit Ha'am in Jerusalem, little transistor radios held to their ears, listening, fascinated, and with every indication that they understood very, very well what had happened.

During the four months of the Eichmann trial, the audience that filled the large, block-like building of light Jerusalem stone, the Beit Ha'am that in ordinary times served as a municipal center for the capital, sat quietly, attentively, in their seats upholstered in Israeli blue, looking down across the hall faced with blond plywood with a handsome paneled wooden ceiling—rather like a Scandanavian theater in the simple, clean effect—toward the glass box where sat the defendant, scarcely moving except to make notes on the proceedings, and, beyond him, on a dais under the seal of Israel in brass relief against a black background, the three judges robed in black. Behind Eichmann in his glass box with its roof sloping forward and downward were two guards, dressed in the British Palestine police uniform, dark-blue caps, now with the badge of Israel, sun-tan uniforms with sleeves smartly rolled up to make a three-inch cuff below the shoulder. These were Orientals, for no Israeli who had any connection with Europe was assigned guard duty for Eichmann, lest the Israeli's feelings interfere with his duty as a guard. Just behind the man in the glass box was a large, glazed schoolroom map of Northwestern Europe, fixed to the wall, with Germany and the occupied and neighboring countries colored in pink and yellow and orange pastels.

The police were deeply tanned as was most of the audience, both Israelis and visitors from Europe and America, but the judges in their black robes were pale, and Eichmann even paler. Except when he was speaking, Eichmann was almost immobile, his bald head sunk in his right hand, a rather large pair of earphones over his head and their cords hanging from his neck like those of a stethoscope. Only his hands were moving, making notes, making notes. He had a slight, rather bird-like look, with vertical cords standing out at the back of his neck. He seemed small and shrunken inside his glass box.

It was very quiet. In spite of occasional verbal pyrotechnics from the prosecuting attorney, Attorney-General Gideon Hausner, the court was quite visibly and audibly restrained, letting the law quietly, exhaustively, take its course.

In the crowd which sat there listening day after day were Africans and Asians, some tourists, and many of Eichmann's own victims, who looked like plain people, decently dressed in business suits for the occasion, middle-class, and sitting there so quietly that one could feel the emotion that filled the hall. Once in a while, someone's back and shoulders would shake as if with repressed sobs. Once a large woman collapsed on the floor beside the witness stand, and once I watched a middle-aged matron in a grey suit, with a white blouse, a wedding ring on her left hand, clutching a small handkerchief convulsively as she told of how she had been thrown naked into a pit with the dead and dying, eventually to crawl out and live again.

There were four secretaries with earphones along the left gallery, and on the right translators' boxes, while visitors to the country who produced their passports could take from the checkroom little transistors with which they could follow the proceedings in English, French, German and Spanish. Even in unfamiliar languages, if one turned the small dial, words like Auschwitz and Führer kept coming through. Each day one could read in the local press the full proceedings in almost any language.

As the man in the glass box explained in convincingly bureaucratic detail what a small cog without power he was, the cumulative effect of incredulity shaded into horror: he said that in truth he himself had been a Zionist, but that his personal convictions were contrary to those of his superiors. He was an expert on Jewish immigration, he said, who wished mainly to put firm ground under the Jews' feet. "Over their heads," said the survivors.

Eichmann spent a great deal of time explaining that he was mainly concerned with the mechanics of deportation, train schedules and border regulations and transport laws, "a very complex situation"— but, as Hugh Trevor-Roper commented, "it needed something like genius for a mere SS Lieutenant-Colonel to organize in the middle of war . . . and in fierce competition, the essential resources, the transport, concentration and murder of millions of people."

"I had to promote Zionism by force," said Eichmann. "I do not believe there is a Zionist functionary of that period who can say that I had hamstrung his work." This came from a man who had said, "With the Jews, my only obligations were emigration and evacuation. My concerns were timetables, technical preparations."

Eichmann went to extraordinary lengths to be a good functionary. For one thing, he learned both Hebrew and Yiddish that he might better deal with the people who were his concern. The international press was out in force to cover the Eichmann trial. Dom Moraes, a young poet from Oxford and the son of Frank Moraes, who is the editor of *The Times of India,* came to cover the trial for several publications, and Ronald Searle arrived to do some of the fine, latter-day caricatures whose technique he acquired mostly as an inmate of a Japanese prisoner-of-war camp.

There has been some objection to the tracking down over fifteen years, throughout Europe, the Middle East and South America, and the abduction of Eichmann, as well described by Moshe Pearlman in his book *The Capture and Trial of Adolf Eichmann,* but it turned out that, even if Argentina were obliged to make a protest at the United Nations, more or less as a formality, against the kidnapping from her sovereign territory of Eichmann by Israeli agents, there was not much in international or national law which could be done once the accused was on Israeli soil. The question became that of the trial itself. The press of the more than thirty countries which followed the trial closely were generally in accord that, lacking an international tribunal as at Nuremberg, Israel was the most appropriate place to try Eichmann. There were some objections to possible imposition of the death penalty. Martin Buber called on Ben-Gurion asking that Eichmann's life be spared if he were judged guilty, on the grounds that his crimes were so monstrous that they fell outside the realm of ordinary punishment and would serve no purpose except perhaps to provide the German people with a feeling of expiation for their guilt. Victor Gollancz, a liberal, a Jew, and a distinguished British publisher, asked for clemency: "I say to David Ben-Gurion with the deepest sympathy and respect, 'Do not kill Adolf Eichmann.' If six million have been slaughtered, what can it profit it to make the number six million and one? . . . Only one thing can lighten that darkness, can redeem and restore . . . to spare—even to forgive. . . . I plead for one thing only, that Eichmann's judges may act in the spirit of what is best in the Old Testament as well as in the New— in the spirit of 'Forsake evil: Do good, and live' and of 'Go and sin no more.' "

The Israeli government replied to Gollancz, who had been a co-founder during the Second World War of an organization rescuing the Jews from the Nazi camps, and after the war supported the State of Israel, German relief and the Arab refugees as well, with the words of Ben-Gurion: "We are not out to punish Eichmann." The purpose of the trial, the Prime Minister explained, was that of a lesson, that "anti-Semitism is dangerous," and that the other nations of the world "should be ashamed of it."

A considerable furor has been caused by a new work by Hannah Arendt, author of an earlier book considered a classic in its field, *The Origins of Totalitarianism.* She stirred up quite a row with *Eichmann in Jerusalem,* in which Eichmann is reduced from being a monster to being "banal." Her recurring theme is that the Jews as victims were accomplices with their murderers in that they submitted meekly and went to their deaths, and were therefore responsible for their own fate. This point of view enraged a great many people, some of whom set out to refute the argument in detail and convincingly. It was done with particular conviction by Norman Podhoretz, the editor of *Commentary,* who wrote in the September, 1963, issue of his magazine an acute refutation called "Hannah Arendt on Eichmann; A Study in the Perversity of Brilliance." Barbara Tuchman, writing in *The New York Times Book Review* about Gideon Hausner's *Justice in Jerusalem,* makes a number of important points of the same sort: "If by coöperation is meant that the Jews, at gun point and outside the ordinary protection of society, went where they were told and did what was ordered without organized resistance, then certainly they coöperated because this was their traditional means of survival. It was bred in the bone during 2,000 years as an oppressed minority without territory, autonomy, or the ground of statehood under their feet." Miss Tuchman points out, as does Podhoretz, that when the Jews learned they had to fight back, it was this same people who resisted so valiantly in the Warsaw Ghetto, and who fought against even more impossible odds in 1948 when they secured the State of Israel. Barbara Tuchman further recalls that literally millions of Soviet prisoners of war were massacred inside the German camps without known resistance, and quotes Hausner's example of the American paratroopers captured during the Battle of the Bulge who were executed by the Nazis after digging their own graves without protest.

The Reverend James Parkes, that excellent historian and humane man, a Church of England priest who has spent most of his life studying relations between Jews and Christians and people of other faiths, wrote an essay for *The Observer* after Eichmann had been judged guilty, in which he said, "An historic guilt lies upon the whole of Christendom for the anti-Semitism and there is an unbroken chain which goes right back from Hitler's death camps to the denunciations of the early Church." Dr. Parkes commented that while all of us are guilty, there *is* a special German guilt, and suggested that the Germans might well learn from Jewish history: "Nowhere in the Old Testament do we find Jews blaming others for their misfortunes. Isaiah, Jeremiah, Ezra are concerned with their own failings, not with the sins of Assyria or Babylon. It is in German history and German *mores* that Germans have to discover and deal with their responsibility."

Eichmann was hanged at two minutes before midnight on the last day of May in 1962, and taken six miles out into the sea where he was cremated and his ashes scattered, following the procedures established at Nuremberg.

There were sixteen Africans watching and listening to the Eichmann trial and a good variety of people from the "other nations" the last time I visited Beit Ha'am, so I think that Ben-Gurion as Prime Minister did achieve what he set out to do, or at least taught people part of the lesson.

There continues to be controversy over the Eichmann trial. Why it continues to bother us as it does was put as well as I know in a short editorial in *The New York Times* on the thirteenth of September in 1965. It was called "One Little Boy":

Why the search for Nazis twenty years after World War II? Why does bitterness still burn as a hot coal in the hearts of millions throughout the world? Why can so many decent human beings not find in their hearts the capacity to forgive and forget? . . . There has just been published in Germany a book entitled "For Theirs Was the Hell." It is a documented account of the fate which befell some of the 1.2 million Jewish children under 16 years of age in Hitler's concentration camps. The few sentences from the story are enough: "Then the guard ordered the children to fold their clothes neatly and march into the gas chamber and crematory. One little boy, less than 2 years old, was too little to climb the steps. So the guard took the child in her arms and carried him into the chamber."

There is the reason—one little boy.

25/ THE VISIT OF PAUL VI

T he first week of January, 1964, Pope Paul VI made a visit of
three days to the Holy Land. Much was anticipated from his
continuation of the ecumenical movement begun so encouragingly
by his predecessor John XXIII, to bring together the many disparate
parts of the Christian Church and to reconcile his faith and church
with those of other religions.

On what he proclaimed to be his Mission of Peace, Paul was to
spend eleven and one-half hours in Israel, and I took advantage
of this by traveling up to Nazareth at the time of the Pope's visit,
accompanied by Ziva Hoogstraal from the CARE staff, while we
checked the food-distribution centers and several Nazareth schools
with vocational-training projects. I was interested to see the new

313

traveling Pope, and even more so to witness his reception by the Israelis, Jew, Moslem and Christian.

Bertie had given me a very small and simple transistor radio, and all the way up to Nazareth I followed with fascination the progress of His Holiness on the first papal tour of the Holy Land since the time of St. Peter. Long before the Pope's plane lit at the Jordanian capital's airport at Amman, the air was electric with broadcasts, reports of the greetings and the blessings dispatched from his plane as he passed over the Arab states on his way from Rome. There were excited descriptions of the places to be visited by His Holiness, heated and alarmed weather broadcasts when the flight encountered rough weather and accounts of any number of dire or wonderful things which might happen. Over the Israeli radio came news that the Chief Rabbis had declined to meet the Pope on his arrival in their country since they considered it unseemly that he had chosen to enter it through the little town Ta'anach near Megiddo, departing from Jerusalem later in the day, rather than entering through their capital, the Holy City. They did not approve of his itinerary. This did not deter President Shazar, who was there at Ta'anach on the Pope's arrival in the early morning. The Ambassadors to Israel were present, led by the Dean of the Diplomatic Corps, who at that time was the Soviet Ambassador, following the usual custom of precedence by date of accreditation.

The Pope's greeting began with *"Shalom,"* thus enraging Jordanian and other Arab commentators who sounded insulted that he should be speaking Hebrew in Israel. The Israelis for their part had not been upset by *"Salaam"* when he had said "Peace" in Arabic on the other side of the frontier. All the while, the Israel government's Departments of Numismatics and Philately had been busy striking special commemorative medallions, engraving postage stamps and preparing special cancellation marks to be used in franking mail from Nazareth that day, all bearing inscriptions in Latin and English celebrating the Pope's pilgrimage to the Holy Land.

In Nazareth, the town was swarming with reporters and photographers. A van belonging to an Italian television company was parked in front of the best hotel, whose rooms had been commandeered by its reporters and those from Radio Luxemburg. The French were reported to have a warship anchored off Israel, with two jets to fly film to Lod and thence out to Switzerland for televising via Eurovision. There was a rumor that a *Paris-Match* plane had arrived with fifty reporters, including ten Israelis. Promoters were selling the holy earth of Nazareth at thirty-three cents for a small bag.

Magen David Adom, which is the Israeli equivalent of the Red Cross, had stationed a hundred and thirty-six people, including ten doctors, along the Pope's path.

During this time, Radio Jordan was, for the Arab world, relatively moderate. Its broadcasts in English were well done, with only a quick reference by King Hussein to "injustices." Then, in an Arabic broadcast on Radio Jordan, the listener was reminded that it was "the Jews who killed Christ," a myth from which I thought the better informed, perhaps more sophisticated, parts of the world had recovered, but quickly was to learn that I was mistaken.

Earlier, Ziva had guided me to a couple of Nazareth schools on our list of distributors which I had not seen before. At the Roman Catholic Jesus School, all two hundred and twenty-five of the children from seven to eighteen were soon going to see the Pope. At the YWCA and YMCA, which here were one, the little girls who had been taking lessons in classical ballet with bar practice and were to perform two numbers called "Ave Maria" and "Flower and Satan" in honor of the visit of His Holiness were having gauze wings sewn on their costumes backstage in readiness for the expected audience of three hundred and fifty. "Firebird," "Swan Lake," "The Blue Danube" and Strauss's "The Baron and the Gypsy" were also in their repertoire. All seemed to be going well except that the neighbors from the Moslem Junior Chamber of Commerce next door sometimes protested that the rehearsals were too noisy. I asked the Y director, a Mr. Yousuf, if everyone were excited about the visit, and he said, "Yes, I think so, everyone. Except the Communists."

We stopped for coffee after visiting the second school, and I heard church bells beginning to chime, suddenly realizing that in Tel Aviv I hadn't heard church bells for a long time, and somehow had missed them. I said to Ziva how nice they sounded. And she looked me straight in the eye and said, "Many people don't like to hear church bells."

Ziva is an exceptionally capable girl, with dark hair and light-blue eyes, one of two sisters who had been hidden as children and saved during the Nazi occupation of the Netherlands where they were born. All the rest of their family except one aunt had perished in the death camps. Perhaps it was because it was early in the morning and I was thinking about the Pope's visit, but I was surprised, and asked why.

"Because it reminds many people," said Ziva quietly, "that they used to ring bells before the pogroms in Eastern Europe."

The crowd was beginning to fill the streets, Franciscan monks, Moslem religious leaders, Italian naval officers, Bedouin in Arab dress wearing *keffieh* and *egal*, substantial Nazareth Arab householders, fathers wearing their tarbooshes planted squarely on their heads, sitting together in front of their houses along the Pope's right of way. Children were clutching little blue-and-white Israeli flags made of paper, and horizontally striped yellow-and-white papal flags to wave at the same time. The day before, at Damascus Gate to the Old City of Jerusalem, in spite of all efforts made to keep the way clear for the Pope from the gate up along the Via Dolorosa, the crush of the pious and the curious had become so great that he could hardly get out of his car, and despite the official ban of all onlookers along the Way of the Cross, and the picked Bedouin guard from the Arab Legion running interference, he was almost crushed. Over my small radio, I could hear police sirens in the background, the dull roar of the crowd around the gate as the announcer on Radio Jordan's English-language program said that the "stalwart church guard is trying to clear the way, trying to help preserve an historic occasion from turning to an historic free-for-all."

A German work, *Pope Paul VI in the Holy Land*, reported the fracas:

> This hour did not seem so peaceful to the Pope's retinue. It is difficult to reconstruct exactly the order of events. Monsignor dell' Acqua fled into an Arabian shop crying "Save His Eminence Cardinal Cicognani." Cardinal Tisserant shielded off blows, aimed by Bedouin guards vainly trying to preserve order. He was later discovered in an inn—"An excusable scandal" was his despairing exclamation. Monsignor dell' Acqua, his clothes torn to shreds, also received a few whacks, before he could save himself, while Don Pasquale Macchi lost his spectacles in the tumult in the Via Dolorosa.

King Hussein, in his usual impromptu way, had come to welcome the Pope at Prince Abdullah Bridge just after the Pope left the airport, and jumped out of his car, himself directing traffic while his Legion fired a twenty-one-gun salute.

One official Arabic Press Translation issued that same day by the American Embassy in Amman quotes an unsigned editorial in the Jerusalem, Jordan, paper *Al Jihad* (The Holy War), entitled "O Your Holiness the Pope," welcoming Paul VI and reminding him that "some Christian states have been the ones who plotted with World Zionism to displace the Arabs of Palestine from their nativeland, to usurp their homeland, lands, properties, wealth, to leave them all fifteen years a prey to hunger, nakedness and humiliation. These powers, by their plotting, have defied the message of Jesus Christ. Your Holiness will see the disasters that Catastrophe in refugee camps, in front-lines, in the tearing apart, in destruction and in devastation, whose remnants are everywhere in Jerusalem."

Al Jihad went on at great length in this vein, informing the Holy Father of Jewish massacres of Moslems, and stating that Israeli Moslems were not allowed to use their mosques which had all been turned into synagogues. The Embassy summary of the editorial ends with the words: "The talk concludes by welcoming the Pope."

The newspaper *Falastin* (Palestine) for the same day went on to remind the Pope that his welcome recalls "the two big crimes committed in the Holy Land . . . here, Jesus Christ was crucified by the Jews . . . here, a nation was displaced from its homeland."

The Jordanian press made a great point of the fact that, at the Pope's departure through Mandelbaum Gate when he left Israel to return to Jordan that night, he had defended his predecessor Pius XII against the charges that he had discriminated against the Jews during the Nazi heyday. This last was correct, for the Pope did make a point of praising Pius XII in his treatment of the Jewish minority during the war, as he made his farewells and thank-yous to President Shazar. It would seem an attempt to deflect charges that Pius XII, known to be oriented toward things German, had failed to speak out against German persecution of the Jews, or to answer the agonized plea of the Roman Catholic Bishop of Warsaw who had described in detail the persecution, and in some cases slaughter, of the Roman Catholics there, and who was asking not for material help or anything more than a statement from the Holy See that the Pope deplored the German genocide; also, the serious questioning of the attitude of Pius XII by the young German Rolf Hochhuth in his play *The*

Deputy; and the publication in Italy by the left-wing, painstakingly careful observer and writer Carlo Falconi on Vatican affairs, in his book called *The Silence of Pius XII,* which reported the murder of a half-million Serbian Orthodox Christians in Croatia and quoted the desperate appeal to the Pope to speak out, sent him by the President of Poland on January second, 1943—emphasizing that only one man in the Roman Curia had challenged this state of affairs— Cardinal Tisserant. It happened that Tisserant was a member of the present Pope's entourage visiting both Jordan and Israel.

One thousand one hundred and fifty newspaper, magazine, television and newsreel reporters and photographers covered the Pope's visit on the Israeli side alone, seven hundred of them coming on special assignment from overseas, and the rest being local press correspondents and photographers, and stringers for the international press, radio and TV.

Security was extraordinarily tight, for Israel honestly feared there might be anything from an attempt on the Pope's life to riots begun by agents provocateurs specifically trained and sent in from across the Arab frontiers, to create an outrage which would shock the world and could be blamed on the Jews.

There seemed to be almost as many police as spectators in the crowd of perhaps twenty-five thousand lining the route to be taken by the Pope's motorcade in Nazareth. At first I had discounted the fears of officialdom as being melodramatic and over-protective, but the more I began to think about it later, the more it struck me as possible that it could have happened anywhere, and certainly in the Middle East with its labyrinthine secret services, plots, counter-plots, espionage and counter-espionage.

Because of Dallas, no one in Nazareth was allowed on rooftops or on upper-stories along the Pope's way, except for the inhabitants of those buildings which had been carefully screened in advance by the police. On the rooftops there were more policemen, armed with walkie-talkies and Israel's Uzzi submachine guns. Still more groups of policemen rode in open Jeeps between all of the cars of the papal entourage, each man equipped with an Uzzi or an automatic rifle, canteen, radio and camera. Spotter planes circled overhead. Members of the riot squad, looking a bit strained after two days of intensive practice, were scattered throughout the Nazarene crowd, each with shield and night stick. The route to be taken by the Pope was not revealed, though I can't see that this made much difference since it had already been published in *Time,* which was available throughout the country.

It was a bright, cold, sunny day when the Pope reached Nazareth. A prize of the equivalent of one thousand dollars had been offered for the best display honoring His Holiness, and, indeed, at the entrance to the city there was a yellow-and-white triumphal papal arch, super-decorated, a bit gaudy and Latino in character, but most effective. By this time, as the Pope entered Nazareth, the Kol Israel radio announcer in French was almost beside himself as he cried, "The Pope is only ten yards away!"

There had been quite a wait, with announcers filling in with bits of papal history, a good deal of Christian sacred music and a talk by General Yadin in excellent English. When he arrived, the Pope himself spoke in French with a rolling Italian accent, his voice strong and firm. He mentioned Abraham, Isaac and Jacob, emphasizing again that his was no more than a pilgrimage of peace. Later that day, when he reached Jerusalem, President Shazar and Mayor Kollek welcomed the Pope to the City of Solomon, the City of David.

Patrick O'Donovan, writing from Jerusalem, and perceptive as usual, then made the point that the most important thing of all historically about the pilgrimage was the meeting between Paul VI and His Beatitude, the Ecumenical Patriarch of the Orthodox Church, Athenagoras, who had suggested it, and had come from Istanbul especially for the occasion. They met on the Mount of Olives where they exchanged the traditional Kiss of Peace.

Pope and Patriarch were to meet again not too long afterward in Istanbul, and yet once again in Rome at the Vatican. A further step was taken at the funeral of Cardinal Spellman. Not only President Johnson and Vice-President Humphrey were there, but Governor Rockefeller and Mayor Lindsay, a four-man delegation led by the president of the New York Board of Rabbis, and Archbishop Iakovos, the Greek Orthodox Primate of North and South America, who had a special episcopal throne to himself. Earlier in the week, when Spellman lay in state at St. Patrick's Cathedral, the Archbishop had been invited to preach there, the first time this had happened in nine centuries. All this seemed to bolster the liberal and ecumenical faction of the Curia at the Vatican in their struggle with the more conservative members, not eager at all for closer ties between Catholics and non-Catholics, between Christians and those of other faiths. There was still a long, long way to go, but a good beginning may have been made on the Mount of Olives.

EPILOGUE

What next?

As the Cold War in Europe, still smoldering fitfully, was gradually burning out, it seemed that the flames were beginning to flicker ever more dangerously in the Middle East.

At the end of the Six Day War, there was introspection in Israel, determination to face a future whose outlines were unclear, like a mountain range partially hidden by haze, beyond which lay still another range, and, beyond that, the unknown.

One thing at least was clear. After withdrawal of Israeli troops from positions held following their victory in 1948 and 1949 over the invading forces of seven Arab nations, and after the rout of the Egyptian Army during the retaliatory Sinai Campaign of 1956, when there were assurances from representatives of the United Nations and the great powers that Israeli's boundaries would not be violated and that she would enjoy free passage of the Gulf of Aqaba and in particular of the Strait of Tiran, which remained her gateway to Africa and Asia, and yet Israel was left to fight without support in 1967 against the massive Egyptian military concentration sent to her southern frontier—at a time when the voice of the government's Radio Cairo announced, "Jews, we are coming to kill you, we are going to exterminate you," and Israel's friends, including the United States and Great Britain, joined most of the United Nations urging Israel to withdraw her troops and to use great restraint in her conflict with the Arabs—Israel's growing belief that she could trust almost no one but herself to ensure her survival hardened into complete conviction.

At the same time, those members of the Arab League, and particularly the immediate neighbors who had declared war on Israel following her invasion of Egypt to incapacitate the Egyptian forces gathering at her frontier, continued to refuse to negotiate directly with the Israelis on common differences, just as they had done since the end of the 1948 war and the armistice agreements calling for such talks. Syria even refused to speak to Gunnar Jarring, the Swedish diplomat and special envoy sent by U Thant to see how the United Nations might be able to conciliate the warriors.

A host of new problems faced Israel. Her mood of anxious, watchful waiting during the two weeks preceding the war when no one knew who might be the first to fire, then the joy at the successful three-day drive of the Israeli forces down through the desert of Sinai to the Suez Canal, the relief at the swiftness of the engagement and the relatively light casualties then and during the next days attacking Syrian positions on the Golan Heights, were succeeded by realization of the formidable tasks which lay ahead.

The Israelis had fought like ones possessed. The first command of the Chief of Staff Itzhak Rabin used the classical phrase of the Essenes, of the struggle of "the Children of Light against the Children of Darkness." Yet all accounts I have seen or heard, including those of foreign correspondents known for both honesty and acuteness of observation, agreed that the Israeli soldiers "fought without hatred." Alfred Kazin, writing in *Harpers* on being "In Israel After the Triumph," described a busload of reporters and photographers traveling through the Sinai, the cameramen enthusiastically shooting every burned-out truck and tank within sight, some of them apparently oblivious to the fact that many of the Egyptians burned with their vehicles, only to be reminded gently by a small, mild Israeli colonel who joined them for the last stage of their trip: "May I say one word? You have seen what we can destroy. Please also notice what we can build."

One of the greatest problems facing the Israelis after their lightning, classical, almost-textbook victory, was rapprochement with the 1,385,000 living in the newly occupied territory, in addition to the existing 300,000 Israeli Arab citizens. The latter, who had been feared by Israeli officialdom as potential fifth-columnists, caused surprisingly little trouble and remained quiet or on the side of the Israeli government during the 1967 hostilities.

At first, when the Mandelbaum Gate was abolished as the only passageway between Israel and Jordan, and then only for the privileged few, Israelis poured by the tens of thousands into the Old City for the first time in nineteen years, in particular to the Wailing Wall, where dusty, sweat-stained soldiers, gun slung over one shoulder, Bible in hand, and wearing the long leather thongs called *tefellin* wound seven times around the arm as prescribed for prayer, could be seen leaning against the Wall and sobbing in gratitude. There were clean-shaven young professors praying with elderly Hassidic Jews wearing earlocks and white beards, wide-brimmed black hats and kaftans, housewifes wearing babushkas, and girls in miniskirts. All Israel had come to pray.

At the same time, thousands of Arabs were streaming from the West Bank of Jordan, from the Old City, and from Gaza into Israel, strolling on the boulevards and sightseeing, meeting their families on the other side for tearful and impassioned reunions. For the first time since 1948, several hundred Moslems now under Israeli government authority set off on the pilgrimage to Mecca and Medina, blessed by the imam of Hebron, who called on them to think especially of their father Abraham while in the holy cities. Americans and other visitors for the first time in two decades were able to visit all of the places of pilgrimage on both sides of the former frontiers without respect to their religion, or the infernal red tape in getting from one side to the other. Pan American Airways' subsidiary, Intercontinental Hotels, lost no time in making arrangements with the Israeli authorities for continued operation of their hotel on the Mount of Olives. The redoubtable Kathleen Kenyon of Oxford applied for and received permission to continue her excavations in Jerusalem and other parts of what had been Jordanian territory, though numbers of Americans and other foreign archeologists held back, fearing this might compromise their work in the Arab lands. Teddy Kolleck, now the mayor of a reunified Jerusalem, announced plans to plant groves and gardens around the walls of the Old City, with *son-et-lumière* spectacles to recall with music, light, and dramatic narration the extraordinary life and history of the city.

Then what had begun as a mingling of the two sides in an atmosphere of curiosity, a degree of fraternity, and even delight in some quarters began to change. Teachers went on strike throughout much of the West Bank. They and many merchants called on all others to boycott any dealing with the Israelis, urged on by Radio Amman from the Jordanian capital which spoke of reprisals against any who might do so. Of all the Arab families who fled across the crumpled but still barely serviceable Allenby Bridge during the heat of the war and the weeks that followed, approximately one hundred thousand did not return to their old homes within the time authorized by the Israelis, and then extended—all supervised by the International Red Cross.

Israeli authorities entering occupied territory found textbooks filled with virulent propaganda against Israel and, by extension, against the Jews in general. This was true even of those institutions supervised by the United Nations, whose officers, largely Palestinian refugees themselves, explained lamely that they had no right to interfere with the schools' curricula. The UNRWA-supervised girls' school at Khan Yunis in Gaza exhibited a crudely drawn, poster-like picture with the caption: ARAB UNITY EXPRESSED IN AN ENCIRCLEMENT OF ISRAEL . . . A MISSILE AND A RIFLE AND TWO HANDS ARE WHAT WILL DO AWAY WITH ISRAEL. A text from the Jordanian Arab Society Second Year High School read: "Like the cry of Cato, the famous Roman orator, 'Carthage must be destroyed,' so you Arab boys and girls must cling to the slogan 'Israel must disappear forever!'" Gaza schoolbooks were even more vicious, those from Syria worse.

Shortly after the Six Day War, Arab guerrillas returned to work, both in the occupied territories and within Israel itself, using the familiar weapons of sabotage and murder, adding intimidation of

Arabs living on the Jordanian West Bank now under Israeli control. Recruited again largely from Palestinian refugees, there were about a dozen of these gangs operating in a loose coalition except for one called El Fatah, growing rapidly in number, and the most active and the most brutal, with training camps in Jordan and across the Syrian frontier.

Russia broke off relations with Israel following the Six Day War, followed by all the other Eastern European countries save Rumania, with whom Israel continued diplomatic relations. Egypt and some of her Arab allies severed relations with the United States and Britain, claiming that it was only air power provided by these two which had made the Israeli victory possible. President Nasser later claimed disingenuously in an interview with William Attwood for *Look* that this was all a misunderstanding based on a telephone call to him from King Hussein announcing that Jordanian radar had picked up American and British planes. An independent American analysis of voice patterns from an Israeli-intercepted telephone conversation between Nasser and Hussein appeared to confirm agreement between the two rulers on blaming military failure on the British and American air forces.

There remained the imponderables. How long would Nasser be able to keep control, in spite of great popular support among his people and through the Arab world, in the face of his hawkish younger officers who were already demanding a fourth round in the struggle with Israel, calling for more Russian arms and Russian technicians, this time emulating the Israelis by planning to strike without advance warning? In spite of her efforts since the time of Peter the Great to obtain a foothold in the Mediterranean and the Red Sea, how long would Russia continue to support her Arab clients with costly losses in arms and influence? How long would Saudi Arabia, Kuwait and Libya go on supporting a bankrupt Egypt? What happened to the German-built rockets which were so proudly wheeled through the streets of Cairo, displayed on television, and then never used? And what about the numbers of Russian technicians, estimated at anywhere from seventeen hundred to seven thousand, in Egypt and the Yemen, capable of using their surface-to-air missiles given the Egyptians, who had simply abandoned them and fled? Nasser blandly denied in his interview with Attwood that there had been any Russian pilots in the Yemen, in spite of the body recovered there of a Russian pilot with incontrovertible documentation. There were also reports from reputable foreign correspondents of Egyptian efforts with bacteriological warfare, simple enough with a few trained biologists so that such a project could be begun in a corner drugstore. This was so far unverified. What had been completely substantiated by the International Red Cross on more than one occasion was the bombing with poison gas of villages in royalist-held parts of the Yemen.

Whether the more hawkish or the more dovelike factions were to win the upper hand in Egypt and Jordan, whether the Israelis were to handle more or less abrasively the Arabs under their jurisdiction, perhaps setting off another war launched by the Arabs, even if probable of failure—for if history has any lesson, it is that nations often act in anything but their own best interest—all this remained to be seen. If in coming generations, the Egyptians master the military techniques at which they have failed so dismally—then Israel might have to cope with such a force of far greater capability, perhaps backed by massive foreign armament.

As against the danger from her neighbors, Israel had made friends in many other parts of the world. She maintained about a hundred permanent diplomatic missions. By leap-frogging the Arab states, she had come up in Burma, Thailand and Nepal, with whom she did a brisk business in scholarships, training missions and trade. The Latin Americas were important to her, too, and her twenty-nine missions in Africa alone gave her the most widespread representation there of any area.

New lessons were being learned: Thanks to Ben-Gurion's determination that neither the Jews nor anyone else forget the lesson of the Nazi holocaust there were reverberations of the Eichmann trial long after it was over. Many millions who had not been touched before remembered witnesses like the Israeli author who lived to tell all he had experienced at Auschwitz, who took the stand and, before he fainted, could say only, "It was a planet of ashes. . . ."

There was always the tantalizing question: what if Russia were to permit departure of all or many who wanted to go to Israel among those of her approximately three and a half million Jews? Israel is pledged to receive all who come, but the resultant social and economic dislocation has been compared as probably equal to that of the Six Day War.

There was greater appreciation among the Arab states and all the rest of the world of Israel's strength and self-reliance. There seemed increasing respect for the Israelis who had more than held their own. Of the more than six thousand young volunteers who poured into Israel to offer their services during and just after the Six Day War, many were not Jewish; one of the first to arrive was a Chinese from Singapore.

Finally, there continued to be progress, now greater, now lesser, of the ecumenical effort initiated by John XXIII to bring together not only the churches within Christendom, but to rid the world of the clerical charges of deicide, of Jews murdering Christian children for unholy rites—with the suffering and the hundreds of thousands of deaths these have caused.

Following the Six Day War, Israel's frontiers were certainly more secure, but her citizens along the border faced mounting, increasingly savage guerrilla attacks. Paradoxically, passage between Jordan and Israeli-administered territory was open as it had not been in years. Trucks of produce, with only cursory examination, rumbled from the West Bank to Amman and returned. Political observers freely predicted both (a) no further war, and (b) massive retaliatory action by either side which would end no one knew where.

From the government of Israel to American rent-a-car services, all hands celebrated the wonderful array of places which now might be visited through Israel: Sinai and the Dead Sea Casino, the Qumran Caves which had sheltered the Dead Sea Scrolls, as well as Jerusalem's Old City, Bethlehem, Hebron and Joshua's Jericho. In spite of the uncertain political temper of the times, groups of tourists found themselves on the Transjordanian Plateau at the Golan Heights and under Mount Sinai at the ancient Monastery of Saint Catherine, in itself one of the fourteen autocephalous bodies of the Orthodox Church.

It would be futile to attempt to predict the future, but if I were forced to wager, I would be quite confident that Israel is here to stay. *Ein brera*: There is no alternative.

APPENDICES

BIBLIOGRAPHY

ALBRIGHT, WILLIAM FOXWELL. *From the Stone Age to Christianity*
(3rd ed.). Doubleday Anchor Books: Garden City, N.Y., 1957.
———. *The Archeology of Palestine* (revised). Penguin Books: New
York, 1954.
ALLEGRO, JOHN M. *The Dead Sea Scrolls* (rev.). Penguin Books: New
York, 1958.
ANONYMOUS. *Belsen.* Irgun Sheerit Hapleita Me'Haezor Habriti: Tel
Aviv, 1957.
ANONYMOUS. *Jewish Exodus from the Arab Countries, The.* Ministry for
Foreign Affairs Information Division, Jerusalem Post Press: Jerusalem,
1961.
ARNOLD, PAULA with FERGUSON, WALTER (plates). *Birds of Israel.*
Shalit Publishers, Ltd.: Haifa, 1962.
ARON, ROBERT. *Jesus of Nazareth: The Hidden Years.* William Morrow
& Company: New York, 1962.

331

Avi-Yonah, Michael. *Jerusalem.* Arco Publishing Company, Inc.: New York, 1960.

Avi-Yonah and Kraeling, Emil G. *Our Living Bible.* Oldbourne Press: London, 1962.

Bartlett, W. H. *Walks About the City and Environs of Jerusalem.* Arthur Hall, Virtue & Co.: London, 1844.

———. *Jerusalem Revisited.* Thomas Nelson & Sons: London, 1863.

Ben-Gurion, David. *Israel: Years of Challenge.* Massadah-P.E.C. Press Ltd.: Tel Aviv and Jerusalem, 1963.

Bentwich, Norman. *The Jews in Our Time.* Penguin Books: Baltimore, 1960.

Berlin, Isaiah. *Chaim Weizmann.* Farrar, Straus & Cudahy, Inc.: New York, 1958.

Berlinger, Michael (ed.) with Berlinger, Se'ev (text) and Avigad, Brakha (Levy) (plates). *Trees and Shrubs in Israel.* Department of Education: Haifa, 1963.

———. *Flowers of Israel.* Department of Education: Haifa, 1963.

———. *Carmel Flowers.* Department of Education: Haifa, 1963.

Black, Matthew. *The Scrolls and Christian Origins: Studies in the Jewish Background of the New Testament.* Charles Scribner's Sons: New York, 1961.

Borchsenius, Poul. *The Son of a Star.* George Allen & Unwin Ltd.: London, 1960.

Bridger, David and Wolk, Samuel (ed.). *The New Jewish Encyclopedia.* Behrman House, Inc.: New York, 1962.

Buber, Martin. *Good and Evil.* Charles Scribner's Sons: New York, 1952.

———. *I and Thou.* Charles Scribner's Sons: New York, 1958.

Chase, Mary Ellen. *Life and Language in the Old Testament.* W. W. Norton & Company, Inc.: New York, 1955.

———. *The Bible and the Common Reader.* The Macmillan Company: New York, 1960.

———. *The Prophets for the Common Reader.* W. W. Norton & Company, Inc.: New York, 1963.

———. *The Psalms for the Common Reader.* W. W. Norton & Company, Inc.: New York, 1962.

Comas, Juan. *Racial Myths.* unesco: Paris, 1958.

Congar, Yves M.-J., O.P. *The Catholic Church and the Race Question.* unesco: Paris, 1953.

Dimont, Max I. *Jews, God and History.* Simon and Schuster, Inc.: New York, 1962.

Duff, Douglas V. *May the Winds Blow!* Hollis and Carter: London, 1948.

Dunn, L. C. *Race and Biology.* unesco: Paris, 1958.

Eban, Abba. *The Voice of Israel.* Horizon Press: New York, 1957.

Bibliography

EL-AREF, AREF. *The Tragedy of Palestine in Pictures.* Modern Library: Sidon, Lebanon, 1962.

ELSTON, D. R. *No Alternative: Israel Observed.* Hutchinson & Co., Ltd.: London, 1960.

ENGLE, ANITA. *The NILI Spies.* The Hogarth Press: London, 1959.

FINER, HERMAN. *Dulles Over Suez.* Quadrangle Books: Chicago, 1964.

FLENDER, HAROLD. *Rescue in Denmark.* W. H. Allen: London, 1963.

FRAZIER, SIR JAMES GEORGE. *Folk Lore in the Old Testament.* The Macmillan Company: New York, 1918.

GERSTER, GEORG. *Sinai.* Ullstein Verlag: Frankfurt and Berlin, 1961.

GLUBB, LIEUTENANT-GENERAL SIR JOHN BAGOT. *A Soldier with the Arabs: The Personal Story of Glubb Pasha.* Hodder and Stoughton: London, 1957.

GLUECK, NELSON. *Rivers in the Desert.* Farrar, Straus & Cudahy, Inc.: New York, 1959.

GORDON, ALBERT I. *Jews in Suburbia.* Beacon Press: Boston, 1959.

GRAVES, ROBERT and PATAI, RAPHAEL. *Hebrew Myths: The Books of Genesis.* Doubleday & Company: New York, 1963.

GREENBLATT, ROBERT B., M.D. *Search the Scriptures: A Physician Examines Medicine in the Bible.* J. B. Lippincott Company: Philadelphia, 1963.

GROLLENBERG, L. H., O.P. with REID, JOYCE M. H. and ROWLEY, H. H. (ed.). *Atlas of the Bible.* Thomas Nelson and Sons: New York, 1957.

HASTINGS, JAMES and GRANT, FREDERICK C. and ROWLEY, H. H. *Dictionary of the Bible.* Charles Scribner's Sons: New York, 1963.

HERSEY, JOHN. *The Wall.* Alfred A. Knopf: New York, 1950.

HOADE, EUGENE, O.F.M. *Guide to the Holy Land.* Franciscan Press: Jerusalem, 1946.

JOINVILLE, JEAN and VILLEHARDOUIN, GEOFFROY. *Chronicles of the Crusades.* Penguin Books: Harmondsworth, 1963.

JOSEPH, DOV. *The Faithful City: The Siege of Jerusalem, 1948.* Simon and Schuster: New York, 1960.

JOSEPHUS, FLAVIUS. *The Jewish War.* Penguin Books: Baltimore, 1959.

KELLER, WERNER. *The Bible as History.* Hodder & Stoughton: London, 1956.

KLINESBERG, OTTO. *Race and Psychology.* UNESCO: Paris, 1958.

LAGERLOEF, SELMA. *Jerusalem.* Doubleday & Co.: New York, 1915.

LAPIDE, PINCHAS E. *A Pilgrim's Guide to Israel.* George G. Harrap & Co., Ltd.: London, 1966.

———. *A Century of U.S. Aliya.* The Association of Americans and Canadians in Israel, The Jerusalem Post: Jerusalem, 1961.

LEARSI, RUFUS. *The Jews in America: A History.* The World Publishing Company: Cleveland and New York, 1954.

LEIRIS, MICHEL. *Race and Culture.* UNESCO: Paris, 1958.

LEVI-STRAUSS, CLAUDE. *Race and History.* UNESCO: Paris, 1958.

LEVY, RAPHAEL and HANFT, BENJAMIN. *21 Frontier Towns*. United Jewish Appeal: New York.

LEWKOWITZ, M. (ed.). *Bites and Stings in Israel*. Kupat Cholim: Tel Aviv, 1962.

LURIE, ESTHER. *A Living Witness: Kovno Ghetto—Scenes & Types*. Dvir Publishers: Tel Aviv, 1958.

MACKAY, CHARLES. *Extraordinary Popular Delusions and the Madness of Crowds*. L. C. Page & Co. and Farrar, Straus & Cudahy, Inc.: New York, 1932.

MAY, HERBERT G. with HAMILTON, R. W. and HUNT, G. N. S. *Oxford Bible Atlas*. Oxford University Press: London and New York, 1962.

MEYER, HERMANN M. Z. *Israel Pocket Atlas and Handbook*. Universitas: Jerusalem, 1961.

MIKES, GEORGE. *Milk and Honey: Israel Explored*. Allan Wingate: London and New York, 1950.

MORANT, G. M. *The Significance of Racial Differences*. UNESCO: Paris, 1958.

NASSER, JAMAL A. *The Resentful Arab*. Published by the author: Jerusalem, Jordan, 1962.

PARKES, JAMES. *A History of Palestine from 135 A.D. to Modern Times*. Oxford University Press: New York, 1949.

———. *Continuity of Jewish Life in the Middle East*. The Anglo-Israel Association: London.

———. *The Meaning of the Torah*. Tooley: London, 1963.

———. *The Concept of a Chosen People in Judaism and Christianity*. The American Hebrew Congregations: New York, 1954.

———. *Toynbee and the Uniqueness of Jewry*. Jewish Journal of Sociology, Vol. IV, no. 1: 1962.

———. *Jews in the Christian Tradition*. The Parkes Library and The Council of Christians and Jews: Barley and London, 1963.

———. *Verdict on Father Daniel*. The Parkes Library: Barley, 1962.

PEARLMAN, MOSHE. *The Capture and Trial of Adolf Eichmann*. Simon and Schuster: New York, 1963.

———. *Ben Gurion Looks Back*. Weidenfeld and Nicolson: London, 1965.

PEROWNE, STEWART. *The Pilgrim's Companion in Jerusalem and Bethlehem*. Hodder and Stoughton: London, 1964.

PINKUS, OSCAR. *The House of Ashes*. The World Publishing Company: Cleveland and New York, 1964.

PREUSS, J. *The Chinese Jews of Kaifeng-Fu*. Museum Haaretz: Tel Aviv.

PRINZ, JOACHIM. *The Dilemma of the Modern Jew*. Little, Brown and Company: Boston, 1962.

PRYCE-JONES, DAVID. *Next Generation: Travels in Israel*. Weidenfeld and Nicolson: London, 1964.

RISCHIN, MOSES. *The Promised City: New York's Jews 1870–1914*. Harvard University Press: Cambridge, Mass., 1962.

Bibliography

ROBINSON, NEHEMIAH (ed.). *European Jewry Ten Years After the War.* The Institute of Jewish Affairs of The World Jewish Congress: New York, 1956.

ROSE, ARNOLD M. *The Roots of Prejudice.* UNESCO: Paris, 1961.

———. *Race Prejudice and Discrimination.* Alfred A. Knopf: New York, 1952.

ROSENNE, SHABTAI (ed.). *6,000,000 Accusers: Israel's Case Against Eichmann.* The Jerusalem Post: Jerusalem, 1961.

ROTH, LEON. *Jewish Thought as a Factor in Civilization.* UNESCO: Paris, 1954.

RUNES, DAGOBERT. *Dictionary of Judaism.* The Philosophical Library: New York, 1965.

———. *Lost Legends of Israel.* The Philosophical Library: New York, 1961.

SACHAR, ABRAHAM LEON. *A History of the Jews.* Alfred A. Knopf, New York, 1948.

SACHAR, HOWARD MORLEY. *From the Ends of the Earth.* The World Publishing Company: Cleveland and New York, 1964.

———. *Aliyah, The Peoples of Israel.* The World Publishing Company: Cleveland and New York, 1961.

ST. JOHN, ROBERT. *Israel.* Time, Inc.: New York, 1965.

SAMUELS, GERTRUDE. *B-G, Fighter of Goliaths: The Story of David Ben-Gurion.* Thomas Y. Crowell: New York, 1961.

SCHILLER, WERNER. *Pope Paul VI in the Holy Land.* Herder & Herder: New York, 1964.

SHAPIRO, HARRY L. *The Jewish People.* UNESCO: Liège, 1960.

SHIRER, WILLIAM L. *The Rise and Fall of the Third Reich.* Simon and Schuster: New York, 1960.

SIMS, ALBERT E., REV. and DENT, GEORGE, REV. *Who's Who in the Bible.* The Philosophical Library: New York, 1960.

SPARK, MURIEL. *The Mandelbaum Gate.* Alfred A. Knopf: New York, 1965.

SYKES, CHRISTOPHER. *Crossroads to Israel 1917–1948.* The World Publishing Company: Cleveland and New York, 1965.

TALMI, EFRAYIM and MENAHEM. *New Israel Guide.* Publishing House Ltd.: Tel Aviv, 1961. (English version by I. M. LASK)

THEODOR, O. *On Poisonous Snakes and Snake Bite in Israel.* The Israel Scientific Press: Jerusalem, 1955.

THOMPSON, EDWARD K. (ed.). *The World's Great Religions, Vol. 2: Religions of the West* (Islam and Judaism). Time, Inc.: New York, 1955.

———. *Volume 3: The Glories of Christendom.* Time, Inc.: New York, 1955.

VESTER, BERTHA SPAFFORD. *Our Jerusalem: An American Family in the Holy City, 1881–1949.* Middle East Export Press, Inc.: Lebanon, 1950.

VOLAVKOVÁ, HANA. *. . . I never saw another butterfly . . . .* McGraw-Hill Book Company: New York, 1962.

WEISGAL, MEYER W. and CARMICHAEL, JOEL (ed.). *Chaim Weizmann, A Biography by Several Hands*. Atheneum: New York, 1963.

WEISS-ROSMARIN, TRUDE. *Jerusalem*. Philosophical Library: New York, 1950.

WEIZMANN, CHAIM. *Trial and Error*. Schocken Books, Inc.: New York and Tel Aviv, 1966.

WILSON, EDMUND. *The Scrolls from the Dead Sea*. Oxford University Press: New York, 1955.

PERIODICALS

CENTRAL BUREAU OF STATISTICS. *Statistical Abstract of Israel* (annual). The Central Bureau of Statistics: Jerusalem.

CENTRAL OFFICE OF INFORMATION. *Israel Government Year Book* (annual). The Government Printer: Jerusalem.

DAGAN, PERETZ. *Who's Who, Israel* (annual). Israel Press, Ltd.: Tel Aviv.

DEPARTMENT OF FOREIGN AFFAIRS. *Israel* (quarterly). Jerusalem.

ISRAEL PUBLISHING COMPANY. *Israel Magazine* (monthly). Israel Publishing Company: Philadelphia.

JERUSALEM POST PUBLICATIONS LTD. *The Jerusalem Post* (daily). Jerusalem newspaper in English, with weekly overseas editions.

JEWISH PRESS, INC., THE. *The Jewish Press*. Weekly newspaper, New York.

MINISTRY FOR FOREIGN AFFAIRS, INFORMATION DIVISION. *Facts About Israel* (annual, available from Israeli Consulates and Government Tourist Offices in the United States and Canada). Government Press Office: Jerusalem.

SHERESHEVSKY, S. (ed.). *"NER": Monthly for Political and Social Problems and Jewish-Arab Rapprochement*. IHUD Association: Jerusalem.

YAD WASHEM MARTYRS' AND HEROES' MEMORIAL AUTHORITY. *Yad Washem Studies on the European Jewish Catastrophe and Resistance* (annual). Yad Washem: Jerusalem.

GLOSSARY

Aliyah	Meaning "ascent," the emigration or return of the Jews to the Holy Land. Youth Aliyah has concentrated in bringing to Palestine and then to Israel children from Nazi Europe and then from the Arab countries.
Ashkenazim	The Jews of Eastern, Central and Northern Europe.
Bar Mitzvah	"Son of the Commandment," the ceremony at which a Jewish boy, reaching the age of thirteen, assumes the religious responsibilities of an adult.
Bedouin	The nomadic Arabs.
B'rith	Hebrew for the Covenant between God and Israel, symbolized by circumcision, ritually performed by Jews eight days after birth, following the Biblical commandment. The fraternal and civic B'nai B'rith is translated as Sons of the Covenant.

337

Cabbalists   Jewish mystics of the sixteenth century and later centered at Safed looking for "hidden wisdom" in the Scriptures, using astrology, numerology, "practical magic" and other occult techniques.

Chief Rabbinate   The central rabbinical authority of Israel, in Jerusalem and presided over by the Ashkenazi and Sephardi Chief Rabbis.

Diaspora   The Greek word for "scattering," used for dispersion of the Jews following conquests of Israel from earliest times. Now, and carrying the sense of exile, the Diaspora is wherever Jews may live throughout the world outside.

Ein brera   Hebrew for "no alternative," often quoted as the reason for the survival, against all odds, by the Jews in Israel.

El Fatah   The strongest, most brutal and most successful of about a dozen groups of Palestinian Arab terrorists operating inside Israel and occupied territories after the Six Day War.

Eretz Yisrael   Hebrew for the Land of Israel.

Fedayin   Egyptian-supported terrorists, largely Palestinian refugees, who made guerrilla raids into Israel from the Gaza Strip and Egypt, in great part precipitating Israel's retaliatory Sinai Campaign.

Gadna   The Israeli youth corps, combining elements of scouting, archeology and para-military training, for boys and girls from fourteen to eighteen.

Habimah   The Israeli National Theatre, founded in Moscow in 1917 with Stanislavsky as its patron and sometime director.

Hadassah   The Women's Zionist Organization of America, founded in 1912 by Henrietta Szold for medical and nursing work in Palestine, since then extremely active as well in Youth Aliyah and allied fields in Israel and other countries.

Hadj   The pilgrimage to Mecca and Medina which the Prophet Mohammed enjoined each Moslem to make at least once during his lifetime.

Haganah   The Jewish underground military organization which became the Israeli Army on the independence of the State.

Hamsin The Arabic, and most frequently used, word for the hot wind from the Arabian desert, in Hebrew called *sharav*.

Hannukah An eight-day autumn festival, also known as the Feast of Lights, commemorating the victory in 165 B.C. of Judah the Maccabee over the generals of Syria, purification and rededication of the Temple at Jerusalem. Now celebrated by the lighting of a special nine-branched menorah, in memory of the small cruse of oil which burned miraculously for eight days at the restoration of the Temple.

Hassidim The Pious, whose original doctrine, though mystical, stressing simplicity and sincerity as more important than learning in communion with God, soon degenerated into fervent following of dynastic *rebbes* (rabbis) called *tzaddikim* (holy ones), who assumed the position of intermediaries with the power to help grant the prayers of the faithful. There remain tens of thousands of Hassadim in parts of Brooklyn, Bnei Brak outside Tel Aviv and the Meah Shearim quarter in Jerusalem, speaking Yiddish instead of Hebrew, which would be profaned outside the synagogue, dressed in the Eastern European clothing of two centuries ago, and refusing to recognize the secular State of Israel since it was not founded by the Messiah.

"Hatikva" "The Hope," Israeli national anthem.

HIAS The Hebrew Sheltering and Immigrant Aid Society, founded in 1884, now the United HIAS Service, helping Jews immigrating to the Americas and elsewhere by preparing for their emigration and assisting upon their arrival with legal, social and economic aid, housing and the reunification of families.

Histadrut The General Federation of Labor to which belong ninety per cent of Israel's labor and over half of her total adult population; an amalgam of trade unions and management, including social services, coöperatives, manufacturing, distribution, marketing, building and banking.

Hora The national dance of Israel, a folk dance originally from the Balkans.

339

Imam	A Moslem holy man, spiritual or temporal leader.
Kibbutzim	Rural settlements in which all land, crops, buildings and equipment are jointly owned, and which provide communal care for children.
Knesset	Israel's unicameral legislature.
Kol Israel	The Voice of Israel, broadcasting in many languages to its own polyglot population, as well as to a multitude of countries in Africa, Asia, Europe and the Americas.
Kosher	Sanction by Jewish rabbinical law, especially of food which may be eaten as ritually clean.
Kupat Cholim	The Histadrut's health-insurance fund covering seventy per cent of the population, with an extensive network of clinics, hospitals, rest homes, child-care centers and other facilities.
Ma'abarot	Transient camps for immigrants to Israel.
Maccabiad	The quadrennial Jewish games, named for the Maccabees who ruled the last independent kingdom in what is now Israel.
Magen David Adom	The Red Shield of David, performing the functions of the Red Cross; affiliated with, but not a member of, the International Red Cross, because of differences over the emblem to be used.
Marranos	"The Damned," those among the hundred thousand in Spain who embraced Catholicism following the persecutions of 1381, and the entire Jewish population of Portugal which was converted forceably, yet many of whom remained crypto-Jews. Suspicion of them launched the Spanish Inquisition.
Menorah	The traditional seven-branched candlestick with an additional candle at the center, used in synagogues and to celebrate holy days, the ancient symbol of Judaism and the emblem of the State of Israel. Nine-branched on Hannukah, the Feast of Lights.
Moshavim	Smallholders' rural settlements with private ownership of property, but with coöperative marketing and equipment.
Nahal	Fighting Pioneering Youth groups of young men and women, assigned after intensive military train-

	ing to border settlements too dangerous or too difficult for ordinary civilian settlement.
Natorei Karta	Guardians of the Gates, ultra-Orthodox Hassidim in the Meah Shearim quarter of Jerusalem, scrupulously observant of rabbinical law according to their own interpretation, frequently involved in clashes with passersby and the nation as a whole over dress, education and details of observance of the Sabbath.
Palmach	The commando force of the Haganah.
Passover	In March or April, a seven-to-eight-day festival celebrating the deliverance of the Jews from Egyptian bondage, and beginning with the Seder supper.
Payot	The earlocks traditionally worn by many ultra-Orthodox male Jews.
Pentateuch	The Greek term used for the first five books of the Bible, "the Books of Moses."
Rabbi	"My master," an ordained Jewish religious leader, officiating at the synagogue's Sabbath services, weddings, funerals and other occasions.
Rebbe	Yiddish and Eastern European form of "rabbi"; as a title, called Reb.
Rosh Hashanah	The Jewish new year, beginning in September or October, and beginning ten days of repentance culminating in Yom Kippur.
Sabra	"Cactus"—a native-born Israeli, popularly described as "prickly outside, sweet inside."
Salaam	An Arabic salutation equivalent to the Hebrew "Shalom."
Seder	The ritual meal on the first night of Passover in Israel and among American Reform Jews (otherwise, occasionally on two nights), as a reminder of the offering of the paschal lamb and the Passover feast in the days of the Temple, and commemorating the flight of the Jews from Egypt. On this and the other days of Passover, only the unleavened bread called matzoth may be eaten, recalling the haste of the Exodus led by Moses. By many Christian scholars, it is considered likely that the Seder was the Last Supper of Jesus and his disciples.

341

Sephardim	Descendants of the Jews expelled from Spain in 1492 and from Portugal in 1496. Speak Ladino, essentially the Castilian of that day.
Septuagint	The translation of the Hebrew Bible into Greek in the third century B.C., probably at Alexandria, by a supposed seventy scholars whose number became the name for this version, predecessor of later translations in English and other languages.
Shalom	The usual Hebrew greeting, meaning "Peace."
Sharav	The hot desert wind from Sinai, usually called by its Arabic name of *hamsin*.
Sherutim	Jitneys which are often second-hand foreign taxis, plying fixed routes at fixed fares in and between cities, accommodating as many passengers as possible.
Shofar	The ram's horn anciently used as an alarm in time of war, or for proclamations of great importance; always used to usher in the Sabbath.
Shtetl	Small Jewish village in Eastern Europe, particularly in Poland or in the Russian Pale of Settlement to which the Jews were confined.
Simhat Torah	The festival of the Rejoicing of the Law marks the end of the annual cycle of the reading of the Torah, and the beginning of the next.
Sinai Campaign	Israel's name for her 1956 invasion of the Gaza Strip and the Sinai Peninsula following increase of the past few years' Fedayin guerrilla raids on Israeli border settlements.
Star of David	Or Shield of David, also known as Solomon's Seal, two interlaced equilateral triangles forming a six-pointed star, an emblem of all things Jewish; in pre-Hebrew times, used as an amulet to ward off evil.
Talmud	The greatest compendium of Jewish law and custom after the Bible, the Talmud was largely written in Aramaic with an admixture of Hebrew, one version being completed in Babylon about 500 A.D., and the other and shorter in Tiberias and elsewhere about 425 A.D. That part of the Talmud called the Halakhah is concerned with the

law, while the Aggadah deals with religion, ethics, history and folklore.

Tel Hebrew and Arabic for a mound or artificial hill of one hundred feet or more covering the ruins of as many as twenty cities of inestimable importance to archeological excavation.

Torah In Hebrew, literally, the Law, the first five books of the Bible, "the Books of Moses," corresponding to the Pentateuch, the predecessor of Greek and English translations.

UNRWA The United Nations Relief and Work Agency for Palestinian Refugees.

Uzi A submachine gun manufactured in Israel; standard army issue there, also exported.

WIZO Abbreviation of the Women's International Zionist Organization, active in many countries (except the United States where its duties are carried out by Hadassah), supporting the United Israel Appeal, the Jewish National Fund reclaiming land, planting trees, child-care centers and vocational and agricultural training for women in Israel.

Yad Vashem Or Yad Washem, meaning the Hand and the Name, the Martyrs' and Heroes' Remembrance Authority, with a museum and archives on the outskirts of Jerusalem.

Yeshivot Talmudic academies at school, college and graduate levels, with both sacred and secular studies, some leading to ordination.

Yiddish A language derived from Middle High German with strong Hebrew and Slavonic influences (written in Hebrew characters), with a rich literature, dramatic and scholarly traditions, once spoken by more than twelve million people, still current among several millions.

Yom Kippur The Day of Atonement, the holiest day of the Jewish year, given to fasting, meditation, repentance and prayer at the synagogue for God's mercy.

Zionism Religious and political movement to establish a national home for the Jews in Palestine, strongest during the late nineteenth and the twentieth centuries.

343

ACKNOWLEDGMENTS

To a thousand and one people whose names I shall never know but who helped me on my way in Israel, many thanks.

And to our neighbors and friends in that country and to their representatives abroad, most especially Danny and Rose Shimshoni, Israel and Dorothy Naor, Claire and Moky Negev, Jacques Medina, Israel and Dita Natzor, Mordechai Arzielli, and Ziva Hoogstraal.

To Ambassador and Mrs. Aharon Remez in London, Ambassador and Mrs. Shimshon Arad in Mexico City, Ambassador Itzhak Shany in San José, Costa Rica, Consul General Michael Arnon and Consul Malka Ben-Yosef in New York City.

For the information services of the government of Israel, much appreciation. Whatever mistakes may remain are my fault, not theirs.

Also to Ted Lurie, editor of *The Jerusalem Post,* and his staff, acknowledgment of continuing assistance.

Acknowledgments

To Ben Touster and his wife Bertha, who know more about Israel than many of its citizens, thanks for sharing with my wife Bertie and me their trips to Tel Aviv, the Galilee and Beersheba, he as head of HIAS and chairman of CARE's board of directors.

To CARE itself, thanks for an extended leave of absence to complete this book.

And to my friends and colleagues, Toni and Lupe Matulewicz and Howard and Odessa Prunty, from all of whom I learned a great deal.

To the Reverend James Parkes for his courageous and unceasing work toward a world in which we can all live together, for his indispensable A *History of Palestine*, and for good counsel whenever my wife and I have called on him and Mrs. Parkes.

To my old friend and mentor, Karl Patterson Schmidt, Curator-in-Chief of Zoölogy at the Chicago Natural History Museum, who at the end of the Second World War did what he himself could to heal the breach by teaching each year in both Germany and Israel.

For Homer Page who, as always, has given generously of his time, helping with both text and pictures. And to William Attwood with thanks for much good advice.

And finally, inadequate thanks to Bertie who began at the beginning, ended at the end, and whose contributions throughout would take another volume this size to describe.

INDEX

347

Index

Index

Index

Index

Index

DATE DUE

FEB 20 '70	NOV 20 '87		
MAR 30 '71			
FEB 17 '72			
MAR 22 '72			
JUN 7 '73			
APR 28 '75			
NOV 4 '76			
NO 8 '78			
MR 1 '81			
AP 22 '81			
DE 7 '81			
DE 14 '81			
MR 7 '82			
JA 28 '83			
OCT 8 '84			
AP 10 '85			
APR 30 '86			
GAYLORD			PRINTED IN U.S.A.

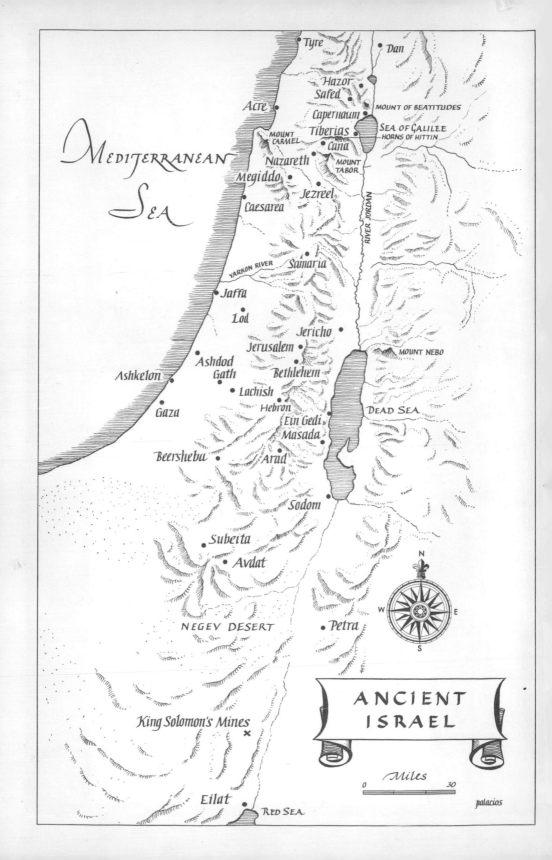